PLANNING AND MARKET IN SOVIET AND EAST EUROPEAN THOUGHT, 1960s–1992

Also by Jan Adam

ECONOMIC REFORMS IN THE SOVIET UNION AND
EASTERN EUROPE SINCE THE 1960s
EMPLOYMENT AND WAGE POLICIES IN POLAND,
CZECHOSLOVAKIA AND HUNGARY SINCE 1950
WAGE CONTROL AND INFLATION IN THE SOVIET BLOC
COUNTRIES
WAGE, PRICE AND TAXATION POLICY IN
CZECHOSLOVAKIA, 1948–1970
ECONOMIC REFORMS AND WELFARE SYSTEMS IN THE
USSR, POLAND AND HUNGARY (*editor*)
EMPLOYMENT POLICIES IN THE SOVIET UNION AND
EASTERN EUROPE

Planning and Market in Soviet and East European Thought, 1960s–1992

Jan Adam
Emeritus Professor of Economics
University of Calgary

150th YEAR

St. Martin's Press

First published in Great Britain 1993 by
THE MACMILLAN PRESS LTD
Houndmills, Basingstoke, Hampshire RG21 2XS
and London
Companies and representatives
throughout the world

A catalogue record for this book is available
from the British Library.

ISBN 0–333–49095–9

Printed in Great Britain by
Ipswich Book Co Ltd
Ipswich, Suffolk

First published in the United States of America 1993 by
Scholarly and Reference Division,
ST. MARTIN'S PRESS, INC.,
175 Fifth Avenue,
New York, N.Y. 10010

ISBN 0–312–08996–1

Library of Congress Cataloging-in-Publication Data
Adam, Jan, 1920–
Planning and market in Soviet and east European thought,
1960's–1992 / Jan Adam.
p.   cm.
Includes bibliographical references (p.   ) and index.
ISBN 0–312–08996–1
1. Europe, Eastern—Economic conditions—1945–1989.   2. Soviet
Union—Economic conditions.   3. Central planning—Europe, Eastern.
4. Central planning—Soviet Union.   5. Mixed economy—Europe,
Eastern.   6. Mixed economy—Soviet Union.   I. Title.
HC244.A516   1993
338.947—dc20   92–28898
                                              CIP

To Zuzana and Julie

Contents

List of Abbreviations

JOURNALS AND PAPERS

Czechoslovak

HN	Hospodářské noviny
NH	Národní hospodářství
PE	Politická ekonomie
PH	Plánované hospodářství (in 1990 it was replaced by NH)
SHN	Supplement to Hospodářské noviny
THN	Týdeník hospodářských novin

Hungarian

F	Figyelő
KSz	Közgazdasági Szemle
Kg	Külgazdaság
Nsz	Népszabadság
PSz	Pénzügyi Szemle
TSz	Társadalmi Szemle

Polish

E	Ekonomista
GP	Gospodarka Planowa
GN	Gospodarka Narodowa (replaced GP)
ZG	Życie Gospodarcze

Soviet

EG	Ekonomicheskaia gazeta
EiZh	Ekonomika i zhizn (replaced EG in 1990)
K	Kommunist
P	Pravda
PKh	Planovoe khoziaistvo
SEG	Supplement to Ekonomicheskaia Gazeta
VE	Voprosy ekonomiki

PoE   Problems of Economics (journal of translations of
             Soviet articles)
CDSP   The Current Digest of the Soviet Press

MISCELLANEOUS TERMS

CC   Central Committee of the Communist Party
CMEA   Council of Mutual Economic Assistance
CP   Communist Party
EM   Economic Mechanism
KJK   Közgazdasági és Jogi Könyvkiadó (Hungarian publisher)
NEM   New economic mechanism
PEA   Polish economic association
PWE   Panstwowe Wydawnictwo Ekonomiczne
             (Polish publisher)
PWN   Panstwowe Wydawnictwo Naukowe (Polish publisher)

Preface

When I was conducting research for my book on economic reforms, I came across many debates about various aspects of this subject. Mainly the debates about the desirable role of planning and the market, which were in the centre of contemplations about the shape of the economic reforms, caught my attention. At that time I decided that once I was through with my book on reforms, I would turn my attention to the evolution of views on planning and market. I had and have several reasons for this. The debates shed additional light on certain aspects of the economic reforms and thus help a better understanding of them. For a long time, of course, the principles of the reforms themselves made up the framework within which the debates could move. But it is also true that the debates had an impact on the design of the reforms, even if rarely on the principles themselves. In the second half of the 1980s, first in Hungary and Poland, later in Czechoslovakia and the USSR, a dramatic change came about: the debates were no longer regulated by the Party line, and the debaters could more or less speak their minds. The relationship between reforms and debates changed. The reforms were much influenced by the views of radical reformers. To capture this new experience on paper may also enrich our knowledge about the development of the socialist economic system.

The book can also be a modest contribution to the history of economic thought in general and to the history of socialist thought in particular. There is a theoretical (which is self-explanatory) and a practical aspect to this. The socialist system, in the form it existed in the USSR and East European countries (it is usually called in the literature 'real socialism'), collapsed. With the collapse of real socialism, the idea of socialism *per se* was largely discredited, but not defeated. There are still political parties in the world, and new parties will probably emerge, whose goal is or will be socialism, simply because the causes which brought about real socialism are far from being eliminated. And there is and will be a desire to know how the ideas about the socialist system developed and why it collapsed.

In a sense, the book which I now present to the reader is a sequel to my *Economic Reforms in the USSR and East European Countries since the 1960s*. I have already started to work on a new book which will deal with the collapse of the socialist system in Eastern Europe. I hope that these three volumes will make a small contribution to the understanding of a great historical experiment that failed.

The topic of this book turned out to be much more demanding and time-consuming than I had originally assumed. It was necessary to sift through a tremendous amount of material and make decisions about what to write about. The selection process is a sensitive issue in many respects. The allotted space and available time allow one to discuss only the debates closely connected with the topic under review and the views of only a limited number of participants in the debates. Many interesting debates which might shed indirect light on the topic had to be omitted. It is not very difficult to determine in most cases who the main actors in the intellectual disputes were and who exhibited originality of thought in the debates. It is, however, not easy to select the second echelon of participants in the debates. Some personalities may be ignored, and this may not make the author popular. But there is an even more delicate issue. One must discuss the past views of many economists, and some of them may not like to be reminded of the positions they took in the past, especially if they were of a dogmatic nature.

I try to give a spectrum of views regardless of whether the individual views had or had not an impact on the process of reforms. Of course, I devote more attention to views which influenced the thinking of economic community, particularly if, at the same time, they influenced the shape of reforms.

My study relies entirely on publications; what has not been published does not exist for me. True, I talked to many authors whose views I discuss here. But what I write about their ideas is not based on those conversations, particularly if they referred to views expressed in the past. My study focuses on the views as expressed in the period under review. Hindsight views are of no importance here, as they are often used to embellish past attitudes. My approach is dictated by my desire to give a true picture of the development of views as they were reflected in publications.

The political atmosphere was, most of the time, not conducive to a genuinely free exchange of ideas. The politicians set the framework within which public views could move. Editors of periodicals saw to it that the set framework was not crossed. In doubtful cases they sought a decision from the Communist Party (CP) secretariat. Of course, there were also times when restrictions on free expression of views were moderate or almost negligible. The more the economy was in disarray, the more the politicians were willing to listen and the greater was the freedom of expression. And this was usually during times of economic reforms. I took these circumstances into consideration when determining the structure of this book. Therefore my study is focused on the periods of the great reforms of the 1960s and the 1980s and discusses the 1970s only exceptionally. In addition, I warn the reader about the political atmosphere whenever necessary.

The reformers of the 1960s put into motion a process on which the reforms of the 1980s were built. The reformers of the 1980s learned from the positive and negative aspects of the 1960s and used them for the expansion of the reforms of the 1980s. Compared to the reforms of the 1980s, the reforms of the 1960s seem to be one-time reforms in the sense that, once they were instituted, their principles did not undergo many modifications. This is more true of the Hungarian reform than the Czechoslovak. Surprisingly enough, in the latter country, the Soviet-led invasion brought about an expansion of the reform, even after the invasion. The 1980s were revolutionary; in the first half most of the reformers still believed in the reformability of the existing economic mechanism. Few economists dared to hope, even if they desired it very much, that the system would collapse in a few years. Maybe this lack of expectation had some impact on their beliefs. In the second half of the 1980s, the number of people who lost their belief in the reformability of the system grew rapidly, and the system soon collapsed.

The different development in the two decades influenced the methodology which I have used in discussing the evolution of views on planning and market. The first part of the book, which deals with the 1960s, is mostly about the published views of personalities, whereas the second part, in which the 1980s are discussed, focuses on events or problems and how they were reflected in publications. This concept is not carried out consistently.

I have tried hard to be objective: to select the best representatives of certain currents of thinking, interpret their thoughts as objectively as possible and choose the most relevant problems for discussion. Despite this effort, I am aware that my study is necessarily marked by subjectivity. No doubt, another author would have approached the topic in a different way, stressed different points and interpreted the ideas of the authors in a slightly or even considerably different way. It is important to stress that the interpretation of views is one of the most difficult problems. Because of limited space, it is often necessary to summarise in a small paragraph or several lines the authors' views, which were originally expressed in tens of pages, or even in a book.

Like other authors, I was faced with making a decision about what my role in the book should be: should I simply report and interpret the views of the participants in the debates without explicitly expressing my own opinion, or should I be an active participant in the debates? It is clear that, by using the term 'explicitly', I take the position that an author cannot avoid the process of a partial revelation of his opinion. After all, the selection and intepretation of the participants' views in the debates betray the author's bias to some extent. In addition, one of the reasons for writing this book is a desire to express myself on the topic discussed. However, I have decided to give a running commentary on ideas expressed only exceptionally. I give my own thoughts about some problems at the end of every chapter. In addition, I explain my views in a systematic way in Chapter 11.

The book is divided into three parts. The first part discusses the debates in the 1960s and the second the debates in the 1980s. The last part is devoted to comments on the debates as well as to the discussion of some problems which were not raised in the debates, but are closely connected with the topic. The first and second parts are made up of five chapters each. In both parts there is a chapter which discusses the common and contrasting features including a theoretical background of the debates in the 1960s (it starts with the 1950s) and 1980s. These common chapters also contain a very brief survey of the political and economic situation as well as economic reforms in the four countries, namely, the USSR, Poland, Czechoslovakia and Hungary, which are covered in this book. In each part, the remaining four chapters are country chapters. The chapters on the 1980s also deal with the transitional period to the market, which means that they also discuss the debates in 1990–91 and in a few cases debates in the beginning of 1992.

I mention the occupation of the participants in the debates only if they had important positions in public and academic life or if the mention of the occupation can add to the better understanding of the debaters' ideas. Where no occupation is listed, it should be understood the debater was or is a university instructor or a researcher.

Finally, clarification is given of the use of certain terms. In the literature, the terms 'system of management of the economy' and 'economic mechanism' are not regarded as fully identical. However, I will use them interchangeably. The terms are meant to express the methods used to operate the socialist economic system. They include planning, regulation system (whose main function is to make sure that plans are implemented) and organisational system. The socialist economic system is a much broader term; it also includes ownership relations. Until the second half of the 1980s, the economic reform was confined to the economic mechanism; later it touched the economic system itself. In my study, I try to respect this difference, though nowadays, for understandable reasons, the terms are mixed up.

I distinguish between the terms 'social ownership' or 'collective ownership' on the one hand, and 'societal ownership' on the other. The term 'social' or 'collective' is used when ownership is considered in the traditional sense, meaning that the means of production are centrally controlled and workers have a negligent say about their use. The term 'societal' is used to express a new concept of ownership which in a sense negates state ownership. As will be shown later, many economists at a certain period, mainly in the USSR, believed that by introducing self-management into enterprises or by changing the nature of state ownership, the traditional exercise of property rights would turn into ownership relations which could be characterised as societal (belonging to society).

The term Eastern Europe was used in the past as a political and ideological term, though some countries included in it were located geographically in Central Europe. Since approximately 90 per cent of my study refers to the period before the collapse of socialism, I will continue for practical reasons to address the three smaller countries under review as East European. When I was putting the last touches to this study, the Soviet Union had ceased to exist. For the reason mentioned above, I will continue to use the term 'Soviet Union' without the adjective 'former', all the more because by now every informed reader knows that the 'Soviet Union' is a historical state structure. The same principle will be applied to Czechoslovakia, which is now called Czech and Slovak Federal Republic.

I will use the terms 'small' and 'large' privatisation as they are used in the countries under review. 'By small' is meant the privatisation of small businesses, catering and service facilities, and 'large' is applied to the privatisation of large enterprises. Middle-sized enterprises are included sometimes in small and sometimes in large privatisation.

Finally, I use the term 'neo-liberals' in my book for social scientists who advocate a *laissez-faire* ideology. The followers of such an ideology believe that the state's role in the economy should be

minimal and in as far as the government does intervene in the
economy, this should be done primarily by monetary tolls. M. Friedman and F. Hayek are the idols of the neo-liberals. Some of the
adherents of the ideas mentioned call themselves liberals, others, as
in the USSR, democrats.

JAN ADAM

Acknowledgements

I would first like to thank the Social Sciences and Humanities Research Council of Canada, Ottawa, for the extended research grants which enabled me to work on this study.

I am obliged to those who read parts of the original drafts and whose comments enabled me to improve the final version of this book. I would like to pay special tribute to professors L. Antal, W. Brus, J. Chapman, H. Flakierski, Z. Hába, C. Józefiak, T. Kowalik, G. Révész, L. Rusmich, Z. Šulc, L. Szamuely, J. Timár, O. Turek and G. Vinokur. I have greatly benefited from consultations with scholars in my field. I am especially obliged to A. Ágh, L. Antal, W. Baka, W. Brus, G. Bager, L. Bokros, L. Csaba, B. Csikós-Nagy, E. Ehrlich, I. Gábor, M. Górski, D. Gotz-Kozierkiewicz, Z. Hába, K. Hagemejer, W. Herer, L. Herzog, I. Hetényi, M. Hrnčíř, I. Illés, P. Juhász, S. Jakubowicz, C. Józefiak, M. Jurčeka, A. Karpiński, M. Kaser, E. Kemenes, J. Klacek, V. Klusoň, G. I. Kočarník, G. Kołodko, S. Kopátsy, K. Kouba, Gy. Kővári, K. Kővári-Csoór, A. Köves, T. Kowalik, W. Krenčik, M. Krzak, J. Lipiński, A. Lipowski, K. Loránt, J. Mujżel, T. Nagy, M. Nasilowski, R. Nyers, K. Porwit, M. Rakowski, G. Révész, L. Rusmich, E. Rychlewski, Z. Sadowski, T. Sárközi, A. Sipos, A. Sopoćko, K. A. Soós, Z. Šulc, M. Swięcicki, L. Szamuely, B. Sztyber, A. Szegő, I. Tarafás, M. Tardos, T. Tepper, J. Timár, J. Trzeciakowski, B. Urban and F. Vencovský. Of course, the sole responsibility for the views expressed in this book, or any remaining errors, is mine.

Most of the materials for this book were collected in libraries and institutes in Europe. My thanks are due to the libraries and their workers: to the Radio Free Europe in Munich, Osteuropa Institut in Munich, Bundesinstitut für Ostwissenschaftliche and Internationale Studien in Cologne, Economic Institute of the Hungarian Academy of Sciences, and Institute for Comparative Economic Studies in Vienna.

I wish also to record my appreciation for the help contributed by my research assistants: Mmes K. Lukasiewicz, J. Ádler-Vértes and Mr P. Slezak in collecting, processing and evaluating materials. Special thanks go to Mrs B. Blackman for the care and patience with which she improved the English of my typescript. To Mrs Langan I am obliged for her care in typing several drafts of the study. To my wife Zuzana, who encouraged me in my work and helped me to collect and process materials, I am very much indebted.

A chapter of the book was published earlier under the title 'The Debate on Planning and Market during the Czechoslovak Reform 1966–69,' *Osteuropa Wirtschaft*, 1990, no. 3. In addition, a small part of my article 'The Possible Role of Market and Planning in Poland and Hungary' in Anders Åslund (ed.), *Market Socialism or the Restoration of Capitalism?* (Cambridge University Press, 1991) was used in this book. I wish to thank the editor of *Osteuropa Wirtschaft* as well as Cambridge University Press for allowing me to use the above material in my book.

Part I

Debates on Planning and Market in the 1960s

1 Common and Contrasting Features of the Debates in the 1960s

In this chapter I will also discuss the 1950s in addition to what the title indicates. I feel that, if a short survey about the debates of the 1950s is given, the reader will have a better understanding of what happened in the 1960s. After all, many of the ideas which governed the reforms of the 1960s were around in the 1950s.

ECONOMIC CONDITIONS

In the USSR, after a slow start to the conversion of the war economy to a civilian one, industrial production grew fast. In 1948, industrial output exceeded the pre-war level: heavy industry was as much as 30 per cent above the pre-war level, whereas all other industrial branches reached the pre-war situation. However, agricultural production, with the exception of grain, did not achieve the pre-war level until 1950. The poor performance of agriculture was the result of the old shortsighted policy of developing the economy at the expense of collective farmers. Agriculture suffered from insufficient investments and very low procurement prices which were far below the cost of production (Ciepielewski, 1987, pp. 302–6).

In the period 1951–5, the Soviet economy, with the exception of agriculture, grew fast on the whole. However, productivity grew at a slower rate than expected. Increased investment outlays in industry did not have the envisaged effect. A great part of the labour force, primarily the part which came from agriculture, had difficulty in mastering the skills needed for industrial production. And, of course, the economic mechanism, which reduced enterprise managers to executors of the will of the central planning bureaucracy and thus put narrow limits to enterprise initiative, hampered the development of the quality factors of the economy.

Czechoslovakia in 1949 and Hungary in 1950 embarked on five-year plans, while Poland began a six-year plan in 1950. These were

3

ambitious plans, designed according to the Soviet concept of economic development. Their purpose was to bring about so-called socialist industrialisation, which, in reality, meant fast development of heavy industry at the expense of consumer goods industries and the infrastructure. The great stress on heavy industry was motivated by military considerations. The Soviet Union was making preparations for a possible hot war, and the East European countries were supposed to contribute to the armament build-up. Naturally, the plans envisaged high increases in the investment outlays and the funnelling of a great portion of them into heavy industry. After the outbreak of the Korean war, the smaller countries accelerated the industrialisation drive. At the same time, collectivisation of agriculture was proceeding at a fast pace (see Karpiński, 1987, p. 161; Průcha, 1974, pp. 294–8; Pető and Szakács, 1985, pp. 151–5).

Under such conditions, great disequilibria in the economy soon became apparent. The amount of wages paid out grew fast due to fast increases in employment; however, output of consumer goods lagged behind. This was caused not only by the neglect of consumer goods industries, but also by the policy applied *vis-à-vis* the newly established collective farms, which were forced to make compulsory deliveries at low prices. Shortages showed up all the more because of price controls. The governments of the smaller countries tried to cope with the new situation by increases in so-called commercial prices (Czechoslovakia), by huge price increases (Hungary in 1951) and by a reintroduction of rationing of consumer goods in Poland (in 1951, after the money reform in 1950 failed) (see Adam, 1979, pp. 8–12).

The smaller countries adopted not only the Soviet concept of economic development, but also its economic mechanism. The introduction of the new coordinating mechanism was plagued by many difficulties; there were not enough experts who knew the Soviet system, and, in addition, it took time to acquaint enterprise managers and bureaucrats with the new system. If the new coordinating system did not work well in the country of its origin, it was not surprising that it worked even less well in the smaller countries when it was first introduced.

1953 was a year of small changes and the beginning of greater changes. Stalin's death was perhaps the decisive factor. The changes affected the internal and foreign policies of the Soviet Union and were soon reflected in the smaller countries. In all the four countries under review there was a trend toward a rearrangement of economic priorities. The new leadership in the USSR, headed by Malenkov, promised to consider consumer demand more, by expanding the output of consumer goods industries. In the smaller countries, the ambitious plan targets were reduced, mainly the targets for invest-ment, and greater attention was devoted to agriculture and the con-sumer goods industry in an effort to improve the standard of living. Of the four countries, Hungary went the furthest.

In the second half of the 1950s, the economy grew quite fast in all the four countries under review. In 1959, all embarked on a new, huge investment drive, encouraged partly by Khrushchev's unre-alistic notions about the Soviet ability to overtake the USA in most important products in 15 years. In the beginning of the 1960s, all the countries (except Poland) experienced a slow-down in their economic growth; in Czechoslovakia, there was even an absolute decline. The slow-down was reflected in a decline in the growth rates of real wages, mainly in the smaller countries, at a time when, for political reasons, it was least desirable. In addition, these countries grappled with foreign trade deficits. The minor institutional changes intro-duced there in the second half of the 1950s did not produce the expected results. The declining rates in population growth were also of concern. All four countries suffered from low economic efficiency. The reforms of the 1960s were supposed to put them on an intensive path of economic growth and thus solve the shortcomings from which they suffered.

POLITICAL SITUATION

In an endeavour to mobilise all segments of the population for the war effort against Nazi Germany, Stalin had eliminated some of the excesses of his repressive regime. Soon after WWII, mainly with the developing cold war, the regime again became more repressive. After the take-over of political power by the CPs in the smaller countries, Stalinist methods were gradually applied there too. The best manifestation was the show trials whose purpose was to scare away activists from any opposition attempt. The show trials were usually geared to the second guard in the leadership: the leader of the CP himself was infallible, just like his real boss in Moscow.

Stalin's death (1953) brought a certain relief from repression. The new Soviet leadership signalled this by executing Beria, Stalin's hang-man, who became, after Stalin's death, a member of the 'trojka'. Events in Moscow were soon reflected in the smaller countries, again to a much greater degree in Hungary than in the two other countries.

The XXth Congress of the Soviet Communist Party (1956) was an important milestone in the development of political life in the Soviet bloc. At that Congress, Khrushchev, the leader of the Soviet Union, revealed Stalin's crimes. The omnipotent dictator, whom propaganda had portrayed as a scientific genius and the embodiment of goodness and angelic qualities, was stripped of his clothes, and there he stood, all at once naked – a disgusting and despised criminal. Khrushchev's revelations were a shock to all the countries of the Soviet bloc; what many had suspected turned out to be true. These revelations came at a time when people were starting to question the communist regime, and they were fuel to the smouldering fire of discontent. Khrushchev's criticism of Stalinism slowly opened the gates for an outpouring of rage and indignation which, combined with other grievances, paved the way for the 1956 riots in Poland and the uprising in Hungary. Both were suppressed: the first by political concessions and the latter by Soviet tanks.

Khrushchev's revelations were also a ray of hope, despite the fact that he soon suppressed the Hungarian uprising with brutal force. People wanted to believe that the man who had the courage to tell the truth, even though it was so horrible, would surely introduce a new epoch. These hopes were strengthened by the release of many hundreds of thousands innocently imprisoned people, and by the gradual rise of a more liberal political and ideological atmosphere.

There was also a change in the relationship between the USSR and the rest of the countries of the Soviet bloc. Stalin had treated the bloc countries almost as if they were republics of the USSR. Khrushchev demonstrated by several acts that he would like to start a new relationship. In 1955, a meeting of the communist leaders of the Soviet bloc decided that the countries (meaning the smaller countries) adhering to the basic principles of socialism should build socialism in accordance with local conditions and traditions. In the same year, Khrushchev visited Yugoslavia to normalise relations with that country, relations which had been almost non-existent under Stalin, who had tried to punish that country for its resistance to his wishes. Considering his treatment of the Hungarian uprising and the Polish political changes in 1956, it is clear that Khrushchev's effort to improve relations did not mean that he was willing to allow any country to deviate substantially from the Soviet model, let alone leave the Soviet orbit.

After the 1956 relaxation, which followed the XXth Congress, a fight against revisionism soon started up again. The uprising in Hungary and the riots in Poland scared the communist leaders and they looked for a remedy in the strengthening of ideological purity.

In the beginning of the 1960s, political relaxation returned to the smaller countries. The worsening economic situation played an important role in this change in Czechoslovakia. In Hungary, it was J. Kádár's desire to bring about a reconciliation between his regime and the opposition. In Poland, where the political situation was always more relaxed than in the neighbouring countries, W. Gomulka, though he parted company with his 1956 political allies, was resolutely against Stalinist methods (see Fejtő 1974, pp. 166–81). The occupation of Czechoslovakia by the Soviet-led invasion reversed the situation to some extent.

DEBATES IN THE 1950s

As mentioned, all the countries under review were faced with serious economic problems. Even when economic growth rates were, on the whole, remarkable – as in the 1950s – other important indicators were unsatisfactory. Economic growth was accompanied by huge disproportions which were reflected in shortages, not only in consumer goods, but also in producer goods. The planners did not manage to coordinate investment activity properly: at times it grew faster than the economy could handle. Technological progress was slow: enterprises did not exhibit interest in it; on the contrary, they often tried to avoid it. Economic efficiency was low, among other reasons, because factor productivity was low and producer consumption, as a portion of national income, had a tendency to increase. The economy could not satisfy the increased demand for consumer goods. At the same time, many products gathered dust in warehouses: because of their low quality, they failed to attract buyers whose demand for quality was increasing.

It became increasingly clear to a growing number of economists that the 'culprit' was the economic mechanism, though the politicians tried to blame the inexperience of the middle echelon of cadres for the shortcomings. It would be unreasonable to expect instant calls for radical changes. The political environment was not conducive to such a demand, nor were economists psychologically ready for it. It should not be forgotten that it was first necessary to get rid of many dogmas which inhibited the clear view of economists. Let me mention some of them. One of the important dogmas which had a great effect on the thinking of economists was the idea of the incompatibility of planning and the market. True, Stalin undermined this dogma by maintaining that the law of value operates to some extent, namely in the circulation of consumer goods, and also influences agricultural production (1952, pp. 18–19). Still, the non-agricultural production sphere was regarded as the exclusive domain of planning. Another piece of dogma which influenced the role of planning was the belief that work expended under socialism has a direct social character. This belief, interpreted simply, meant that planners got a blank cheque of approval for their activities. An obstacle to the analysis of the potential role of the market was the belief, advocated by Stalin, that commodity-market relations result from the existing two forms of ownership, which in other words meant that once the cooperative ownership was removed market relations would cease to exist. The so-called law of the faster growth of production of producer goods than consumer goods, whose primary purpose was to underpin ideologically the drive for the fast development of heavy industry, principally affected economic policy, but the dogma also had an indirect effect on the working of the economic mechanism.

Law of Value

A frequent topic of debate was the law of value, more in the USSR than in the smaller countries. When Marx used the term – the law of value under capitalism – he usually talked explicitly about it as a law which dominates price movements (*Capital*, vol. III, p. 176). Here, Marx had in mind that prices oscillate around value under conditions of simple commodity production and around a transformed value, price of production, under capitalism. However, the law of value is not fully explained by this. On another page Marx writes 'Only as an inner law, *vis-à-vis* the individual agents, as a blind law of Nature, does the law of value exert its influence here and maintain the social equilibrium of production amidst its accidental fluctuations' (*Capital*, vol. III, p. 858). From this quotation and other indications it is clear that what Marx meant by the law of value was not only the forces which determine the exchange ratios of commodities, but also the allocation of resources (human and non-human) to various branches of production under a commodity producing system based on private ownership (see also Sweezy 1968, pp. 52–3). In brief, if the Marxian view on the relationship between prices and values is disregarded, the law of value is more or less what is called the market mechanism in non-Marxian economics.

When economists in socialist countries talked about the application of the law of value under socialism in the 1950s and 1960s, or even in the 1970s, it was not always clear what they had in mind. Judging from the debates, one could argue that there were on the whole two definitions of the law of value: a narrow one and a broad one. We disregard here the simplified definition, which saw in the law of value nothing other than the necessity to calculate expenditures and receipts in value terms. Those who conceived the law of value in the narrow sense saw in it only a law of price formation. Many adherents of this definition believed that an overhaul of price relations, which were quite distorted, would improve economic efficiency. Since they believed that price distortions resulted from bureaucratic arbitrariness and from disregard for objective criteria, they saw the cure in the use of Marx's teaching on prices. The advantage of this approach was that, on the one hand, they could defend themselves against attacks by alluding to Marx and, on the other hand, prices could be based on some relatively objective gauge.

To Marx, prices tend to correspond to values, or, more precisely, price relations tend to be determined by values. The term 'tend' here is only to make clear that Marx, when talking about prices and values, took into consideration the role of supply and demand, and therefore prices corresponding to values could arise only if supply and demand were fully in equilibrium. What the adherents of the narrow definition called for was prices to be brought into line with the cost of production. (It will be shown later that the term 'cost of production' has been ambiguous.) They did not by any means want to bring about an overhaul of the price system by spontaneous forces. What they had in mind was to use the law of value as a guide to the authorities' decision-making about prices. However, they were against its application to the regulation of production. To them this activity, including the allocation of resources, was to be carried out consciously by the planners, who, in their decision-making, were to be guided by the law of planned, proportionate development of the economy and the basic law of socialism (meaning that the aim of production under socialism is enhancement of the material and cultural standard of the population and not profit as it is under capitalism).

The second group saw in the law of value not only a guide for setting prices, but also a regulator of production. This regulating function was supposed to be accomplished by prices and by the adjustment of production to the relationship of supply and demand through the inflow of resources (human and non-human) when they were needed and the outflow when they were in excess. Prices were to correspond to social cost of production. This does not, of course, mean that all prices set by the authorities must be in line with the law of value. If there are good reasons for social preferences prices may deviate from the law of value. If disequilibrium occurs in the relationship of supply and demand and, as a result, the existing prices set according to the cost of production do not correspond to equilibrium prices, the cure need not be in price changes. In the case of equilibrium prices for certain products being higher than the set prices, some suggest (for example, Brus, 1956) increasing output, or, in other words, changing the production plan. The rationale behind this suggestion was multifold. The desire to maintain equivalent exchange was only one reason. Another was probably the assumption that the supply could often be increased, but it had not been because of the planners' wrong estimate of demand. It might also be an indirect criticism of the planners' reluctance or inability to pay thorough attention to market demand.

The adherents of this view did not necessarily want a market economy. What they wanted was for the planners, in setting production targets, to take demand more into consideration. In the course of time, this wish developed into a demand that the plan reflect the anticipated market. Even if some economists thought about giving the market a greater role, as long as they believed in planning, long-term investments were regarded as the exclusive domain of planning. Nobody wanted prices to determine all investment activities.

The law of value is closely connected with commodity–money relations. It can operate only where commodity–money relations exist. However, commodity–money relations are not a sufficient precondition for the working of the law of value; they may exist, as in the centralised system, and yet the law of value has a very limited scope for operation.

The discussion about the law of value was combined, mainly in the beginning, with a debate about the reasons for the existence or survival of commodity production and its place in the economy. The debate was, of course, influenced by the ideas of the debaters concerning the structure of the management system. Those who viewed the existing system of management as satisfactory, or believed that only some minor changes in the system were needed, tried to explain why commodity production was *still* needed. For some time, they used Stalin's explanation, namely, that as long as two forms of ownership, state and co-operative, survived, commodity production would exist. When this went out of style, some other explanations were used, for example, the internal contradiction of social labour or the need to distribute income according to labour, as Kronrod did (Kronrod, 1958; see also Zauberman, 1960; and Astakhov, Voznesensky, Volkov and Judkin, 1958).

For economists who believed that the system of management should be substantially reformed, the question was not so much why commodity–money relations exist, but why their scope should be extended (see, for example, O. Šik's views in Chapter 3).[1] With the start of economic reforms, particularly in Poland and Hungary, the question about the survival of commodity production was gradually replaced by questions about where the dividing line between planning and the market should be, and what the realm of the market should be. More and more economists took market relations as given, an integral part of the system of management, and were concerned more with theoretical and practical questions about their utilisation than with a question which had doctrinaire connotations.

In the 1950s, in the countries under review, there was also a debate on prices in connection with the law of value. The Soviet debate will be discussed in Chapter 2.

Economic Mechanism

Calls for radical changes in the EM came only after the XXth Congress of the Soviet CP in 1956, and these were primarily in Poland and Hungary. But, even before 1956, some Hungarian economists openly advocated changes which indirectly challenged the existing economic mechanism. Hungary was the first country in which Stalin's death generated changes. In June 1953, M. Rákosi, with some members of the Politbureau, including Imre Nagy, were invited to Moscow. Judging from what happened afterwards, it is plausible to assume that the Hungarian delegation was taken to task. After his return from Moscow, Rákosi – keeping on the post of first secretary of the CP – vacated the post of prime minister, which was taken over by Imre Nagy. The latter, apparently having the trust of Moscow, immediately started modifying the strategy of economic development and even appointed a committee with the task of looking into possible changes in the system of management (Pető and Szakács, 1985, pp. 240–1; Szamuely, 1986, p. 15).

The more relaxed political atmosphere in Hungary generated the first major criticism of the economic mechanism. For example, S. Balázsy (1954) called for an overhaul of the system of indicators by reducing them to two: valued added and transfer of accumulation to the budget. Otherwise, enterprises should be left free to make decisions about their activities, with two important exceptions: (i) planned changes in the lines of production would have to be approved by the authorities, and (ii) investment would be the domain of planning (see also Szamuely, 1986, p. 16).

Gy. Péter, head of the National Statistical Office, in his more generally conceived paper, 'The significance and the role of efficiency in the planned management of enterprises' (1954), also criticised the traditional system for focusing on assignment of a huge number of targets and indicators, which only made the tasks of enterprises more difficult, instead of concentrating on efficiency. To this end, he suggested, on the one hand, giving managers the maximum possible freedom in decision-making and, on the other, subjecting them to control of their performance from the viewpoint of economic efficiency. Profitability should be the gauge of efficiency, and for this purpose profit should become the indicator of material incentives. The buyers should become the controllers and judges of enterprise performance. To make the system work, prices should reflect the law of value, and in order to make definitely clear the direction of his views, he added that they should reflect demand and supply. He also suggested including in the cost of production the price of land and a tax on working and fixed capital.

In his concept, planning was still supposed to play an important role. It was supposed to determine, among others, macroproportions and the distribution of investment between sectors of the economy, and a few indicators (for more, see Berend, 1990, pp. 22–4).

Considering that Balázsy's and Péter's papers[2] were written in 1954 and indirectly called for the giving of an important role to market forces, one has to admit that they were courageous deeds which were only possible during the short period of liberalisation engineered by Imre Nagy. With his forced resignation in 1955, a period of dogmatism again took hold, but only for a short time.

This part would not be complete without a mention of J. Kornai's work (*A gazdasági*, 1957, new edition in 1990) which, no doubt, had an impact on the reforms. In it, the author gave an analysis of the real not the supposed, working of the economy, based on the example of the textile industry. He criticised the excessive centralisation of management, the system of assigning targets, the irrational price system, and so on, and described their adverse consequences. As he himself stressed in his introduction to the new 1990 edition of his book, this was the last time he took on the role of a naive reformer.[3] In his suggestions for reform, which were more or less similar to those of Gy. Péter, he emphasised the need to change the whole economic mechanism at once (1990A, p. xii). He took the same position on planning as Gy. Péter.

After the XXth Congress, mainly in Poland and Hungary, the intellectual community, particularly writers and artists disillusioned with the system, gradually started to criticise the system and to call for changes (Fejtő, 1974, pp. 88–95). The new movement also had its reflection among economists. In Poland, the Second Congress of Economists, held in June 1956, gives good insight into the thinking and mood of the economists. Some economists used the forum to vent their frustration with the scientific conditions, and indirectly with the economic mechanism and political system. They were given such an opportunity by O. Lange, who, in his paper dealing with the state of the economic sciences, gave quite a rosy picture. They criticised the unsatisfactory state of research, the imposition of Marxist political economy as a monopoly of truth, the lack of information, the neglect of real economic problems, and so on. (*Dyskusja*, 1956).

Approximately at the same time Polish and Hungarian economists were occupied with the idea of reforming the system of management. It is not clear how close the contacts and exchange of views were between the reformers of the two countries. What is clear is that reformers of both countries were influenced by the reforms in Yugoslavia.

It is worthwhile comparing the ideas about the proposed changes in both countries. Needless to say, the ideas in both countries were quite divergent; here, only the mainstream views will be discussed.

In my opinion, the Theses of the Polish Economic Council, which was chaired by O. Lange, represented the mainstream thinking of the reformers (*Dyskusja*, 1957, pp. 261–78).[4] In Hungary, two important documents resembled in purpose the Polish Theses and more or less reflected the mainstream thinking of the reformers. One is a paper by six economists (henceforth Bokor et al., 1957) who were part of a larger group engaged, with National Bank and Planning Office authorisation, in the preparation of a proposal for a change in the system of management. A second document is a reform proposal sponsored by the National Economic Committee, the supreme body for economic coordination, which was finished in 1957 (whereas the first was initialled at the end of 1956). It is best known in the form in which it was published by its chairman, Professor I. Varga (1957), a well-known economist before the war. The Polish document, compared to the two Hungarian ones, is shorter: it is presented as an outline and therefore does not deal with the reform problems in great detail. All three documents suggest changes in planning, in the position of enterprises and in the regulation of enterprise activities.

All three documents accept planning more or less as the fundamental coordinating mechanism.[5] The stress is on medium-term and long-term planning; the role of annual plans is de-emphasised. In the Polish Theses, special importance is attached to economic analyses in macro-economic planning, and it is suggested that due regard be given to prognoses of future development. There is no difference in the documents when it comes to important investments: all are in favour of leaving decisions about them to the centre. The old system of financing investment from the state budget should be abandoned instead, most of the investment should be financed from enterprise resources and bank credit.

Enterprises should receive considerable autonomy. They should work out their own plans and determine most of their output mix in accordance with their interests. The centre should assign targets to enterprises only exceptionally; according to the Polish Theses, this should be done only in cases where producer goods are allocated to enterprises because of shortages. Enterprises should have the right to administer their financial assets, which should also include depreciation.

The Polish Theses counted on workers' councils and attached great importance to them. They were seen as an instrument of democratisation which, by their very existence, would help to bring about more decentralisation (see, for example, Lange, in *Dyskusja*, 1957). In some economic circles this attitude to workers' councils has survived up to the present. The Hungarian proposals took workers' councils as given, but made it implicitly clear that the reform was not linked to their destiny. The workers' councils there were soon disbanded.

The question was: how was the centre to coordinate its plans with enterprise plans? Or, more precisely, how could the centre make enterprises follow the objectives of its macroeconomic plans? All three documents agreed that economic levers should be used. Material incentives linked to profit should play an important role. In addition, fiscal and monetary instruments should be used. The Hungarian documents also suggested using allocation of producer goods as an instrument for guiding enterprises.[6] This was certainly contrary to Polish thinking. Polish reformers regarded allocation of resources as an integral part of the centralised system, a logical extension of the assignment of targets. One can only speculate why the Hungarian economists took a different position. Unlike Poland, Hungary was, during the Second World War, an independent country to some extent and controlled the war economy through allocation of resources. Some Hungarian economists were personally involved in, or had knowledge about, the war economy, and therefore the habit of allocating producer goods as an instrument for managing the economy did not seem strange to them.

In wage and price control, the Hungarian proposals went further than the Polish. Bokor et al. proposed abandoning the setting of the enterprise wage–bill from above and controlling wages by fiscal policy. The authors of the Theses did not call for a termination of wage–bill regulation; they only suggested replacing the existing wage growth indicator, gross value of output, by net output. The Polish document demanded that, in the suggested reform of producer prices, due regard should be given to the social cost of production, the need for equilibrium and world prices. The Hungarian proposals seemed to go beyond these demands. They contained the idea of grouping prices into three categories: fixed, maximum and free.

Disregarding some differences, the reform proposals pointed in the same direction. Polish and Hungarian reformers saw a possible improvement in the economy in restricting the role of planning, giving more rights to enterprises and managing enterprises by economic levers instead of by direct orders. Even if they did not talk much about the market (in the Theses the term does not even turn up), they counted on it having a role in the management of the economy. If the assignment of targets is removed, it is clear that its place can only be taken over by the market. Though the concepts of the reformers developed in the documents of the 1950s were not adopted by the authorities,[7] and few of the suggestions were applied to the existing system of management, the work of the reformers was not in vain, particularly in Hungary, where the 1968 reform was strongly based on the suggestions of the 1950s.

In the Soviet Union, the rejuvenation of intellectual life after the XXth Congress developed at a much slower pace than in the smaller countries. Stalin's destructive work was much more profound at home than abroad. In the economic sciences, in many positions of responsibility in the universities, the Academy of Sciences and research institutes, there were people who linked their careers to Stalin and his teaching. And they could not and did not want to place themselves at the head of a movement against the old dogmatic thinking which might undermine their positions; on the contrary, many of them hampered the process of rejuvenation. Pressure on economists to become active came from an unexpected place, from above (Judy, 1973, pp. 226–7). Seeing many signs of a poorly working economy, the political leaders felt the need of the help of economists in order to be able to cope with the problems faced by the economy.

There was also another source of inspiration for a rehabilitation of political economy: this was a part of the old generation who had received their training in the 1920s or even earlier. Some of them were former prisoners who were released by Khrushchev. Important roles in this revival were played by Nemchinov, Novozhilov and Kantorovich, mathematical economists. Thanks to their endeavours, a new branch, mathematical economics, which had been completely neglected before, came into being (see Lewin, 1975, pp. 134–5). Many talented young people joined the new field, some of them because this branch seemed to be less exposed to ideology than economic theory.

The mathematical economists must be credited with the introduction of mathematical methods in planning, and with the effort to base central planning on rational decision-making. At their urging, the first input–output table for the USSR was compiled for 1959 (Ellman, 1971, p. 2), the next followed later. Their activities were not welcomed by the whole community of economists; on the contrary, they had to put up a good defence against frequent attacks.

Of course, the Soviet leaders were not looking for proposals for a radical overhaul of the system of management. What they wanted were proposals for improvements within the framework of the existing system. They wanted suggestions for improvements in planning techniques and price formation, better formulas for the computation of investment effectiveness, suggestions for more effective territorial allocation of investment, better indicators of performance, and so on.

There is not much one can say about Czechoslovakia that would be in the same league in systemic thinking as what was said of Hungary and Poland. Published articles about the system of management moved within the framework given by the minor economic reform, which was approved in 1957 and was in effect from 1959 to 1961. The proposals which served as a basis for the reform were not published, and therefore no evaluation of their concept can be given. Knowing the dogmatic thinking of the Czechoslovak leaders, one can speculate that the economists involved in designing the concept of the reform did not dare suggest a radical reform. I would not be far from the truth in saying that already at that time some Czechoslovak economists were convinced about the need for a far-reaching reform (see also Chapter 3).

DEBATES IN THE 1960s

In the sixties, Czechoslovakia and Hungary embarked on economic reforms which broke out of the traditional framework of the management system. The USSR introduced a reform too, but this did not go beyond the limits of the traditional system. Poland carried out a reform in 1973 which, in its conceptual design, was somewhere between the Czechoslovak and Hungarian on the one hand, and the Soviet on the other.

In the Hungarian and Czechoslovak reforms, and to a lesser extent in the Polish, planning was supplemented by the market. Most economists accepted the idea that the market has a role to play in the coordinating of economic activities. It became clear that the strict centralisation of decision-making was untenable, that decentralisation was needed, and that many of the decisions made by the central planners, particularly micro-economic decisions, should be delegated to associations or enterprises. Some economists substantiated the need for decentralisation by arguing that the objectives pursued in centralisation were in substance fulfilled. To them, centralisation resulted from a desire for industrialisation with great stress on heavy industry, or a restructuring of industry where a great deal of industrialisation had already been achieved. An economy based on market mechanism would have hampered a restructuring of the economy in the direction mentioned.

Others argued that it was impossible to manage effectively from one centre an economy which was becoming more and more sophisticated, with increasingly intricate relations within individual enterprises and between enterprises, that the centre could not take care of the hundreds of thousands of products, and that, therefore, market equilibrium could not be ensured. Of course, one of the reasons for the centre's inadequacies had to do with the lack of information and the impossibility of quickly processing what information there was. However, even if all the information could be processed instantly, the problem could not be regarded as solved since there was no guarantee that those who could provide reliable information were willing to do so. In addition, rigid centralisation hampered the initiative of enterprise managers, and this in turn affected innovations and economic efficiency detrimentally.

Once the decision is taken that enterprises must be given greater autonomy and the system of compulsory output targets and central allocation of producer goods is removed, the market is the only institution which can fill the resulting vacuum. In such a situation, the question arises of where to set the dividing line between the two coordinating mechanisms: what should the functions of planning and the market be? As is known, socialism is characterised by the desire consciously to guide the economy to certain goals. How can the new demand for the market be reconciled with the old goal of guiding the economy consciously? It was clear that the role of the market, as Stalin defined it, was no longer sufficient. In decentralised conditions, the market must also have an effect on production; otherwise its coordinating effect cannot be felt. At that stage of thinking most economists were against exposing all production to market forces. They believed that the dividing line between the two coordinating mechanisms should run somewhere between simple reproduction (static economy) and extended reproduction (dynamic economy). They were willing to allow the market to have an important part in simple reproduction, but a much smaller role in extended reproduction. It was believed that decisions about extended reproduction, as long as they referred to major investments which have an important effect on the structure of the economy or technology, should be reserved for planning. In this way the achievement of social preferences could be guaranteed. In addition, it was argued that planning was needed because present market prices, even if they were applied, could not provide reliable information about the future structure of the economy.[8] Furthermore, the centre had better access than enterprises to information needed for rational decisions about major investment projects.

This differentiated approach to simple and extended reproduction also influenced the views on planning. In the traditional system, the stress was on annual plans, which contained compulsory targets and limits. With the removal of plan targets and limits, the role of the annual plan, even if it was still drawn up, necessarily changed and declined. Naturally, a demand was voiced to shift the focus of planning to medium-term and long-term plans. The rationale behind this demand was that changes in the structure of the economy, if they were of major dimensions, required a longer time span for their implementation.

Economists, who followed more or less the official stand according to which the economic reform was designed in Czechoslovakia and Hungary, talked rather about the utilisation of market forces. For them, planning was to remain the leading coordinating mechanism. They associated socialism with a planned economy. The market which they wanted to allow was to be a planned market. In this model the market was to be regulated, on the one hand, by central decisions about the distribution of income and the distribution of investment among sectors of the economy and industrial branches and, on the other, by certain limits being set on the working of market forces; some of the limits were to be of an administrative nature, such as not allowing enterprises to diversify their production without approval from above and leaving intact the existing administrative associations, and others were to consist of indirect methods. Wage regulation and price formation were not to be without controls, though, of course, these controls would be much smaller and of a different kind than before the reform. In addition, it was suggested that enterprise performance should be evaluated. To this end, the size of the incentive fund was to be linked to the chosen indicator of enterprise performance. This last proposal, combined with a continuation of the ministries' right to appoint top managers, was to give the authorities an effective control over the activities of enterprises.

In a reformed system of management, where enterprises are given a great deal of autonomy, it is obvious that they must have the right to work out their own plans which reflect their own interests. The question can be posed: how should central plans and enterprise plans be coordinated? How can the centre make sure that social preferences assert themselves? Both groups realised that direct macro-decisions alone could not guarantee that enterprises would follow the centre's goals, and that the autonomy given to enterprises might be used for a partial frustration of the central planners' plans. Therefore they agreed that the economy should be regulated by economic levers, by fiscal and monetary policies, and that regulation primarily of taxes, but also of amortisation rates, tariffs, credits, interest rates and exchange rates, should be used in managing the economy in line with planned objectives. All these tools were supposed to influence enterprise costs, profits and revenues and thus act as an incentive (or disincentive) to enterprise activity in a certain direction.

None of the economists, even the most radical, suggested bringing about substantial changes in the predominant role of state ownership. It was believed that the market could work by giving enterprises autonomy and that enterprise autonomy, combined with incentives and other factors, would create sufficient room for the working of market forces. Of course, they were in favour of the extension of the private sector, but this perhaps was motivated more by other considerations than by the belief that the working of the market required private ownership. The expansion of the private sector was expected to contribute to a renewal or preservation of market equilibrium, and at the same time counter possible trends towards unemployment in the state sector. It was also motivated by political considerations, the expectation that the expansion of the private sector would contribute to the political stabilisation of the system.

The vast majority of reformers were party members, working in universities, the Academy of Sciences, and research institutes, and therefore they did not dare deviate very much from the Party line. The prevailing ideology of that time still held that state ownership, understood very broadly, was the basis of socialism. Propagation of ownership pluralisation would not have been well received. In addition, most of the reformers themselves, mainly in Czechoslovakia, even if they were not happy with the approach of the public to state ownership,[9] did not even consider the need for far-reaching privatisation.

The market was understood to be a market for products. The idea that a fully-fledged market can exist only if, at the same time, room is made for a capital market and a labour market did not surface until the 1980s. True, it was felt that the existing arrangement in which enterprises could use retained profit only within the enterprise or for deposit with the bank for extending loans, hampered capital mobility and thus the efficient use of capital. Nevertheless, only a very few people called (and in addition, in uncertain terms) for the overhaul of the financial system, from which one could draw the conclusion that they had the capital market in mind. In the 1960s the capital market was regarded as a capitalist institution, which was too much in contradiction with socialist production relations, mainly with the principle of distribution of income according to labour, and, therefore, there was a reluctance to challenge the system. In addition, many still believed or wanted to believe that the market could work well without a capital market.

Nor did economists call for a genuine labour market, in the sense that hiring and firing would be subject to micro-economic efficiency considerations. At that time, full employment belonged among the unalienable principles of socialism. It was unthinkable to entertain an idea which might lead to unemployment. This attitude to employment probably was partly responsible for the accepted view that labour was not a commodity, though, in practice, the market (wage differentials) had a certain impact on its distribution. The main argument used in defence of the thesis that labour was not a commodity was that a worker as co-partner in state ownership could not sell labour to himself.

Needless to say, not all economists favoured far-reaching reforms. Few denied the existence of commodity money relations; even some anti-reformers called for their expansion. But they regarded commodity money relations as a temporary phenomenon. Some believed that with the development of productive forces the need for the market would disappear; others hoped that with the perfection of the information system and data processing, planning would be improved to the extent that the market would become superfluous.

Some argued that socialist commodity relations were different from market relations. They alluded mainly to the fact that the socialist economy was based on state ownership, whereas a market economy on private ownership. Under socialism, the goal of production was consumption and use values, whereas in a market economy profit was the goal.

In the foregoing pages I have analysed on a general level the views on the concept of economic reforms in Hungary, Czechoslovakia and Poland. The economic-scientific activity in Poland was perhaps more vibrant and fertile in new ideas than in other countries, if the 1950s and 1960s are taken together. The spectrum of thinking of the Polish reformers was much broader. Not only this, but the thinking of the Czechoslovak and Hungarian reformers was also influenced by the Polish reform literature, mainly Brus' book (1972) which will be discussed in Chapter 5.

The Polish situation was the result of several factors. The room for freedom of expression was greatest in Poland, considering the situation in the countries under review. The intellectual community, including economists, managed to carve out a certain autonomy, whose strength fluctuated from time to time. Polish economists have managed to preserve their own organisation – the Economic Association – as an important institution for an open exchange of views and a channel to the political élite. The worst times in Poland were better than the worst times in other countries.

In addition, O. Lange and M. Kalecki, two internationally known economists, returned home to Poland from the West, where they had lived between the two wars and during the Second World War, and they helped maintain continuity and contact with Western economic thought. It was no accident that in Poland, even at the end of the 1950s and more so in the 1960s, economic calculation under socialism, a topic of great debate in the West since the end of the 19th century, became an important subject of dispute. This happened at a time when this topic was taboo in other countries; not only this, the vast majority of economists did not even know about it.

Poland had two specialities. On the one hand, there was a group, associated with the name of A. Wakar, which started out as believers in and propagators of a market economy, to end in practice as defenders of the existing system. On the other hand, there was a group, associated with the name of M. Kalecki, which did not really want substantial changes in the economic mechanism. It believed that, to cure the ills of the economy, improvements in planning and changes in economic policy were primarily needed. Similar views were also expressed in other countries, but nowhere were they professed by an economist of Kalecki's stature, nor were they backed up by proper research (see Chapter 5).

The views of Soviet economists on our topic were quite different from economic views in the smaller countries. This was not only because the Soviet reform differed so much from the Hungarian and Czechoslovak. The whole environment in the Soviet Union was more conservative than in the smaller countries, where the memories of the recent past were still alive. The break with Stalinism proceeded much more slowly in the USSR and under much greater resistance. And this also had, no doubt, an impact on published views.[10]

The discussion on Liberman's reform proposal, which was by no means radical, showed clearly that dogmatic views had deep roots. Many economists rejected his proposal, not because they felt that it would not turn out as promised, but only because some concepts were not in line with what they understood under Marxism. R. Judy (1973, p. 238), who took the trouble to classify the positions taken by authors in the debate on Liberman's proposal which took place in 1962–5, found that thirty-one authors out of ninety-three opposed it in principle.

The conservative economists were, in substance, against any meaningful reforms. They did not mind some changes in the techniques of planning, incentives, indicators, and so on, as long as they did not diminish the role of the centre. Some hoped to strengthen and stabilise the centre's role by disseminating computer technology.

The Soviet scene had a speciality in optimal planners who put forward their theory of optimal planning in the form of a programme in 1966, but had started to publish their ideas much earlier (Ellman, 1973, p. 4). They did not really aspire to replace the existing economic mechanism by a new one. What they wanted was to improve the existing system by optimisation of planning and pricing for the sake of improving economic efficiency (see Chapter 2).

The activities of optimal planners had an echo in other countries to different degrees. They fed illusions in some circles, including the USSR, that, with the perfection of computer technology and mathematical methods, market relations would become superfluous.

The debates, including the ones on Liberman's proposals, viewed from the vantage point of our topic, did not mean great progress in furthering the idea of combining planning with the market. In my opinion, the importance of the debates lay primarily in the fact that they threw a great shadow of doubt on the traditional system of management.

Notes

1. The reader who is interested in more information about this topic is advised to consult J. Kosta (1974, pp. 88–111).
2. Of course, there were more authors involved in criticism (see for more Berend 1988, pp. 41–54; Árva 1989).
3. He believed for a long time that the socialist system was irreformable and regarded Brus and O. Šik and other reformers as naive.
4. This was preceded by a debate about the model. Some preferred to put the market in a superordinate position, others wanted to make planning and market complement each other, and some preferred no changes at all (see Glówczyk, 1968; and also *Dyskusja*, 1957).
5. 'It is necessary to point out as a basic principle', wrote Bokor et al. (1957), 'that only *a socialist state and a state building socialism* can apply a planned economy'. This quotation comes from Szamuely's book (1986, p. 168) where the article was republished.

6. Bokor et al. took this position explicitly (Ibid., p. 171) and Varga implicitly (1957).
7. In both countries, needless to say, there were economists who applauded the government stand.
8. O. Lange writes (1973, Works 2, p. 336) in his famous paper, 'The Computer and the Market', '. . . because present prices reflect present data, whereas investment changes data by creating new incomes, new technical conditions of production and frequently also by creating new wants . . . In other words, investment changes the conditions of supply and demand which determine equilibrium prices. This holds for capitalism as well as for socialism'.
9. It was no secret to the reformers that state ownership in the form it existed did not generate a feeling in the workers that they were the owners and therefore they must care about its efficient utilisation nor did it eliminate alienation.
10. This situation was also to blame to some extent for the use of esoteric language and for adherence to the old terminology. In the smaller countries, Western terminology was spreading quite rapidly, whereas in the Soviet Union mostly Marxist terminology, often deliberately ambiguous, was used.

2 The USSR

INTRODUCTION

The debate in the USSR (henceforth the term Soviet Union is always understood as the former), which lost its vigour for some time, was boosted by the new Party Programme adopted at the XXIst Congress in 1961. To create the preconditions for an early transition to communism, the new Party Programme exhorted communists and non-communists to improve the management of the economy, to use resources more efficiently, and to promote economic efficiency. It underscored the importance of incentives and a better satisfaction of demand. It also stressed the importance of the 'extension of operative independence and initiative of enterprises on the basis of the state-plan targets' (*The New Program*, pp. 439–43).

The quotation shows clearly that the Programme was not intended to bring about revolutionary changes. Yet it encouraged a new debate which no doubt had an effect on the ensuing economic reform in 1965. The willingness of the authorities to listen to the economists was also motivated by the difficulties which the implementation of the seven-year plan encountered (Zaleski, 1967, p. 70). Most of the important indicators of performance were lagging behind the plan targets. In agriculture the situation was the worst: the plan target for the seven years was a 70 per cent increase in gross agricultural output, but in reality the increase was only 15 per cent.

After some experiments, the Soviets embarked on an economic reform in 1965. This was not a radical reform; it was a far cry from the Hungarian or Czechoslovak reforms. It did not transgress the framework of the traditional system. The assignment of compulsory plan targets and the central allocation of producer goods – the two main characteristics of the centralised system – were in substance preserved. The number of plan targets was substantially reduced, but with the collapse of the reform their number started to grow again. A promise was given that a market for producer goods would be gradually introduced, but little was done to make the promise come true.

The reform was primarily focused on improvement of the incentive system. Its purpose was, on the one hand, to encourage enterprises to have a greater regard for market demand (to this end, the incentive fund was linked to sales and profit) and, on the other, to accept taut plans (to this end, overfulfilment was rewarded less than fulfilment of plan targets). (For more about the economic reform, see Campbell, 1968; Grossman, 1966; and Adam, 1989).

The question may be posed: why did the Soviets not opt for a far-reaching reform as the Hungarians and the Czechoslovaks did? First, in the Soviet Union the pressure for reform was not as strong as in Czechoslovakia. Part of the political leadership was lukewarm about the reform and, when it did not fulfil the expectations pinned to it, turned against the reform and brought it to a halt. But even the part of the leadership which was in favour of the reform was not prepared to take the risks which a far-reaching reform would mean with regard to ideology. The leadership was simply not ideologically prepared for a radical reform. The fear that a radical reform might strengthen centrifugal forces in a multinational country, as the former USSR was, surely played a role.

It is possible to distinguish three groups in the Soviet debate. One, conservative, was in principle against any meaningful reforms. This group objected to reforms in the name of Marxist orthodoxy. A second group was reform-minded; with some simplification it can be said that it rallied around E. Liberman's reform ideas. Liberman's suggestions were, to a great extent, implemented in the 1965 reform. Finally, there was a group of mathematical economists who wanted to improve the working of the economy, primarily by optimising planning.

In this chapter I will discuss the conservative view only very briefly in connection with Liberman's views, in order to have more space for the reformers' views and the price debate.

LIBERMAN'S PROPOSAL

In his 1962 paper, *Plan, Profit, Bonuses*, published in *Pravda*,[1] E. Liberman[2] (1966), a Professor at Kharkov University, returned to some of his ideas published in the 1950s and elaborated on them. He called for an increase in enterprise autonomy by reducing the number of indicators binding on enterprises to two: volume of output including mix, and date of deliveries.[3] In setting the dates, the planners should take into consideration the contracts between suppliers and buyers. Otherwise, enterprises should be free to compile their own plan which also covers capital investment. He made it explicitly clear that large investments and rates of growth should remain at the discretion of the centre. He pinned great hopes on his idea of long-term normatives of profitability to make enterprises behave rationally. He explicitly called for setting such normatives for all branches of production. Profitability to him had to serve as a synthetic indicator for estimating the performance of enterprises and for motivating enterprises to aim for higher economic efficiency.

The bonus fund was to be fed from profit on the basis of a long-term normative, set for branches of industry or groups of enterprises. Differently from the paper of the 1950s, where he defined profitability as profit over production costs, he here proposed that profitability be computed as a ratio of profit to fixed and working capital. The change in the definition of profitability was to be a stronger incentive to enterprises to try to fulfil their targets with minimum resources (human and non-human). Waste of resources would, namely, reduce profitability. In addition, fulfilment of planned targets should be rewarded by the set normative. For example, if an enterprise agreed to produce profitability at 5 per cent and the normative was 0.2, the 1 per cent of profit could be channelled into the bonus fund. However, an overfulfilment of the planned target in profitability was not to be considered fully for bonus purposes. What should count was only the average rate of the two figures: planned and actual profitability. This proposal aimed at making enterprises interested in accepting plans corresponding to their capacities, thus bringing to an end a situation in which enterprises were interested in concealing their reserves.

The idea of long-term normatives was supposed to give managers a feeling of certainty with regard to bonuses. Not only this, but planning based on the level achieved and favouring poorly performing or speculating enterprises at the expense of hard-working ones was to be removed, or, more precisely, applied only once in a long period (say five years). This does not mean that the normative was supposed to be the same through the whole period; the promised stability was to lie in the fact that the normative would be known in advance for the whole period. Otherwise, the size of the normative was to decline, since it was assumed that profitability would increase.

E. Liberman was aware that his proposal about profitability was vulnerable, due to the lack of rational prices, and, as will be shown later, some of his opponents used this circumstance as an argument against his idea about profitability. The author did not call for a radical overhaul of prices; he only tried to assure his opponents that price increases were not on the cards, since buyers in their own interest would fight such tendencies.

Liberman's proposal did not cover the whole system of management; rather it referred only to some important aspects of the traditional system. In addition, the aim of his proposal was not to get rid of the traditional system, for it was designed in a way that would improve the system without really removing it. Liberman did not call for the elimination of annual plans with the assignment of binding targets. Though his proposal implicitly assumed a role for the market, he did not discuss it, which is one of the weaknesses of his approach. Had he done so, he would have had to struggle with the problem of drawing a dividing line between planning and market. He would also have discovered that there was a conflict between assigning binding targets to enterprises and giving them a free hand in investment, except in large investment. If enterprises are to produce what the centre wants them to, where is the guarantee that they will find the producer goods which they need for their investment? It is possible to remove the assignment of binding targets and still control investment, but not vice versa. A similar conflict arises if production targets are set, but inputs are free in the market, as Liberman indirectly suggested (see also Smolinski and Wiles, 1963).

Liberman probably knew that his two papers (see note 3) would be attacked, as he was suggesting operating the economy differently from before and, in so doing, he demolished some of the dogmas. And, for many economists, this was intolerable. No wonder that his papers provoked a great debate. It would exceed the scope of this paper to discuss in detail the arguments of the opponents and supporters. In addition, it would not serve any purpose to mention all the names of the discussants.[4]

REACTION TO LIBERMAN'S PROPOSAL

Many of the participants in the debate not only took a position on Liberman's proposal, but used this occasion to present their own views on how to solve the problems confronting the economy. Naturally, the opponents of Liberman's proposal were not a monolithic group. Some of them advanced arguments from the old arsenal, permeated with dogmatism. Some used the weaknesses in Liberman's proposal to reject, more or less, the whole proposal. There were also debaters whom it is difficult to classify as adherents or opponents of Liberman.

The first group of opponents included economists who attacked Liberman from conservative positions. For example, the former finance minister, A. Zverev (1966), criticised Liberman's definition of profitability as non-Marxist. The idea of calculating profitability as a ratio of profit and fixed and working capital was proof to him that Liberman believed that profit was also produced by fixed assets. As is known, Marx believed that profit was created by workers' surplus labour. In addition, Zverev disliked Liberman's suggestion about price formation, in which profit should be divided up according to invested capital.

Liberman's proposal aimed for decentralisation, for enterprises to be given greater autonomy and for their activities to be influenced indirectly by profitability as a synthetic indicator. Some opposed decentralisation in the belief that computer technology enables planning to be improved without the need to make any systemic changes. They saw the main shortcoming of planning in the inability of the planners to process quickly the huge amount of information about the many thousands of relationships needed in order to make correct decisions with regard to targets. Computer technology was supposed to eliminate this shortcoming. Such a position was taken, for example, by M. Fedorovich (1962) (for more see Smolinski and Wiles, 1963), who also argued that profit was a more arbitrary indicator than cost of production (see also Felker, 1966, p. 63).

Many argued against the idea of making profitability the only synthetic indicator. Some substantiated their stand by alluding to the fact that profitability was not an accurate gauge of enterprise performance. As is known, profitability depends on factors beyond enterprise control. Enterprises differ in their technical equipment; therefore productivity and profitability can be different even if all other conditions are the same. Many alluded to the price irrationalities which gave some enterprises an advantage. Under such conditions, the application of profitability would mean a violation of the socialist principle of distribution of income.

Even some of the economists who supported Liberman expressed concern about the impact of price irrationalities on profitability. However, they did not use this fact as an argument against Liberman's proposal.

B. Sucharevskii (1966), a labour economist,[5] drew attention to another important weakness in Liberman's proposal. Sucharevskii suggested that market disequilibrium might be generated if the decision about the wage-bill was left to enterprises. Consumer goods are not produced in all sectors of the economy. As a result, fast increases in heavy industry production might generate incomes which might not be covered by consumer goods. Under the existing conditions of giving high priority to heavy industry production this was, no doubt, a valid point.

Almost all of the opponents rejected the idea that investment decisions should be left to enterprises. The arguments were not always the same. But most had in common the fact that such a step would deprive the authorities of the most important instrument of planning.

Among the first who rushed to back up Liberman was V. Nemchinov (1966), a reputable mathematical economist. His support was all the more important because he was the chairman of the Academy of Sciences' Scientific Council on the Scientific Foundation of Planning and the Organisation of Social Production. He argued in favour of profitability by juxtaposing it indirectly with gross value of output which served in practice as the main indicator. He underscored the shortcomings of gross value of output and wrote, ' . . . society is interested in the growth of the final product rather than of the intermediate product'. To make the management system more efficient, he called for an end to allocating investment funds without charge. (For more about this problem, see p. 33.)

Nemchinov also urged an expansion of enterprise rights and the abandonment of 'petty supervision'. His proposal to organise a market for producer goods was in line with Liberman's ideas, but not with his suggestions about output targets. Nemchinov's proposition about close co-operation between enterprises and the planners with regard to the volume and mix of products was a quasi-solution to the problem.

In a debate going on in *Voprosy ekonomiki* (Nemchinov, 1966A) he again backed up Liberman and defended him against ideological accusations. What was important was that Nemchinov maintained that neither he nor Liberman wanted to make profitability a universal index.

Some of Liberman's proponents, who backed him up directly or indirectly by arguing convincingly about the need for reforms, and who accepted the idea of a synthetic indicator, supported profit against profitability. To mention some: Academician V. Trapeznikov (1966), who put great stress on economic levers, mainly on the role of flexible prices in managing the economy; L. Leontiev (1966); and Vaag and Zakharov (1964). The latter argued that profitability could turn out to be an obstacle to the introduction of progressive techniques under certain conditions.

In his 1964 article (1966B), Liberman defended profitability against profit by alluding to the fact that profit depends on the size of enterprises, whereas profitability does not. (The 1965 economic reform adopted profitability as one of the main indicators of the size of the bonus fund, but also gave a certain role to profit.) Nevertheless, Liberman agreed with some modifications of his original plan. He no longer insisted on profitability being a universal index; he admitted that in some branches, due to special conditions, another indicator could be applied. In addition, he agreed to consider in the determination of the size of the bonus fund the role of labour cost. To this end he suggested that the normative should be expressed as a fraction of a percentage of the wage-bill or wage-bill per employee. The first suggestion was included in the 1965 reform.

OPTIMAL PLANNERS

As already indicated in Chapter 1, the 'Libermanists' were not the only reformist group; the optimal planners also played an important role.[6] Surely they are and will be remembered for their technical and organisational suggestions on how to improve planning, the collecting and processing of data, national accounts and the flow of information, and for their successful push to introduce input–output tables and linear programming more than for their systemic proposals. They wanted to bring about a change in the working of the economy by basing decisions 'on rational (objective, scientific) grounds' (Ellman, 1971, p. 14) for the purpose of promoting economic efficiency. They also wished, no doubt, to make changes in the working of the EM, but these could be accommodated even within the existing system. Their intention was to improve the existing EM rather than replace it. Planning was still viewed by them as the best possible coordinating mechanism, though they believed that it needed big improvements, mainly in the internal consistency of short- and long-term plans, the stability of plans, the integration of physical and value planning and the evaluation of the flow of information – to mention only the most important ones. Much of their research was devoted solely to finding ways to improve the techniques of planning and thus to optimise planning. Their interest was also geared to designing a more rational price system as a guide for a more efficient allocation of resources and better computation methods for the evaluation of investment projects. This does not mean that they denied the market any role. Most of them were interested in decentralisation, and this must be combined to some extent with the market. The role they attached to the market was, however, a limited one.[7]

For want of space, only Nemchinov's and Novozhilov's views will be discussed.[8] I have selected economists who were preoccupied with the systemic as well as the technical problems of the economic mechanism.

In one of his papers, Nemchinov (1966B) developed what he called a cost-accounting system of planning. Considering the elements of the system, one could call it, with some simplification, a contractual system of planning. In the existing system, enterprises were assigned output targets and allocated inputs in order to be able to implement the targets. To him such a system was bureaucratic and inefficient because, among other things, it hampered the initiative of managers and workers. He preferred instead a system in which the planning authorities and enterprises had a choice. To this end, the authorities should announce their production plan and the enterprise submit ' . . . preliminary proposals concerning the conditions under which it is prepared to fulfill one or another plan order for the delivery of goods, specifying the assortment, quality, time limits, and prices' (p. 177). In turn, economic and planning authorities should distribute the orders to the best bidders, judged from a national economic viewpoint. Once enterprises accept the offers, they become binding on them.

Such an agreement, which has the form of a contract, is to Nemchinov a combination of planning and *khozraschet* (cost-accounting or more precisely self-financing). Such a system in the author's view would allow both the national economy and producing units to achieve optimums in their activities.

The contractual relationships should not be limited to one year, but should be concluded for a longer period, and renewed and supplemented in accordance with the requirements of the production process.

The products produced according to the specification of the contract should be bought by economic agencies whose jobs would undoubtedly be to sell them to buyers. To make the system rational, the economic associations and other superordinated organisations –

hinted the author – would have to be subject to the rules of *khozra-schet*, as enterprises were.

The supply of producer goods should no longer be rationed, but should be available in wholesale trade.

The system described constituted only a foundation. To make it work, additional building blocks must be appended. Nemchinov attached great importance to public and enterprise funds from which incentives, investment and technological progress would be financed. The funds should be financed from profit and their allocation and replenishment should be regulated by long-term normatives set by laws.

Needless to say, the price system must also change. He did not call for a radical change, for market prices. What he suggested was that the old practice of separate price and production planning should be terminated and that, instead, prices should be planned in coordination with production and consumption, with the help of mathematical methods (shadow prices), in order to create equilibrium between supply and demand. In addition, he urged that prices be made more flexible; fixed prices should be maintained only for particularly important commodities. Most prices should only be 'controlled'. Prices for non-mass products should be set by enterprises. As to price formation, the price of products should be made up of production costs, a charge on fixed assets and, of course, profit. For more discussion of this, see the price debate.

In Nemchinov's system, charges on fixed and working capital were to play a very important role. They were to present a minimum return on the use of assets by enterprises and repayment for the use of assets given to enterprises without charge by the authorities. In addition, the charges should encourage enterprises to make an efficient use of assets, all the more since profitability was to be calculated in terms of profit over assets.

V. Novozhilov (1970), one of the representatives of the group which favoured optimal planning, used the terminology of the conservatives but bent it to his own needs. He asserted that democratic centralism was the only possible principle for the management of the economy under socialism. By democracy he understood the involvement of the masses and enterprises in decision-making. Centralisation, whose role was enhanced by increasing large-scale production and the 'increasing complexity of economic connections', consisted for him of two forms: direct and indirect. Direct centralisation should be primarily applied where feedback from commodity–money relations is slow to appear, as in investment, technological changes, and development of heavy industry (p. 26).

Indirect centralisation has the advantage of subordinating all decisions to the plans without really excluding decisions from below. And now here is the interesting element which deals with the framework within which enterprises are supposed to make decisions.

> Indirect centralization in the solution of a particular class of economic questions consists of establishing norms for calculating costs and benefits by means of which the localities, guided by the principle of 'maximum benefits and minimum costs', may themselves find the variants that correspond most to the national economic plan. . . . The most important decisions are regulated in a twofold manner, directly and indirectly, and all the remaining ones are regulated only indirectly, through planned norms for calculating costs and benefits (p. 37).

From this statement and others, it seems that Novozhilov expected efficiency mainly from normatives ('The Russian term 'normativy' was incorrectly translated into 'norms'.)[9] worked out by the planners and not from the working of the market.

The combination of direct and indirect centralisation – to him – widens the circle of problems which can be solved jointly by the centre and enterprises, and this allows the interests of both to be respected.

Alluding to the New Economic Policy applied in the 1920s (NEP), Novozhilov argues that democratic centralism ' . . . presupposes a planned utilization of the law of value as an automatic regulator, i.e., as a regulator with feedback. Such a system of management was basically created at the very beginning of NEP, consisting of the plan and economic calculation, *khozraschet*' (pp. 26–7). The coordination of both is very important and complicated and can only be achieved gradually. The level of coordination is an indication of the degree of perfection of the management system.

According to Novozhilov planning can only be effective if it respects the law of value, which is to him not only a law of prices, but also a regulator of production. However, he did not have in mind a spontaneous, but a planned operation of the law of value. 'The planned use of the law of value can subordinate all economic decisions to the plan, if planned prices and the system of economic calculation are formed in conformity with the law of value' (p. 275).

In the following page he writes: 'The plan as a form of realization of economic laws must be the regulator' (p. 276).

Novozhilov urged optimal planning which to him meant primarily the working out of optimal plans and optimal prices. To him this could be achieved if the production structure and prices were determined jointly.

What Novozhilov really suggested was improving planning by utilising the law of value and *khozraschet*. But the law of value was not to operate spontaneously; instead, its assumed operation was to be quantified and offered to central planners and also to enterprises, to each in his realm, as a guide for decision-making.

THE PRICE DEBATE

The price debate was an integral part of the law of value debate. It started soon after the XXth Congress of the Communist Party in 1956. The focus here is on the debates of the 1950s and 1960s, mainly the latter. Most Soviet economists acknowledged that the price system was distorted. Since the effectiveness of the planning system as a whole and its individual components depended on the rationality of the price system, its overhaul was felt to be a primary task.

In Chapter 1 I have already indicated some of the shortcomings of the price system. Here let it be added that realisation prices for producer goods (wholesale prices) and consumer prices (retail prices) were differently formed. (This phenomenon is often called a two-level price system.) Wholesale prices were set according to the formula of production cost plus profit, whereas retail prices also included a turnover tax whose purpose was, among others, to ensure that prices clear the market. Since retail prices were rigid, the turnover tax could not long fulfil this task. As a result, wholesale prices as a whole were set below social costs, whereas retail prices were above them. In addition, prices for many producer goods (raw materials, some machines) were set intentionally low in order to stimulate investment. Furthermore, because of the infrequent adjustment of prices and the differences in the number of stages of processing which individual products went through, the differences in the profitability of products were excessive. Last but not least, in setting wholesale prices, scarcity was not given much consideration and some social costs (land, water, natural resources, as long as labour was not applied to them) were entirely neglected.

In the price debate which was primarily a debate about industrial prices (wholesale prices), three groups can be distinguished. One held that no substantial changes were needed. M. Bornstein (1964) calls this group traditionalist. The second group believed that the problems of the price system could be solved by changing the way that the surplus product (profit + turnover tax) is divided between prices. The third group advocated unorthodox solutions: it can be said that it favoured quasi-opportunity cost prices.[10]

The traditionalist group included many highly positioned economists who were known for their conservative thinking. To mention some: L. Maizenberg (Deputy Director of the Price Bureau in Gosplan), Academician K. V. Ostrovitianov, L. Gatovskii, V. Diachenko and S. Turetskii. They objected mainly, on the one hand, to the suggestion of the second group that the surplus product should be divided evenly into prices according to a certain formula. For example, V. Diachenko (1966) argued that the equalisation of profitability would deprive prices of their active influence and make them into a technical accounting tool. L. Maizenberg (1966) advocated the existing system of dividing the surplus product according to the cost of production, while S. Turetskii (1961) argued that the application of a production price formula would bring about a price increase in heavy industry products of 200 to 250 per cent and, consequently, a price increase in the whole economy. On the other hand, they objected even more strongly to the adherents of opportunity costs, whom they regarded as holders of anti-Marxist views. As is known, the Marxist tradition viewed marginalism, utility, and scarcity as subjective concepts, introduced with the purpose of undermining the Marxist labour theory of value. The critics of marginalism also voiced more practical objections; they mainly deplored the fact that it would lead to higher prices (see Sharpe, 1966, vol. II, p. 129). (For more, see Bornstein, 1964, Zauberman, 1960, and Bergson, 1960.)

The second group was divided into three subgroups. One defended the existing principle of distribution of the surplus product according to the size of the production cost, but with one difference – that the rate of return would be made uniform for all enterprises.

Another group called for the distribution of the surplus product according to the size of the wage-bill. This concept was defended by S. G. Strumilin (1960), one of the best known Soviet economists, and Ya. Kronrod (1957). It can be said that they did so with the object of applying Marxism in its purest form. In Marx's concept of value, only labour creates surplus value, and the rate of surplus value is measured in relation to paid out wages. Such pricing would make sense only if the planners wanted to encourage greater labour intensity of products, which was not the case (see also Zauberman, 1960). Needless to say, such pricing, in the final analysis, must work against technological progress, mainly if producing enterprises have an interest in using more capital-intensive input, and against increases in labour productivity.

Of the three groups, the following was the most innovative and courageous. It suggested a uniform rate of return depending on fixed and working capital. This concept is similar to Marx's production price, but in the eyes of dogmatists it presented a heresy, since, in Marx's teaching, it was only valid for capitalism. I. Malyshev was the first who came up with the idea. In the beginning, he was opposed by many, some of whom (for example, V. Nemchinov) later changed their views (*Diskuse* . . . , 1957). He was supported, among others, by V. Sobol (1966), editor-in-chief of *Vestnik statistiki*, L. Vaag (1966) and Z. Atlas, as well as by E. Liberman. They argued that such pricing would encourage enterprises to substitute capital for labour and to utilise capital assets more efficiently. In addition, they called for the introduction of a charge on capital assets, which was supposed to stimulate economising on capital assets, so that only assets which could be used efficiently would be kept.[11]

The members of the opportunity-costs group had in common a desire to derive prices from an optimum plan worked out on the basis of mathematical methods, mainly linear programming and input–output methods. These shadow prices were supposed to help to draft the plan and also be used as operational prices. The optimal planners' prices had to reflect demand and scarcities of factors of production. To this end, they called for prices to contain a capital charge and a differential rent.[12] In the view of the proponents of opportunity costs, the construction of prices in the way mentioned was consistent with Marx's labour theory of value and ensured an optimum allocation of resources. Finally, they were against the two-level price system.

One of the principal masterminds of the opportunity-costs school was L. Kantorovich, a mathematician with a great interest in planning. He developed his ideas in a 1939 paper which is credited with introducing the early form of linear programming, and later in a book (*The Best Use of Economic Resources*, 1965), for which he later received the Nobel prize. His views about pricing were commented on quite widely (Bornstein, 1964; Nove, 1968, p. 312; Ellman, 1973, pp. 94–108). Here only his ideas, as expressed in a symposium held in 1965, will be reproduced.

To Kantorovich (1966), the main purpose of prices is to have a guide 'for most optimal decisions' and a reliable gauge of economic efficiency resulting from decisions made in the interest of the national economy. Therefore, in setting prices, he stresses the need to take into consideration not only direct 'but also indirect outlays, as well as the unrealised possibilities in other branches as a result of assuming given resources to a given branch' (p. 136) – in other words, opportunity costs.

In his paper, L. Kantorovich argues that prices should include, besides production costs, costs reflecting capital output-ratio and also a rent, if extracting industries are involved. Thus the industrial price in his formula is made up of

$$P = C + W (1 + p) + ekF$$

where C is material expenditures per unit of product, W is the wage, p the growth rate of wages, F the assets per unit of output, e the percentage rate of production assets, and k is the differentiation coefficient in accounting of assets. e is in fact a charge on capital assets; its percentage should depend on the expected labour savings due to investment and should be determined on the basis of a long term plan for the development of the economy. k should be used as an incentive to promote the technical level of production and also to expand productive capacities where shortages exist. An increase in k, thus allowing higher prices, will stimulate more intensive utilisation of the assets.

In extracting industries, a rent should be paid by enterprises which work in better natural conditions or in a more favourable geographical location than the average. Enterprises working in worse conditions should receive a discount from the charge on assets.

The shadow prices of Kantorovich, derived from an optimum plan, have in common with the concept of production prices the same objective, an increase in the technical level of production and a better utilisation of assets.

V. Novozhilov was perhaps the most active and prolific member of the group. He developed his price theory gradually; his monograph *Cost–Benefit Comparison in a Socialist Economy*, published in a volume of papers edited by V. Nemchinov (1964), was an important stage in this development. His book, *Problems of Cost Benefit Analysis in Optimal Planning* (1970), can be regarded as a completion of the work on pricing.[13]

In brief, Novozhilov, in his *Problems*, takes the position that prices should conform to the law of value. But this is no easy task; it assumes an optimal organisation of the socialist economy, which in turn presupposes the realisation of planned proportionality of production and economy of labour. The author writes, ' . . . the essence of the law of value is the connection between the labor equivalence of exchange and proportionality of commodity production' (p. 271). The complete realisation of the law of value also means the fulfilment of optimal plans and this shows that optimal prices 'are another aspect of the optimal plan' (p. 274). On the other hand, plans to become optimal must be based on optimal prices.

And now let us turn to his concept of prices. Novozhilov argues that, in the first volume of *Capital*, Marx's definition of socially necessary labour time as an average magnitude is correct under equal technical and natural conditions. With the development of productive forces and the use of poorer natural resources, the utilised means have different effectiveness. Therefore, prices can no longer be equal to the average cost; instead, they are equal to marginal costs (1970, pp. 284–8). He resorts to quotations to show that Marx used marginal concepts not only when he was discussing differential rents.

The concepts of value, characteristic of simple commodity production, and of the price of production, valid for capitalism, are not appropriate for the socialist economy. In an optimally organised, planned economy, the socially necessary labour costs of each product are determined by what Novozhilov calls minimum differential (marginal) costs. He calls them minimum differential costs because they are incremental costs which appear in total costs as a result of producing an additional product. These costs are minimal if output is equal to requirements (p. 307) or, in other words, if supply and demand are in equilibrium. Since, according to Novozhilov, socially necessary costs are equal to marginal costs, 'prices always tend toward differential (marginal), socially necessary, labour costs' (p. 309). Prices include, besides direct labour costs, scarcity charges which are made up of investment effectiveness norms, differential and obsolescence rents, and interest for the time factor (Holubnychy 1982, p. 385).

V. Nemchinov is usually placed among the adherents of opportunity costs; M. Bornstein (1964) calls him the more cautious member of the school since his views are dressed more in Marxist terminology than is the case with Kantorovich or Novozhilov.

V. Nemchinov believes that the market mechanism is not the best mechanism for figuring out the amount of labour society can expend on individual products. Under conditions of planning this can be calculated successfully through computations on electronic computers. Objective price formation does not need the market. 'The market is only one of the mechanisms imitating the complex objective process of price formation and acts only in certain phases of the historical evolution of society' (1972, p. 210).

Price formation presents a transformation of the value, determined by the amount of labour embodied in products, into its components: material costs, labour costs and surplus product. This split is needed in order to 'differentiate the value in relation to various conditions of labour expenditure and to be able to utilise efficiently the existing labour resources, production funds and natural wealth' (1972, p. 232).

Price formation goes through several phases. After value is transformed into prices, planning prices are compiled; they present a social evaluation with which individual enterprises compare their production costs and estimate their expected profitability. In the last phase, prices are adjusted in such a way that no losses arise.

Unlike the second group, which counselled a distribution of the surplus product on the basis of an even rate according to a formula, Nemchinov called for the individualisation of the rate according to the size of the fixed and working funds of enterprises and the conditions for labour expenditure (1972, p. 216–17).

CONCLUDING REMARKS

Compared to economic thinking on our topic in smaller countries under review, the thinking of the Soviet economists was much less radical. It moved within the framework of the centralised system. As already mentioned in Chapter 1, the environment in the USSR was much more conservative: dogmatism had much deeper roots, mainly in the thinking of the older generation, than in the smaller countries. In addition, the self-interest of the older generation, who were in leading positions, suggested a need for caution. It is certainly no accident that the Academy of Sciences meetings, which called for a discussion of the ongoing debates about the economic mechanism, always came to the conclusion that the old centralised system should be preserved (Šulc, 1966).

It would be wrong not to see that both groups, the Libermanists and the optimal planners, played a positive role on the whole. What they suggested was mostly progress compared to what had existed before. When evaluating their contribution it would be incorrect to apply current criteria and forget the conditions under which the ideas came about. They introduced new, fresh air into the musty and stagnant environment of thinking and shook it up, broadened extensively the body of topics to be discussed and made economic thinking a more enjoyable activity. Their debates created favourable preconditions for debates in the smaller countries. There the resistance of the Party's bureaucracy to new ideas could be disarmed by alluding to the Soviet scene. And this was at that time a powerful argument.

Both groups, the Libermanists and the optimal planners, supported and had influence on the direction of the 1965 economic reform and saw in it a realisation of their ideas to some extent. Whereas the Libermanists saw the solution to the economic problems facing the Soviet Union in a better incentive system and more effective indicators, the optimal planners saw it in greater regard for economic calculation and value relations. On the whole, the former thought more in systemic terms than the latter.

Liberman's proposal did not go beyond the framework of the centralised system, but considering the existing economic mechanism, it was basically innovative and a step in the right direction. In particular, the suggestions for giving enterprises quite extensive autonomy, cutting plan targets to two, and making profitability the only success indicator, to which the size of the bonus fund was to be linked, were, no doubt, an improvement over what had existed before. Profitability in Liberman's proposal was not a planned indicator, as it usually was in a centralised system, and what was no less important, it was to be computed in a new, unorthodox way. Had these suggestions been applied consistently, it might have brought about a better working of the economy. Though theoretically sound, the idea of long-term normatives was in practice almost impossible to realise.

M. Ellman, who devoted great attention to optimal planners, argued when dealing with their impact on the economic mechanism (which is the only interest for my study) that optimal planners 'provided a theoretical basis for the use of value relations' (1973, p. 109). Several pages further on, he stressed that optimal planners' ideas were similar to market socialism (1973, p. 133).

In my opinion, the first evaluation statement is correct, but I have great doubts about the second, at least as far as it refers to

Nemchinov and Novozhilov. Even Nemchinov, who went further than Novozhilov in his reform blueprint, did not advocate a fully fledged market. Rather, he wished to imitate the market or, more precisely, apply the law of value, combined with some market activities.

Nemchinov's proposal for a cost-accounting system of planning was meant as a step in the direction of decentralisation and, in this sense, it was innovative. It probably influenced the reforms of the 1980s. To make a judgment about its practicality, one would need to see it in an elaborated form.

The changes suggested by optimal planners, such as the introduction of a capital charge, greater price flexibility, marginal pricing, the inclusion in price formation of the extent of capital intensity, and payments for the use of land and other natural resources make economic sense. Some of the proposals (the capital charge, recognition of capital intensity as a price factor) were integrated in the 1965 reform, and some appeared in a modified form in Gorbachev's reform of 1987 (for example, charge on water, stumpage fee, price flexibility).

The suggestions mentioned were an integral part of the optimal planners' effort to base planning on scientific grounds by using modern mathematical methods and computer technology. Without intending to make any judgment on the merits of their technical suggestions for improving planning (since this is beyond the scope of this study, let alone my capacity), it can be said that this was a worthy endeavour.[14] No doubt, Soviet planning techniques were quite unsophisticated and very labour intensive; every effort to improve them could be welcomed, as long as it was not meant as a substitute for economic reform.

The price debate, which was to a great extent sterile, meant, however, some movement in thinking about pricing which had an effect on the 1967 price reform. And this meant some progress, considering that it adopted the production price at the branch level, a solution which was unthinkable in the 1950s for ideological reasons.

It seems that there were economists who wanted to go much further in reforms than Liberman and the optimal planners suggested. No doubt they wanted to give enterprises more leeway in decision-making, but it is not clear how far they intended to go. They called for a clearly defined dividing line between what should be planned and regulated by the centre, and what should be left to the decision-making of enterprises. Generally, it was suggested that the central authorities should concentrate primarily on macro-economic issues, whereas enterprises would attend to the micro-economic areas (see Lewin, 1975, pp. 165–6). To make enterprises follow the state plan and in this way coordinate their economic activities, it was suggested that rules for the formation of certain value categories (as for wages, prices), normatives and the use of monetary, fiscal and investment policies should be established by the central authorities. So far so good. One may have the impression that this concept was not much different from what many reformists in the smaller countries advocated. Of course, whether or not it was so can be found only after a detailed analysis of the whole suggested model has been made. To make a judgment, the precise role of the centre is of crucial importance. Needless to say, divergency of views existed on this matter. For example, A. Birman (1964), after making a plea for a division of decision-making along the lines mentioned, gives a more detailed description of the model. Then it turns out that his model assumes the assignment of targets to enterprises, though in a limited number. The five-year plan (this is what he surely had in mind when talking about long-term indices) should include targets for growth of volume of production in value terms, level of profitability, expenditure, quotas, and so on, and annual plans would have output-mix targets. In another place, when he defines the role of the centre, he expects it to determine prices and, for a transitional period, rationing of producer goods. In other words, the most important features of the centralised system are to remain. The same is true in a modified form of G. Lisichkin's book on plan and market (Lisičkin, 1967). Perhaps the explanation for this phenomenon is that reformers, though they had in mind a radical reform, did not dare to divulge their real thinking due to the existing situation.

Notes

1. Many of the articles quoted here are taken from M. Sharpe (ed.) (1966) *The Liberman Discussion*, vol. I, and *Reform of the Soviet Economic Management*, vol. II. In the bibliography it will be indicated by an abbreviation: in Sharpe I, or Sharpe II.
2. There were other participants in the debate who preceded him (see Felker, 1966, p. 58); however, Liberman's contribution, due to its content, attracted great attention at home and abroad.
3. In his article in *Voprosy ekonomiki* (1966A, p. 66), Liberman formulates the assigned targets a bit differently. He talks about 'volume of marketable output of a specified nomenclature and appropriate quality'. It is not clear which of the two papers was written earlier.
4. Liberman had to compete for some time with another proposal for a

synthetic indicator. The author of the other proposal was F. Tabeyev, head of the Tatar Economic Council, who favoured the 'normative value of processing' as the main synthetic indicator. (For more, see Felker, 1966, p. 58; also Vaag and Zakharov, 1964).

5. B. Sucharevskii was also a member of the State Committee on Labour and Wages.

6. In writing this paragraph I have made much use of Ellman's book (1973).

7. The main institute of the optimal planners was the Central Economic Mathematical Institute of the USSR Academy of Sciences. The ideas of the Institute were presented in a book edited by its leading scientific workers (Fedorenko, Bunich and Shatalin, 1970). According to the book, enterprises should still be assigned targets, though only for key products, and allocated inputs. Wage rates and prices for key products were to be set from above. Enterprises were supposed to pay charges for the use of capital goods and natural resources. The difference between the existing management system and what these optimal planners suggested was primarily in enterprises being encouraged to apply the 'local optimality criterion' to the targets given by the authorities, and in the flexible prices (see Ellman, 1971, p. 17).

8. The reader who is interested in knowing more about optimal planners is advised to consult, besides Ellman's books already mentioned, Sutela (1991) and Katsenelinboigen (1979).

9. By normatives we understand proportions in which money variables (revenue, net income, profit) are distributed between the state and enterprises and within enterprises. Norms are primarily a technical relationship (norms of labour intensity) or a relationship between certain performance and reward (performance norms).

10. In writing this section, I have relied on M. Bornstein's article (1964).

11. At the second meeting of the Scientific Council on Problems of Price Formation, which took place in March 1963, it was stated by the chairman that the greatest support was received for a compromise proposal, through which the surplus product would be divided in proportion to labour costs and in proportion to fixed assets (Chernysheva 1964). The wholesale price reform carried out in 1967 accepted in substance the idea of the production price (for more, see Adam, 1989, pp. 45–6).

12. The differential rent has, on the one hand, to mitigate the differences in income resulting from natural conditions and, on the other, to value natural resources appropriately when decisions are made about investment projects. In the USSR, the regionally differentiated agricultural procurement prices represent a quasi-differential rent.

13. The reader who is interested in the development of Novozhilov's views on pricing should consult V. Holubnychy, 1982, pp. 420–6.

14. P. Sutela (1991, p. 39) believes that the methods of the optimal planners were too crude and rested on the unrealistic assumption that enterprises were interested in economic efficiency.

3 Czechoslovakia

INTRODUCTION

The economic reform in Czechoslovakia in 1966–9 was put into motion by the resolution of the Central Committee of the CP. The 1965 resolution made it clear that planning was to remain the fundamental instrument of the management of the economy and, in order for it to become more effective, it should utilise commodity–money relations. The role of the market in the reformed system was not elaborated on very much in the resolution; it was indicated by the stress given to the need for more rights to enterprises, for greater room to be given to the assertion of special interests, and for the constant renewal of the harmony between social and special interests. It also implied that the balancing method of plan formulation, which was criticised in the resolution as ineffective, would be supplemented by economic calculation and the pressure of the market (*Život strany*, no. 4, 1965).

The Action Programme of the CP, which was adopted in April 1968, devoted greater attention to market forces. This was at a time when the reformers' position was significantly strengthened by the new First Secretary of the CP, A. Dubček, who was favourably disposed to the reformers. But even the Action Programme put narrow limitations on their working. It called for a 'renewal of the positive functions of the market as a necessary mechanism for the functioning of the socialist economy and a verification of whether the work of enterprises was expanded purposefully. We do not have in mind a capitalist market but a socialist market and not its spontaneous but regulated utilisation'. (*Rok* . . ., 1969, p. 130).

The preparations and, even more, the inception of the implementation of the reform culminating in the Prague Spring gradually removed the tight control over society, and a liberal atmosphere came into being. This was also reflected in a rejuvenation of intellectual life, the best demonstration of which was an ending of the artificial uniformity in views. This was a period of great debates; the focus of the debate in the economic field was the role of planning and market in the reformed system. Needless to say, some economists opposed the promised role for the market in the official documents.

45

On the other hand, the number of economists who wanted to go far beyond the official reform grew in the course of time and the views on the relationship of planning and market underwent substantial changes. In the beginning the question was: what should the role of the market be? This meant: what should be left to the market and what could planning not perform well? Later the question was turned around: what should the role of planning be? This meant: what should be left to planning and what could the market not perform well? In the beginning economists usually talked about a combination of planning and market; later the order was changed – the market moved to first place. Putting the market in first place was not always a matter of priority; in some cases it resulted from the method of examining the combination of the two coordinating mechanisms. Since the problem was how to renew the market, what role should be carved out for it and, as a result, what planning should not do, it seemed to be logical to start with the market (Kožušník, 1968). Some suggested starting with the market for historical reasons.

There was also quite a development in understanding the scope of the market. Initially, the market meant primarily a market for commodities. Later, when the economists realised that the reform did not develop in line with expectations, and when the political situation in the meantime became more favourable for reforms, there was a push for the extension of the market. Calls for the establishment of a capital and labour market started to be voiced, primarily in 1969.

In this chapter, I will discuss not only the debate about planning and market itself but also some aspects which are closely connected with the way planning and market are combined.

PLANNING AND MARKET

As to the combination of planning and market, four groups of views can be distinguished. Of course, this division is artificial as far as it refers to the last three groups of views, since there are no clear dividing lines between them, especially if we take into consideration the years 1968–9 when a radicalisation in systemic thinking took place. At one end of the spectrum there was the traditional view which was represented by J. Vejvoda. At the other end of the spectrum was the view represented by several young economists who gave to planning only a supplementary role. To them the market was to be the main coordinating mechanism. In the middle, there were two groups whose views were that planning should continue to play an important role. The difference between the two middle groups was really in the mix of planning and market. The second preferred a regulated market, and the third saw in planning and market more or less two complimentary coordinating mechanisms.

To J. Vejvoda (1966), planning is conditioned by the direct social character of labour. Since, at the existing level of productive forces, the socialisation of labour is realised at the level of enterprises, market relations survive. However, they are limited to a corrective role in a planned economy: namely, they correct the proportions set by the plan, and in this way they incessantly renew equilibrium relations between enterprises. To give market relations a regulative role in the generation of proportions, as happens in a capitalist system, would mean introducing relations among enterprises based on the principle of different owners. Vejvoda implies that such a step would be wrong, since enterprises in a socialist economy belong to the same owner, and, as a result, planning would be undermined. For the same reason he opposes the idea of equilibrium prices generated by market forces (more about this later).

Vejvoda does not explain what the thesis about market relations, which are defined in one place 'as a form of a realisation of the plan', should mean in practice. From the whole tenor of his argument, one must come to the conclusion that he was not in favour of any substantial changes in the system of management (compare Kožušník and Kodet, 1967).

The representative of the second group of views seems to be O. Šik. The statement's indefiniteness follows from the realisation that Šik's writings must be read differently from those of other authors.[1] He was, no doubt, the leader of the movement for the reform; his leadership position resulted from being, among others, a scholar and a politician at the same time.[2] As a politician, he had to be very careful in his formulations in order not to supply the opposition with ammunition against the reform. It should not be forgotten that in leading party circles there was, in the beginning, tremendous opposition to a major economic reform. Not only this, but even factory workers were also sceptical of the reform, fearing instability and unemployment – ideas instilled to a great extent by CP leaders who opposed the reform.

The topics of Šik's papers and the argumentation at the time were determined largely by the debate about the reform, and even more by the economic situation and the development of the reform. His views on the whole underwent certain changes.

In his 1964 paper, O. Šik directed his fire primarily on the ills of the economy, the reasons for these ills and how to cure them. He subjected the existing centralised planning system with its assigned targets and ideological underpinnings[3] to sharp criticism. 'He who thinks that the most important thing is fulfilment of all the plan targets, even though production satisfies increasingly less the needs of the consumers, makes a fetish of the plan in reality and makes of it a self-purpose, even if he proclaims one hundred times the opposite.' The idea that everything must be determined by the centre and that without such determination production would not take place is Stalinist. And this, Šik claims, is also the source from which the notion came that the 'market should not regulate a socialist economy.'

Why Šik believes that the market should be an important component of the system is discussed in his book *K problematice . . .* (1965) which was later translated, with some changes, into English under the title *Plan and Market under Socialism* (1967), and also in a paper delivered at a conference (1965A). In his book, where he develops his ideas in great detail, Šik sees the necessity for market relations 'in contradictions between concrete labour expended and the socially necessary expenditure of labour' (1967, p. 169). In simple words, this means that there is a contradiction between what individuals produce and what society needs. The traditional system, with its plan targets and the way it sets them, and incentives linked to quantitative targets, did not motivate people (neither managers nor workers) to aim for an 'optimum development of production'. As consumers, these same people, of course, wanted more, new and better products. This conflict can be solved only by commodity–money relations (market).

O. Šik also tries to answer the question about the reasons for the conflict. He sees them in the circumstance that the work, due to the incompletely developed productive forces, has not yet reached the creative stage and therefore one could say with Marx that work is not yet 'life's prime want'. People only work in order to make a living and, as a result, strong incentives to work are essential. This also means that decisions of enterprises are influenced by self-interest and, consequently, the old thesis about the identity of interests between society or, more precisely, government and enterprises is groundless.

An understanding of these relations means that a system of incentives must be designed in a way which will motivate the enterprise collective to work efficiently. And this can only be achieved with the help of the market. If enterprise collectives are made to realise that their well-being depends on the performance of their enterprise in the market and this, in turn, depends on the extent to which it is able to respond to demand in terms of quantity, quality and cost, but mainly to the latter two, a powerful incentive to work will be created (Šik, 1965A).

As to the relationship between planning and market, Šik (1964) believes that macro-proportions, including major investments, should be determined by the plan which, in turn, should be in line with anticipated long-term changes in market demand. The market is to him a market regulated by the 'planned determination of the main processes of distribution of national income'. Micro-proportions, with some exceptions, should be determined by the market. Its impact should be felt through prices which should reflect the real development of the costs of production.

In his English brochure (1966), where he apparently was especially careful not to be accused of abandoning socialism, he writes: 'harmony between production and the market is achieved primarily through long-term plans determining not only the main trends and structure of production but also the basic trends of the home market. And the fact that these plans basically define the distribution of national income . . . determine the movement of prices for the basic goods, predetermines also the general trend of demand and of the economic macrostructure. Consequently, socialist planning will continue to be the basic means for dovetailing production with the market' (p. 13).

The views expressed by M. Sokol, a high bureaucrat in the Planning Office, also belonged to the second group. They represented, however, a mixture of the official policy and his own, the latter mainly when he indulged in pointing out future trends. What is presented here is in substance the concept of the enacted reform.

According to Sokol (1965), the role of the plan necessarily changes when enterprises are given greater autonomy in an acknowledgment that they are quasi-autonomous units and when many directives are replaced by economic tools. To him, the role of the plan is in the macro-economic sphere, where it determines macro-proportions as well as economic tools for the indirect management of the economy. From the foregoing, it is clear that he attaches great importance to the plan in investment activities: it should determine their direction and also decide about important investment projects. With the development of the reform, the centre should rely more and more on indirect methods, on credit and the interest rate. The same is true about important tasks in technical development. The centre should be involved in the determination of all proportions which go beyond the branch interests or which are difficult to anticipate, and in projects which entail a lot of risk. Finally, the plan should ensure international division of labour. All these tasks are necessarily reflected in some compulsory targets.

Economic equilibrium is expected to result not only from the application of economic tools but also from the setting of orientation targets which are not binding on enterprises. However, if great disproportions arise, binding targets can be assigned.

K. Kouba is a good representative of the third group. He expressed his views primarily in two articles. In his 1965 article he calls for the combination of plan and market as two complementary coordinating mechanisms which make economic rationality possible. To him, the reformed system should be designed so that in it the plan becomes the anticipation of the market, fostered by economic aims and the direction of economic development. On the other hand, the market itself is influenced by the choice of variants of development and the application of preferences. Thus the aim of the plan is, among others, to set goals for economic and social development. Its realm should be, however, limited to the determination of certain macro-economic proportions, and should not, by any means, cover micro-proportions.

On the whole, his paper is quite abstract; it does not discuss in any detail how the two coordinating mechanisms should 'coexist'. The reason for this lies perhaps in the topic of the paper, which is entitled 'Plan and Economic Growth'. In this context it is worthwhile mentioning that he subjected the balancing method to criticism, arguing that it is unable to equilibrate supply and demand and causes disproportions by setting the growth rate from the anticipated growth of individual branches of the economy, instead of from the anticipated growth rate of national income and structure of consumption.

In his 1967 article, which is a shortened version of a longer article published in a book edited by him (1968), he is no more specific about our topic. He introduces, however, some new ideas about planning. To him, socialist planning is an instrument of 'coordinating economic activities, harmonising interests and setting a preferential scale of goals'. The difference between socialism and capitalism is not in planning and market, but in the aims set independently of market forces. A socialist economy needs market impulses to work efficiently, but it is not a market economy. Unlike a market economy, where profit is not only an incentive, but also the aim of economic activity, the socialist economy needs profit only as an incentive and signal. Socialism 'is a system with a higher targeted behaviour' (*cílové chování*). For all these reasons, the plan is to him more than the model of the future market.

These views of Kouba underwent a great change in the direction of the fourth group. This statement is based on an outline for the further development of the reform (*Náčrt základní . . .*, 1969) completed by a collective under his headship.[4] Considering that his judgment had great weight among his peers, one can assume – and the author himself confirmed it – that the outline reflected his views. In the outline, the role of the plan was

> to synthesise the elements of economic policy on the basis of knowledge of economic processes, enable coordination of the economy, solve systematically macrostructural and interbranch relations, support progressive structural changes, safeguard smooth and balanced development and assert societal priorities to a purposeful extent. At the same time *market processes* act as a general environment of the economy. (p. 21)

No doubt, the outline assigned a much greater role to the market than previous studies had, all the more because it also contained a proposal for the creation of a market infrastructure, including a money market 'properly modified by socialist production relations' (p. 57). Considering that this outline was worked out in the beginning of 1969, under Soviet occupation, it was quite a daring document.

Some representatives of the younger generation belonged to the fourth group. P. Pelikán (1967) believes that the combination of the coordinating mechanisms must be such that the market determines prices at which producing units and consumers exchange products and services. In addition, material incentives should be derived from the market. The role of the state is to intervene when the market fails and also to set non-economic goals. In addition, its role is to be a powerful participant in the market; as such the state can determine a portion of production and investment and thus stabilise the market. To him, planning is a supplement to the market mechanism. In talking about planning, he has in mind indicative planning: a set of information about supply and demand in the future market.

O. Kýn is a good example of the radicalisation of systemic thinking. Being one of the few economists who knew Western literature, and being articulate and dynamic, he had quite an influence in reformist circles. In his 1964 paper titled 'The Role of the Plan', he criticised the traditional concept of planning, according to which plan fulfilment was identified with meeting national interests. To him, reality 'always deviates from the conditions assumed by the plan' (1964). This does not mean that planning has no role to play. Kýn sees its function primarily in harmonising interests and decisions on the long- term development of the economy (investment). In his 1968 paper, he takes a position *vis-à-vis* planning and market similar to Pelikán; the first is to him only a supplement to the latter. He maintains that the 'substance of socialism is not planning', but lies in 'humanisation of human society and in elimination of exploitation of various kinds'.

Marketisation of the economy had more enthusiastic adherents in the Czech lands than in Slovakia. In the latter, there was some concern that the market might hamper further equating of the economic level in Slovakia with that in the Czech lands. In their Outline of the further development of the reform (*'Náčrt d'alšieho . . .'*, 1969),[5] Slovak economists maintained that 'economic evening out in Slovakia will be more complicated in a management model based on market relations', and therefore suggested a series of measures to ensure further equalisation.

The first, and even more the fourth, group of views on the desirable combination of planning and market were far from what the official reform intended. In the existing internal and external political conditions and the prevailing thinking of the public, it was unimaginable that the Czechoslovak leaders would even consider making the market the fundamental coordinating mechanism. It should not be forgotten that at that time planning still had many followers, even in the West, and that France still applied some planning.

It could be argued that the majority of academic and non-academic economists held more or less the views of the second and third groups. In a nutshell, they wanted a management system in which there was a division of coordinating activities between planning and market. Planning was supposed to be limited to the determination of macro-proportions; mainly the determination of long term investment was to remain in the hands of the centre. It was also accepted that the plan must play a role in foreign trade. The market was to determine most of the micro-proportions. In planning the anticipated development of the market should be taken into consideration, the market in turn being influenced by the planned macro-proportions.

The ideas about the combination of planning and market determined, of course, the views on subsystems, such as price determination, wage regulation, financing of investment, and so on.

The adoption of the Action programme of the CP in April 1968 created a platform for reformers to push for further changes in the system of management. Despite important changes in the system of management of the economy, when compared with what existed before, the market was still very weak. Many institutional obstacles prevented it from functioning properly. To mention some: the price system was not reformed sufficiently, the authorities still interfered a lot in enterprise affairs, monopolisation prevailed, the monobanking system remained intact and the state monopoly of foreign trade was changed only a little (compare Kožušník, 1968A). In addition, what existed of the market was primarily a market for commodities.

In 1968, and even more in 1969, calls for a capital market were increasingly voiced. Understandably, the demands for a capital market had fuzzy contours in the beginning. Some economists were uncertain about how far it was productive to push, but perhaps, even more, had ideological inhibitions about pushing for changes which smacked too much of capitalism, and some probably did not have a good idea of how a capital market works. Therefore, initially, the demand was formulated generally, as a call for a financial market. To my knowledge, the first fairly systematic formulation of the demand was in the study of Horálek et al. (1968). But even here it was timid and limited in scope. They stressed the need for a flow of capital where it could be used most efficiently. However, they excluded the possibility of joint stock companies on a large scale, as well as investment by one enterprise in another. Instead they suggested that enterprises with surplus capital should loan to other enterprises at an interest rate set between the creditor and debtor.

In their Outline mentioned (*Náčrt d'alšieho* . . . 1969), Slovak economists, who dealt with the problem of the capital market in greater detail, did not go much further than Horálek et al. In the outline mentioned, worked out by a collective headed by K. Kouba (*Náčrt základní* . . . 1969), the idea of a money market was specified quite clearly, but was still restricted in its scope; no mention was made in it about joint stock companies or the stock market.

AUTONOMY AND SELF-MANAGEMENT

It was clear that, if the centralised system was to be abandoned, enterprises were supposed to get genuine autonomy. However, the authorities were not prepared at that stage entirely to forgo control over enterprise activities. Of course, the control was not to be exercised as before, directly through binding targets and allocation of inputs, but indirectly, primarily through economic regulators, and also, more directly, by limits to enterprise decision-making about investment activities.

The scope of the debates was, of course, not limited by the authorities' set rules. Economists who were in favour of abandoning for good the old directive system were looking for a theoretical underpinning for the autonomy of enterprises. The government interfered in the affairs of state enterprises as the representative of the state, which, in socialist countries, was the owner of the means of production. Considering this circumstance, it is clear that the solution to the problem of government interference lay in changing the exercise of property rights.

There was not just one approach to this problem. Some economists, for example, D. Plachtinský (1966), argued that state ownership of the means of production was realised and concretised in enterprises, hence there was state enterprise ownership and the right of enterprises to autonomy. Plachtinský saw the proof of his statement in the fact that state enterprises enter into different relationships among themselves, and between themselves and the state. He tried to back up this reasoning by alluding to the circumstance that, in the reformed system, enterprises were supposed to finance investment activities from their own resources. In other words, if they were not owners, they would not be asked to behave in this way. In his opinion, enterprise ownership was the real cause of the existence of 'commodity production'.

Needless to say, the argument is not very convincing, considering the very limited autonomy of enterprises under the directive system. The allusion to new rights and obligations in the reformed system is even less persuasive: on the one hand, it smacks of circular argumentation, and, on the other, it tries to base its thesis on the actions of the authorities as if they were the embodiment of consistency.

Nevertheless, a similar view was accepted by many economists (see Ernst, 1968). On the other hand, a few economists opposed such views. The motivation behind their opposition was not the same. Some objected to enterprise ownership, because they were adamantly opposed to any decentralisation, and some, such as E. Löbl (see Ernst, 1968), because they disliked the idea of self-management which can be inferred from enterprise ownership.

Other economists approached the problem of government interference more practically; they simply argued for the transfer of property rights to enterprises. For example, B. Komenda (1969) argues that state ownership is a form of societal ownership which is 'alienated from its own purpose' and will come to an end as enterprises become 'economically independent market actors' (p. 874). To him, this does not mean the end of societal ownership; on the contrary, it means a better realisation of it.

The transfer of property rights from the state can, in substance, be accomplished in two ways. One method is to transfer them to a non-state institution outside enterprises and leave to the managers the right to steer enterprises in the name of the non-state institution. Such a step means a separation of ownership and management. The other option is to transfer them to enterprises, or, rather, to the representatives of the working collective of enterprises, a solution which can mean an integration of ownership and management.

In the beginning of the reform, the idea of self-management had few adherents and was hardly discussed in the literature. The initial documents about the reform contained no indication of the upcoming introduction of self-management in enterprises. Though Czechoslovak reformers took over many elements of the Yugoslav reform, self-management was shunned. It seems that there were two reasons for this. To advance the idea of self-management meant identifying the economic reform with the Yugoslav system and, what is worse, identifying it with a most hated concept in the official circles of the USSR. Secondly, many economists believed that the expected benefits from self-management were greatly outweighed by costs. It is worthwhile mentioning that Horálek et al., who were among the best-known reformists, did not even mention self-management in their comprehensive outline of the further steps needed in the reform (1968). But slowly the views changed, mainly as the threat to the reform from inside and, above all, from outside increased. Self-management started to be viewed as a useful two-pronged instrument which can protect enterprises from government interference and also gain workers for the reform.[6] The idea of self-management gained considerable credence when it was included in the Action programme of the Party (*Rok . . .*, 1969, p. 127). In June 1968 the government published provisional rules for setting up workers' councils. The rules were quite flexible in the sense that enterprises were allowed certain choices. In substance, the workers' councils, apart from their right to elect top managers of enterprises, were supposed to play an advisory more than a decision-making role (Kosta, 1973, p. 191; Golan, 1973, pp. 42–6).

This is not to say that Czechoslovak economists embraced self-management with no worries and concerns. B. Ward's paper (1958) was known to some of them. They were not, however, worried that self-management might lead to unemployment (see Kocanda and Pelikán, 1967). Most concerns were focused on the possible effect of self-management on wage growth and thus on price movement, and on investment activities.

B. Komenda (1969) fears that self-management may create an ownership relation to the accumulation fund which would hamper labour mobility. In his scheme labour will move only if such a move is accompanied by the flow of its share in capital, which is not easy to accomplish. In addition, workers may also have a claim to the net income and a share in returns on investment with all the consequences. To prevent such a development which would, among other things, destroy collective ownership, he suggests regulating the income of enterprises as well as the wages.

Komenda's fears were not warranted since such a possibility could only arise if enterprise collectives became the owners of the means of production, and thus collective ownership turned into group ownership, a scenario which had few adherents, since most followers of the self-management solution were willing to give the working collectives only the exercise of some ownership rights and not ownership itself.

K. Kouba (1969) believes that workers' councils cannot be successful managers unless there is a favourable environment, by which he means an efficiently functioning market with rational prices, conditions which did not exist in Czechoslovakia.

In an attempt to reconcile self-management with an efficient use of capital, B. Urban (1969) suggests combining self-management with a non-state institution responsible for the management of the means of production. He calls for the creation of a Fund of national wealth which would include the means of production of enterprises. The management of the fund is to be entrusted to an executive nominated by workers' councils, the State Bank and the government, and to be appointed by Parliament and reporting to Parliament.

In Urban's opinion, this executive organ should have many important tasks once it is fully instituted. It should work out an optimal national plan including suggested structural changes, which should be considered as an alternative to the state plan. Urban does not mention the mechanism which will bring about a compromise between the two plans.

The executive should also have the function of a founder in the sense that it makes decisions about allocation of capital, establishment of new enterprises and liquidation of existing ones. Finally, it should be authorised to enter into general collective agreements with the Trade Unions.

What Urban suggests is only a general open-ended draft. Nevertheless, it is an idea which emerged in a different form in Hungary in the 1980s.

REGULATION OF ENTERPRISE INCOMES: GROSS INCOME VERSUS PROFIT

The economic reform was supposed to give enterprises quite a lot of autonomy in decision-making about what to produce, how to produce, where to buy inputs, and so on. In return, enterprises were supposed to be self-financed, responsible for wages and to a great extent for investment. They were expected to raise the needed revenues by producing goods in a mix and quality which the market demanded and at costs which it could absorb.

At that stage of thinking, the authorities were not prepared to leave enterprises to themselves; they believed that it was still necessary to maintain control over the behaviour of enterprises by subjecting them to various regulations and to an evaluation of their performance. The question, what should the evaluation indicator be, was of great importance, since the indicator was supposed to be not only a gauge of performance, but also an incentive, and thus an object of maximisation and taxation, and finally a guide to decision-making. The choice was between gross income and profit, and almost always the former was selected (only in a small percentage of enterprises did profit become the indicator).

The choice of gross income was not generally approved of. Many economists argued in favour of profit. It is interesting that mostly the reformers who argued for maximum decentralisation were in favour of gross income, whereas many of their opponents argued for profit. It is not clear whether the choice was influenced by the Yugoslav system. If it was, the supporters of gross income did not admit it.

The views of the reformers and supporters of gross income were perhaps most articulately explained by Z. Kodet (1965) and M. Sokol (1968). According to Z. Kodet, in the final analysis only one important aspect was decisive in the selection of gross income, and that was the desire to create conditions for an economic regulation of wages.

Like M. Sokol, he believes that the use of profit as an indicator and base of taxation would not allow the direct assigning of the wage-bill from the centre to be abandoned. Kodet does not explain why, but he must have had in mind that such a system would not force enterprises to use objective criteria for wage formation. If managers of enterprises are entitled to make decisions about wages, they may be tempted to pay excessive wages and thus reduce the amount of profit. Such a step may lead not only to unwanted (from the viewpoint of society) wage increases, but in addition will reduce state revenues due to lower profits. The only way to counter such a danger would be to regulate wage increases directly. By contrast, taxation of gross income, which means simultaneous taxation on the portion earmarked for wages as well as profit, reduces the danger mentioned and therefore enables an economic regulation of wages to be introduced. In addition, the adoption of gross income makes possible a regulation of both wages and bonuses by a single evaluation indicator.

M. Sokol (1968) believes that promoting profit to an indicator would mean taxing it as in a capitalist economy. However, profit has a different position under socialism than under capitalism. Unlike profit under capitalism, which is used for the private consumption of capitalists and for investment, profit under socialism is earmarked primarily for investment and therefore should not be the main object of taxation. Instead, he suggests making wages the main target of taxation 'which is in line with the fact that in our conditions there is (in enterprises) a greater interest in wages than profit'. The choice of gross income, which contains both wages and profit, as a basis for taxation fits Sokol's suggestion.[7]

J. Kosta and B. Levčík (1967) argue that taxation of profit under capitalism is acceptable since capitalists are interested in its maximisation and protect it from the working class. By contrast, under socialism there is no class which is dependent on profit due to its position in production and which would defend profit against the workers.

The main argument against gross income was that, serving as a base of taxation, it did not act as an incentive to more efficient performance. Assuming that two enterprises have the same gross income, they will pay the same tax, regardless of the amount of profit and the methods of production. In taxation terms, enterprises are treated in the same way whether they perform well or poorly, which is against the spirit of the reform (Bránik, 1967, p. 26). The reform, namely, set as a goal the termination of the old practice which rewarded enterprises with a poor performance at the expense of those performing well.

Some argued against gross income in the belief that abandoning the old system of direct assignment of wages would lead to disparities between incomes and the consumption fund (see O. Šik 1964).

The argument of the supporters of gross income that the selection of profit as an indicator would not allow the direct assignment of the wage bill to be abandoned was not very convincing. The Hungarian reform showed that this was possible even under profit. True, the Hungarian reform did not give enterprises such leeway in wages as the Czechoslovak, since wage increases were controlled primarily by a normative linked to gross income per employee, and tax was only the second line of defence.

On the other hand, what J. Bránik suggested would have meant, in the final analysis, adjusting the tax rate to the methods of profit production in individual enterprises, which would have opened the door to arbitrariness.

The promise of the reformers that the adoption of gross income would prevent unwarranted increases in wages did not turn out to be realistic, partly because the stabilisation tax was a weak restraint on wages at a time when enterprises were gaining revenue due to the failed wholesale price reform. As a result, the government also introduced a tax on profit which undermined the idea of having gross income as the only indicator.

PRICES

In the centralised system of management, the vast majority of prices were set by the centre. Once they were set, they did not react flexibly to changes in supply and demand. Naturally, they were not scarcity prices. In addition, individual price circuits (retail, wholesale, agricultural and foreign trade prices) were mutually separated. A reformed system of management in which market forces were to play an important role could not have such prices. Therefore, it was clear that a price reform was needed. Obviously, there was disagreement about how far the price reform should go. At one end of the spectrum were economists who, in substance, wanted to preserve the status quo in the price system and, at the other end, there were economists who called for the creation of market (equilibrium) prices. Compromises filled the middle ground.

From the foregoing it is clear that Vejvoda's (1966) views reflected a desire for the preservation of the status quo. His point of departure was that the economic structure should be regulated by the plan and not by prices. In a market economy, prices are the result of the relationship of supply and demand, but, at the same time, prices shape this relationship by their feedback. In Vejvoda's view, it seems (his explanation is quite obscure) that the relationship of supply and demand should not determine prices; what it should affect is the realisation of prices. The plan should be adjusted so that goods can be sold at existing prices.

He also advances another reason for his objection to equilibrium prices. Applying such prices means giving enterprises a lot of say about the price level. Since enterprise workers are interested in wage increases, they will use their influence to induce price increases as a source of wage increases, which will in turn generate inflation. Under socialism, price increases do not serve accumulation as in the capitalist system. Equilibrium prices – argues Vejvoda – necessarily lead to a deepening of conflicts between society and enterprise collectives.

The other end of the spectrum was marked by views calling for equilibrium prices. Komenda and Kožušník were perhaps the best-known representatives of this view. It would be wrong to assume that they wanted mechanically to transplant the prices of market economies into Czechoslovak conditions. Their price reform left some room for government intervention (planning), mainly in the transitional period. A similar position was taken by Horálek et al. (1968). In a joint article, Komenda and Kožušník (1964) call for an introduction of equilibrium prices, determined by the relationship of supply and demand, which should become the only factor in exchange relations between enterprises. Unlike the prices determined from above which always favour some enterprises more than others, these new prices are supposed to be an objective criterion of enterprise performance. Equilibrium prices must be flexible prices and are thus in conflict with the idea of what I would call rigid stability prices, which necessarily lead to an ossification of the structure of production.

Komenda and Kožušník are against government price control of new products, as long as they are substitutes; however, they do not mind intervention, if the new products are complementary and exposed to price increases. The speed of the changing relationship between supply and demand is for them an important criterion for government control. In the case of engineering and consumer industries' products, where the relationship between supply and demand changes rapidly, no price determination from above should be allowed. In the event that central control is still needed, it should be exercised by so-called limited prices. Prices should be set from above in the case of products for which the relationship between supply and demand changes slowly, as is the case with basic raw materials and energy.

These conclusions served as a theoretical basis for the grouping of prices which the reform introduced.[8] This does not mean that Komenda and Kožušník agreed with the way the grouping was handled. Komenda (1966) criticised the price grouping, mainly the fact that the official prices were rigid, contrary to original intentions.

CONCLUDING REMARKS

I have discussed only the most important aspects of the debate about planning and market. There were also debates about the administrative organisation of enterprises, which was an instrument of monopolisation, about investment systems, wage regulation, and so on. Problems of economic policy, which were closely connected with the system of management, were also hotly debated.

The tenor of the debates was much influenced on the one hand by the Marxist ideology to which everyone paid tribute, to varying extents, and on the other by the long insulation from the development of Western economic thought. Of course, the two factors were interrelated. The term 'insulation' perhaps does not express properly the real state of affairs in the beginning of the sixties. Perhaps a better characterisation of the situation is the fact that many economists knew little about non-Marxist economic theory. They did not even know what the West contributed to the theory of socialism. When the economic reform started, only a few knew about the important debate in the West on economic calculation under socialism. After the seizure of power by the communists in February 1948, all non-Marxist academics were pushed aside or left the country, so the new generation was left to itself to find out what was on the other side of the Iron Curtain. As a result of all this, only a few economists, when the debate about the desirable shape of the reform started, had a good idea of how a market works. Needless to say, this lack of knowledge had an important effect on the debate.

The development of views on the relationship between planning and market was also influenced by slow progress in the economic reform, and by political events. The political leaders only reluctantly agreed to economic reform under the pressure of the worsening economic and political situation and therefore – as already mentioned – they tried to limit the reform as much as possible. Under the pretext that substantive problems must first be solved, such as, for example, the renewal of market equilibrium, the agreed principles of the reform were put into effect only slowly and inconsistently. In response to such a policy, the reformers pushed for more changes in the system of management, arguing that in a reformed system such problems could be solved more easily.

With the advent of A. Dubček to power, the demands of the reformers were treated with greater sympathy, and this indirectly encouraged reformers to make even greater demands. The threat from outside, which culminated in the occupation of Czechoslovakia by the Soviet-led invasion, radicalised the reformers. The invasion did not bring the reform to a halt instantly; on the contrary, the period after the invasion, up to the resignation of Dubček in April 1969, was marked by further development of the reform (it was characterised mainly by the democratisation of management structures) and new ideas about how best to reform the system.

Still, uncertainties in the minds of the reformers about how best to combine planning and market did not disappear. They resulted mainly from perplexity about what the market can do and what should be done in order to make it function well. This resulted not only from a lack of theoretical clarity and from insufficient theoretical erudition, but more often from ideological confusion. For example, some economists were aware that without a capital market it was not possible fully to develop market forces. But they had ideological inhibitions about suggesting doing what was necessary.

Considering that the economic reform, including the pre-reform debate, was relatively short-lived, the extent of the development of ideas about the market was quite an accomplishment. After all, almost all the ideas which characterised the Hungarian reform of the 1980s, which was the most advanced, were already present in the Czechoslovak debates, though often in an embryonic state.

An idea which was absent from the debate is that functioning of the market presupposes pluralisation of ownership. The majority of even the most radical economists believed that the market could be made workable if enterprises were given full autonomy. They did not assume that the reintroduction of private ownership on a larger scale was needed.

Notes

1. There is also another reason for this ambiguity. Šik was a passionate fighter for market forces. In 1962, he published a book under the title *Ekonomika, zájmy, politika* (*Economics, Interest and Politics*) (1962) which was a refreshing piece, considering the ideological conditions at that time. Its main message was that market relations were a necessary, integral part of the socialist economy. Nor should one forget his publications abroad, in which he unambiguously argued for some market socialism, with the market the main coordinating mechanism. Since this book deals only with discussions in Czechoslovakia in the period 1966–9, Šik's later publications are disregarded here.
2. He was the director of the prestigious Institute of Economics of the Academy of Sciences and, what is more important from a political aspect, he was a member of the CC.
3. He mainly ridiculed the thesis that under socialism expended labour has a social character automatically.
4. The outline was compiled by research fellows of the Economic Institute (M. Horálek, B. Komenda, Č. Kožušník, among others) and representatives of the Economic Secretariat of the Prime Minister (M. Sokol, among others). Needless to say, the outline had no effect on the management system, since it was not completed until A. Dubček was ousted.
5. The Outline ('*Náčrt d'alšieho . . .*', 1969), which takes positions on various aspects of the reform, was prepared by a group of Slovak economists affiliated with the Commission for Management by the Slovak National Council.
6. This is confirmed in Lang's paper (1970), written for the purpose of discrediting the idea of self-management.
7. To this end, the authorities made taxation a criterion of efficiency and introduced in 1967 a uniform tax rate on gross income for industrial enterprises, and a tax on the wage-bill (stabilisation tax) which was a proportional tax in substance.
8. Three price categories were introduced: fixed, limited and free.

4 Hungary

INTRODUCTION

In the 1966 resolution, the CC of the Hungarian Socialist Workers' Party (Communist Party) laid down the principles of the 1968 economic reform. 'The underlying features of the economic mechanism should be an organic combination of centrally planned (*tervszerű*) management of the economy with commodity relations and an active role for the market, based on collective ownership of means of production' (Party Resolutions and Decisions, 1978, p. 459). Following that, the writers of the resolution make it clear that the two elements of the reformed economic mechanism, planning and market, are not to play an equal role. The 'terms of working' of the market are to be determined by the plan. The market should not be left to itself but should be regulated and managed so that it can contribute to the implementation of national economic plans. On the other hand, the market, with its feedback, influences the plan and puts checks on it (ibid., p. 459). In brief, the market is supposed to be a supplement to planning. It is worth stressing that the expanded role of the market is not to be combined with important changes in the collective ownership of the means of production.

Though the space carved out for the market was quite limited, the reform meant great change in the economic mechanism. This reform and the Czechoslovak reform were the only two radical reforms in the 1960s.[1] They expanded enterprise decision-making substantially and freed enterprise managers from the straitjacket which assigned targets had meant for their decision-making. They also allowed enterprises to choose suppliers according to their own considerations. Enterprises also got more say in wage determination, employment, pricing and investment decisions.

In return, enterprises were supposed to be self-financed: besides covering material costs, they were to earn money for wages and investment and to make a profit. It was hoped that enterprises, in pursuit of their own interests, which would be reflected above all in maximising profit, would also improve economic efficiency and satisfy market demand. Only if they were able to sell their products in the market, which would not be possible unless they responded to the demand of the market, would they be able to make a profit. Since market demand was supposed to be influenced to a great extent by government investment and government-sponsored exports, enterprises in their own interest were expected to follow the state plan voluntarily.

In addition, the authorities reserved to themselves the right to intervene directly, especially when the security of the country was at stake and when foreign trade obligations had to be fulfilled. They also counted on indirect intervention with the help of fiscal, monetary, wage and price policies (for more, see Adam, 1989; Berend, 1990, pp. 137–47; and Révész, 1990, pp. 60–83). Finally, the right to appoint enterprise managers gave the authorities the guarantee that they would not lose control over the activities of enterprises.

The 1968 reform was not preceded by extensive debates (Szamuely, 1986, p. 44). The Hungarian reform was a reform from above, without great pressure from below. In the face of a worsening economic situation, part of the Hungarian leadership believed that a proper response to the new situation would be an economic reform. The internal political situation was quite favourable for economic reform in the sense that the government was not afraid that the economic reform would touch off demands for political reform. The government made efforts to gain the support of the people[2] and was successful to a great extent. The international atmosphere was also favourable – the Soviets themselves were engaged in debates about reform – and this helped to convince the rest of the leadership to go along. Some personnel changes, mainly the fact that R. Nyers became the secretary of the CC which had nothing to do with the reform, strengthened the reform-minded wing in the highest governing body of the CP.[3]

Debates about the reform went on mainly in the reform committees which prepared the reform blueprint. They were based on materials prepared in advance (Hetényi, 1989, pp. 12–14). Of course, the debates behind the scene were *partly* transferred to the columns of magazines and journals. Economists looked in this way for support for their stand. But once the decision about the direction of the reform was made, the publications mostly defended the concept of the reform.

In their considerations of the blueprint for the 1968 reform, the reform committees made much use of the results of the working committees of 1957, all the more as some prominent reformers of that period, for example G. Péter, participated in the preparation of the reform. Needless to say, the public debates in the 1960s were a follow-up to some extent to the debates of the second half of the 1950s.

The reform committees did not have an entirely free hand in designing the blueprint. In a 1988 interview, T. Nagy[4] (Ferber and Rejtő, 1988, p. 42[5]) mentioned that he was told not to come up with suggestions for self-management, with solutions which might lead to unemployment, and with proposals for changes in the organisational system. Only the first and third constraints require some explanation. It appears from a 1988 interview with R. Nyers (Ferber and Rejtő, 1988, p. 25) that J. Kádár was very much against self-management, apparently as a result of his experience with workers' councils in 1956–7. In addition, the Trade Unions opposed the idea, since they saw in self-management a threat to their position. The politicians did not want changes in the organisational system which might antagonise the bureaucracy.

Here I would like to confine myself to the debates on planning and market and some connected problems, in the period preceding the 1968 reform up to 1972, when a reversal started.

PLANNING AND MARKET[6]

With some simplification, it is possible to argue that, in the period under review, two groups of views on the combination of planning and market existed. According to the views held at one end of the spectrum (which could be characterised as conservative), planning is the natural coordinating mechanism of socialism and the market should be applied only because planning has not yet been put fully on a scientific basis. Commodity money relations were regarded as a necessary evil. The other end of the spectrum was dominated by views which did not transgress the official ideas of the reform. I will call them reformist views. They can be summed up by saying market relations also exist in socialism, and their use should be substantially extended, mainly in the microsphere, for the sake of improved economic efficiency. They should, however, be regulated by planning. Though there must have been some economists who were in favour of a fully marketised economy, their views did not appear in the press. In the prevailing thinking of that time, which was marked rather by fear of the market (see Berend, 1988, p. 239), such views were regarded as extreme. Besides the views mentioned, it is also important, for the sake of completeness, to mention the views of T. Liska, who did not have many followers, but whose ideas did not leave people indifferent.

The Reformist Views

Many economists shared reformist views. Due to limited space, mention can only be made here of the contribution of some of the authors. One author (see L. Árva, 1989) maintained that the debate about the reform started with T. Nagy's paper on the law of value (1964).[7] This was an important paper, primarily for two reasons. First, in discussing the law of value, the author took a clear anti-Stalin position, though he did not mention Stalin's name. Second, he examined the socialist economic system, perhaps for the first time in Hungary, from the viewpoint of two possible models, probably under the influence of W. Brus.[8]

Nagy takes the position that the existence of value categories, such as prices or cost of production, does not mean that the law of value is in operation. A permanent deviation of price relations from values, without having an effect on production, means only an impediment to the law of value. To put it in other words, the working of the law of value must also be felt, according to him, in production, in that the law of value regulates it.

The author then examines the law of value from the viewpoint of two possible models, centralised and decentralised. In the latter the market can only be a regulated one under socialist conditions. Government decisions about the distribution of national income into accumulation and consumption, as well as about the allocation of the bulk of the accumulation fund, should form the framework within which the market can work. In addition, the government should exercise its influence on the market by regulating prices and taxes primarily.

The foregoing, applied to the law of value, means that T. Nagy takes a similar position to Brus, as Nagy himself makes clear. The law of value is not only a regulator of prices to him, but also – as already mentioned – a regulator of production. Yet, the law of value is not an absolute regulator, its working is restrained by social preferences in the structure of consumption and income distribution. In addition, the law of value does not regulate the main direction of the economy. 'In this respect [writes Nagy] central decisions and orders are needed.' In brief, the decentralised system which he favoured meant to him a centrally planned economy with a regulated market.

One of the best representatives of the reformist group was the main architect of the reform himself. R. Nyers, who was the secretary for economic affairs of the CC of the CP, and, as such, the initiator and mover of the reform, had a very pragmatic approach to the reasons for the need of the reform and its principles. Being not only a very good and experienced economist but also a politician in a very high position, he knew very well what the economy needed and what the limits under the existing conditions were. Hence, he tried to have the reform designed in a way that would be acceptable to the highest bodies of the Party, mainly to J. Kádár, the leader of the Party. His expressed views were therefore, not necessarily always a precise reflection of his genuine thinking. Considering his papers, and particularly his speeches in CC meetings, one cannot fail to see some development in his views concerning our topic on the combination of planning and market. One can only speculate whether the 'development of views' was the tactic of a politician who presents his programme gradually in order to make it more acceptable, or the genuine result of a longer concern with the topic, including discussions with members of the reform committees.

In one of his first papers on the reform (1965), R. Nyers mentions the following reasons for the reform: after explaining that the economic mechanism is bound to change with the evolution of productive forces, he maintains that changes are needed in order to create an environment which is more conducive to the working of the economic policy. The existing EM is not able to ensure a proper harmonisation of the interests of individuals, enterprises and society. Without a reform, an increasing conflict between enterprise and societal interests is unavoidable. With this reasoning, the author indirectly destroys one of the 'principles' – more precisely, the wishful thinking principle – on which the traditional system was based, namely, that there was no conflict of interest between enterprises and society.

A change in the EM is also needed, the author argues, because of the exhaustion of the extensive sources of growth. The transition to an intensive type of economic growth, of which productivity growth becomes the primary source, cannot be implemented in the old institutional framework. The traditional system is not conducive to an optimal increase in economic efficiency.

As to planning itself, he sees its shortcoming primarily as based on two faulty hypotheses: first, that planning is a one-level activity, and second, that it is possible to plan everything from the centre.

Finally, even in this short survey of Nyers' ideas about the shortcomings of the management system, it is worthwhile mentioning that he criticised the way the *khozraschet* principle was implemented, mainly the fact that enterprises did not operate within their own revenues.

When he explained the need for reform to the meeting of the Central Committee for the first time in 1964 (1968, pp. 84–5), Nyers, judging from his speech, was very general with regard to the direction of the reform. What he needed at that meeting was approval for the start of the reform committee's work, and the less specific he was the better, though he had the Politburo's sanction. Only later did he start to explain the concept of the reform. In his interview with *Népszabadság* in April 1965 (1968, p. 98) he called for a more purposeful combination of central planning and commodity–money relations. In November 1965, when the CC met to discuss the guidelines for the reform worked out by some 200 economists, Nyers, was, of course, specific.

First, he made clear that there was a need for a substantial overhaul of the EM. In the new economic mechanism (NEM) greater room must be given to market relations and connected categories. In other words, to him, planning and market are not incompatible coordinating mechanisms. The market is to be, however, a regulated market, not a spontaneous one as it is under capitalism. The main distinction between socialism and capitalism is, according to him, that in the former '*the labour force even in the future cannot become a commodity and that not the market, but conscious, state planned management will have the decisive role in extended reproduction, in investment*' (1968, p. 140).

Furthermore, enterprises should be given greater autonomy. However, they should remain in state ownership and the directors should be nominees of the state. Enterprises should work out their own plans: they should be allowed to determine their output plan and make decisions about the best use of resources. The handing down of binding targets is not needed in a planned economy. However, as long as NEM is not fully established, only a reduction in binding targets is possible. Needless to say, a contradiction exists between allowing enterprises to determine their output and assigning them binding targets. It seems that these contradictory statements reflect the disagreements in the reform committees. A minority in the committees insisted on maintaining binding targets (see interview with T. Nagy carried by Ferber and Rejtő, 1988, p. 42).

In the May 1966 meeting of the CC, when the final principles of the reform were approved, Nyers had already suggested eliminating binding targets while retaining for the authorities the right to impose quotas 'if enterprise effort clashes with societal interest' (1968, p. 189).

To calm fears that enterprise activity might deviate significantly from the five-year plan objectives, he mentioned the tools which the authorities have at their disposal to make sure this does not happen. The authorities appoint managers and evaluate the performance of enterprises. This in itself gives them great influence on the behaviour of managers. In addition, the authorities determine, among other things, major investments, the amount of investment credit, and its distribution among sectors of the economy and industrial branches (1968, p. 188).

Judging on the basis of his writing, B. Csikós-Nagy favoured an economic reform along the lines approved or even a more radical one. He belonged to the tiny group of very good economists with a solid knowledge of Western economic theory. His prolific writing, which covered a wide range of topics, helped others, mainly the younger generation, to orient themselves in the intricacies of a market economy. But due to his past and his position (he was the chairman of the Price Board until the middle of the 1980s), he was careful in his pronouncements. In his 1964 paper, he supported T. Nagy's (see Árva, 1989) stand on Brus' two models. In his 1966 paper on two phases of the discussion about prices, he succinctly explained the difference between a regulated market in the suggested NEM and market relations in the traditional system and the role of prices. In NEM 'the national economic optimum . . . is not produced on the basis of regulation by the central plan, but as a final result of real market processes' (1966).[9] This interpretation of the role of the market went, of course, beyond the spirit of the reform. However, several sentences later, he made it clear that the regulated market 'of the socialist planned economy should not be contrary to planability (*plánovitost*)'. To him the role of planning should be 'a consciously regulated growth of the economy on the basis of an economic policy concept, equilibrium, stability, regulation of incomes'. No explanation is given as to how the centre should achieve equilibrium and stability.

In his 1968 paper on the socialist monetary system, Csikós-Nagy touches on the problem of capital flow and the banking system. Faithful to his cautious approach, he does not challenge the existing rule forbidding the extension of credit between enterprises and the use of surplus funds of one enterprise for investment in another. The author only timidly suggests that even the free flow of capital within the banking system may bring advantages. To this end he also proposes examining whether a multiple banking system would not better serve the flow of capital.

There were other well-known economists who professed reformist views and were engaged in designing the reform blueprint. To mention some: I. Hetényi, later the finance minister, O. Gadó and J. Wilcsek. The latter stressed in his writings the need to create proper conditions for profit to become the main incentive and guide for decision making, one being a flexible price system (1965). He also pointed out the advantages of the market and competition (1967).

Finally, I. Friss should also be mentioned as one of the representatives of the reformists. His importance lies, however, in providing arguments for the abandonment of the old, traditional system rather than for the adoption of the new. In the 1950s and the beginning of the 1960s, he was known in economic circles as a faithful and dedicated adherent of the old system and opponent of reforms, and his positions, first as the head of the economic department of the CC and, later, the director of the prestigious Economic Institute of the Academy of Sciences, lent him credibility. Since he was not known as an opportunist, his criticism of the old system helped smash some of the dogmas on which it was based. True, he did not maintain that the various laws of socialism (for example, the basic law of socialism, the law of proportionate development, the law of distribution according to work, were wrong, but that the conditions for their working in the Hungarian situation did not exist in many cases. He suggested 'that the laws of the socialist economy we, the successors [to Marx, Lenin] must conclude from the analysis of our own experience' (1967). And, what is the most important, he concluded that planning must be supplemented by the market.

The Conservative Views

Gy. Sík (1966) can be regarded as the representative of the other end of the spectrum. He saw in the approved reform a regrettable, but necessary retreat from the correct trend of socialism. To him, the intended expansion of the autonomy of enterprises was an instrument rather than a goal, since the trend under socialism is to centralisation. However, centralisation requires planning based on scientific methods, and, in their absence, the law of value should be allowed to regulate output and therefore it would be wrong to assign targets to enterprises from the centre. Planning cannot be scientific unless a clear-cut method is available for measuring economic efficiency, and unless there are methods for comparing objectively the advantages of different development proposals. The author puts great hope in the development of mathematics and computation techniques to a level which will allow optimisation of planning and thus the basing of planning on a scientific foundation. Once planning becomes scientific, no incentives will be needed, nor any market, which is probably what he had in mind.

Gy. Sík's opposition to the assignment of targets to enterprises was limited to simple reproduction. However, he was very much for government control when extended reproduction (investment) was involved. Unlike many other economists who believed that government control should be limited to major investments, Sík advocated government decisions about almost all investments. To give enterprises a free hand in decision-making about investment would mean – he argued – rewarding enterprises for good work in the past, and this would, in his view, be wrong, since only the centre can make correct decisions about future development (Sík 1966).

At first glance, it is clear that Sík underestimated and misunderstood the role played by material interests in motivating people. He did not see that even the best computation techniques cannot ensure correct decisions, simply because nobody can force enterprises to give accurate information, which is the basis for computation, if this is not in their interest.

Among the critics of Sík's views, it is worth mentioning K. Szabó and M. Mandel (1966). The first was for many years the head of the department of political economy of the Marx's School of Economics and as such was quite influential. The authors criticised Sík's suggestion that all investments should be under the control of the centre. They advocated the view that microdecisions should be left to enterprises, whereas macrodecisions should be the domain of the government. Yet even the macrodecisions should be handed down, not directly, but indirectly. Szabó and Mandel were, however, not very specific as to indirect methods. The ambiguousness of their thought was increased by their suggestion that planning should 'create a uniform movement from which would integrate the simple and expanded reproduction into an interlocking process' (1966, p. 445). (See also Szamuely, 1984, p. 47.)

The conservative views on planning and market were shared by other economists, though they approached the problem in a different way. For example, T. Morva, who was a member of the three-man secretariat, was against dropping compulsory output targets (Berend, 1988, p. 222). He believed that the problems faced by the economy could be solved by changes in economic policy (see his interview with Ferber and Rejtő, 1988).

The need for changes in economic policy, mainly the abandonment of the trend to maximum growth and autarky, was also stressed by other economists. For example, F. Jánossy (1969) was one of the proponents of such ideas. But to him, changes in economic policy had to be coupled with systemic changes.

T. Liska's Views

T. Liska was a maverick of Hungarian economic theory. It is necessary to stress right away that his radical views are combined in places with conservative ideas. In his 1963 article ('Critique and Concept, Reform Outline of the Economic Mechanism'), which was among the first in a lengthy list of publications with unorthodox views and innovation and often unrealistic suggestions which shocked many readers, he made a strong appeal for market relations. To him, production under socialism is geared to the market and not to the satisfaction of needs. The latter requires an economy with much more developed productive forces than socialist countries have. Market relations result not from special ownership relations (let me add, and thus from production relations) but from the state of productive forces. Because productive forces are not yet sufficiently developed, the market is needed to prevent losses from occurring. Considering that this argument was used at a time when much dogmatic thinking was still the rule of the day and it was very easy to interpret his views as anti-Marxist, the author's approach was, no doubt, courageous.

The institution of market relations must start, according to Liska, with a reform of the price system. He mentions 25 reasons for the need to replace cost pricing, one of them being that the existing cost-price formation cannot serve as a reliable gauge and information for rational decision-making. The new prices should result from world prices.

He calls for the integration of the Hungarian economy into the world economy. This is not to be regarded as an anti-CMEA manifestation; Liska is against any economic bloc and in favour of a global international economy. He takes the communist leaders' pronouncement about the need for international co-operation not as an expression of propaganda, but as an acknowledgement of the trend to a single international market.

His stress on market relations did not mean that he was prepared to abandon planning. Of course, he wanted a modification of planning, above all, a cessation of the practice of assigning compulsory targets to enterprises, which, according to him, made the whole planning process a formality, all the more as it was happening when rational prices were lacking. In the existing management system, planning and rational decision-making became two conflicting terms. Because money and prices were passive instruments, the socialist economy was deprived of its most important tools.

Liska expects that rational prices would allow effective planning and make it possible for profitability to become a synthetic indicator. He believes that planning allows more developed organisational forms and a higher level of monopolisation than capitalism does. To him, in the process of plan preparation, the best and most efficient plan projects are selected among the many competing for resources. To make the projects realistic, a supplementary control by the market is needed.

It can be assumed that in what he had to say about planning he was referring to a rejuvenated planning. But even so, his belief that planners select the most efficient project seems naive in the light of experience and our present knowledge about planning.

In his book *Ökonosztát* (which was written in 1963–5, first circulated as *Samizdat* (underground literature) in 1965, and again published in 1988), T. Liska elaborates on the ideas expressed in his 1963 article, and gives answers to his critics. For our purpose, the first part is the most important because in it he confronts the readers with an ultra-radical plan for the re-organisation of the socialist economy. The *ökonosztát* is, according to the author's definition, 'an economic automatism (market mechanism), which works automatically according to the socialist goals and properties' (1988, p. 33). To put it in a simplified way, Liska suggests entrusting the banking system with the running of the collective property. In the banks' hands the collective property turns into credit capital. The banks lease enterprises, land and investment projects to the people who are willing to pay the most in organised auctions. If no lessee is found, the banks are empowered to appoint trustees to operate certain businesses (pp. 239–40). After the leases expire, the assets are again leased to those who are willing to pay the most.

The purpose of this arrangement is to promote economic efficiency by encouraging entrepreneurship. Collective ownership is not abolished, it is only modified into personal societal ownership. Nobody owns any means of production except his own human capital. Liska sees this socialist system as superior to the capitalist system, since everyone is given an equal opportunity to be an entrepreneur.

Liska's *ökonosztát* is supposed to be an anti-bureaucratic system in which the role of the state is minimal, or, at any rate, smaller than in the most liberal state, and where planning only exists to the extent needed to put the system into motion.

Liska's book had a great response; some praised it and some criticised it but only a few ignored it. It was criticised, because it reminded people of the utopias which have been written in the course of history. I. T. Berend (1983, p. 342) characterised Liska's *ökonosztát* as a system comprised of progressive elements, but conservative and utopian. He found the idea of a society composed of bidders and competitors unrealistic. Also, the role attributed to government seemed to him incorrect, a view shared by R. Nyers. The latter was also critical of the fact that Liska attributed a minimal role to planning and relegated democracy to free entrepreneurship (1988, p. 17). Some admitted that auctions could be a good idea when small businesses are involved, but they would not be good for large businesses (see, for example, M. Tardos, 1983, pp. 365–9).

VIEWS ON PRICING

Hungary played, to some extent, a pioneering role in pricing. As is known, in the 1950s and 1960s Soviet and East European economists were occupied with the question of how to divide up the accumulated 'surplus product' in industry into the prices of products, whether according to cost of production, as was the practice at that time, or according to the amount of wages (value price), or according to invested capital (production price) (see Chapter 2). The production price was rejected by many because Marx regarded such a price as characteristic of the capitalist system. The Hungarians were the first to accept the idea of production prices and use them in their industry, but in a modified form, as a two-channel price, meaning that the profit should be divided according to two principles: according to invested capital and to wages (for more, see T. Nagy and Sz. Esze, 1963).

The debate about the formula for distributing profit revolved around the question of how best to express the social cost of production (value). When news about the upcoming reform started to leak out, the debate about prices, of course, focused on new concepts. B. Csikós-Nagy, in his already mentioned paper dealing with the two phases of the price debate in Hungary (1966), stressed that in the second phase of the debate (connected with the upcoming reform) economists barely talked about social costs of production, price centre, two–price level, which were concepts known from the first phase of the debate.[10] The debate was focused instead on 'real' market prices, and entirely neglected social production costs.

Csikós-Nagy indirectly expresses disapproval of this approach and takes the reader through a short course in the history of price theories. He takes the position (in which at that time Marxist economists, who fought for more rational prices, believed) that a rational structure of consumption can be achieved at prices which correspond to social costs of production. And such prices and market (equilibrium) prices are not the same. There may be prices which equate supply and demand, but which deviate from social costs of production and thus from an optimum structure of consumption and production. And after all, he argues, prices are determined by *the relationship of planning and market* (my italics). Since, in the re-formed system, the market is going to play an important role, prices will play one too, but they will not be market prices. In NEM, price relations will reflect the social cost of production, the value judgment of sellers and buyers (supply and demand) and social preferences. In his 1982 book, which deals with economic policy, Csikós-Nagy labels the price system, which came about through the 1968 reform, as a mixed system (1982, p. 232).

This mixed system in practice meant that three different price forms came into being: fixed (applied to some basic materials, agricultural products and important foodstuffs), limited (could move within a certain range, applied to some raw materials and consumer goods) and free prices (agreed between sellers and buyers). Furthermore, the authorities committed themselves to bringing consumer prices gradually closer to production costs.

In his paper about the socialist monetary system (1968) Csikós-Nagy argues that, in the third phase of the price debate, the stress should be on what the second phase had failed to do, that is, on considering prices as an integral part of the monetary system. In this connection, he also touches on the exchange rate and currency convertibility, and indirectly defends the decision to base the exchange rates on the average cost (instead of marginal costs) incurred in producing commodities for one dollar, by arguing that marginal costs only make sense if convertibility exists, and it cannot exist because of the system of trading in CMEA countries.

B. Csikós-Nagy's views were more or less shared by most authors specialising in prices (see T. Nagy, 1967; Vincze, 1969; Sulyok, 1968). True they also touched on problems which Csikós-Nagy did not mention, or did so only in passing, but the underlying approach was the same in substance.

For example, in his 1967 paper (titled 'The Price and Socially Necessary Costs in Socialism'), T. Nagy also tackles the impact of world prices on domestic prices. The more a country's economy is 'involved in international division of labour and the more freely the market mechanism works in international trade, the more international value relations determine the domestic price centre relations in the long run'. He does not forget to mention that in practice domestic prices deviate from world prices for various reasons (in developing countries for the sake of protecting the domestic market). In the socialist countries, planning is an additional factor of price deviation, and for this purpose various tools are used (tariffs, subsidies and quotas).

Even T. Liska (1963), who vigorously defended the idea of world prices as the basis for the domestic prices of tradable goods, acknowledged that it was impossible to stop deviations from world prices entirely. Of course, he wanted to reduce them by keeping impeding factors to a minimum.

In the large number of papers written on prices besides T. Liska's, I. Hagelmayer's paper (1968) can also be evaluated as a voice which diverged from the general line. His divergence was, however, presented in a very timid way. To him, the working of the law of value presupposes free prices; such prices are brought closer and closer to value by economic processes. In other words – in contrast to other economists who called for prices corresponding to social production costs without really suggesting how this process should come about, but mostly assuming that it would be the result of government action – Hagelmayer is quite specific: he prefers that this process be achieved by market forces. Of course, he acknowledges that this cannot be achieved instantly without causing great disturbances in the economy.

CONCLUDING REMARKS

The reform debates which found their way into publications covered many topics other than those discussed in this chapter. There were discussions about the proper performance and incentive indicator, whether profit or gross income (most debaters favoured profit), the best strategy of economic growth, how to improve planning, to mention some of the important topics.

The reformists' thinking in Hungary in the 1960s – as far as it was reflected in publications – did not differ much from the thinking in Czechoslovakia or, for that matter, in Poland. Most Hungarian economists believed in the need for a reform and believed that the system, though marked by shortcomings, was reformable. (There were certainly economists who did not like the system and wanted its elimination, but only a few doubted its viability.[11]) This was also clear from the direction of the proposals for reform. Nobody challenged collective ownership or called for its fundamental reorganisation. It is interesting that when T. Nagy got his 'marching orders' from the CP (see p. 66), in the sense that he was told which items should not figure in the reform blueprint, ownership was not even mentioned. Apparently the political leaders did not even expect that such ideas might crop up. It is also true that collective ownership was regarded as a fundamental feature of socialism and therefore challenging collective ownership would have meant challenging socialism.

The market suggested was not only to be regulated and to serve planning activities, but in addition was limited to commodities. The approved reform blueprint did not envisage a capital and labour market, because the introduction of such markets would smack too much of capitalism, an idea which was totally unacceptable to Kádár, since it was in contradiction to his political conviction. Even if he did not mind, he had to consider Soviet sensitivities. To allow a labour market would mean going back on the promise of full employment.

S. Kopátsy (1969) was perhaps the first to challenge the adopted concept of the market, and called for the introduction of a quasi-capital market. He was probably allowed to do so in a journal because the devised system of investment in NEM produced overinvestment. According to the author, all state enterprises should be turned into joint stock companies and their shares should be evenly distributed among twenty banks entrusted with handling the property. The directors of the banks should see to it that investment funds flow to enterprises which are able to use them best. The finance minister should be responsible for ensuring that the tendencies in the stock market are in accordance with government policies and plans. However, Kopátsy does not explain what kind of tools the finance minister should use in order to achieve the task mentioned. The author stresses that such an arrangement will strengthen collective ownership because it will make it more efficient. It also has the advantage of separating ownership from management, which the author regards as important. Three years later, M. Tardos (1972) came up with a similar suggestion which he elaborated on in 1982.

The suggestions about a capital market had no great echo in the 1960s and even less in the beginning of the 1970s when the reform came to a halt. The reform even left the monobanking system intact in substance. B. Csikós-Nagy (1968) maintained that this was a deliberate decision, stemming from the conviction that indirect management of the economy requires a centralised bank and credit system, and that the monobanking system was to be *the* tool by which the market was to be regulated. True, the reform promised to make the banking system a 'partner' of enterprises (see Csapó, 1967); however, in practice, the monobanking system remained an administrative organ once it was entrusted with the task of seeing to it that, in extending credit, the objectives of the plan were also taken into consideration. Only in the second half of the 1980s did the capital market, after a long discussion, start to be gradually introduced.

Compared to the situation in Czechoslovakia, including the period from the occupation until the ousting of A. Dubček from his leading position (a period which was fertile in radical thinking), the spectrum of views in Hungary was narrower: in Hungary radical views like those in Czechoslovakia did not appear. It seems that two reasons were responsible for the difference. The 1956 suppression of the uprising in Hungary was still fresh in the minds of economists and therefore more self-control and self-censorship was exercised. J. Kádár was quite popular at that time, and most economists trusted the authorities' judgment about the possible limits for reform and maybe even for ideas.

In Czechoslovakia, the initiative for the reform came from below. The intellectual community was involved in a protracted fight with the political leadership about the direction and scope of the reform, and this bred frustration as well as radicalisation. The fact that the Hungarian reform was initiated from above and that a big collective of economists and other social scientists (200) participated in the formulation of the blueprint proposal added to this trust.

Notes

1. True, in some circles there is a tendency to belittle the importance of the reform. Its significance should not be viewed through the prism of present ideas about economic systems but through the conditions of the 1960s, and what the reform meant for the future development of the socialist system. For example, to J. Kornai (1986) the reform only meant relaxation of the bureaucratic coordination of the shortage economy.
2. Travel abroad was gradually expanded. People who left the country in 1956 could return home for good or for a visit. The atmosphere for creative intellectual work improved; the number of taboos slowly declined.
3. S. Kopátsy argues (1989) that J. Kádár allied himself with the reformers because he was afraid of the Stalinists.
4. Nagy served as the head of a three-man secretariat which steered the work of the reform committees, which were entrusted with the preparation of proposals for the reform.
5. This book is a collection of interviews with some of the economists who participated in the working out of the official reform blueprint for the 1968 reform.
6. The book edited and introduced by L. Szamuely (1986) was very helpful to me in sorting out my ideas about planning and market.
7. S. Kopátsy (1989, p. 10) regards T. Nagy and Gy. Péter as the only real reformers.
8. In the article T. Nagy mentions only Brus' teaching material. It can be assumed that the material also contained some mention of the two models, since Brus' book in Polish appeared in 1961 and the material in 1964.
9. This is a translation from Slovak.
10. This statement is an exaggeration, easily refutable. It was probably said in order to make a point.
11. J. Kornai was one of the economists, who – as it turned out from an interview with him (*Mozgó Világ*, 1990, no. 4) – after 1956 no longer believed in the reformability of the system.

5 Poland

INTRODUCTION

Unlike Czechoslovakia and Hungary, Poland did not carry out a major reform in the economic mechanism in the 1960s. The changes made in the 1960s were of a minor nature and were primarily geared to an improvement in the incentive system. In 1968, the ruling Polish CP (officially called the Polish United Workers' Party) took the decision to introduce an economic reform, starting with 1971. It was to be focused on the incentive system. Changes were also to be made in the planning of prices and in foreign trade regulation, to mention the most important features. The reform was not supposed to be by any means as radical as the Czechoslovak or Hungarian reforms; it was not to transgress the centralised model. An integral part of the reform was supposed to be a radical consumer price reform whose purpose was primarily to reduce subsidies on basic foodstuffs and bring about a restructuring of personal consumption (decrease the demand for food, mainly meat, and increase the demand for durable goods and textiles) and thus renew market equilibrium (for more, see Adam, 1979, pp. 27–8). The price increases, which were offset to some extent by price reductions, touched off riots which brought down W. Gomulka. This also meant an end to the economic reform.

The new CP leader, E. Gierek, committed himself to a new economic strategy which was supposed to ensure, on the one hand, high growth rates and, on the other, increases in the standard of living. As a first step in the implementation of the latter pledge, price increases were rescinded. Gierek also promised an economic reform, which was instituted in January 1973. This reform, which incorporated some elements of Gomulka's reform, was by no means radical. Its underlying idea was that by establishing large economic units – WOGs, as they were called in abbreviated form in Polish – which would be given greater economic autonomy, incentives would be created for more efficient performance. The WOGs in fact meant a strengthening of the monopolisation of the economy and, for this and other reasons, could not work as expected. The strategy of economic development which was based on the idea of modernising the economy by borrowing investment capital abroad turned out to be a failure. The economic crisis which arose after a short period of fast growth in the economy and standard of living brought the reform to an end (for more, see Adam, 1989 and Fallenbuchl, 1986.)

Two questions may be posed: why did Poland opt for a different policy than the other countries under review, and why was the reform limited in its scope once Poland decided to reform the economic mechanism? After all, its economy was not in much better shape than the economies of its neighbours. True, Poland did not experience a great decline in economic growth in the beginning of the 1960s as Czechoslovakia did; however, its economy was marked by great disproportions, and in 1960–70 real wages almost stagnated. This was one of the main reasons why workers reacted to price increases with riots.

To answer these questions, one must speculate to a great extent. The answers lie in the political situation at that time. The Polish CP was quite factious and Gomulka had a difficult time balancing the aspirations and ideas of the different factions. Gomulka himself was not very reform-minded. Soon after becoming First Secretary, he started a campaign against part of the intelligentsia, including those who had helped him to power, in the name of a fight against revisionism (see Kowalik, 1989). He was afraid that a far-reaching reform, which was advocated by the 'revisionist faction', would strengthen the revisionist stream in the Party. Fear of the moral help the Czechoslovak reform might give to the reform movement in Poland was also the motive for his support of the intervention in Czechoslovakia (see Fejtő, 1974, p. 227). When in 1968, after student demonstrations, the liberal and what still remained of the revisionist faction in the CP were deprived of their influence (see Bielasiak, 1983, p. 15), Gomulka felt free to embark on a limited reform. A radical reform was also out of the question for external reasons.

The external situation was not much changed a few years later when Gierek embarked on an economic reform (Kowalik 1986), a phenomenon which Gierek surely did not regret very much. Some believe that the new strategy of economic development as an option in the beginning of the 1970s was also motivated by the consideration that such a step would make a genuine economic reform unnecessary.

Poland's 1960 and 1970 systemic changes were by no means pioneering, and contributed little to the evolution of the EM in the direction of decentralisation. This does not mean that Poland did not participate in generating ideas about the reform of the centralised system. As will be shown later, Polish ideas, especially those of W. Brus, played a role in the systemic changes in Hungary and Czechoslovakia.

In Poland, as in other countries, the economic community was split. To put it generally, there was, at one end of the spectrum, a classical, conservative group, and next to it was a group of converted conservatives. Both groups were against substantial reforms and thus, in practice, they favoured the preservation of the existing system with some modifications – the first because it believed that the system was good, and the second because it did not believe in mixing systems. The other end of the spectrum was dominated by reformists of different stripes who are very difficult to classify, as will become transparent later.

THE CONSERVATIVE POINT OF VIEW

The classical conservative attitude was influenced by Marxist orthodoxy and, in the case of some individuals, by opportunism. B. Minc can be regarded as one of the representatives of Marxist orthodoxy. His views on our topic can be gathered from, among others, two articles, one dealing with the law of value and the second directly with our topic. In the first article mentioned B. Minc adhered in substance to Stalin's views about the law of value, though he argued differently. According to him (1961), the law of value is marked by general and special features. In each historical epoch, features common to all epochs are present, but each epoch is also distinguished by particular features. He lists the following four general features: (1) the law is inseparably linked with commodity-money relations; (2) due to the working of the law of value, prices are based on costs of production and a portion of the global surplus value; (3) the law of value regulates prices of different kinds; and (4) prices are based on average costs. Minc explicitly states that prices tending to equate values is not a general feature of the law of value. To him, the best proof of this lies in the socialist reality. If prices in socialist countries which deviate considerably from values were a violation of the law of value, this violation, which has already lasted for a long time, would have necessarily been felt in economic growth. Since the economy is growing well, the law of value is not violated.

For Minc the law of value in socialism does not regulate production; this is regulated by the plan. The regulative function, as a specific feature of the law of value which is linked to other historical epochs, has no place under socialism.

In brief, it can be said that to Minc the socialist reality, including pricing, is in no way contrary to the working of the law of value. Under such conditions there is no need for any changes.

Alluding to J. Galbraith's work, *The New Industrial State*, Minc's paper, which deals directly with the question of plan and market (1969), takes in substance the position that the market is an institution of the 19th century when the economy was characterised by small economic units. With the increase in the size of enterprises, the developing need for research in order to further technological progress, and the expansion of the time horizon for economic activities, the role of the market as a regulator of production is quite limited, even under capitalism. Therefore, suggestions for making planning rely on the market, which is of a short-term nature, can only have detrimental effects in the form of disproportions. And to want to support planning by a future market is a contradiction in terms (1969, p. 304).

Poland was distinguished by a group which for some time was in the opposite camp and in the 1960s in fact defended the traditional system. This was not a large group, but, because it was by its nature more of a school, with an acknowledged scientific leader by the name of A. Wakar and with disciples, it gained respect and influence in the economic community.

According to this school, the difference between economic systems is not in the location of decision-making, but in the nature of economic calculation. It distinguishes indirect and direct economic calculation. The indirect is characteristic of a market economy where prices play an active role by providing a choice of alternatives. The traditional system is characterised by direct calculation in which prices do not play an active role (Wakar and Zieliński, 1961).

The activity of Wakar's school can be divided into two phases. In the first phase, in the 1950s, it worked on a model of indirect economic calculation adjusted to a socialist economy. It used as a basis for its model the works of Lange and Lerner, written for the Western debate on economic calculation in the 1930s. This happened at a time when Lange had abandoned the positions taken in the 1930s (Kowalik, 1987, p. 390; Grabowski, 1961).

In 1961 in an article written together with his disciple J. Zieliński, Wakar made it clear that their interest had shifted to an improvement of the traditional system. They accounted for their about-face by pragmatism, by alluding to the fact that the traditional system was the reality and would remain the reality, and the many suggestions taken from indirect calculation could not improve the system (1961, pp. 39–40).

In a collective work of the school (*The Theory Outline of the Socialist Economy*, 1965), edited by A. Wakar, the authors formulated their positions more clearly. In the introduction, they criticised the critical attitudes to the traditional system taken by many economists, including themselves. 'Apart from the positive features of this period which we value very highly, we also see in it features of weakness and immaturity; at this time reformative enthusiasm prevailed over the calm deliberation of a practitioner or theoretician' (p. 5). They also criticised economists for overestimating the role of the market, as if a socialist economy could not be managed by other means. The sharpest criticism was levelled at attempts to design a mixed system. According to them, the indirect and direct calculations each have their logic, and attempts to transplant some elements from the indirect to the direct may be harmful (p. 174). In other words, efforts to reform the traditional system by supplementing it with market forces has no chance for success. Needless to say, this was an attack on reformers.

Let me now briefly discuss their views about direct calculation. They call the system so because in it, economic activities are coordinated by commands, and also because calculations are made with the help of physical magnitudes and no active role is given value categories. In a broader sense, direct calculation includes the principles of working out plans which are known by the term 'balances of the national economy', as well as making rules for the realisation of plan objectives (pp. 86–7).

Prices in the system of direct calculation are only a reflection of physical magnitudes; they act primarily as an instrument of aggregation. They play a passive role in the working out of plans; they do not serve as an instrument of choice in the selection of a plan variant (p. 93). Prices also serve as a tool for handing down plan targets and as a gauge of their fulfilment. In decisions about plan fulfilment as well as in the design of the bonus system, prices play a pragmatic role according to the authors, who write: 'The only criterion for setting prices is their impact through the system of calculation and incentives on the fulfilment of the plan in accordance with the rules (*zalozenia*) of the central organ of planning' (p. 334).

The authors did not close their eyes to the shortcomings of the economy (sellers' market, lack of full market equilibrium, waste of raw materials), but believed that these could be overcome by a tightening of the system and by some socio-economic changes (democratisation of political and social life, development of self-management) (p. 86).

Wakar's school was criticised by many. Most of the criticism was levelled at the idea of the inadvisability of mixed calculation systems and of the neglect of value categories (see, for example, Wilczyński, 1963; Sztyber, 1963; Gordon, 1962). Some even doubted the sincerity of the authors. One author suggested (Grabowski, 1961) that what Wakar and Zieliński wanted to prove indirectly was that von Mises was correct in arguing that under socialism economic calculation was impossible. Others argued in a debate about economic calculation that the views of Wakar's school were close to von Mises' (see Bosiakowski, 1963). It did not help the school much when such a staunch conservative as B. Minc proclaimed in a debate that the development of the school's view was of a Marxist nature (see Bosiakowski, 1963).

REFORMERS

In the 1960s there was a large group of economists in Poland who believed that the working of the economy could only be improved if much greater room was given to market forces. To mention some names: W. Brus, O. Lange, E. Lipiński, J. Mujżel, W. Trzeciakowski, Cz.Bobrowski, J. Popkiewicz, and so on. The question was, however, how to harness the advantages of the market without giving up what was regarded at that time as one of the fundamental properties of socialism, central planning. M. Kalecki was also a reformist, but, as will be shown, of a different kind. The limited space in this book allows only the discussion of a few contributions.

W. Brus

There is no doubt that W. Brus' contribution deserves the greatest attention. His book *The Market in a Socialist Economy* (1972)[1] represents a new era in ideas about the socialist system by providing theoretical arguments for the need for, and the possibility of, combining planning with the market. It was received in reformers' circles, mainly in Czechoslovakia and Hungary, almost as a guide to reforms.

In his book, Brus shows that a socialist economy can be guided not only by the traditional centralised system, but also by a decentralised system in which a planned economy is combined with an application of the market mechanism, that a decentralised system is in line with socialist production relations and that social preferences, which the planning system has to ensure, are achievable in a decentralised system too. In other words, a decentralised system is not contrary to a planned economy (1972, p. 184).

He makes it clear that the combination of the two coordinating mechanisms is not only compatible with, but also desirable in, a socialist economy, thus implicitly admitting that the market mechanism is a systemically neutral coordinating mechanism. To him, the main question in the debates on the model of functioning of the socialist economy is how to combine the advantages of planning and market, and centralised and decentralised decision-making.

Of the three groups of decisions – macro-decisions, choice of consumer goods and jobs, and micro-decisions – the last group is the basis for a distinction between centralised and decentralised systems.[2] In a centralised system, the third group of decisions is also in the hands of the central planners, whereas, in a decentralised system, it is left to enterprises (pp. 62–3). Once enterprises are no longer assigned aims and methods of production from above, and are left to themselves to make decisions about these matters, the market and with it profitability must necessarily increase in importance. From where else can enterprises obtain impulses and signals for their successful activities, of which profit is the basis?

The market mechanism, which Brus called for, was not to be spontaneous but regulated. When the author spoke of a regulated market, what he had in mind was an arrangement in which enterprises have quite a lot of autonomy; however, prices are parameters given to them, or, more precisely, prices are set by the authorities or 'by special measures of economic policy' (p. 132).

The author maintains that the scope for using the law of value is not the same as it is for using the market mechanism. To him the law of value works fully if 'supply and demand balance at price ratios which correspond to value ratios'. Brus, of course, supports a broad definition of the law of value in the sense that he also regards it as a regulator of production and investment. Since he believes that the government has to set social preferences and make sure that they are achieved even at the cost of deviating from the operation of the law of value, this law is not 'an absolute, general regulator of output and exchange proportions. It retains this role only within the limits determined by autonomous decisions at the level of the central authority and primarily by decisions on investments and on certain current preferences' (p. 127). The market mechanism can be used not only when the objective is to achieve proportions which are in line with the law of value in the sense of the principle of equivalence of exchange, but also when the objective is to achieve different proportions for the sake of social preferences.

Decisions in a decentralised system, unlike those in the centralised system where almost all macro- and micro-economic decisions are made by the central planners, are made on different levels. The central authorities make direct decisions, primarily about the distribution of income and the allocation of investment among the branches (pp. 139–140). In addition, the centre has the right to establish and liquidate enterprises. Almost all other decisions are left to enterprises. This means that they are allowed to determine what to produce, how to produce and where to buy input (only in the case of serious shortages of producer goods would direct distribution be applied – p. 174), how much to pay in wages, and what to do with profit after taxes are paid. All these decisions are guided by the interest in profitability whose level is determined by market forces.

The market mechanism – as already mentioned – is to be regulated, on the one hand, by the direct decisions of the central planners, and, on the other, by indirect decisions – economic levers. In a decentralised system, plans are worked out on different levels. They are not hierarchically integrated. However, the primacy of the national interest must be preserved. Direct decisions may not be enough to ensure the pre-eminence of the central plan over enterprise plans; therefore they must be supplemented by indirect decisions in order to put certain restraints on the working of the market mechanism. Or, to put it in Brus' words: 'the market [in a decentralised system] is not a means of subordinating production and exchange proportions to spontaneous processes, but an instrument which serves to adjust individual enterprise activities to overall social preferences as expressed in the plan' (p. 144). To this end the government has to use price, wage, fiscal (tax, amortisation allowance) and monetary (credit) policies. These affect enterprise profit by affecting the costs and revenue of enterprises. Since these measures have a different effect on costs and revenue in individual branches and enterprises, they become important instruments for influencing the decision-making of enterprises concerning volume and structure of output, techniques of production, investment, and so on (p. 144).

W. Brus believes that the decentralised system has potential for many properties which cannot come to fruition in the centralised system, due to its nature. He alludes to the potential for increased economic efficiency, the flexible adjustment of the production structure to market demand without interference from above, and more balanced economic growth. The decentralised system also allows a shift in the focus of planning activities from short-term to long-term and thus enables a more thorough analysis of mainly long-term economic processes. Finally, the author does not forget to stress the favourable conditions the decentralised model creates for the participation of workers in decision-making and for the elimination of alienation (pp. 147–157).

It has already been mentioned that in Brus' view certain important economic activities must be subordinated to general social criteria, and their concrete choice should result from direct calculation (and not from the market). Brus has in mind major investments primarily, but he also means the choice of basic types of production and sometimes even basic methods of production (pp. 175–7). 'The choice of general and long-term *directions* of investment must be of a direct character in a planned economy' (p. 135). To subject investment decisions to the law of value would be to 'act under the influence of the law of value [meaning primarily prices] for today, and perhaps for the relatively near future' (p. 120). And current prices are not a reliable source of information for him about future development. This does not, of course, mean that prices have no role to play in major investment projects; their role, however, should lie more in determining the methods to be used in the implementation of long-term investment projects than in setting the aims themselves (p. 126).

When it comes to prices, W. Brus tries to reconcile two aims: to secure price flexibility and to maintain prices as parameters, which are independent of enterprises (p. 182). The reconciliation would be simple if prices were determined in the market. However, Brus would like to see government involvement in pricing, especially in the case of basic consumer and producer goods. He also mentions that in some cases price controls can be limited to setting maximum or minimum prices. In areas of production where competition is strong, no controls should be applied.

When talking about the scope of the market mechanism, Brus had only commodities in mind. He made it clear that the flow of capital cannot and should not be subject to market forces in a socialist economy. Investment by one enterprise in another, apparently with the intention of sharing in profit, would 'contravene the socialist nature of productive relations' (p. 142). He probably had in mind that sharing in profit would violate the principle of socialist distribution of income according to labour.

O. Lange

A chapter written on planning and market cannot, of course, ignore the intellectual contribution of O. Lange and M. Kalecki, the two internationally well-known Polish economists, even if their main work (and this refers more to Kalecki than Lange) on our topic was written in the 1950s. Readers have the right to know what kind of positions the two took, since it is known that both professed a left-wing world outlook before the Second World War.[3, 4] In addition, the influence of both on economic thinking was long-lasting, enduring at any rate beyond the 1950s. Both, as well as W. Brus, were heavily involved in the 1956–7 efforts to reform the Polish system of the functioning of the economy, as the EM was called in Poland. O. Lange was the Chairman of the Economic Council, an advisory body of the Council of Ministers and M. Kalecki was one of the deputies. Both (Kalecki with some qualifications) were in favour of the economic changes as formulated by the reform blueprint (known under the name Model outline or Theses – in Polish, *tezy modelowe*), which was worked out under the leadership of the Econ-omic Council (see Chapter 1). Both defended it against the criticism of the Planning Commission (Osiatyński[5] 1988, p. 39). What is said about the two is also true of W. Brus.

T. Kowalik (1987), who edited and annotated Lange's collective works, contends that Lange was obsessed with the idea of decentra-lisation and democratisation of the socialist system. But he also mentions that Lange wavered in his views. Judging from Lange's 1956–8 views, which will be discussed later, one would not expect him to have objections in principle to Brus' decentralised model; this statement is probably less true about M. Kalecki. But O. Lange is also the author of 'The Computer and the Market' and 'From Balanc-ing . . . to an Optimal Plan' (Works 2, 1973[6]), which could be read as a statement against radical reforms; at any rate they did not help the reform movement.

On the whole, it is possible to argue that O. Lange was more liberal in his views on the economic mechanism than M. Kalecki. This is quite clear when a comparison is made of the model presented by O. Lange in his 1956 paper 'How I see the Polish economic model' with

Kalecki's three papers (see pp. 93–4). True, O. Lange shares with Kalecki the basic principles of the model, namely, central planning and workers' councils. They are also in agreement that central planning must determine the distribution of national income between consumption and accumulation and the pace and direction of economic development. Furthermore, the wage fund must be planned and prices controlled. However, when it comes to specifics, the differences become apparent. O. Lange assumes that the central plan will cover only important products such as coal, steel, basic raw materials, fertilisers, machines and consumer goods of mass consumption. In addition, Lange has much greater confidence in incentives than Kalecki has, and calls for the authorities' reliance on incentives above all. He does not mention output targets. Relations between enterprises should be governed by contracts; allocation of producer goods should be an exception, if equilibrium cannot be achieved by price increases (Works 2, pp. 484–6).

In this paper, he even calls for political changes, for the instituting of a second chamber of *Sejm*, which should be made up of the representatives of workers' and peasants' councils. This new chamber should serve as an 'organ of economic democracy', an idea which he abandoned (p. 599) when the political situation changed, but which cropped up again in the middle of the 1980s.

One is not very surprised that O. Lange took a relatively liberal position in 1956. After all, he was the mastermind of the concept of market socialism in 1936–8. At that time he suggested, in his *On the Economic Theory of Socialism* (1938), a model of socialism in which the means of production were to be nationalised, consumer prices were to be determined by market forces and there would be a free choice of jobs. The planning board sets producer prices and ensures market equilibrium by adjusting prices by the method of trial and error, in response to the signals of the market. According to T. Kowalik (1987A), Lange became more radical during the war in the direction of letting market forces play a much greater role in his model.

O. Lange's 1956 views are a far cry from his war views. Probably he adjusted them under the pressure of new realities as many other people did. He was vulnerable because of his past membership in the Social Democratic Party. This may also have been the reason for his negative attitude to a possible publication in Poland of his papers on market socialism from 1936–8.

He consoled himself and others with the idea that the centralised system was only a transitional phenomenon due to industrialisation. He first touched on this idea in an interview (Works 2, p. 512), returned to it in his contribution to a volume on problems of political economy under socialism *Zagadnienia . . .* (1960), which was edited by him, and developed it in greater detail in his presentation in India, 'The Role of Planning in a Socialist Economy' (Works 2, pp. 384–5). In the first stage of socialism, planning and management are very centralised because fast industrialisation requires central disposal of scarce resources. It is possible to characterise this stage as a war economy. These administrative methods are not characteristic of socialism. When the socialist society starts to abandon administrative and bureaucratic methods and when, in the management of the economy, the working of economic laws is gradually given more scope, the transitional period comes to an end.

His hopes for reform were soon dashed by the Party's abandonment of reforms and by the paralysing of worker's councils. O. Lange retreated to his ivory tower and ceased to occupy himself with practical systemic problems.[7] Instead, he started to lecture and write on econometrics, optimal decision-making, cybernetics, and so on – disciplines, he believed, that future reformers would need (Kowalik, 1987).

Not long before his death, in 1965, Lange wrote two papers, 'The Computer and the Market' and 'From Balancing the Plan Towards the Choice of an Optimal Plan', which are of importance for the topic under review, especially the first. In the paper 'The Computer and the Market', Lange contends that were he to rewrite his *On the Economic Theory of Socialism*', he would not argue for stimulating the market through trial and error, but would instead suggest using computers. 'The market process with its cumbersome tatonnements appears old-fashioned. Indeed, it may be considered as a computing device of the pre-electronic age' (Works 2, p. 333). Further on in the text, O. Lange waters down the importance of the computer and discusses the significance of the market. The market has, however, the shortcoming of not being able to 'provide a sufficient foundation for the solution of growth and development problems. In particular it does not provide an adequate basis for long-term economic planning' (p. 336). He completes his reasoning that the computer 'fulfils a function which the market never was able to perform' (p. 336).

In the second paper, he contends that, due to the rapid development of mathematics, planning in socialist countries is entering a new stage; coordination with the help of material balancing, which is characteristic of the first stage, is being replaced by optimal planning.

The two papers were probably written under the influence of Soviet optimal planners, all the more so because those planners' activities coincided with the 1965 Soviet economic reform, on which O. Lange pinned great hopes (Kowalik, 1987).

M. Kalecki

M. Kalecki was a reformer, but of a different kind from those to whom reform meant an expansion of market forces. He favoured a reform which would primarily rationalise economic policy and planning. His views about the preferable system were clearly formulated in several of his concise papers, three of which are important for this discussion.

In his 1957 paper 'Let us not Overestimate the Role of the Model', M. Kalecki made it clear that he did not see changes in the model of functioning of the economy as a panacea. He did not share the view of many economists, who blamed the economic mechanism for the disproportions which had arisen as a result of the six-year plan. To him the disproportions were the result of the content and direction of the plan rather than of the systemic arrangement. Excessive investment, disregard for investment efficiency, too optimistic expectations in agricultural production, foreign trade and so on were the culprits, argued M. Kalecki (Works 3, 1982, pp. 107–8). In other words, the author believed that the main reason for economic troubles should be looked for in economic policy and in shortcomings in planning

M. Kalecki favoured a model which combined central planning and workers' councils, as he made clear in his 1956 paper 'Workers' Councils and Central Planning'. He believed that such a combination was a precondition for the fast development of the economy. Workers' councils were supposed to protect the workers against abuses, shield enterprises against excessive bureaucratisation and centralisation, and promote the initiative of workers (Works 3, 1982, p. 94).

In both the '56 and '57 papers he defines central planning, which, according to him, should cover production, the most important product mixes, the wage-bill, major investments, price control[8] and the allocation of basic raw materials. It seems that the last mentioned item was not to be a permanent feature of the system but rather the result of existing economic conditions.

He did not share the view of economists who wanted planning of production to be replaced by incentives in the hope that this would stimulate enterprises to utilise the productive apparatus effectively. He believed that profit, which was usually suggested as a synthetic incentive, could not meet such expectations in a socialist system. A combination of targets and incentives seemed to him the most effective way to improve performance. In one of his papers published in 1957, 'The Scheme of a New System of Incentives and Targets' he suggested using net product as an indicator for assigning output targets. The growth of the wage-bill should be linked to the growth of net output. Bonuses should depend on the increment in profit compared to the previous year. Enterprises should pay a charge on investment funds received from the centre (Works 3, pp. 118–24).

Since he believed that the improved working of the economy depended on improvements in planning, Kalecki devoted much of his time and energy to research on planning and related problems' and to practical considerations for drafting plans in his capacity as advisor to the Planning Commission.

J. Osiatyński (1988) maintains that Kalecki revolutionised planning by stressing that the planning process should start with consumption, and that consumption must be the planners' focal point. All other targets must be adapted to the consumption target. Before, the drafting of the plan had started with the extrapolation of growth trends in individual industrial branches (p. 177). To Kalecki the demand for a change in planning was natural since he was convinced that the main purpose of socialism is to increase the standard of living. Full employment to him was one of the instruments for achieving this goal.

In addition, Kalecki insisted that in the planning of investment projects their efficiency should be strictly considered. To this end, new methods of calculation of investment efficiency were worked out under his supervision (Osiatynski, 1988, pp. 180–1). He also pushed for plans to be more realistic, and one of the methods he advocated was the working out of more variants of the plan, which has the advantage of allowing the involvement of the public in decision-making about plan objectives.

Kalecki's book on economic growth (1963) brought him additional fame. This theoretical book was to serve a very practical purpose: to show how individual macro-economic magnitudes, such as national income, consumption, investment and the labour force, are related to each other, and how changes in one magnitude affect others. On the other hand, it showed the barriers to economic growth and the consequences if they were not respected.

The theories and equations developed in the book were used in all East European countries for various computations of economic growth. K. Laski used them in his book (1967) to refute Stalin's dogma: the law of the faster growth of production of producer goods than of consumer goods.

Other Contributions

J. Pajestka[9] can also be regarded as one of the reformers, though closer than Brus to what can be called the middle of the Polish spectrum of views. He expressed his views in several places; here, I will discuss only his paper at a conference (which together with other contributions was published in a book entitled *Plan and Market* (1969)), in which he repeated views professed in other articles, and his contribution in a panel discussion (1967).

To him (1969) planning fulfils two functions: conceptual–strategic and dispositional–coordinative (*dyspozycyjno-koordynacyjne*). The first is geared to the choice of long-term development and is reflected in long-term plans. The second function lies in a coordination of economic activities. It is reflected in annual plans. According to the author, the stress in planning should be shifted to the first function. However, he is against dropping annual plans which, to him, are an important instrument for fulfilling the long-term plan. At the same time, Pajestka believes that the assigning of targets is not needed (1969, pp. 22–4). In the panel discussion (1967), he expresses the view that planning should cover primarily long-term changes in the structure of the economy, the distribution of income and the development of science and technology.

To make planning more effective, the central planners should utilise societal initiative and activity to the maximum. This should be achieved by allowing enterprises and associations to participate in the formulation of plans, and by decentralising the operative management. In order to implement these postulates, mainly the second one, it is necessary to subject enterprises to self-financing and the market. Both should be influenced by economic methods: prices and fiscal tools. (In the 1967 panel discussion, he suggests leaving the authorities to determine the prices of the most important products.) He takes the position that long-term development should not be subject to market forces. With this approach, the role of the market is already defined to a great extent. According to Pajestka, the market is primarily important in making the supplier in daily economic activities respect the buyer's demand and achieve this at minimal cost. In planning production for consumption, market demand should be the guide; however, demand should be influenced by price policy (1969, pp. 31–4). In other words, the market should determine the micro-output mix of enterprises and the allocation of resources connected with it.

Pajestka regards such a division of roles between the two coordinating mechanisms as a utilisation of market forces. He does not explicitly say so, but implicitly he believes that this is how the leading role of planning is maintained.

J. Mujżel, a prolific writer, expressed his view on our topic in several publications. In his 1968 article, he took the position that central planning should focus on problems which can be most done on this level best, primarily macroproportions. For him, effective decentralisation can be achieved, provided self-management bodies are equal co-managers of enterprises. He attached great importance to the making of decisions on the basis of realistic calculations of foreign trade operations.

In his 1969 publication, he returns to the political aspects of economic reform, a topic which he touched on in the article mentioned above. He takes as a point of departure the existence of conflict between political and economic criteria for action. In the situation which existed at that time in Poland, he had to acknowledge that, according to Lenin's thesis, primacy must be given to politics. Simultaneously, he maintained that the development of the economic mechanism depends on the strength and the progressivity of the state and the CP (1969, pp. 98–9).

K. Porwit (1968) accepts J. Pajestka's definition of the two functions of planning. To him, long- and middle-term planning should be based on a system of hierarchical optimisation, utilising mathematical methods and computer technology. In short-term planning, the market should play an active role. Economic levers, used for the management of enterprises, should be subordinated to the objectives of the plan.

CONCLUDING REMARKS

In this chapter I have confined myself for space reasons to the topic under review in the narrow sense. It seemed to me more important to devote more space to the analysis of the thinking of the economists discussed than to add several paragraphs on the price debate which did not represent great progress in ideas about pricing anyhow.

In contrast to the economic reform itself, Poland was far ahead in the evolution of ideas about how to reform EM without abandoning the basics of socialism. This was the usual phenomenon; perhaps the Hungarian scene was to some extent an exception. In Poland, however, the gap between what the economists suggested doing and what the authorities were willing to do was perhaps the largest.

The gap was due on the one hand to the authorities' politically motivated opposition to economic reforms. On the other hand, in Poland more than in other countries, conditions existed for the rise of theories which did not negate socialism but which looked for new arrangements of the EM in the area of the combination of planning and market. Even in the most repressive period in Poland, scientific contacts with the West were not interrupted, and the existence of such renowned economists as Kalecki and Lange helped the germination of ideas. The opposition of the political leaders to reform may have added to the intellectual dissent.

Of the Polish reformist literature of the 1960s, W. Brus' book was the most important: it represented a milestone in the history of ideas about the socialist economic system. Its importance lies primarily in providing theoretical arguments against the view that the traditional economic model, as conceived in the USSR in the 1930s, was the only possible model of socialism. He shows that a decentralised model, which has many advantages over the centralised, is compatible with socialism. Brus' concept of a decentralised model also shatters the Marxist idea about the market as an institution linked inseparably to capitalism. His study is an indirect defence of the market as neutral coordinating mechanism.[10] His ideas about planning and the market influenced a whole generation of economists and were reflected in the design of the reforms in Czechoslovakia and Hungary. W. Brus also shows, as K. Laski (1961) stresses in his review of Brus' book, that a decentralised system creates a better environment for democratisation, or, more precisely, for workers' participation in decision-making.

Even many of those who praised Brus' book in the 1960s and 1970s criticised it in the 1980s, mainly for the role it attributed to the government in major investments. Some of the criticism was ahistoric: it disregarded the conditions and environment in which it was written, and the way ideas develop. In addition, the contention that Brus' system could not work was never really tested in practice.

It has already been mentioned that M. Kalecki looked for the cure to the ills faced by the Polish economy primarily in a change in economic policy and an improvement in planning. He remained faithful to these ideas even in the 1960s.[11] In other words, he put more stress on non-systemic factors; therefore there is a tendency to underestimate them. No doubt, without systemic changes, the economy could not improve. But it is also true that a wrong economic policy, mainly the obsession with economic growth and huge military expenses, which was characteristic for the traditional system, was also to blame for the troubles in the economy. Not only this, but the wrong economic policy aggravated the working of the economic mechanism. Thus, drawing attention to economic policy was a legitimate and a very useful purpose.

Those who called for improvements in planning, whether from the vantage point of economic policy (as M. Kalecki did) or from a technical viewpoint (as O. Lange did), had, no doubt, a legitimate point. After all, planning as a science or as a practical coordinating mechanism was relatively young and there had not been much experience with it. In addition, it was in practice subservient to the industrialisation drive understood quite simplistically, at any rate without due regard to other factors which have an impact on industrialisation. A proposal to focus on consumption or on analyses showing the relationship between consumption and accumulation can be highly useful for making plans realistic. The techniques applied to the drafting of plans were quite simple and without great sophistication. The balancing method used is good for finding out what can be produced, but less useful for figuring out what is optimal. Therefore, suggestions for the optimisation of planning could only be welcome. This is the positive side of the drive for planning optimisation. It may also have a negative side if it is intended to take the place of systemic reforms. It is not entirely clear what kind of message Lange intended with his article 'The Computer and the Market', but it is probable that in some circles it was used against a systemic reform which would give greater space to the market.

As in Hungary and Czechoslovakia, the suggested expansion of the market was almost always limited to commodities. At that stage of thinking, it was hardly imaginable that a demand for a capital and labour market, which seemed to be in contradiction with the principles of socialism, could be made. In addition, it was not felt that a decentralised system cannot work if a capital and labour market are excluded.

Notes

1. The book was published in Polish in 1961 with the title *General Problems of Functioning of a Socialist Economy*. W. Brus was a chairman of one of the two departments of Political Economy at the University of Warsaw.
2. W. Brus uses the term 'model' instead of 'system' in order to be able to abstract from many concrete features.
3. O. Lange achieved fame before the war by participating in the debate about economic calculation and by suggesting that a socialist economy can become efficient by simulating the market.
4. Before the Second World War, M. Kalecki was associated with the left-wing movement. His famous writings on capitalism were marked by his ideological beliefs (Kowalik, 1989, p. 435).
5. J. Osiatyński was the editor and annotator of the Collected Works of M. Kalecki.
6. The bibliographical data from Kalecki's and Lange's papers are quoted, if not otherwise indicated, from their collected works.
7. This is important to mention in light of the fact that Lange was the Chairman of one of the departments of Political Economy at the University of Warsaw and wrote a textbook on Political Economy.
8. The oligopoly price practices in the West were partly responsible for his opposition to enterprises being allowed to set prices (Osiatyński, 1988, p. 53).
9. J. Pajestka was Deputy Chairman of the Planning Commission in the 1960s.
10. Nowadays most economists who favour marketisation of the economy take an opposite position, believing that the market economy cannot work without substantial privatisation of the means of production.
11. I visited Kalecki in 1965 and informed him about the goals of the impending economic reform in Czechoslovakia. When I finished, he told me that what was needed was an improvement in planning.

Part II

Debates on Planning and Market in the 1980s and 1990–1992

6 Common and Contrasting Features of the Debates in the 1980s and 1990–1992

This chapter is devoted to the common and contrasting features of the debates in the 1980s and 1990–1992 in the countries under review. To make the debates more understandable, a very brief survey of the economic and political conditions, as well as the economic reforms, is given. These surveys deal mostly with the situation as it developed until the collapse of the socialist system. The situation after that time is discussed only briefly. In all the surveys, comparative aspects are mentioned. In the country studies, some of the points mentioned here will be elaborated.

ECONOMIC CONDITIONS

In the first half of the 1970s, the economic situation was quite good in all the countries under review, though the seeds of the decline to follow had already been sown. The economy grew relatively fast; the standard of living reached its peak. These were the most successful years. Referring to Hungary, B. Csikós-Nagy called these years the golden age. The rising standard of living in Hungary and Poland, but mainly in the latter, was to a great degree the result of loans taken up in the West, mostly from recycled petrodollars.

In the second half of the 1970s the pendulum of economic growth swung in the opposite direction, to varying extents in individual countries. It was mainly the Polish economy which suffered a serious setback. The Soviet reversal in economic growth did not come till later. CMEA turned out to be helpless in the face of an unfolding crisis which was in part the result of a recession in the West. This was all the more momentous because CMEA determined to a great degree the economic development, including technological progress, and the economic policy of the countries under review. It was to some degree responsible for the widening gap in technology between the member countries and the West. There were many suggestions about how to modernise and adjust this institution, but not much happened, one reason being that the Soviets did not care enough.

In the 1970s, the Soviet economic situation started to deteriorate; this trend continued in the 1980s and developed into a crisis in the second half of the decade. Though economic growth rates in the second half of the 1970s declined and even stagnated in some years of the 1980s, the Soviet Union, unlike Poland, experienced an absolute decline in output only in the 1990 for the first time. In the 1970s and the beginning of the 1980s, increased armament, which withdrew not only resources from the civil sector but also the best qualified and brightest cadres, was an important factor of the economic crisis, whereas in the second half of the 1980s the crisis was, in a nutshell, the result of badly thought-out economic policy.

Another main reason for this development was the exhaustion of extensive factors of growth (investment and labour). The USSR, like other countries under review, did not manage to offset the exhaustion of these factors of growth by higher productivity. Extraction of raw materials and fuels, which play a paramount role in Soviet exports,[1] shifted more and more to regions with poor climatic conditions and often difficult access to deposits, and thus became more costly. The Soviet Union did not manage to reduce the material and fuel intensity of products, the retirement rate of fixed assets did not improve (in *Perekhod* . . ., 1990, it is maintained that in many branches fixed assets were not renewed for 15 to 25 years) and labour productivity, particularly in the 1980s, remained low. As a result of these and other factors, the capital–output ratio in the manufacturing sector increased from 2 in 1975 to 3.5 in 1987 (*The Economy* . . ., 1990).

The Soviet Union had quite a good record with regard to inflation. In the 1980s, when inflationary pressures increased compared to the 1970s, inflation was on the average less than 2 per cent, even in the second half of the 1980s (*The Economy* . . ., 1990, p. 49). This figure probably refers to open inflation; even if repressed inflation is taken into consideration, inflation in the USSR was below that in the USA and Canada. In 1991, a dramatic reversal has occurred; inflation is now more and more out of control. Wage, price and credit policy are to blame for this development in the first place. Wages were allowed to grow much faster than prices, and price subsidies and subsidies to enterprises, which were anyhow high, continued to grow. For these and other reasons, which will be discussed in Chapter 9, huge shortages of consumer goods came about.

Relative to Poland and Hungary, the USSR in 1991 was not much indebted to the West; however, its debt has almost doubled in the last five to six years.[2] What is worse is that, due to the lack of sufficient convertible commodities and hard currency, Soviet foreign trade has suffered a setback. It has been forced to rely on barter to a great extent.

E. Gierek's (First Secretary of the Polish CP) new strategy turned out to be an immense failure. The strategy aimed at restructuring and modernising the industry with up-to-date technology, bought in the West with Western credits, and simultaneously improving the standard of living of the population. The imported technology was excessive and could not be effectively absorbed, and the assumption that loans would be paid back by commodities from the modernised enterprises did not materialise, partly because of the slump in the West. The huge increases in wages, which were not matched by increases in consumer goods, were inflationary. In addition, indebtedness grew fast and with its servicing costs[3] and the balance of payments deficit. It took Polish leaders some time to react to the severe problems. In 1976 they decided to reduce investments and shift resources to consumer goods branches in order to arrest the rapidly unfolding market disequilibrium and also to prevent indebtedness from increasing. As a result of these and other measures, economic growth rates were brought down to an extent unprecedented in other countries. In the period 1979–81, national income produced declined by 21 per cent.

The martial law of December 1981, which outlawed Solidarity (for more, see p. 109), was also put into effect for economic reasons (as M. Rakowski, the former prime minister, mentioned in his recent book – 1991, p. 36). It enabled the Polish leaders to renew, at least for a while, the semblance of market equilibrium by huge price increases. The widespread shortages existing at that time threatened to bring the economy to ruin.

In the period 1983–5, the situation improved: the economy started to grow again and inflation was brought down to a manageable rate. However, the authorities did not manage to cure the many ills which afflicted the economy. Growing subsidies contributed to the budget deficit. This, combined with a failure to restrain wage increases, caused inflation to accelerate again. Huge price increases in 1988, whose purpose was to cope with market disequilibrium, only added to inflation without achieving the objective. Exports to non-socialist countries did not increase, and as a result indebtedness continued to grow. Imports from non-socialist countries were slashed to such an extent that the development of the economy was necessarily unfavourably affected in the long run. No great progress was achieved in the restructuring of the economy ('Report . . .', 1987).

In Czechoslovakia, as in other countries under review, economic growth started to decline in the second half of the 1970s and continued to decline on average in the 1980s. In the period 1978–88, the growth rate of national income used was only 1.5 per cent on the average; if this figure is deflated the growth rate is below zero (Komárek, 1989). Economic stagnation was due to several factors, one being the old, irrational and ineffective structure of the economy, marked by the hypertrophic role of heavy industry, which was one of the main reasons for the Czechoslovak distinction of having much higher consumption of energy and steel per unit of production than most advanced industrial countries. Heavy industry required a great amount of investment, and, for a long time, the heavy industry lobby saw to it that the industry got it even at the expense of light industry and services. In the second half of the 1980s, there were attempts made to redress the balance, but without success. Nor was there success in the effort to narrow the lag in technology behind advanced industrial countries. The existing economic mechanism did not exert sufficient pressure on enterprises to innovate. Technological progress was also hampered by the slashing of imports from the West, where Czechoslovakia could have got the machinery needed for modernisation. Imports were reduced because the number of competitive products which could find a market in the West was declining, and, for political reasons, Czechoslovakia did not want to increase its indebtedness. On the contrary, it tried to reduce it. As a result, the share of foreign trade with the USSR increased at a time when trade with Hungary and Poland was declining (Altmann, 1987, pp. 169–72). To cope with the worsening terms of trade, Czechoslovakia increased, *inter alia*, investment in energy (mainly coal), at the cost of huge pollution, in order to reduce the need for imports.

Despite all the difficulties, Czechoslovakia, like the USSR, had a good record in coping with inflationary pressures. It also suffered from shortages, which were a further reason for the declining growth rates, but these were not of the Polish magnitude and did not much affect the supply of consumer goods to the population.

Hungary was also in bad shape economically. It was heavily in-debted, even more than Poland in relative terms, its terms of trade had deteriorated considerably, and it suffered from a foreign trade deficit. At the end of the 1970s, the Hungarian authorities decided to abandon the old policy of ambitious economic growth: they slashed investment outlays and imports and thus decreased economic growth. The result of this operation was that the rate of GDP growth declined on the average to 1.8 per cent in 1978–87, from 5.6 in 1970–8.[4] Of course, such a decline meant that technological progress fell even further behind the West at a time when it was accelerating there. Needless to say, it also impeded the structural changes which were slow in any case. And these structural changes were all the more needed because Hungary was forced to reorient its foreign trade, the volume of which increased immensely (from 8 per cent of GDP in 1938 to 40 per cent in 1987). In 1962, 65–70 per cent of foreign trade went to members of CMEA; in 1987 this number declined to below 50 per cent.

In the second half of the 1980s, Hungary had increasing difficulty maintaining a balanced budget, though its enterprises were supposed to surrender up to 80 per cent of their profits. And this was one of the reasons for the accelerated inflation. In the period 1970–8, it was on average 4.7 per cent, whereas in 1978–87 it increased to 9.7 per cent. In 1988–9, it was 15 per cent on average. (For more, see Révész, 1990.)

Despite the worsening economic situation, Hungary had the best record among European socialist countries for satisfying consumer demand. Stores were quite well stocked and the product mix, as well as the quality, were superior to other countries under review. This attested to the positive effect of the reform, despite its shortcomings, on market equilibrium.

POLITICAL CONDITIONS

Nowadays, all four countries under review struggle, with the odds against them, to establish a genuine democratic system. The fight for the elimination of the one-party state has not proceeded in the same way in all the countries. Poland has gone through a turbulent political development in the last two decades. The same can be said about the last several years of development in the USSR. Compared to these two countries, Hungary in the last two decades has been, to put it metaphorically, an island of tranquility. Czechoslovakia has had more or less the same record as Hungary with the difference that its tranquility was achieved by repressions up to the 'velvet' revolution.

After N. Khrushchev's 'thaw', a freeze followed. L. Brezhnev did not bring back Stalinism; nevertheless he instituted a much more repressive regime than there had been under Khruschchev. Having secured 'stability' at home, Brezhnev turned his attention to the outside world, mainly in pursuit of three targets: strengthening the Soviet position in the arms race with the USA; expansion of the sphere of USSR's influence and making sure that the loyalty of Eastern Europe remained strong.

In their armament policy, the Soviet tried to achieve parity with the USA. This was a costly venture in terms of a percentage of GNP, considering that the Soviet GNP was only a fraction of that of the USA.[5] Nevertheless, the Brezhnev administration pursued this goal with obsession, disregarding the consequences it had for the Soviet economy and the economy of Eastern Europe. The windfall from the explosive increases in prices of oil and gold was squandered on the military instead of being used for the modernisation of Soviet industry and for aid to struggling Eastern Europe. This policy, which was pushed hard by the military, did not change when the Reagan administration stepped up armament with the purpose of destroying the Soviet economy.

The advent of M. Gorbachev to power gradually brought a crucial change to the Soviet scene. It is not yet certain whether M. Gorbachev had from the beginning a clear idea about Soviet socialism marching towards a dead end (which he himself accelerated by his policies), or whether he intuitively behaved as if Soviet society was facing an impasse. At any rate, he came up with programmes to change Soviet society. *Glasnost* and *perestroika* became the two mainstays of his policy. The first meant a new thinking about the relationship between CP and government on the one hand and the people on the other, between the centre and the nationalities, between the republics themselves, between the USSR and its allies and between the Soviet Union and its rivals. The new leadership was determined to replace relations based on coercion and confrontation with voluntary co-operation. It was particularly interested in reducing international tension as a way to gradual disarmament, thus easing the burden of military expenditures. To this end, it abandoned Brezhnev's doctrine,[6] an action which opened the way for the independence of East European countries. The policy of *glasnost* immensely strengthened the centrifugal forces in the

USSR and contributed to the disintegration of the Union.

Glasnost stirred up political life: on the one hand, conservative forces in the CP arrayed themselves against far-reaching political and economic reforms, and, on the other, radical forces pushed for more reforms. In August 1991, the leaders of part of the conservatives attempted to usurp power; their failure brought about a dissolution of the CP and a weakening of forces which favoured the preservation of the Soviet Union, the opposite to what the plotters wanted.

As already mentioned, Poland was often in crisis. If we disregard the 1956 riots, Poland was the scene of four conflicts between workers and the government because of huge price increases. All of the price increases (with the exception of the one in 1976) shook up the regime. The first price increase, in 1970, which took a heavy toll on lives, brought down W. Gomulka, and the third, in 1980, E. Gierek.

The price increases in 1980 gave birth to Solidarity, a new trade union, which forced the government to certain economic and political concessions (for more see Chapter 8). Since Solidarity's aspirations classed with the government's, the latter, under the leadership of W. Jaruzelski, outlawed the new trade union and arrested its leaders, headed by L. Walesa.

Solidarity could not be muzzled fo long; it retreated underground and continued its activity. The more the economic situation worsened, the greater was Solidarity's popularity. In 1987, the Polish leaders, this time encouraged by the IMF, again decided to resort to huge price increases, though past experience should have deterred them from such an action. And again the country was plunged into a crisis, and the political leaders finally recognised the need for dialogue with Solidarity, which took place in 1989. In this dialogue Solidarity was legalised and allowed to participate in the political structure; in return it recognised the Party's leading position for one parliamentary session, but Solidarity outmanoeuvred the CP and took over power.

In Hungary J. Kádár continued his policy of balancing the interest of the Soviet Union with the aspirations of his people. He supported Soviet foreign policy even at times when it went against the grain, in order to have greater manoeuvring room at home. This does not mean that he was not a devoted communist – he certainly was. J. Kádár was, however, a communist of a different brand from Brezhnev: he could be characterised as an enlightened communist who believed that socialist ideas could be best achieved if they were reconciled with people's interest.

Kádár's regime was a dictatorship; however, it used repression in a measured way. It tolerated dissent as long as it did not go beyond certain limits. It understood how to manoeuvre effectively. It resisted reforms which were not to its liking, but, when the pressure became too strong, it was prepared to enter into compromises. This was the case in 1984 and 1987 with the economic reforms, and later with political changes. This was also the reason that, up to the last years of the regime, no powerful opposition came into being, though the economic situation worsened.

In contrast with that of Poland, the opposition in Hungary came mostly from within the Party itself; Hungarian propaganda managed to isolate Hungary from the 1980 events in Poland. This was all the easier because Poland was not a role model for most of the Hungarian intelligentsia.

In the second half of the 1980s, mainly when it became clear that M. Gorbachev was not going to enforce Brezhnev's doctrine, and when the economic crisis had not eased but on the contrary had deepened, opposition to Kádár's regime inside and outside the CP started to grow with Western help. In 1988, J. Kádár was ousted, and this was the beginning of the end of the socialist regime (for more, see Chapter 7).

G. Husák failed to honour his promise to introduce a Kádár-like regime in post-invasion Czechoslovakia. Czechoslovakia instead got 'normalisation', a government term for the renewal of the pre-reform situation to a great extent. The reform was largely dismantled and a wide-ranging purge in the Party, which affected approximately half a million people, was carried out. Thousands of people were fired from their positions, and many of them were forced to accept manual work. In no other socialist country did the government apply such repressive methods to such a large number of people. It will be the task of historians to explore how this was possible in a country which was distinguished for its pre-war democratic traditions.

The Czechoslovak leaders did not use only repression: for some time they combined the normalisation process with an increase in the standard of living. Unlike leaders in most other countries, who endeavoured to be independent of Moscow as much as possible, the Czechoslovak leaders slavishly imitated Moscow up to the advent of Gorbachev to power. Though they reluctantly followed the example of the USSR as to economic reform, they resolutely shunned *glasnost*.

There was no strong active opposition; perhaps a majority hated the system, but only a few wanted to take the risk of actively opposing it, for fear of the consequences. The end of the regime came not so much from the activities of the opposition as from the changes outside the country, which made the communist leaders understand that the end of their rule was inevitable.

ECONOMIC REFORMS

The reforms will be discussed briefly, only to the extent needed for the understanding of the chief topic. The reforms varied in their radicalism and time of introduction. First, the common and contrasting features of the Hungarian and Polish economic reforms before the collapse of the socialist system in those countries will be discussed, and then attention will be devoted to the Soviet and Czechoslovak reforms. Finally, I will discuss the common and contrasting features of the approaches to the transition to a market economy.

Reforms before the Collapse of the Socialist System

Compared to the 1960s, the 1980s in Hungary and Poland saw reforms which expanded the role of the market in two directions. First, the market was no longer supposed to be limited to being an adjunct to planning. It was to be gradually extended to the competitive sphere. In the final stage of the socialist regime, the authorities were willing to agree to a market socialism where the market would be the coordinating mechanism and state ownership would still have a dominant position.

Second, compared to the 1960s when the market was limited to commodities, the reforms in the 1980s envisaged a gradual application of the market to capital and labour. The authorities finally acknowledged that in order to make the market work, enterprises must have the right to use their retained profit according to their interests, make profit on such an operation, and acquire capital wherever and in whatever ways it was advantageous for them. This change also meant that enterprises would be allowed to make decisions about investment. To this end, the mono-banking system was liquidated: the National Banks in Hungary and Poland were restricted to the functions of a central bank, and commercial banks were instituted. In addition, enterprises were allowed to convert into joint stock companies and to issue bonds. The institution of a stock market was to complete the operation of an idea which was first implemented in Hungary and later in Poland.

In both countries, a partial labour market had already existed in the 1960s. However, enterprises were deeply involved in the endeavour to safeguard the government policy of full employment. The 1980s brought a change in the sense that enterprises, in their hiring and firing policy, were to be concerned purely with economic efficiency aspects, whereas the concerns for full employment were to be in the realm of the government.

Both reforms envisaged an increased use of economic levers – monetary and fiscal policies – to influence economic development. What is important to underscore is that the governments committed themselves to using interest rate and money supply regulation as active tools for controlling inflation and fluctuations in the economy.

The 1960s reforms, as well as the Polish one in 1973, did not challenge collective ownership. In the 1980s, the authorities acknowledged the need to overhaul the old concepts of ownership for the good working of the economy. The leaders of both Hungary and Poland accepted the principle that all forms of ownership should be treated equally, and legal conditions were created for the expansion of the private sector. It was still assumed that state ownership would preserve its dominant role, though in a modified form. The reforms in both countries (the same happened later in the USSR and Czechoslovakia) entrusted most property rights of the state to self-management bodies in enterprises. The purpose of this operation was to reduce the centre's ability to interfere in enterprise affairs and thus to enhance the autonomy of enterprises.

The USSR and Czechoslovakia had a similar development up to 1989; Czechoslovakia, at first willingly and later reluctantly, followed the Soviet example. In the Soviet Union, in the period 1979–86, minor systemic changes with negligible effect on the economy were carried out. Czechoslovakia followed suit. In 1987 the Soviets carried out a reform which Gorbachev labelled as radical. Had it been carried out in the 1960s (instead of the 1965 reform) one could agree, though with some qualifications, with such an adjective. The reform can be characterised as a watered-down version of the 1968 Hungarian reform, combined with some elements of the East German system. Czechoslovakia again followed the Soviet example more or less.

The Soviet Union came up with ideas and solutions for ownership relations, such as leasing of industrial assets and land, which did not appear, or were not implemented, in other countries. Leasing of land deserves special attention. In the 1980s, the authorities were long reluctant to allow private ownership in agriculture, and this stand was more or less followed in the literature. Since agriculture was in trouble, despite various measures to improve it, the Soviets tried to follow the example of China, where leasing had a very positive effect on agriculture.[7]

Transition to a Market Economy

The transition means a transformation into a market economy of economies at different stages of combining planning and market and at different degrees of stability. A market economy requires private ownership (the extent of which is contentious), free prices, an environment conducive to competition, freedom for economic actors to act according to their interests – of course, within the set rules of the game – and an open economy. There must be an important role for the government, mainly in the transitional period (for more, see Chapter 11). The transformation is easier the more the economy is stabilised and the more its structure corresponds to domestic and foreign demand. The foregoing can be summarised by saying that transformation means, on the one hand, a series of macro- and micro-economic systemic changes, and on the other, privatisation.

In the economic literature dealing with former socialist countries, the term 'stabilisation' is usually used as another name for a series of macro- and micro-economic measures – apart from privatisation – needed to achieve a market economy. The word is used in this way because it is assumed that the countries were, when the transition started, in a state of gross economic instability, an assumption which could be challenged in the case of Czechoslovakia and to a lesser degree with regard to Hungary. Thus, stabilisation is usually understood in the literature in a broad sense; it includes not only stabilisation in the narrow sense – but also provisions facilitating a transition to a market economy, such as the creation of market prices and an environment conducive to competition, liberalisation of foreign trade and the introduction of convertibility of the currency, to mention the most important items. Stabilisation in the narrow sense means a renewal of market equilibrium, stoppage of inflation, restoration of a balanced budget and stabilisation of the value of the currency. Needless to say, the two groups of necessary measures are closely inter-twined.

The transition to a market economy was not handled in the same way in the four countries under review. As to the methods applied in order to achieve transformation of the economy, Poland opted for shock treatment, whereas Hungary, its partner in spearheading the reform movement, resorted to a gradual solution. Czechoslovakia used a moderate form of shock treatment. In 1990, the Supreme Soviet in the USSR approved the proposal to transform the Soviet economy into a market economy. Before the *putsch*, it seemed that the Soviets would rather proceed cautiously and gradually. After the collapse of the USSR, Russia and the former co-members of the Union have decided in fact to follow in the footsteps of Poland with some modifications.

The gradual Hungarian approach to the problem of transformation can be explained by several factors. Though shortages in Hungary existed, they were by no means as catastrophic as in Poland. The different situation was largely due to the fact that Hungary started the process of marketisation earlier than Poland. Inflation in Hungary was quite high, but substantially lower than in Poland, where hyper-inflation was devastating the economy. In addition, Hungary had a long tradition of tackling its economic problems by gradual changes, whereas Poland moved rather by great leaps. A classic example is how the two countries handled the need to equilibrate the economy with the help of price adjustments.

As to privatisation, there is one important difference, if the differ-ences in pace, which are of no great magnitude, are disregarded. Czech-oslovakia is engaged in distributing a certain portion of its assets at a small charge, Poland has legislation which enables it to go the same route, whereas Hungary wants to get market prices for state assets.

COMMON AND CONTRASTING FEATURES IN THINKING

No great changes occurred in the 1970s in economic thinking. The first half of the decade was under the influence of the 1968 occupation of Czechoslovakia by Soviet-led armies, and of the lesson given to Czechoslovakia for its attempt to reform the economic mechanism. The occupation changed not only the attitudes of a great part of the ruling élites in Czechoslovakia, but also of those in the other countries. Before the occupation, the political élites in most East

European countries viewed the reforms as a solution to economic problems, whereas, after the occupation, they regarded them as a source of internal instability and a threat to national sovereignty. Reforms ceased to be a welcome option. Some lethargy, like that which follows defeat, set in. The reluctance to engage in reforms was strengthened by the quite favourable development of the economy. When the standard of living is rising, dissentient thinking is usually discouraged. In the second half of the 1970s, the economic situation started to worsen and continued to deteriorate throughout the 1980s (with the exception of some years) in all the countries under review. As a result, the countries again started to look for some systemic changes, and intellectuals began to raise their heads. This happened first in Poland where Solidarity was born.

The 1980s meant a dramatic change in economic thinking about the socialist economic system; this was true primarily about the second half of the 1980s. The movement for changes was spearheaded by Polish and Hungarian intellectuals; the Soviet and Czechoslovak intellectuals joined them later. Of course, if not for Soviet *glasnost* and *perestroika*, who knows whether the dramatic changes in Poland and Hungary could have taken place at all.

In the first half of the 1980s, even in Poland and Hungary, the vast majority of economists still believed in the reformability of the existing economic mechanism and in planning as an important coordinator of economic activities. At that juncture, economists did not think that privatisation of the state sector was needed; they believed that the market could fulfil its economic functions without privatisation of the means of production, provided enterprises were autonomous.

From the middle of the 1980s, Polish and Hungarian reformers were absorbed with the idea of how to create conditions for the working of the market. Though they started to lose faith in the reformability of the economic system, they took into consideration the prevailing realities and retained the idea of a system where planning would play an important role. The idea of a fully fledged market economy came only later. The reformers came more and more to believe that market forces could only work if capital and labour markets existed simultaneously and ownership relations were radically changed. Therefore, they called for an expansion of the market to capital and labour. As to ownership relations, they demanded the creation, first of all, of conditions for the expansion of private ownership and the setting of all forms of ownership on the same footing. The idea of transforming most state into private enterprises surfaced, together with the demand for a fully fledged market economy.

Soviet thinking went in the same direction as the Polish and Hungarian, with differences in time and in the extent of support. It caught on later than in the two countries mentioned; when a large number of Soviet economists embraced the idea of a free market economy, both Poland and Hungary were already engaged in the transformation of their economies into market economies, though with different methods. In contrast with Poland and Hungary, there was tremendous opposition in the USSR to a full-grown market economy. It should be borne in mind that the Soviet CP until the August 1991 *putsch* was the best organised power.

Though in Czechoslovakia the old repressive regime (true, with some rotten teeth in the last years) existed up to the time of the 'velvet' revolution and though it continued to propagandise against radical reforms, most economists favoured the idea of a market economy and managed to find ways to air their views. The lessons from the 1968 reform were not forgotten, and the ongoing changes in the thinking of neighbouring economists also had their impact. There were, of course, disagreements about the role of some socialist principles. Some still preferred market socialism.

It can be argued that in all the four countries under review, economic thinking developed in general in the direction of an acceptance of a fully fledged market economy. Needless to say, this path in thinking had its national (country) features which will be examined in the following pages. When talking about differences, I have in mind a situation where a certain idea of how to solve a particular problem is favoured by many economists in one country, whereas in another country the same idea has few followers.

There were several important differences in thinking between the Polish and Hungarian economists before the collapse of the socialist system, as well as about the question of how to transform the socialist system into a market economy. One occurred at the beginning of the 1980s, when economists of both countries were grappling with the problem of how to prevent the authorities from interfering in the affairs of enterprises, and thus ensure a substantial expansion of enterprise autonomy. In Poland, most economists, supporters of the government reform as well as radicals who opposed government reform policy, saw the introduction of self-management into enterprises as a suitable instrument not only for blocking unreasonable government interference, but also for fulfilling some other functions.

The idea of self-management had few supporters among the radical reformers in Hungary who disliked government reform policy, though it was included in the economic reform which was implemented in 1985. Most radical economists in Hungary preferred holding companies as a solution to the problem mentioned.

The difference in outlook certainly had to do with the birth of Solidarity, and a relatively long-lasting tradition of appreciating the self-management idea in Poland. In that country, the idea had historically much deeper roots than in Hungary (see Chapters 1 and 5). It was regarded by reformers as an important ingredient of any economic reform. It was, therefore, no wonder that Solidarity, a new trade union and worker movement led by workers, embraced the idea and made it part of its ideology. After all, L. Wałęsa, who now professes to be a follower of capitalism, was not against socialism in 1980; his programme was largely based on the reform ideas of the 1956 reform blueprint worked out under the leadership of O. Lange. Many intellectuals supported Solidarity; self-management was one of the reasons. This is not to say that all members of Solidarity were enthusiastic supporters of the idea; there probably were many, especially those who saw Solidarity's fight only as a stage in the effort to bring down the socialist regime, who had doubts about the self-management institution.

In Hungary, once self-management was eliminated in 1957, there were no great efforts on the part of the reformers to have it reinstituted. Neither was it an issue when the nature of the 1968 economic reform was determined. In the 1980s most reformers approached the problem of self-management from a business-like view point; for them, the idea did not have emotional connotations as was the case with many Polish economists. Nor was it an article of ideology. They believed that shunning self-management would eliminate a potential reason for economic inefficiency and were not willing to pay a price for industrial democracy which is one of the objectives of self-management. Western theories already had an impact on their thinking.

The idea of converting enterprises into holding companies caught on in Hungary (for more, see Chapter 8). This was not an entirely new idea, but in the beginning of the 1980s, when it seemed to be closer to realisation than ever before, it won in competition with other concepts, mainly with the self-management idea. At first glance, it seemed to be a reasonable tool to block interference in enterprise affairs and at the same time promote economic efficiency.

In addition, it seemed to be realistic since it did not formally affect state ownership.

In the second half of the 1980s, the idea of holding companies was combined with a conversion of enterprises into joint stock companies whose shares should be owned by other state enterprises: banks (cross ownership), insurance funds (institutional ownership), etc. Even these changes could not be classified as privatisation, since they left state ownership formally intact. Some attacked this solution as an attempt to avoid privatisation, which the authors certainly did not have in mind.

In Poland the idea of holding companies did not catch on, even at a time when many supporters were abandoning the idea of self-management. Instead, many economists started to demand quick privatisation of state enterprises. Polish economists came up with this idea first, at a time when Hungarian economists were still pursuing the conversion of state enterprises into cross and institutional ownership. Polish adherents of privatisation argued that only a market economy based on private ownership could ensure an economic turnaround, and that there is potentially a strong link between ownership and motivation, and this can be utilised, provided it is a form of ownership in which the owners can be fully identified. To them state enterprises, judged from this angle, should be regarded as ownerless.

During the first phase of Gorbachev's administration (up to 1989), the idea of self-management was quite popular. Its primary objective was to turn state ownership into societal ownership. There is some ideational connection between the desire to institute societal ownership and privatisation. Both try to make ownership more real (the goal of societal ownership is to give workers the feeling of being co-proprietors), but with this, of course, the common ground ends.

The debates about systemic changes in the USSR concentrated on questions about socialism more than in the other countries under review. Social scientists tried to find an answer to many questions related to socialism. What went wrong with socialism? Why did it lose in competition with capitalism? Was the idea of socialism wrong from the beginning, or only because it was distorted by Stalin? What should the shape of renascent socialism be? Does the adoption of a market economy mean the end of socialism? – to mention some of the questions.

One could argue that social scientists tried to clarify for themselves what kind of system they wanted and then looked for ways to achieve it. After all, socialism was first instituted in the USSR and lasted longer there than in other countries. Two or three generations in the Soviet Union did not know any other system, and therefore socialist ideas dominated the minds of intellectuals more than in other countries. The greater isolation of Soviet intellectuals from Western thought and the relentless propaganda about the superiority of socialism also had their effect. In brief, the ideology of real socialism put down deep roots in the Soviet Union. Perhaps the most important factor shaping the difference between the Soviet Union and the smaller countries was that socialism in the former was an indigenous phenomenon, while, in the smaller countries, it was regarded by many as a foreign product imposed on them by a foreign power which was viewed by many with contempt.

The difference in the intensity of socialist ideology perhaps also explains why, in the Soviet Union, in contrast with the smaller countries, mathematical economists headed the opposition to the union government reform policy and belonged among the radical or most radical economists. Shatalin, Yavlinskii and Yasin are mathematical economists or have worked in the institute for mathematical economics. These academics have apparently not been as much affected by ideology as their colleagues in institutes for and departments of political economy. It is known that many bright young people who were interested in political economy, but disliked the ideological dish in which it was served, specialised in mathematical economics. Perhaps tradition also played a certain role. As has already been shown in Chapter 2, mathematical economists played a chief role in the 1960s reform movement.

The debates in the countries under review also showed differences in thinking about the transformation process. In Poland and Czechoslovakia the debates were concentrated more on macro-economic problems connected with the transition to a market economy, because both countries resorted to shock treatment. It seems that in Czechoslovakia the clash between the adherents and opponents of shock treatment was on the whole more bitter than in Poland. This was perhaps because, when Czechoslovakia was on the verge of deciding about the methods of transformation, the first negative results of the Polish venture were already known. In addition, many believed that their country, which was in a much better economic situation than Poland, should not resort to risky methods which might upset the economy and the standard of living of the population. Finally, personal reasons also played a role. In Poland, neo-liberals might have been in a stronger position than in Czechoslovakia, and what is important to stress is that L. Wałęsa supported shock treatment and made no bones about it. Many did not want to challenge him, all the more because they did not have an alternative plan tested in practice for coping with hyperinflation, and had some trust in international financial institutions. Therefore many sat on the fence for a while, and only started to voice their criticism when the negative results of shock treatment started to show up in very drastic forms.

In Hungary, shock treatment did not have many adherents. When J. Kornai, influenced by some of his colleagues from Harvard University, came up with the idea, he was attacked by many very well-known economists. Apparently, when the economists considered the costs and benefits of such a treatment, they drew the conclusion that it would harm the economy. After this attack, few economists defended the idea of shock treatment.

It seems that in the Soviet Union, up to the aborted *coup d'état*, the adherents of a gradual transition to a market economy had the upper hand. This is quite understandable if one considers that the idea of the transition to a market economy itself was for many economists a shock to which they could not become reconciled. Others needed time to adjust to the idea. Seeing the first consequences of shock treatment in Poland and comparing the political situation and the national structure of the population in the Soviet Union with that in Poland before it ventured on shock treatment, it is no wonder that most Soviet economists were daunted. In addition, they were encouraged in their views by the opposition of Gorbachev to such radical measures as shock treatment.

After the attempted *putsch*, the victory of Yeltsin over his rival Gorbachev, and Yeltsin's commitment to radical reform, economists were in a new situation, and this could not be without an impact on their thinking.

There is also a difference in thinking about methods of privatisation in the countries under review. The main bone of contention is the question whether state assets should be sold at market prices with some discount for workers, or distributed among the adult population without charge or for a nominal charge. Even before Solidarity came to power, some Polish neo-liberals, wanting to achieve a quick privatisation, but aware that the savings of the population were only a small percentage of the value of state assets and doubtful of the willingness of people to invest very much, came up with the idea of a free distribution of part of the state assets. When the socialist system collapsed in the smaller countries, many foreign economists pushed this idea; some, though having nothing in common with socialism, used socialist arguments to make their point.

In Hungary, the idea has had few followers; economists there view privatisation more pragmatically and less ideologically than in other countries under review. This has also been reflected in some calls to put greater stress on privatisation through the creation of new private units.

Czechoslovakia is the country where the greatest debate about the distribution of bonds for a nominal charge for the purchase of state assets has been going on, the reason being that the idea is in the process of implementation. Many economists have opposed the idea, but the government has nevertheless pushed ahead.

Notes

1. In the document containing Shatalin's programme, it is argued that in the 1970s the USSR lived to a great degree from exports of fuels and raw materials (*Perekhod . . .* 1990, p. 15).
2. According to a Soviet source, the gross external debt in 1990 amounted to approximately $35 billion (Ibid., p. 18). In November 1991, it was estimated at $80 billion (*The New York Times*, 28 November 1991).
3. In 1980, the servicing costs of the debts amounted to 101 per cent of Polish exports (Jędrychowski, 1982, p. 99).
4. If the terms of trade are taken into account, the growth rates were considerably smaller, 3.9 and 0.5 per cent respectively (see *Gazdaságpolitika . . .*, 1988, p. 3).
5. According to an American study (*The Economy . . .*, 1990, p. 51), the Soviet GNP per capita in 1989 was no more than 10 per cent of that of the USA. The figure seems to grossly underestimate the performance of the Soviet economy.
6. In brief, this doctrine meant that socialist countries make up an eternal community which should see to it that all members remain loyal to socialism. In other words, the USSR would not allow anyone to quit the community.
7. While the Soviets often had to grapple with insufficient agricultural output, other countries, mainly Hungary, and to a lesser extent Czechoslovakia, had problems with a lack of foreign markets and with low world prices. In both Hungary and Czechoslovakia, collective farms did well on the whole.

7 Hungary

INTRODUCTION

In the period 1972–9, the economic reform more or less stagnated, after some recentralisation provisions in the beginning of the period. The reason for this stagnation was political to a great degree: it was the echo of the 1968 Czechoslovak events. Pressure to do something about the EM started to build up in the second half of the 1970s when the economic situation began to worsen.

The economic and political situation probably caused a standstill in the evolution of systemic ideas. True, there was a debate in 1974–5 about ownership (see Lengyel, 1988, p. 23) which did not have much impact on systemic thinking. It was soon overshadowed by the 1977–81 debate about the organisation of industry (see Lengyel, 1989, p. 160) which drew attention to the excessive concentration of industry.

In the beginning of the 1980s changes set in. In 1980 the authorities introduced a competitive price system whose purpose was to link domestic producer prices with world prices, and in 1982 they created a legal framework for the expansion of the private sector and for the legalisation of many previously illegal activities. They also reduced the concentration of industry. Even before this, they had decided to abandon the policy of maximum growth (for more, see Révész, 1990, pp. 108–118). At the same time the Hungarian Socialist Workers' Party (henceforth, CP) solicited proposals for improving the EM. The CP's challenge was answered by young economists, both as individuals[1] and as a group,[2] and by others. This young generation was different from the old: it was more liberal in its thinking, less bound by Marxist ideology and less influenced by the consequences of the 1956 uprising. The environment was also different: the authorities were much more tolerant of dissent, and connections with foreign peers gradually became easier so that a better knowledge of Western thinking became possible. Their proposals, many of which found their way into publications, attested to their belief in the reformability of the economic system. In co-operation with the older generation,[3] they called, however, for a radical reform, one which would expand substantially the sphere of market forces. This was to be achieved by dramatically reducing government interference in the

122

affairs of enterprises, by strengthening incentives, by making money an integrating force for the whole economy, by bringing about rational prices and a more efficient use of capital and labour, and so on. T. Bauer (1982) called openly for a second reform.

The CP was not prepared to accept the calls for reform. Kádár himself rejected them by saying that no reform of the reform was needed since the reform (meaning the 1968 reform) was successful (Berend, 1988, p. 384). Even before this, the *Társadalmi Szemle* (no. 2, 1983), the CP's theoretical journal, tried to counter the position of the 'young Turks' by soliciting the views of some economists about the 1968 reform. In addition, the journal initiated a report by experts[4] from central agencies and enterprises which was published with the title 'The further development of our management system in the services of building socialism' (*TSz*, no. 11, 1983). The young economists, however, remained defiant (see for example, Bauer, 1983).

The 1983 debate on planning also shed light on the thinking of a group of the best-known economists. It showed that there was quite a change in the attitude of most participants. None of them rejected the idea of planning, but most of them approached it pragmatically, no longer as something which was necessarily needed because of socialism.

Despite this locking of horns, the young economists continued to co-operate with the CP; they took part in the preparation of the 1984 Party resolution. The final text of the resolution went beyond the principles of the 1968 reform: it brought about limited self-management institutions in enterprises, so-called enterprise councils (instituted in most enterprises) and collective managements (in smaller enterprises) were given many rights previously kept by the centre. This was intended to reduce government interference and strengthen market forces. Enterprises got more say in wage regulation, pricing and investment. In the dismantling of the state monopoly in foreign trade a further important step was taken.

The changes introduced were not to the liking of the young economists; they were a far cry from their ideas about systemic changes and changes in economic policy. Their disappointment was increased by the resolutions of the CP Congress in 1985, in which they saw a backing-down from previously promised priorities (Lengyel, 1987, p. 141).

All this dissatisfaction did not make them throw in the towel; on the contrary, they decided, with the help of some other economists and social scientists, to put together a comprehensive study of the economic situation and the kind of reforms needed. The study was called 'Turning Point and Reform' (Antal et al., 1987), and was a watershed in the development of systemic thinking. Judging from the written text only, one can hardly argue that it was a clear rejection of the socialist system, though the text included some passages from which one can draw such a conclusion. At any rate, the blueprint reflected a profound disappointment with the system and deep doubts about its reformability. These young reformers had already managed to rally a large part of the interested public. With this study their reputation and influence increased. The CP again tried to counter their influence by publishing a 'standpoint', written by an advisory group of the CP (see 'Standpoint' . . ., 1987).

The promises of the 1984 CP resolution were implemented slowly and inconsistently, and the economy, after a short-lived recovery, started to go downhill again. In 1987, the authorities came up with a stabilisation programme which promised to stabilise the economy and accelerate its restructuring. The authorities also committed themselves to an acceleration of the economic reform by giving greater scope to market forces (*Nsz*, 4 July and 19 September 1987).

The CP also tried, with some ideological and political concessions, to placate the growing dissent within and outside the CP. The call for political changes gained an increasingly broader base. In May 1988 at a CP conference, J. Kádár and his closest supporters were ousted from the Politburo.[5] The new Politburo was mostly made up of reformers; some of them were determined to transform Hungary into a democratic society. The conference also decided on the transition to a socialist market economy. K. Grósz, the new leader of the CP, certainly did not want a multi-party system, but under pressure from inside and outside the CP he had to agree to one. In two meetings of the CC (see *Nsz* 23 February and 1 April 1989) the CP made it official.

Once it became clear that the authoritarian regime was at an end, great political activity started throughout the country. In the CP the reform movement, which called for discarding and sweeping away all vestiges of Stalinism and for orienting the CP towards social-democratic values, won. At the Congress of the CP, which took place in October 1989, the CP changed its name to Socialist Party and elected a new leadership with R. Nyers at the top. A minority split from the new party and re-established the old party.

In the March and April 1990 parliamentary elections, a right-wing coalition won. It committed itself to a market economy based on private ownership.

In this chapter I will first discuss how the systemic views developed in the first half of the 1980s when belief in the reformability of the system still survived. Then I will discuss the evolution of this thinking from the second half of the 1980s, which was marked with a speedy loss of belief in the reformability of the system, until its collapse. The last part deals with debates about a transition to a market economy in the period after the collapse of the system.

DEBATES IN THE FIRST HALF OF THE 1980s

The worsening of the economic situation pushed the CP into defence and created a more favourable atmosphere for criticism, which was usually combined with some suggestions for a cure.[6] There were also, of course, critical voices aimed directly or indirectly at the fault-finders.

Apart from a general debate, there were also debates about property rights, planning, restructuring of the economy, pricing, the banking system – to mention only the most important ones. Taking the suggested remedies together, one can see contours of market socialism emerging. In the first half of the 1980s, collective ownership was still taboo; what many critics wanted was to reduce dramatically government control over the nationalised means of production.

Criticism of the System

Criticism was directed at the EM generally and at changes carried out in 1980–2 in particular. J. Kornai and T. Bauer may have given the most comprehensive critical evaluation of the changes. J. Kornai (1982) argued that the hardening expected in the budget constraints of enterprises due the competitive price system had not materialised and that enterprises behaved as before. He found the reason for this phenomenon in the artificial nature of the price system – that it was not the result of market competition but of a design worked out at a desk. T. Bauer (1982) took a similar position when arguing that, without integrating the Hungarian economy in the world market and without having competitive imports, it was difficult to have competitive prices.

J. Kornai also believed that the deconcentration of industry which had been carried out was not sufficient in light of the excessive concentration, and he also indirectly criticised the slow expansion of the private sector. But his main fire was directed against the existing economic mechanism. According to him, the state sector was not yet regulated by market forces; it was not equipped with a mechanism which would curb its investment drive and force it to adjust to changing demand. Moreover, the Hungarian economy, though to a much smaller extent than other socialist economies, was suffering from chronic shortages.

Kornai's statement about shortages enjoyed credence, since support for it could be found in his book *Economics of Shortage* (1980), which was very well received and gained him renown at home and abroad. In this book J. Kornai shows that the socialist system necessarily produces shortages of goods as well as of labour, and that the socialist system is therefore supply constrained, unlike the capitalist system which is demand constrained. In other words, shortages are not an accidental phenomenon, but a necessary product of the working of the socialist system.

The shortage phenomenon was closely linked to what Kornai called 'soft budget constraint', a lack of sufficient pressure on enterprises to behave rationally when cost and outlays were involved. The behaviour of enterprises was due to the state's paternalistic approach; it bailed out enterprises if they got into financial trouble, which is, of course, an invitation to inefficiencies.

T. Bauer (1982) characterised the 1980–2 provisions as radical because they touched areas which, before, had been regarded as taboo. He apparently had in mind the expansion of the private sector. Bauer recognised with satisfaction that Hungary was ahead of other countries in the reform of the EM; he nevertheless regarded the changes as unsatisfactory and called for a new, second reform. Though the directive system had been abandoned, the economy was not yet regulated by the market; the economy was run by a peculiar consensus according to which enterprises were voluntarily trying to meet the targets which, they believed, were expected of them. And this was, of course, not satisfactory to him.

It is worthwhile mentioning that Bauer also warned that CMEA countries would not be able to compete with the West in armament and technological progress unless the decline in economic growth was reversed.

It has already been mentioned generally what the CP did in order to neutralise the criticism. Now, this will be elaborated upon, and the views of B. Csikós-Nagy and A. Szegő will also be discussed.

In my opinion, the answers given by the respondents to the questions asked by the CP's theoretical journal, *Társadalmi Szemle* (no. 2, 1983) were mostly lukewarm: they were formulated carefully in order not to create the impression that they were critical of the views of the young reformers. Csikós-Nagy stressed the importance of preserving freedom of research and of instituting further reforms. R. Nyers maintained that there was no need for a second reform, but there should still be a substantial change in the economic mechanism.

The report of the experts (*Társadalmi Szemle*, 1983, no 11, pp. 11–29), mentioned above, tried to convey the message that the CP was aware of the problems and was doing its best. According to the experts, the main endeavour should be focused on the development of socialist entrepreneurship. To this end, changes should be made (it did not mention what kind) which would enable successful entrepreneurs to be rewarded. The need for a further strengthening of market forces and purposeful regulation was also stressed.

B. Csikós-Nagy (1982) believed that in the transformation of the management system monetarisation of the economy was more important than decentralisation, all the more because the latter is also dependent on non-systemic conditions (in some sectors, centralisation is efficient, for example, electric power). Only if the economy were monetarised would the authorities be able to administer it with the help of monetary and fiscal policy. He understood that to make such an economy function, rational prices and their linkage to world market prices were needed. He did not, however, explain how a market economy – of the kind he had in mind – could arise if the economy was excessively monopolised.

A real attack on the young reformers came from A. Szegő (1983), a research worker. In essence, she posed the question: why does the non-cadre intelligentsia[7] abandon Marxism in favour of neo-liberalism; why is M. Friedman becoming its idol instead of Marx? The answer she gave was that the intelligentsia resented its status in society; it resented being subjected to the general 'proletarisation'. Furthermore, the intelligentsia did not receive any compensation for the loss of its privileges; the possibility of vertical mobility, which brings advantages to workers and peasants, was no consolation.

She indirectly accuses the radical reformers of 'salami tactics'. They call for a regulated market though it cannot work. Do they not do so in the hope that, once the authorities adopt their concept of a regulated market, it will be easy to convince them to take the next step to a marketised economy, if it turns out that the previous concept does not work? She also criticises the intelligentsia for suggesting that the regulated market should be expanded and for not really analysing the connection of such a concept with ownership relations; she further hints that such an analysis would show that the expansion of the market is impossible unless collective ownership is reduced to a formality.

The answer to her attack was published in the same issue of the journal, written by L. Antal (1983), one of the leaders of the young radical reformers. The title given to the paper – 'Conceptual indictment, without proof' – was enough to indicate on its own that the radical reformers were not happy with Szegő's attack. Antal denied that the radical reform movement had any intention of eliminating the planned economy.

Understandably, the cures suggested were not all the same. It is, however, possible to argue that most critics still believed in the reformability of the system. They wanted to expand the scope of market forces without denying planning an important role in the coordination of economic activities. For example, according to Bauer (1982), it was necessary to create an economic mechanism in which the plan and market were integrated. The former should focus on macro-processes, the latter on micro-processes. L. Antal (1983A) called indirectly for a more radical reform: leave to the government only the decisions which cannot be made efficiently by the market; the latter should also take care of the allocation of labour and capital, with some qualifications. He also advanced the idea of 'grass root democracy' and a transformation of ownership functions.

Property Rights

The 1968 reform did not put an end to government interference in the affairs of enterprises. Government intervention by fiscal and monetary policies, which are applied even in market economies, is disregarded here. The interference which was exercised primarily by the branch ministry as the supervisory and control body took on different forms. The ministry's interference was facilitated by enterprises' dependence in many respects on its benevolence. The relationship between the authorities and enterprises was not one-sided. Enterprises, mainly large ones, used their bargaining power to extract various advantages: to influence the nature of regulators to their benefit, and to get subsidies and tax breaks. In this way, the original idea of making the regulation system uniform was eroded.

The reformers wanted to change this unhealthy state of affairs which hindered economic efficiency. The branch ministry derived its power from being the representative of the state as the owner of the means of production. It is not far from this fact to the idea that a change can be brought about by entrusting the property rights to someone outside the government. In substance, three proposals were presented on this idea (T. Liska and Kopátsy's proposals, which have already been discussed in Chapter 4, are disregarded here). One was to transfer the property rights to holding companies, the other to enterprises, and the last to enterprises with outside participation (the so-called corporative solution). The first proposal meant a clear separation of ownership and management, the second an integration of the two functions, and the third was somewhere in the middle. The proposals were usually associated with certain names, the first with M. Tardos, the second with T. Bauer, and the third with T. Sárközy, though none of the ideas was new.

According to Tardos (1982) between four and ten independently functioning and competing holding companies should be established in the competitive sphere. Each enterprise, together with a group of enterprises – the way the grouping will be done is not discussed – will be subordinated to a holding company which will be headed by an executive body appointed by the Presidential Council of the National Assembly. The holding company should have the right to control the activities of enterprises, establish new enterprises, liquidate existing ones and reallocate capital. To Tardos the holding company has not only to prevent the authorities from interfering in enterprise affairs but, even more, it must be an instrument for promoting interest in the expansion of enterprise capital (therefore the holding company should be guided in its decision-making by long-term profitability) and for establishing a capital market. To achieve all these goals he is willing to sacrifice some of the rights of enterprises.

L. Antal (1982), who takes a similar position to Tardos, calls the special institution the ownership–entrepreneurial bureau. Initially, the members of the bureau are appointed by the Council of Ministers; later, the bureau itself will determine who its members will be. They will have the same rights as Tardos' holding company, and it is expected that their interest in the expansion of capital will be ensured by giving them low salaries and high dividends.

Among the various methods for transferring property rights to enterprises, Bauer (1982) prefers self-management. He is not oblivious to the various objections to self-management; he discusses briefly the well-known observations by Ward (1958) and some other objections. Bauer agrees with some of them; others he refutes. He devotes special attention to potential critics who call for the separation of ownership and management, and indirectly reject self-management in the belief that this hampers capital movement (see Balázsy, 1984). Bauer maintains that separation weakens the profit motive and that self-management can be adapted in a way that will promote capital mobility, which is the main purpose of separation. The latter view is also shared by R. Nyers (1986) and K. A. Soós (see Antal 1985).

Bauer did not, however, discuss the objection which Tardos (1982) raised, which is that self-management cannot be effective in large enterprises, and therefore smaller units within enterprises must get almost complete independence – as was the case in Yugoslavia with the basic units of associated work – which weakens the enterprise in its quest for efficiency. Nor did he discuss the danger of inflation, which may result from self-management's short-term interest in wage increases. Not because he was unaware of the problems, but because he excluded from consideration the return of large- and middle-sized enterprises to private hands, Bauer had to choose between self-management and other methods of enterprise ownership, and he gave preference to the first. However, he did not object to the application of other methods to some enterprises and preferred co-operative self-management.

Finally, it is worthwhile mentioning that Bauer does not try to sell the idea of self-management by alluding to ideological or political arguments. There is no mention of either of the known arguments about self-management, that it gives meaning to collective ownership and eliminates alienation, or of the potential of self-management as a tool of democratisation of the economy and the political system.

The corporative approach (see p. 129) means that all the interested groups in enterprises – management, representatives of the workers, the Party and trade unions, as well as the state administration – participate in the strategic decisions of enterprises. Operative decisions remain in the hands of directors. I have not managed to find any of Sárközy's articles in which the author outlines the specifics of this solution and its advantages. There are some hints in his 1982 article and in Sipos and Tardos (1982).

The Role of Planning

The 1983 debate (*Vita* . . ., 1984) gives good insight into the thoughts about planning of well-known reformers in the beginning of the 1980s. The debate revolved around nine papers, four of them prepared by research fellows of the Economic Institute, and discussed the following questions: what should be planned; what should the role of planning in the management system be; what should the role of annual and long-term plans be; what is the relationship between planning and economic policy; how should state and enterprise plans be harmonised; and how should the planning system be democratised?

In his summary, R. Nyers maintained that none of the participants in the debate challenged the need to combine planning and market. Some derived the necessity of planning from the value system of socialism, and others saw planning's task primarily in promoting efficiency and correcting the market's shortcomings (*Vita* . . ., 1984, p. 32). I. Hetényi, the former minister of finance and deputy chairman of the Planning Office, who introduced the debate, evaluated it in retrospect in the following way: 'In the debate the unanimous view was that there was a need for national economic planning and the planning should be developed in a way that supports a decentralised, better working market' (1989, pp. 69–70).

Of course, there were quite important differences of view on the role of planning, the relationship of planning and economic policy, types of plans and democratisation. As to the role of planning, it is possible to say that three groups of views crystallised in the debate. Á. Balassa (at the time of the debate one of the highest bureaucrats in the Planning Office) believed that the role of planning, as designed in the 1968 reform, was in substance correct and no change was needed (*Vita* . . ., 1984, p. 70). Planning's function according to him is, among other things, to detect the possibilities of economic development, and to determine the growth rates, equilibrium conditions, and the main proportions. The state should help to implement the most important structural changes, primarily by research, but also by investment activities. Balassa believed that, as to energy, basic material production and technology, government interference should be direct, whereas, in the competitive sphere, indirect and direct methods should be used. In brief, Balassa's views were in line with actual government planning activities.

According to Tardos, the main functions of the national plan are:

to determine the changes in global earnings and price level, the proportion between consumption and accumulation, and the main direction of foreign relations; to develop the infrastructure and protection of the environment; to keep inequities within limits; to develop social policy; and, finally, to ensure continuous economic growth and full employment. In the functions enumerated, there is already a difference between Tardos and Balassa (for example, Tardos would like to limit government involvement in earnings to a determination of global earnings and exclude government from distribution of earnings by wage regulation, which is not Balassa's view), but the difference becomes more profound when the issue is the material sphere. Both believe that the government should take care of the development of the infrastructure. In the material sphere, however, the views diverge: unlike Balassa, Tardos, as a convinced adherent of the market mechanism, wants the government and planners to stay out of production. To him, the government role in the development of the material sphere should be limited to the setting of priorities and 'the determination of the degree of their support' (*Vita* . . ., p. 189). In other words, if the government feels that a certain branch or line of production should be developed preferentially, the government should make it known, and organisations which are willing to involve themselves in such a project should get government support. In brief, M. Tardos suggested solutions which A. Lerner proposed in his *Economics of Control* (1947).

Tardos' views are in line with his opposition to the centralisation of decision-making about the allocation of resources in the hands of government or the National Bank, and with his favouring the development of a capital market.

L. Antal (*Vita* . . . 1984, pp. 59–63) in substance agreed with Tardos about the functions of the plan, but demanded that the existing hierarchical harmonisation and coordination be replaced by collective agreements. He had in mind collective agreements not only about basic wages and working conditions, but also about the distribution of subsidies and what to do about inefficient enterprises. These agreements should be concluded between the representatives of the interested parties and the authorities. Probably Tardos had a similar solution in mind. Otherwise, one could question his idea of planning the proportion between accumulation and consumption if government is not allowed to interfere directly in the material sphere.

T. Bauer (*Vita* . . . 1984, pp. 111–14) took a middle position; he saw an important role for the government in major investment. On the other hand, the government should not interfere with what he called natural enterprise investment (what is called induced investment in the West). In addition, he suggested excluding from planning trade contracts with CMEA countries. The rationale behind this suggestion came from experience: the concern about fulfilling trade contracts was seen to be one of the reasons for government interference in enterprise affairs.

The debate took place as the political leadership prepared for new moves in economic reform. The previously mentioned Party resolution of April 1984 brought no important changes in planning itself: 'The national economic plan [reads the resolution] is the instrument for the assertion of the societal interest and the basic instrument of management' (*Népszabadság*, 19 April 1984).

DEBATES IN THE SECOND HALF OF THE 1980s

In the second phase the main focus of the intellectual activity of a great many reformers, more precisely radical reformers, was on their advocacy of a market economy and their proposals for achieving it. For ideological reasons, they still used the ambiguous term 'regulated market', but, in fact, what they had in mind was a market economy. In this endeavour, the reform blueprint 'Turning Point and Reform' (Antal et al., 1987) played a very significant role. It was written under the auspices of I. Pozsgay, the then general secretary of the Patriotic People's Front, which gave it some political protection and also enhanced its credibility, since I. Pozsgay was known for his nonconformism. Indeed, the blueprint was not suppressed; it was, however, published after some delay. Its publication encouraged more people to go public with their views.

It has already been mentioned that the reform blueprint can be regarded as a reflection of deep doubts about the reformability of the socialist system. J. Kornai's paper in the *Journal of Economic Literature* (1986), which is only an analysis of the Hungarian system without any explicit suggestions for reforming it, takes implicitly the view that the system is not reformable. In the author's eyes, reformers who wanted in the past (or now want) to reform the system by supplementing it or combining it with the market were (are) naive. 'The faith placed in the harmonious, mutually correcting duality of "plan" and "market" (or, in the language of the present paper, bureaucracy and market) is the centrepiece of the pioneers' naivete' (1986, p.

1729). There is an irreconcilable conflict between indirect bureaucratic control and the market, and therefore the concept of dividing up the coordinating activities between planning (extended reproduction) and market (simple reproduction) cannot work effectively. To Kornai the bureaucracy cannot be made to respect the division of decision-making, and the profit motive in enterprises is 'illusory' if they cannot make decisions about growth and technical development.

As already mentioned, in 1987, the CP came up with a stabilisation plan which also promised to accelerate economic reform. At a CP conference which took place in 1988, the newly elected leadership of the Party committed itself to create 'conditions for the working of a socialist market economy' (see Supplement to *Nsz*, 23 May 1988). The rumours about impending radical changes in the economic system, and even more the official announcement of the changes, sparked a debate among others about market socialism in general, and also about ownership relations and planning. Market socialism is usually defined as a system based on preponderance of collective ownership where the market is the dominating mechanism.

Promotion of Interest in the Expansion of Assets (Capital)

This is an important and well thought out concept and goal; it can be argued that its achievement is connected with many important changes crucial for the good working of a market economy. No doubt, the point can be made that the expansion of capital assets presupposes a modification of how property rights are exercised and an introduction of a capital market. Likewise, the argument can be made that rational prices are needed. In addition, no ideological objections can be made to this concept. One could even speculate that the legitimate demand for the expansion of capital served as a cover up for more controversial demands.

The promotion of interest in the expansion of capital (interest in the expansion of property as one of the masterminds of this concept, L. Antal (1985) called it) was intended to strengthen the profit motive. The architects of the 1968 reform counted on the profit motive to be a strong incentive for the promotion of efficiency and a guide to decision-making, but their expectations did not materialise, for several reasons. Enterprises were, in so many respects, dependent on the authorities that it was more important for them to follow the wishes of the authorities, including the CP, than the profit motive. Due to the weakness of market forces and the lack of a rational price system, to mention the most important reasons, profit did not become an objective gauge of performance. As a result, the amount of profit remaining with enterprises depended more on government withdrawals and subsidies[8] than on the market (Kornai and Matits, 1987, pp. 71–2).

To the extent that profit was pursued as a goal it was judged from a short-term vantage point. There were no forces at work to make managers interested in long-term profit. The stress on expansion of capital was intended to make sure that 'current profit would not grow at the expense of future profit' (Tardos, 1987, p. 24).

Interest in the growth of capital, which was to be understood primarily in terms of growth in the capacity to produce profit, aimed at stimulating enterprises to make the most efficient use of capital, which involved not only the most efficient use of profit for investment, but also a permanent restructuring of the existing stock of capital in order to be able to preserve and expand its value (Antal, 1985).

Such a handling of capital presupposes, of course, its free movement; it should be allowed to flow where it can produce the greatest return. If an enterprise can achieve a greater return on its capital by investing it in another enterprise instead of in its own, it should have the right to do so.

Most economists believed that interest in capital expansion could only be achieved by a special institution, a property organisation, outside the state administration, which would be entrusted with looking after ownership functions. Some of the suggestions for a property organisation have already been mentioned.

Some of the advocates of the idea of interest in capital growth give preference to a state institution (for example, K. Szabó, 1985; J. Bársony, 1986). K. Szabó (1985) takes the position that the special institution should not interfere with the self-management of enterprises, whereas some others, for example, Tardos, for whom economic efficiency has precedence over all other considerations, are in favour of a managerial solution (1982).

It is clear that not only managers, but also workers, must be made interested in long-term expansion of capital if the idea is to have a chance of success. Workers who are close to retirement, or those who do not intend to work in one enterprise for long, are more interested in short-term benefits (wages, bonuses) than long-term ones. But even young workers, who would like to link their productive activities with the enterprise for which they work over the long term, may be reluctant, for various reasons, to give up short-term interests to the extent needed. Therefore, some economists came up with some incentives which would stimulate the interest of workers in the long-term expansion of capital. All the suggestions have in common that workers should, like their managers, share in the long-run increment in capital. L. Kotz (1987, pp. 56–62) presented quite a detailed proposal.

'Turning Point and Reform'

'Turning Point and Reform' (Antal et al., 1987) – an important milestone in the evolution of ideas about the socialist EM – was the work of a large collective of social scientists in 1986. A team of young researchers of the former research institute of the Ministry of Finance, headed by L. Antal, were the initiators and masterminds of this blueprint proposal. It was discussed first in various forums and later with CP officials. One of the important questions discussed was whether the blueprint should include a demand for political reform, that is, for democratisation of the power structure. According to L. Lengyel (1987, p. 145), who was one of the editors of the blueprint and wrote its history, some of the debaters posed the question whether such a demand would not scare away the otherwise reform-minded leadership. Some even raised the question of whether an authoritarian system could not tackle the economy more effectively, having in mind the South Korean, Taiwanese and Turkish cases. The debaters soon agreed that under socialist conditions a combination of political dictatorship and competitive market was incompatible.

The authors of the blueprint proposal gave a scathing criticism of the existing system of management as well as of the economic policy. They mainly criticised the fact that the government had not made noticeable progress in restructuring the economy.

The blueprint called for a 'comprehensive, radical, democratising and decentralising market reform'. 'Comprehensive' referred to the change in economic policy, decisive steps in the transformation of the economic mechanism into a market economy, and a societal–political reform, all to happen simultaneously. By 'radical' they were thinking of the exercise of self-criticism by the authorities, and a complete break with previous behaviour (Antal et al., 1987).

As to the transformation of the economic mechanism, the blueprint called for an overhaul of the tax system, the introduction of a more realistic exchange rate, and liberalisation of imports. It also called for the introduction of a capital market and the abolition of the mono-banking system. All this in the name of making monetary management paramount.

The blueprint also suggested opening the door to various forms of ownership with great stress on joint-stock companies. Self-managed enterprises were encouraged to give up voluntarily certain or all decision-making rights. Furthermore, it called for splitting up enterprises which were in a monopoly position in order to create a greater number of actors in the market.

In the first version of the document, the authors suggested increasing trade co-operation with East European countries which had already embarked on reforms and treating the Eastern and Western market equally (Lengyel, 1987, p. 153). Apparently, for political reasons, they later decided to forgo such a demand.

Restructuring of the economy was mentioned as one of the main goals of economic policy and it was indicated that it could not be achieved without unemployment (*Medvetánc*, 1987, p. 22[9]).

The change in thinking is best seen in how the authors treat macro-economic policy and planning. From their stand on macro-economic policy, it is clear that neo-liberalism and monetarism made significant inroads in the theoretical arsenal of the Hungarian reformers. They suggested, namely, switching the main stress from fiscal policy to monetary policy. Regulation of the money supply should become the focal point of economic policy. Administrative limitations should be replaced by monetary restrictions which should play a key role in the management of demand.

As for planning, according to the text published in *Közgazdasági Szemle*,[10] it should undergo great changes. Existing planning, which was permeated by natural balancing, should be replaced by planning in value terms. The main focus of the new planning should be on the drafting of a macro-financial plan and on its preservation. The departure point should be the working out of preconditions for internal and external equilibrium. In the non-competitive sphere, mainly the infrastructure, the role of planning should be more important and direct.

The text in *Közgazdasági Szemle* was accompanied by a 'standpoint' written by some members of an advisory group of the CC ('Standpoint . . .', 1987).[11] The writers of the 'Standpoint' mainly reject the part of the study which deals with planning and which really adds up to a rejection of planning. They maintain that the study overestimates the importance of monetary policy, and that it alone cannot solve such current problems as a restructuring of the economy. Government coordination policy is indispensable and cannot be given up. Neither can the government leave to the market and to representatives of interest groups the harmonisation of conflicting interests. On the other hand, the writers of the 'Standpoint' recognise the need to revitalise and modernise planning, and call for a greater role for financial instruments in planning. 'It is necessary to create a planning system which would be more open, flexible and willing to accept and absorb the impacts of the market' ('Standpoint . . .', 1987).

Market Socialism

The debate about market socialism took place primarily in *Társadalmi Szemle* (the theoretical journal of the Party) and *Gazdaság* (the journal of the economic association). This was at a time when it was already possible to express one's views more or less freely, and some used this occasion to vent their anger and frustration with the system. Of the debates, the one in *Gazdaság* was the most important; the editors of the journal selected the debaters[12] and, of course, the most known, reputable and influential economists; in addition, they tried to get a representative sample of holders of different ideas, and asked them to answer two questions: (1) what is market socialism? and (2) can it work, and under which social and economic conditions?

All the participants in the debate in *Gazdaság* (1989, no. 2) agreed that a transition to a market economy was needed, but most of them argued that the term 'market socialism' was inadequate. L. Szamuely titled his answer 'The Squaring of the Circle', arguing that market economy and socialism, understood in the Marxian tradition, are in contradiction. A. Hegedűs, the 1956 prime minister under Rákosi, argued that the term market socialism was only cosmetic. A market economy cannot take care of socialist values (egalitarianism, solidarity); these must be upheld by other institutions. T. Nagy suggested that the title was confusing and that a better one would be a socialist-type (*jellegü*) market economy. L. Lengyel maintained that there is only one market economy; it is neither socialist nor capitalist. To him the market economy is, in a sense, systemically neutral. He also suggested that a market economy should first be constructed, and only then could, and should, come socialism.

In a debate in *Figyelő* (1988, no. 50), R. Nyers takes the position that the term 'market socialism' is rather political; it includes a market economy including capital relations, combined with a socialist policy, focused primarily on preferential treatment for ordinary people.

When it came to the question about what to preserve from socialism, views differed very much. On the one hand, there was the view that a market economy was needed, and everything which had to do with socialism was useless. This did not, of course, mean that *social* institutions were not needed. M. Tardos can be regarded as the best representative of this view in the debate. According to him, socialism, based on collective ownership, and a market economy are conflicting institutions, and the CP state, which manages the economy, cannot accept a market economy which works against the CP state. In addition, the 'socialist' market economy cannot be efficient, since it considers only the interests of labour and neglects the importance of capital. The only solution to the problems which Hungary faces is a return to a market economy and democracy.

J. Kornai did not participate in the debate, but took up a position in regard to market socialism in his *Road to a Free Economy* (1990), and it was a harsh one. According to him, the idea of market socialism has, in practice, collapsed and has no chance of revival. The market mechanism based on private property is the natural coordinator of economic activities, and, in addition, it would be futile to expect that a state enterprise can behave like a private one. He writes, 'state ownership permanently recreates bureaucracy, since the state owned firm is but an organic part of the bureaucratic hierarchy' (p. 58). As in his 1986 article, here again he maintained that the 1968 reform only replaced direct bureaucratic regulation by an indirect one (p. 59).

The other end of the spectrum of the mentioned debate in *Gazdaság* was represented by academician R. Hoch, who argued that the reforms showed that it was possible under conditions of collective ownership to change the expanding market from a sellers' market to a buyers', and to create market conditions for stimulation of innovations. To him, market socialism should be marked by the following features: planning, existential security (full employment), limits on wealth and income differentials, equal opportunity, predominance of collective ownership, and the participation of workers in the management of enterprises.

In the *Társadalmi Szemle* summarising debate, Hoch (1989) makes it clear that he is not an adherent of self-management, which was introduced in 1985. He does not, however, explain what kind of workers' participation in management he has in mind.

In the middle of the spectrum of views, the respondents attributed a certain role to socialist features. For example, L. Lengyel maintained that all ownership forms should be treated equally: none of them should be given preference. Planning should play a role in the infrastructure development, and protection of the environment. Without planning, it is difficult to improve the quality of life.

T. Nagy suggests converting existing state ownership into community (*közösségi*) ownership. By this he means turning state enterprises into joint stock companies, whose shares are owned by special banks, holding companies, or insurance companies. Planning should play a role when the market is not able to solve problems satisfactorily. It should also be involved in the foundation of a long-term strategy of development.

Ownership Reform

The campaign to increase interest in the expansion of assets was only an overture – not clear whether intended or unintended – to an ownership reform debate which eventually put privatisation on the agenda. In the second half of the 1980s, the debate first concentrated on the pluralisation of ownership and how to achieve it. In this connection, the demand was formulated so as to treat all forms of ownership in the same way. Only later was the predominance of private ownership put on the agenda.

The demand for pluralisation of ownership is not really a revolutionary demand if one considers that the CP itself agreed to the expansion of the market and to private ownership. It can be reconciled even with the idea of market socialism, an idea which the CP toyed with in 1988–9. Different forms of ownership are not contrary to the idea of the predominance of state ownership, particularly if the latter itself changes its nature. Neither are they contrary to self-management (compare Bársony, 1989).

The demand for pluralisation intensified the debate about how to change state ownership. Many argued that ownership by the state is ownership by everyone and thus by no one – that is, state ownership is an ownership without real owners. A real owner is the one who takes care of the property and sees to it that it is efficiently used and expanded. The state, according to those with a negative view on state ownership, cannot fulfil this function. It was suggested identifying the real owner, the final owner who could behave in such a way. Gy.

Matolcsy (a former high official of the new government) started one of his articles (1989) with 'The model crisis elimination can be started with the finding of the real, final owner'. Obviously, the concept of the final owner was nothing but an ideological preparation of the ground for the predominance of private ownership.

There were considerable differences in views as to how to conceive the ownership reform. Some stuck to ideas expressed at the beginning of the 1980s, but others abandoned their positions. M. Tardos (1988A) still favoured, among other solutions, the distribution of state property between holding companies, this time with the explicit precondition that the distribution should be at random; he was probably influenced by the criticism that holding companies might turn into monopolies. If enterprises were to be turned into joint stock companies, then he would prefer property rights to be transferred to insurance and pension funds and to local governments.

Needless to say, these solutions were regarded by Tardos as only temporary because of lack of capital, and probably also because it was too early to come up with demands for all-out privatisation. After all, in an earlier study (1988) on the same topic, he had suggested that private or group ownership was a better solution than these 'artificial' institutions.

S. Kopátsy has always held the view that in a modern society pension funds are the most effective owners. He came to this conclusion on the basis of his study of the ownership of Western corporations. He suggested (1988) creating approximately twenty pension funds (separate funds for miners, construction workers, trade employees, etc.) which would own the shares of enterprises in the competitive sphere. The day-to-day operation of the shares should be left to the banks; the pension funds should shift the shares from one bank to another, depending on the gains made by the banks.

T. Liska's ideas, this time in favour of the distribution of all state property among the population (a concept known under the name of personal collective ownership – *személyes társadalmi tulajdon*), had some supporters (for example, Bársony, 1989; Síklaky, 1989). However, in Hungary, in contrast to Poland and Czechoslovakia, this idea did not take deep roots. Many regarded it as a utopia, an illusion which could not work (see Matolcsy, 1989).

The self-management idea did not fare much better. L. Lengyel (1988, p. 31) mentioned that, after the appearance of 'Turning Point and Reform', the idea of self-management, including the self-management introduced in 1985–6, became subject to attack and ridicule. Many saw self-management as an obstacle to the expansion of market forces and to the promotion of economic efficiency (for example, Falusné Szikra, 1988). Some therefore wanted to use new legislation then in preparation – the transformation law which set the rules for turning enterprises into joint stock and limited liability companies – to limit the right of self-managed enterprises to such an extent that, in practice, an end would be put to their existence. However, the architect of the transformation law, T. Sárközy, in the new law, managed to maintain for self-managed enterprises the right to make decisions about their conversion. The debate which developed around this question (Sárközy, 1989; Bokros, 1989) was, in fact, a concealed debate about two concepts of future privatisation. (See below for further discussion.)

Planning

In the summer of 1988, the K. Grósz government decided to have a strategy worked out for the transition to a market economy. To this end, the Consultative Council for Economic Management published a detailed outline of the reform concept ('Outline . . .', 1988). The outline was written very much in the spirit of the 'Turning Point and Reform', with the difference, of course, that the 'Outline' was a government document and therefore had to respect government policy. In a nutshell, the document committed the government to market socialism, that is, to a system in which the market is the dominant coordinating mechanism and where communal (*közösségi*) ownership prevails. The word 'communal' should be stressed, because, by using it, the authors wanted to indicate that it would no longer be the old form of state ownership. As for planning, the document is very brief. Its main role should be in strategic planning, that is, restructuring the economy and also playing a role in harmonising long-term economic and social policy.

The debate on planning concentrated primarily on three topics: what should the role of planning in a socialist market economy be, what type of plans should be given priority and how should democratisation of planning be achieved? Most of the participants in the debates took the transition to a market economy as given, and tried to tailor the changes in planning accordingly. Some, however, could not reconcile themselves to the new reality. Of course, the attitudes to planning changed radically within a very short period of time; planning became a bad word, and any association with it was not advisable. I will focus my attention on the first point and concentrate primarily on the debate initiated by the journal of the planning office, *Tervgazdasági Szemle*. The latter asked a few reputable economists to express themselves on several questions pertaining to planning, especially its role in a socialist market economy. Most of the respondents were people who were associated with planning. Others may have been approached too, but did not care to answer.

I will start with K. Lóránt (1988), an official of the planning office, who in my opinion expressed to a great extent the views of his workplace, even if he was not part of the debate mentioned. According to him planning should be focused on what he called strategic planning, government management and coordinative activity. By strategic planning he meant the determination of the goals of the economy, especially with regard to structural changes and the development of the economic mechanism. By economic management he understood the implementation of the strategic goals. This did not mean that he favoured a return to operational planning; what he wanted was for the government to focus only on important processes. Coordinative activities should consist in coordinating regulative activity with regard to pricing, wages, foreign trade, etc.

In responding to questions posed by the journal mentioned, M. Németh (1988), at that time a high official of the CP secretariat who would soon become the last prime minister of socialist Hungary, attributed many roles to planning, even those which perhaps belong rather to functional ministries, if the solution of short term problems is the issue. He wanted to involve planning in stabilising the economy, in working out provisions for the restriction of demand and for the renewal of a balanced budget. Németh also wanted to use planning to transform the economy into a market economy. This approach is understandable, considering that he regarded the plan as the government programme of activities. He disagreed with those who believed that market forces alone would bring about the desired structure of the economy; in his view, planning was needed for an accelerated restructuring of the economy.

B. Csikós-Nagy (1988), responding to the same questions as those mentioned above, took the position that planning is an integral part of the economy. The question is not whether to plan, but how to make planning successful. In the socialist countries planning had to function in an autarkic environment and in a shortage economy. To make planning successful, an open economy policy is necessary.

Csikós-Nagy further believed that planning should be involved and play a leading role in formulating and coordinating economic policy, because the planning office was the best 'brain centre' of the government, and he also felt perhaps that this institution could best defend the national interest. Unlike other economists, he was against dropping annual plans; he did not believe that budget programming could entirely replace annual plans.

In many respects I. Hetényi (1989) takes a different position from the two previous authors, in a larger study which gives a very good critical survey of planning since the 1950s and which was sponsored by the Institute of Social Science. Of course, he too attributes an important role to planning in a socialist market economy. First, his critical comments on planning after the 1968 reform will be mentioned. He believes that planning was given too ambitious a role, which was not only to take care of the economy, but also to formulate societal economic policy for which it had no good preconditions. The fact that politicians regarded increases in the standard of living as the foundation for achieving the consensus of the people led to plans which were too taut. The excessive meddling of the CP in the economy made matters worse. The desire to involve enterprises and the public in planning to a greater decree had a double effect. On the one hand, it enabled planning to reflect conflicting interests in a more balanced way, and on the other, group interests got a voice even when that was contrary to national interests.

He believes that planners should be kind of government controllers and evaluators of concepts and programmes prepared by the ministries. Planning should be pluralised, mainly the short term, in as far as it refers to mitigating fluctuations in the economy (*konjunkturális jellegű*). In addition, the focus of planning should be on problem solving strategic planning, and structural policy. He does not believe that the planning office should become the centre of economic policy formulation and the harmonisation of interests (1989, pp. 82–6). In his response to the question of *Tervgazdasági Fórum* (1989A), he takes more or less the same views as those mentioned above.

The response of G. Báger (1989), a former high official of the planning office and under the new non-socialist government the chief of the programming section of the ministry of finance, to the questions mentioned is already marked by the knowledge that a change in regime is forthcoming. He assumes a market economy, managed primarily by monetary policy. Still, he believes that planning has a role to play, primarily in forecasting. Its function is to forecast macro-economic development and influence it (he does not say how), and also to forecast the 'motion room' available to economic and social policy. Planning should no longer be involved in structural changes; instead it should examine the conditions under which macro and technological changes can take place. It should also examine monetary and budgetary connections and their impact on the economy. He distinguishes long-term strategic planning, whose task is to help open the economy, expand exports and advance technology. The mid-term (three years) should primarily forecast trends in economic and structural changes. Annual programmes should ensure the development of the market and influence the development of the economy.

A. Szegö and Gy. Wiener (1988), who volunteered to respond, take as their point of departure the unrealistic assumption that there is going to be a debate about whether to introduce a market economy or rejuvenate socialism. They are in favour of the latter course; they suggest achieving it by rejuvenating planning, introducing self-government on a societal scale and radically changing the CP. Planning should be restructured according to Kalecki's model. They are not very specific about details. According to them, planning should bring about a closer link between the estimated growth of GDP, planned investment, budget and foreign trade. They subject monetary policy to sharp criticism.

As in 1983 (see p. 128), L. Antal (1988) rebuffed the authors in the same issue, maintaining that they attach subversive intentions to the market reform effort and suspect that reformers want to liquidate socialism quietly.

DEBATES ABOUT THE TRANSITION TO A MARKET ECONOMY

The three right-wing parties which make up the government coalition have not had any great pool of talented experts in their ranks; this has been reflected in the quality of leadership and of ministers. In addition, there has been no consensus among the parties on how to solve some important problems connected with the transformation. What is worse is that the chief party (the Hungarian Democratic Forum) has been plagued by internal bickering. For all these reasons the government did not know for some time what to do with the political power which it had gained, and it lost precious time (see L. Csaba, 1991).

Nevertheless, the new government came up with its own three-year transformation programme, which got the approval and financial support of the IMF ('IMF study . . .', 1991). It was soon replaced by a four-year programme. The collapse of trade with the USSR was listed as an official explanation for the programme replacement. Probably this played a certain role, but the fact that little of the three-year programme was achieved and there was an exchange of ministers of finance responsible for economic policy was perhaps more important.

The new programme, known as Kupa's programme after the current minister of finance, is, like the old, based on the idea of gradualness, and is more realistic. It promises a turnaround in 1993 in the currently declining economy (In 1990 the GDP declined by 4.2 per cent and in 1991 by 8 per cent – Hungarian Statistical Year Book for 1990 and *F* 1992, no. 23.) a reduction of inflation to a single number in 1994, and the achievement of convertibility at the same time. Liberalisation of foreign trade should be more or less completed in 1992. No mention is made of prices, because they have in the meantime been freed, with some exceptions. As to privatisation, no time targets are given, though the government puts it at the centre of its activities. No free distribution of shares is mentioned. Finally, the programme envisages the completion of the legal infrastructure in 1991–2 (*Kupa Programme*, 1991).

Many government critics agree that Kupa's programme has not yet had a distinct impact on the economy. For example, M. Petschnig (1991), a senior researcher in the Finance Research Institute, maintains that the government has not advanced the transformation process very far beyond the point where it was left by the last socialist government of M. Németh, which, according to her, made a lot of unpopular provisions, for the sake of transformation, which hurt the Socialist party in the elections.

Despite all its weaknesses, the government has not been swayed by the idea of shock therapy, as was applied in Poland and Czechoslovakia. Perhaps the populist wing in the chief government party, and the fact that the majority of economists were opposed to such a policy, had to do with this. After all, Hungary was in a much better economic situation than Poland when the new government took power, so that shock therapy might have caused a much worse situation than there is now and probably would have generated social unrest. The Hungarians do not have as much trust in their government as the Poles had in 1989.

The choice of a gradual transformation has not protected the economy against further aggravation. Inflation has continued to increase (from 25 per cent in 1989, to 29 per cent in 1990, and 38 per cent in 1991), unemployment has reached more than 6 per cent with a prediction that it will soon reach 10 per cent, and the budget deficit has reached an unprecedented level (Lengyel, 1991). Besides reasons which have to do with government policy, some international factors have contributed to the current state of the economy.

Strategy of Transformation

Naturally, once it became clear that the socialist system would be replaced by a market economy, a debate about the strategy of transformation developed. As usual, proposals of groups and of individuals came to light. Group proposals consisted of official proposals and private proposals. Of the latter, the so-called Blue Ribbon (1990),[13] in which foreigners participated in large numbers, and an indigenous project called the 'Bridge' (1990)[14] deserve attention. It seems that the former aroused greater interest that the latter, though several of the authors of the second proposal became high officials in the new government. Individual proposals, written in the form of papers, were usually focused on a few topics. If focused on the whole range of problems connected with the transition, the papers were written on a general level. The only exception, to my knowledge, is the study by J. Kornai (1990).

The debate on the transition to a market economy revolved around many problems. Let me mention the most important ones. One was pricing, understood broadly. Despite great progress in the liberalisation of prices, many were still under the control of the government. The contested question was whether to liberalise prices with one stroke or gradually. Most economists agreed that the Hungarian currency must become convertible in order for Hungary to have a fully fledged market economy. Again, the question was: should the Polish solution be followed, or should convertibility be achieved by stages?

Neither question, liberalisation of prices or convertibility, can be discussed without considering their effect on inflation, mainly if the option is 'by one stroke'. In 1990, the inflation rate was quite high anyhow and it had a tendency to increase. What should be done about wages? Should they be controlled, or left to market forces?[15]

The debate has also been focused on the question of how to

achieve a restructuring of the economy in accordance with domestic and foreign demand. Needless to say, the new government relies primarily on market forces to do this job. It regards planning as something which is completely identified with the old regime and which should disappear with it. And, indeed, the planning office has been abolished, and part of its agenda, related mainly to prognostication, has been transferred to the ministry of finance.

I will use Kornai's book (1990) as a platform from which to explain his own views, which had a mixed response in Hungary, as well as views of groups and individuals. Kornai regards himself as a liberal in the European sense. To him, individual autonomy and sovereignty are among the highest values. He is against 'subjection of the individual to the interests of the state and to the collective interests ordered by movements, parties or leaders' (p. 180), and believes that a market economy based on private ownership can bring about such freedoms and make the economy efficient.

In his book Kornai suggests that the stabilisation programme, which is centred on stopping inflation and restoring a balanced budget, should be carried out within a year. The introduction of convertibility of the Hungarian *forint* should follow soon after. To him, inflation is primarily the product of government behaviour and it can be stopped if the government so wishes. He has a very simple but questionable cure for inflation, once a democratic government is in place. What is necessary is to allow the free play of prices. There will be an increase in prices; however, if macro-demand is put under strict control (of wages among other things), the price increases will be only a one-time phenomenon (pp. 112–14).

When discussing the restoration of a balanced budget, which is also supposed to be one of the anti-inflationary instruments, Kornai devotes great attention to taxation. He repeats several times that he is against *progressive taxation*: taxes should be impersonal and neutral to distribution; they should not punish or reward. In his suggested tax system there is a consumption tax (value-added tax), payroll tax paid by the employer on paid-out wages, and a profit tax, but there is no place for income tax.

His objection to progressive taxation has probably to do with his view of the need to create conditions for 'embourgeoisement'. For this reason he also objects to any propaganda against the rich. This does not mean that he is against welfare; he would like, however, 'to set sensible upper limits' to it (p. 202).

Kornai's views were challenged. The Blue Ribbon report suggests fighting inflation by tight monetary and fiscal policies, without calling for a surgical operation as J. Kornai does. Furthermore, it proposes control of wages, and also the prices of monopolies and in certain areas of agriculture and food. It is, however, against price freezes and administrative wage determination (1990, pp. 63–5).

J. Kornai was also directly criticised for his suggestion of shock therapy, mainly with regard to the stopping of inflation. Here the attack was waged primarily by Csillag and Soós (1990).[16] They argued that in Hungary there was no need for shock therapy. Furthermore, Kornai's cure for inflation would lead to a decline in output and an increase in unemployment.

Privatisation

Much more attention has been devoted to privatisation than to other questions of transformation, the main reason being that privatisation has not proceeded as smoothly as expected. Furthermore, the spectrum of ideas on the role of privatisation has broadened in the course of time.

Privatisation in Hungary started before a new government, based on entirely free elections, was established in the summer of 1990. Already the socialist government had adopted several laws (corporation law in 1988 and transformation law in 1989, to mention the most important) which enabled managers, in co-operation with the self-management bodies, to make enterprises fully autonomous and, under certain conditions, to privatise them (see *Hungary*, 1991, p. 68; Stark, 1991; and E. Balcerowicz, 1991). Since it was not always difficult to manipulate self-management bodies, top managers were in fact mostly in control of enterprises. Privatisation, which came about on the basis of the laws mentioned and was called spontaneous, was subject to sharp criticism, primarily by the new government. Needless to say, managers used it in some cases to enrich themselves by seeing to it that the assessment of the assets was set low. It is interesting that the socialist government of M. Németh did not intervene, even though, if it had wanted to, it could have (Móra, 1991; Voszka, 1991).

The passivity of the old government was not accidental. Many believed that privatisation should be left to managers because of their skills and experience, and if, in the process of privatisation, they made a fortune and rescued their positions, this would not be unheard of. After all, a bourgeoisie was needed, and talented and experienced people would remain in managerial positions. In new governmental circles and among their supporters, however, spontaneous privatisation was not acceptable for many reasons. The new government wanted to show a new standard of morality and use the abuses of state ownership against the old regime. After all, most top managers were members of the CP nomenclature. In addition, the new government wanted to use privatisation to reward its political loyalists and to create a mass base for its political parties.

In 1990, the new government centralised privatisation by creating a State property agency. In the beginning of its activity, the agency reported to parliament, but later it was subordinated to the government (for information about the role of the agency and its performance, see *Information* . . ., 1990; and *Hungary*, 1991). The promises that the agency would accelerate the process of privatisation have not materialised. In the year which has elapsed since the establishment of the agency, not much progress in privatisation has been made (Voszka, 1991). It takes time to organise an agency, get acquainted with pertinent problems and formulate a strategy. The uncertainty about compensation of former owners has also complicated the process of privatisation. Furthermore, there is no agreement among politicians on how to go about the privatisation strategy. Finally, the old problems have not disappeared, namely, the shortage of capital and the lack of a fully-fledged market infrastructure (see also Horváth, 1991). Recently there have been calls to restore a greater role to managers in the process of privatisation.

The privatisation debate revolved around the following questions: should it be privatisation or reprivatisation;[17] should the new owners pay the market price, or a price which would give them an easy start; should shares be distributed without charge; how should foreign capital be treated; who should carry out privatisation, enterprises or a special agency, and so on. Most economists have focused their attention on the elimination of state ownership, though they have disagreed on matters of pace and privatisation methods. In the course of time, some economists have started to question the idealised role of privatisation and the suggested methods for its achievement.

The views of the majority are well represented by J. Kornai and M. Tardos, though they disagree in some respects. It seems that J. Kornai (1990) was influenced by Western economists when the stabilisation problem was an issue. In many aspects of privatisation, he parted company with foreign economists, many of whom, along with the IMF, urged rapid privatisation as a precondition for the establishment of a market economy. Kornai takes the position that privatisation will take time. 'Embourgeoisement', which is a precondition for bringing about a dramatic change in ownership relations and which was interrupted in 1949, is a lengthy process (1990, p. 54). His desire is to create a new middle class from which 'pioneers of economic progress and founders of large enterprises would eventually emerge as a result of the market's natural selection process' (p. 51).

Unlike many, primarily foreign economists, Kornai maintains that state assets should be sold at real market prices. He makes it explicit that he is against distributing shares without charge, but he does not mind selling shares with some discount to employees. Leasing of state property is an acceptable method to him. In order to promote privatisation, bank credits, designed for this purpose, should be extended. Foreign ownership should be allowed, but only to the extent that it is in the national interest. Therefore, a limit on foreigners' purchases of Hungarian property should be considered (pp. 80–8).

J. Kornai is very critical of the suggested ownership reform (which is for some only a transitional solution), namely, to turn state enterprises into joint stock companies whose shares are owned by other state enterprises (cross ownership) or pension funds, state owned insurance companies, municipalities, and so on (institutional ownership). To him this is only a monopoly game and a simulation exercise. He is not in favour of a large dispersal of ownership; he wants 'tangible' owners and he prefers individual shareholders, or a group of shareholders, having at least 20 to 30 per cent of shares. This approach results from his contempt for and frustration with state ownership, which he regards as an impersonalised form, where the risks of the undertaking are not borne by those who use it, so that it is necessarily inefficient. Everything which reminds him of state ownership is suspect to him, including institutional ownership in the West. He writes 'germs of socialism are already present in today's capitalism' (p. 76).

Kornai's views were challenged. The Blue Ribbon Commission report calls for rapid privatisation. Since there is not enough private capital in the country, it suggests, as Kornai has, a special line of credit for Hungarian citizens to buy shares. Unlike Kornai, however, it suggests selling or allocating enterprises to institutions and opening the door to foreign capital without limits.

Kornai was also criticised for his idea of discriminatory treatment of state enterprises. In the Hungarian text (1989), which appeared earlier than the English (1990), Kornai suggests a strict regime for the state sector, including the introduction of upper limits and quotas (*kontingensek*) for certain macro-economic categories concerning the state sector (credit, investment, wages, imports, and the purchase of foreign currency) (1989, pp. 30–2). These same controls should not be applied to the private sector. In the part of the English text which deals with the state sector, the controls are scaled down, probably under the influence of the criticism. The critics argued that the controls suggested by Kornai would necessarily lead to a revival of the old system of plan targets and bargaining (see Bauer, 1989; Csillag and Soós, 1990; Szegvári, 1990; and Tardos 1990).

M. Tardos, who recently became the leader of the parliamentary faction of the chief opposition party (Free Democratic Association), maintains that there is a need for rapid privatisation, but there is no optimum way to go about it. He discusses the various possible courses of action, including free distribution of assets, their advantages and disadvantages, and takes a lukewarm position in favour of distribution. He resolutely rejects reprivatisation and suggests replacing it by compensation. Finally, he calls for privatising the privatisation process and limiting the State property agency to a supervisory role, with its direct involvement only in the most important cases of privatisation (1991). A similar claim on the agency was made by E. Voszka (1991).

The experience gained with privatisation in Hungary and neighbouring countries, and the passing of the initial revolutionary excitement, have led some economists to a more sombre contemplation, and this has resulted in quite different thinking from before. E. Voszka, who has devoted a lot of research to privatisation, tries in her study (1991A), which is titled 'Privatisation Illusions', to show the origins of so many illusions. She mentions that it is an error to assume that every decline in state ownership can be regarded as privatisation and that the new owners must necessarily be interested in a competitive market economy. Another illusion is to assume that privatisation alone will bring about a market economy. She also regards as illusory the expectation of an improvement in economic efficiency from various free forms of asset distribution.

A. Köves, the deputy director of the reputable Institute for economic and market research and information, is more blunt in his two contributions. In the first (1991), he takes the position that privatisation must progress slowly and that adherents of rapid privatisation do not take into account changes which have occurred in the former socialist countries: as central planning was abolished, the monopoly of state enterprises was broken, CMEA was dissolved, and a new relationship between the government and enterprises was established. The assumption that privatisation will arrest inflation is not supported by new research; he alludes to the study of M. Petschnig and E. Voszka (1991). Furthermore, rapid privatisation will not create a new team of managers and will not restructure the economy.

A. Köves expresses concern that economists, when discussing change of ownership relations, consider almost exclusively the privatisation of state enterprises and devote almost no attention to the second source of privatisation as a possible strategy, namely, the establishment of new private enterprises. In his second contribution, an interview (1992), he returns to the idea of building a private sector from below and maintains that 'perhaps this is a slightly slower process, but based on safer foundations, than an artificial creation of owners'. In both items, he rejects the idea of a free distribution of shares, arguing that such a method will not create more efficient enterprises.

CONCLUDING REMARKS

In this relatively short chapter, it was impossible to capture the whole richness of ideas which marked the 1980s. I could only concentrate on some milestones in the development of thinking on the topic under review. Many additional topics, which shed light on the way the ideas developed in this eventful decade, had to be neglected.

From the foregoing, it is possible to observe that quite a straight line without any great deviations runs from ideas about the need to restructure property rights to the ideas of transition to a market economy based on private ownership. One cannot escape the question whether this development was only the result of the economic, political and social development, or whether Hungarian authors, when formulating the idea of restructuring property rights, already knew that this was only an overture to further demands which would result in a final demand for a transition to a market economy. This is an intriguing question for which I do not have a clear-cut answer.

No doubt, the decline in the standard of living in the 1980s, which was, to a great degree, the result of high indebtedness and low prices for agricultural products on world markets, played an important role in the gradual radicalisation of the views of the intelligentsia, including economists. Of course, the old grievances of the intelligentsia –

among others, the low appreciation of its services in terms of financial rewards; financial restraints on travel abroad; and some limitations on freedom of expression – played an increasing role (for more, see Chapter 11). The more opportunities Hungarian social scientists were given personally to compare their position in society with that of their peers abroad, the greater was their frustration with and alienation from the real socialist system. IMF and World Bank officials can claim credit too for the changes in the views of the intelligentsia.

The question can be posed: what was the contribution of the 1980s to the body of economic ideas about socialism? On the one hand, the 1980s contributed to a better understanding of the working of the indirect system, as L. Antal (1985A)[18] called the EM, which was brought into existence by the 1968 reform. The analyses of EM were, in general, more and more critical of the system as time went on, and with this the belief in the reformability of the socialist system declined, and vanished entirely in the second half of the 1980s.

Two comments on this negative assessment are in order. In the criticism of the working of the system, it very often happened that no distinction was made between phenomena resulting from economic policy provisions and those due to the working of EM. Without such a distinction, it is very difficult to draw correct conclusions about the working of the system.

Many economists came to the conclusion, from the working of the system in Hungary, that an arrangement in which both coordinating mechanisms (planning and market) play an important role (for the sake of simplicity let us call it here 'the decentralised system') or even market socialism have no chance of working efficiently. Neither the decentralised system nor market socialism was given the opportunity to stand the test of time. The former system was not properly developed, and what did exist was mostly in operation when the economic situation was worsening. In addition, the decentralised system lasted only a short time, and there was no time even to establish market socialism.

On the other hand, the contours of market socialism were worked out. When the last socialist government was already prepared to accept it, it was too late; new forces were arrayed to take over political power; even most of the architects of the concept were no longer interested in it.

In many studies, the market, mainly private ownership, is portrayed in colours which are too rosy. These studies give the impression that once market relations and private ownership are in place, prosperity is ensured. In reality, market relations are a precondition, but not a sufficient one, for an efficient economy. Not all the countries which have a market economy do well. To make market relations an instrument of economic efficiency requires, among other things, proper working habits and, what is perhaps more important, a market economy culture, an attribute which can only be gained in a long process. In addition, the economic efficiency of modern enterprises, which determines the performance level of an economy, depends very much on the capabilities of their managers to innovate and organise the production process (see Chandler, 1990, pp. 594–605). Without these additional elements market relations may produce meagre results.

The privatisation debate has shown that some authors have a tendency to absolutise the importance of private ownership. For example, J. Kornai, in the book mentioned (1990), approaches the process of privatisation itself with a great degree of pragmatism, unlike many other economists. He apparently understands that a rushed privatisation will not help the economy. However, when it comes to the comparison of private and non-private ownership, he is carried away. He takes the position that only private units can work efficiently, a position, which, as will be shown in Chapter 11, is contrary to experience. His call for 'tangible' owners (see p. 151) is an impractical demand in the light of present experience and development in the West (Compare Kopátsy 1990[19]).

The debate has also shown that economists focus excessively on transfer of state enterprises into private hands as a method of privatisation, while neglecting another potential method of privatisation, namely, the creation of new private enterprises. Had this been pursued firmly, there would not have been such pressure for a rapid privatisation of state enterprises, which caused uncertainty in enterprises and had a negative effect on their working.

Notes

1. Known economists like L. Antal, T. Bauer, L. Lengyel, K. A. Soós, I. Csillag and Gy. Matolcsy belonged to this group.
2. One collective work was prepared by the Communist youth organisation in the ministry of finance. Some of its members are very well-known economists nowadays.
3. Here M. Tardos should be mentioned primarily.
4. The team of experts was headed by F. Kozma.

5. People who are supposed to know maintain that J. Kádár agreed to resign, provided that some of his closest supporters would remain in the Politburo. The new leader, K. Grósz, did not, or could not, honour his promise.

6. J. Kornai was an exception. As he himself suggested in an interview (*Mozgó Világ* 1990, no. 4), he did not want to advise a non-democratic government.

7. By this she meant the intelligentsia which is not directly in the services of the CP and State apparatus.

8. The Hungarian ministry of finance found that in 1982 profit went through 290–300 redistributions (Kornai and Matits, 1987, p. 71).

9. Besides the text of 'Turning Point and Reform' which circulated in *samizdat* (underground literature), there are published versions, one in *Medvetánc* (1987, no. 2) and one in *Közgazdasági Szemle* (1987, no. 6). The latter is a shorter version and was published after it was discussed with CP officials.

10. The version in *Medvetánc* does not discuss planning at all.

11. The writers of the 'Standpoint' are well known economists and former party and government officials. To mention the most important ones: Ivan T. Berend (former president of the Academy of Sciences), B. Csikós-Nagy (former chairman of the Material and Price Board), I. Hetényi (former minister of finance) and R. Nyers (former member of the Politburo).

12. They also solicited the views of foreign economists (*Gazdaság*, 1989, no. 3).

13. The masterminds of the Blue Ribbon Commission report were probably M. Tardos and I. Hetényi (both Hungarians) and P. Marer (American professor).

14. Among the authors of the report were B. Kádár and M. Kupa, now ministers, and L. Csaba, who was the coordinator.

15. Of course, privatisation was the most contentious problem.

16. Interestingly enough, both parties to the debate argued that they have the backing of J. Sachs of Harvard University.

17. Reprivatisation means that the nationalised assets are returned to their owners.

18. In his book, which had quite an impact on Hungarian reformers, L. Antal distinguishes between an indirect and a decentralised system. In the latter, the role of planning is substantially reduced in favour of a self-regulating market (for more, see Adam, 1989, pp. 4–5).

19. S. Kopátsy, who also favoured privatisation primarily with the help of pension funds, criticises the government for wanting to sell large enterprises to private owners.

8 Poland

INTRODUCTION

The 1980s in Poland started with the rise of Solidarity in the shipyards of Gdansk. It was an independent trade union, founded during the strike to protest a substantial increase in consumer prices. After negotiations, a protocol of understanding was signed between the government and Solidarity[1] as a trade union, in which the government pledged to seek input from Solidarity when decisions were made about the standard of living, and to institute a strike law. In return, Solidarity committed itself to refraining from becoming a political party and to acknowledging the leading role of the Party, and collective ownership as a basis of the socialist system. Finally, the government promised to carry out an economic reform (*Glos Wybrzeza*, 1 September 1980).[2]

The rise of an independent trade union, an unparalleled occurrence in the socialist camp, gradually created a more liberal atmosphere in Poland, and this, in turn, made an environment conducive to intellectual activity. In the economic sphere, the main focus of intellectual activity in the beginning of the 1980s was on the impending economic reform and the government stabilisation programme. The debates showed that the spectrum of views was quite broad; there was no unanimity either in the ranks of economists faithful to the Party or in Solidarity. With some exceptions, the views did not go beyond what can be characterised as a socialist ideology. There were not even any calls for market socialism; planning was still regarded as useful, and state ownership was not challenged. This is even true about Solidarity's programme adopted at its first Congress which took place in October 1981. Though Solidarity, in the time since its rise, had been substantially radicalised and had acquired political ambitions, the programme was by no means anti-socialist.[3] It called for an economic reform which would combine planning, self-management and market. There should be separation of the management of enterprises from the political sphere; enterprises should be autonomous, and the government should influence their activities primarily by economic instruments. Planning should be democratised and correspond to the needs of the people. The right to a job should

157

be maintained. Market equilibrium should be renewed primarily by the expansion of output ('Programme', 1981).

The martial law imposed in December 1981, the outlawing of Solidarity, and the arrest of its leaders brought far-reaching changes to the thinking of economists. Martial law stopped the debates for some time, but when they started again, it could be felt that many authors had changed their allegiance. Not only did Solidarity gain more sympathisers and supporters, but in many economists' minds martial law strengthened doubts about the reformability of the system. With each failure of the economic reform, which was instituted in a limited form in 1982, the loss of belief in the reformability of the system spread.

When the debates started again, they were geared primarily to an evaluation of the working of the 1982 reform. As it became clearer that the new reform was not working as its architects had promised, one reason being that its principles were modified at the expense of the autonomy of enterprises, allegedly only temporarily, a wave of criticism started to build. At its edge it was directed against planning.

Criticism became more vocal when market equilibrium, after some improvement, started to worsen and, simultaneously, the inflation rate rose again, and kept on rising, even when in 1987 the government announced the second stage of the reform.

In 1989, the government agreed to a dialogue with Solidarity which ended in a round-table agreement, according to which the Party agreed to democratise the political system and introduce a market economy.

In the same year, a Solidarity government was formed which committed itself to stabilisation of the economy and privatisation in order to create a market economy along the lines of advanced capitalist countries.

PRE-MARTIAL LAW DEBATES

Nature of the Economic Reform

In 1981, the Party leadership published its reform project (*Project*, 1981) which contained the main principles of the pending reform. Half a year later, after a heated debate, the CP published the final version of the reform (*Directions* . . ., 1981).

In a nutshell, the reform promised to bring to an end the assign-

ment of plan targets (except for central investments), give an important role in the centrally planned economy to the market mechanism,
create autonomous enterprises, most of which would be managed by
employee councils, put all ownership forms on an equal footing
without affecting collective ownership as the foundation of the socialist system, democratise planning and bring changes in administration
(*Directions* . . ., 1981, pp. 10–22, 33).

This time several organisations, groups and individuals came up
with their own reform blueprints; some of them were published
before the CP's project and some later. All called for the elimination
of the administrative system (or, as it was called in Poland, directive-
distributive system) and the expansion of the market. They put much
greater stress than the official reform on a radical reorganisation of
the government administration and the elimination, or at least the
restriction, of branch ministries, including the branch departments in
the Planning Board.[4] This demand was connected with the belief, on
the one hand, that the branch ministries, as the bearers of group
interests, had achieved too much power and had pushed the economy
in a direction which was contrary to the national interest, and on the
other, that, with the elimination or restriction of branch ministries,
the direct bosses of enterprises, the interference in enterprise affairs
would decline. Furthermore, all the blueprints called for self-
management in enterprises. Some were convinced of its need, and
others saw it as a good move against government interference in the
affairs of enterprises.

There were not many demands for dramatic changes in ownership
relations. There was, to a great extent, consensus about the expansion of the private sector, but nobody challenged the predominance
of collective ownership. In connection with self-management, some
authors called for the institution of enterprise ownership.

Of the reform blueprints, L. Balcerowicz's and the Economic
Association's proposals will be discussed first; both were published
before the CP's reform project and differed from each other to a
great extent. What is important to stress right away is that in 1980
Balcerowicz, who later became the finance minister in the first two
Solidarity governments, and as such the architect of the shock treatment as a way to put Poland on a transition to a market economy, was
still calling for a reformed system which, in substance, meant a
combination of planning and market.

The reform blueprint, attributed to L. Balcerowicz, was in fact a
collective work, headed by him (1980).[5] It called for many changes,

including in planning, in order to create an environment conducive to the expansion of market forces. To this end, the blueprint suggested, among other things, demonopolisation of the economy and the liquidation of the mono-banking system. However, an important role was still attributed to planning. It was supposed to focus on strategic problems, on the structure and growth rate of the main sectors of the economy, and on the main structural branch changes in industry, including investment. It was also to focus on the development of consumption, mainly collective consumption, and the main trends in research and development. Of course, the methods used in planning should be in line with the developing market forces. Central investment should be limited to the infrastructure and to extractive branches. In other sectors, the central authorities should limit the regulation of investment activity to the extent needed in order to make sure that it was in line with the plan. The authorities should become investors only if indirect methods failed.

In 1980, most economists did not want to go as far as Balcerowicz did, which is clear from the blueprint put together by a large collective representing the Polish Economic Association (PEA). In its detailed blueprint ('Polish Economic . . .', 1980), which was edited by J. Mujżel and J. Pajestka, it stated: 'Central planning is the basic principle of the socialist system'. In brief, the role of planning should be: to forecast future conditions on a world and country scale as well as future societal tendencies and aspirations, make rational choices in basic strategic matters, and make sure that they are implemented, and finally protect the national interest.

The role of planning is best seen in how investment decisions and financing are handled. The PEA blueprint called for central decisions about investment in technical infrastructure, in large industrial enterprises which aim at changes in the structure, and in large programmes intended to satisfy certain societal wants. While the first kind of investment should be financed from general revenue, the last two would be financed only partially.

The PEA also called for restructuring and limiting the central apparatus, but did not advocate the elimination of branch ministries. Its blueprint did not talk much about the market, but it was assumed that its role would increase substantially by giving enterprises autonomy, and making them self-financing and self-managed.

Both the PEA and Balcerowicz and his group returned to the topic of how to reform the economic mechanism. The Economic Association did so in its Congress which was held after the Party published its reform project. The personal makeup of the newly elected leadership, as well as the resolutions of the Congress, were already marked by the new realities in Poland, the great political influence of Solidarity. And this was, of course, reflected in the resolution on the reform. In it a central place was given to autonomy and self-management; the latter had been given only little attention in the previous 1980 blueprint. The relatively short resolution also discussed the instruments to be introduced in order to prevent enterprises from using autonomy and self-management in conflict with societal interests, which indicated that the resolution was probably a compromise in which non-Solidarity members accepted the idea of self-management and, in return, Solidarity members agreed with some limitations on self-management. The same impression is obtained from the proposed structural changes in the administration; it only called for the severe restriction of the branch ministries (*Z.G.*, 1981, no. 12).

The Balcerowicz et al. (1981) study was rather a concretisation of the reform principles suggested in the 1980 blueprint. What was perhaps of significance was the proposals about planning; instead of an annual plan the authors suggested drafting a two-year plan whose purpose was to stabilise the economy and implement a reform. The plan should have a prognostic and a determinative part; in the latter, problems and not branches should be tackled.

The next two reform blueprints to be discussed were also a reaction to the Party's reform project. J. Beksiak's (1981) blueprint[6] harshly criticised the CP reform project for not taking into account the fact that the main reason for the crisis was the inadequate economic system, blaming instead the autocratic running of affairs and faults in the economic policy. The author called for the creation of a body independent of the political organs, which would be in charge of economic policy, planning and the development of the market. The blueprint attached great importance to the development of different forms of ownership. There was, however, no mention of private ownership in its enumeration of various forms; instead, family ownership was listed.

Beksiak also suggested modifying the right to a job by making the government responsible for seeing its implementation, whereas enterprises should be free to tackle employment according to criteria of efficiency.

The proposal of NET (Siec) (1981), a grouping of Solidarity organisations in some large enterprises, was probably an early reaction to the final official document of the reform. As to planning, NET agreed in many respects with the official version of the functions of planning. In order to reduce the monopoly position of the planners, NET suggested that two planning institutions should exist, one (the main) with the Sejm and the second with the government.

As to the role of the market, NET went further than the blueprints mentioned before. Among other things, it suggested the expansion of the private sector – but within certain limits. Once these limits (no specifics were mentioned) were reached, private enterprises should be turned into mixed enterprises in order 'to reduce incentives for luxury consumption'.

Stabilisation Programme

In July 1981, the government came up with a programme for over-coming the economic crisis and stabilising the economy. It envisaged an economic recovery in 1985–6 to the 1978 level of production (an annual increase in production of 3–4 per cent). Since, in the mean-time, the population had increased, the achievement of the 1978 level of output per capita would have required even more years (see interview with Z. Madej, the chairman of the Planning Commission, 1981).

The government programme was attacked by S. Kurowski, one of the experts of Solidarity, who may have been the first to come up with a shock-treatment proposal. But he did not have the full support of Solidarity, since R. Bugaj, who was a high functionary in Solidarity, challenged his ideas. Thus a debate developed between the two, which was joined by other economists, including CP faithfuls. The latters' criticism was directed against S. Kurowski.

Kurowski's programme was different from the state programme, especially in two aspects. It suggested restoring the economy to its 1978 level in three years, by increasing the national income by 55 per cent (1981).[7] He wanted to achieve such an ambitious leap forward by restructuring the economy (conversions, as he called them). He suggested reducing investments in producer goods substantially and using the saved capital for eliminating the idle capacity in manufac-turing. The labour released should be used in, among other things, the coal industry and services. He proposed shifting fertilisers and other producer goods from the socialised sector of agriculture to the private, and making the state sector sell machines and equipment to the private sector. He believed that two-thirds of the estimated foreign currency treasured by the population could be used for the latter purpose. And, finally, he aimed at reducing military spending.

S. Kurowski, in co-operation with some colleagues (Kurowski et al., 1981), offered his alternative programme, as he called it, combined with a proposal for restoring market equilibrium, to the first Congress of Solidarity for adoption as its policy. His suggestions for restoring market equilibrium were quite radical; they meant a freeze on a certain amount of savings in the bank, and a compulsory loan to the government in the form of a progressive tax. In addition, he suggested two variants; according to both, prices of foodstuffs should be increased to the level of production costs (elimination of subsidies), with full compensation being given.

R. Bugaj, who chaired the committee for coping with the crisis and economic reform, also submitted, together with some of his colleagues (Bugaj et al., 1981), a proposal to the Congress. Compared to Kurowski's proposal, it was distinguished by moderation. He too suggested decreasing investment to the extent possible, selling unused machinery to the private sector and giving some preferences to the private agricultural sector. However, he regarded Kurowski's expected effects concerning economic growth as exaggerated and an illusion.

R. Bugaj's opposition to Kurowski's proposal was even stronger when the issue was restoration of market equilibrium. He warned against provisions which politically might endanger the economic reform, such as the one-time huge price increases suggested by Kurowski.[8] R. Bugaj argued that the stress must be on production expansion, and price increases should be used as a secondary tool. (In a panel discussion about the economic crisis, in which C. Bobrowski and M. Nasilowski, among others, participated, he suggested that an annual 30 per cent increase in prices would be acceptable.) Alcohol, gasoline and luxury goods should be an exception; their prices should reflect production costs and clear the market. He made it clear that the brunt of the renewal of equilibrium should not be borne by the weak layers of society.

As could be expected, Kurowski was attacked by CP loyalists. His unrealistic concept for recovery easily lent itself to criticism, which was voiced by S. Albinowski (1981). A more powerful attack, coloured by ideology, came from one of the editors of *Życie Gozpodarcze*, M. Mieszczankowski (1981). The editor picked out not only the weak points of the recovery programme (he, along with others, argued that investment could not be reduced to the extent suggested, if priority sectors were to grow[9]), but also contended that Kurowski's suggestion to sell machinery to the private sector was nothing but a step-by-step strategy with the end goal of liquidating socialism.

Kurowski must have known that neither the CP nor Solidarity could accept his concept of market equilibrium renewal. The latter could not afford to antagonise people in a situation in which it was engaged in a permanent fight with the government. And, indeed, in its adopted programme, Solidarity accepted Bugaj's proposal. One can only speculate why Kurowski came up with such a drastic plan. He probably believed that this was the only way to cure market disequilibrium, and as economists very often do, he failed to take into consideration the political viability of his concept.

There was also a debate about the causes of the economic crisis. As usual, some authors focused on economic causes, while others added non-economic ones. Needless to say, the views were much influenced by the ideological outlook of the debaters. Some authors blamed Solidarity for the crisis (see Bugaj and Kowalik, 1986[10]). In his paper, W. Kuczyński (1984) tried to refute these accusations by showing that the crisis had started before 1980 and that the economic situation was much affected by the 1980 harvest failure.

W. Herer and W. Sadowski argued that the crisis was caused by lack of regard for the barriers of raw materials and foreign trade (Bugaj and Kowalik, 1986). The authors reconfirmed their view in a 1988 book.

Naturally, in such a debate the question necessarily arises about the extent of responsibility of the socialist system itself for the crisis. Certainly, there were many scientists who held the view that the socialist system was crisis prone, but only a few dared to go public with such ideas. M. Mieszczankowski (1984) resolutely rejected such a view, and the view that the crisis had to do with the rise of socialism in a less developed country, as Poland was.

Self-management

Most politicians and economists accepted that one of the components of economic reform must be self-management. The Gdansk Protocol of Understanding was quite specific on this score. Self-management was not a new idea: in 1956 the newly elected leadership, headed by W. Gomulka, after the riots in Poznan, had committed itself to institute self-management in enterprises. However, as soon as Gomulka consolidated his power, he started to dismantle the institutions introduced by the economic reform and, at the same time, to restrict the power of the self-managed bodies.

It must be made clear right away that though the idea of self-management was regarded as a necessary ingredient of the economic reform, there was no great enthusiasm for it either in the CP or in Solidarity. The CP adopted the idea because it believed that this would placate its critics. However, only under pressure did it agree to give self-management bodies much greater rights than they had had in 1958. It budged only partially from the position that top managers must be appointed by the founder (for more, see Adam, 1989).

Solidarity hesitated for several reasons. It was afraid that the self-management bodies might turn against it, because the interest of the two bodies might clash. Solidarity was also afraid of the responsibility resulting from self-management, mainly at a time when the economy was in a mess (see Jakubowicz, 1981). Under some pressure, the leadership of Solidarity adopted the idea of self-management in April 1981 (*Tygodnik Solidarność*, no. 13, 1981).

Debates about self-management showed that there were quite great differences in views about the need for self-management, its organisation, functions, and so on. On the one hand, there were true believers in self-management; some derived their belief from socialist ownership and the idea of industrial democracy, others from general humanistic values. Some of these believers, for example, Jakubowicz, defend the idea even now when the Polish economy is in the process of transition to a capitalist system and the idea of self-management has lost its appeal in the wave of enthusiasm for private ownership.

On the other hand, there were people who favoured self-management, not because they saw it as a goal in itself, but because they felt that it could be used as an instrument for other goals. This group of people was made up of CP loyalists as well as followers of Solidarity. Many CP members accepted the idea of self-management in the belief that it would contribute to the relaxing of social tensions. Many followers of Solidarity believed that self-management would reduce the possibility of government interference in the economy, serve as a guarantee of economic reform, and undermine the 'nomenclature' (see, for example, Paszyński, 1981).

Of course, there were many people who did not care for the idea of self-management at all. Some believed that it was contrary to the 'socialist' principle of one man management (see Debate in *ZG*, 1981, no. 14). Others believed that self-management was at variance with a desire for the promotion of economic efficiency.

Sz. Jakubowicz (1981) mounted a passionate defence of the idea of self-management. To him, management without the participation of workers necessarily means bureaucratisation and prevents workers from identifying themselves with enterprise goals. Self-management is a way to make the socialisation of the means of production a reality. To this end, he advocated the principle that the enterprise personnel should be recognised as the sovereign actors, and the representative body of the self-management institution (workers' councils) had to be equipped with powers which would allow it to manage enterprises. The workers' councils, which should arise from secret and direct balloting, should be independent in their decision-making, and top managers should be elected by the self-management bodies.

Self-management should engulf factories, enterprises, and associations, but should not be structured hierarchically. The parliament should have a second self-management chamber.

Judging by this article and others, it seems that Jakubowicz took the position that self-management should not be extended to workshops. According to J. Grosfeld (1981), another true believer, there were disagreements in Solidarity about the extension of self-management. The higher echelons of functionaries in Solidarity advocated the principle that self-management should be limited to enterprises, whereas Solidarity functionaries in enterprises wanted to have self-management in smaller units. Grosfeld argued that this boiled down to the question: was self-management a goal or an instrument? He implied that those who saw it as a goal must opt for its application even in workshops.

Most adherents of self-management wanted its representative body to be separate from the trade unions. J. Staniszkis, an activist of Solidarity and a known sociologist, took the position in a panel debate (*ZG*, 1981, no. 48) that the trade unions themselves should exercise self-management rights, arguing that the workers' councils had lost credibility because of their dismal past. She also expressed disagreement with W. Kuczyński, another activist, who argued that the trade unions should focus on distribution problems while workers' councils should concentrate primarily on production problems. She believed that this was an artificial division of power.

It seems that the known advocates of self-management did not consider very much the possible negative effects of self-management, mainly on wages, inflation, employment, etc. Many of them were carried away by enthusiasm for the idea of self-management, so that they could not or did not want to see the possible dark side of the institution in question. For example, J. Grosfeld (1981) saw self-management as an instrument of motivation and a tool to extricate the country from its economic crisis.

POST-MARTIAL LAW DEBATES

In April 1983, martial law was lifted, and scientific activity was gradually normalised. The feeling of freedom, which had existed before martial law, did not return in its entirety. One of the first government provisions during martial law had been to increase prices by approximately 100 per cent. However, people did not react to the unprecedented price increases as they used to in the past, since they were suffering from the after-effects of martial law. In addition, part of the population was already psychologically prepared for price increases (Kuczyński, 1984).

The three-year plan for 1983–6 was fulfilled in many respects. However, many problems continued to plague the economy. Economic equilibrium was not restored and wage growth was not brought under control. Indebtedness grew. Inflation, which had been brought down during the three-year plan, began to grow again.

The second stage of the economic reform announced in 1987, and the subsequent government 'Programme' based on it, constituted new attempts to cope with the problems mentioned. The 'Programme' (1987) promised, among other things, to stabilise the economy, expand the autonomy of enterprises, and give a greater role to market forces by dropping all discriminatory provisions against the private sector.

Popular support in general and the support of the intellectual community in particular, which were needed in order to make the reform provisions work, were available only to a small extent. Many in the intellectual community were weary of socialism and saw the 'Programme' as a manoeuvre of the CP élite to prolong its rule.

In 1987 the authorities decided to reduce price subsidies substantially and increase consumer prices considerably in order to stabilise the economy. This time, they consulted the population through a referendum. Though the population rejected price increases, the government went ahead with smaller price increases (27 per cent).[11] The manoeuvre did not succeed; strikes and threats of strikes produced higher increases in wages than in prices. As a result, the crisis deepened, and Solidarity, which had already gone into a decline, became active again; the people's dissatisfaction infused it with new energy and determination. In this hopeless and precarious situation, the CP saw no other solution than to accept Solidarity's call for a dialogue, which came about in 1989.

The 1983–9 debates were focused on various subjects. Here I will confine myself to the debates on the shortcomings of the 1982 economic reform, planning, market and ownership reform.

Evaluation of the 1982 Reform

The economic community was split concerning the evaluation of the reform. Most objections were aimed at the process of its realisation; many felt that it deviated too much from the reform concept and that the authorities were not really interested in its being implemented consistently. Many felt that the reform did not really bring great changes to the working of the management system. This view was quite widespread in enterprises (see Panel debate, *ZG*, 1985, no. 13).

Z. Sadowski (1985), a non-party member, the deputy prime minister in 1987–8 and later the Chairman of the Polish Economic Association, did not agree with such views, which he characterised as pessimistic. He maintained that the pessimism was spread by opponents of the regime who did not believe in the reformability of the system. The pessimism was also fuelled by the price increases, the unrealistic expectation of rapid improvements, the frustration of the younger generation which saw its hopes for prosperity dashed, etc.

In a 1991 study, Z. Sadowski took the position that the systemic changes started in 1981 were initially 'orientated towards market socialism', which was supposed to be a market economy based on a predominant share of state ownership combined with one-party rule. Many economists, including Sadowski, supported the reforms, seeing them as a beginning of changes in the economic system which would bring about other changes in due course in the political system, which would eventually culminate in pluralism and democracy (1991, pp. 46–7).

J. Pajestka (1984, p. 43), who was at one time the deputy chairman of the Planning Commission and later the head of the Economic Institute of the Academy of Sciences, took a position similar to Z. Sadowski's in 1985, arguing that the economic reform had become the object of a political struggle. People who were against the government did not want to support the reform because this would strengthen the government.

J. Pajestka advanced also the view that the reform was hampered by being carried out in a very difficult economic situation, and therefore administrative methods had to be used, which many interpreted as a deviation from the reform. He also had another explanation, to which he returned in a modified form in his other writings. According to it (pp. 37–9), a conflict developed between the aspirations of the people and the development of the economy. (The conflict was, of course, the doing of the CP itself by using uncritically slogans about the superiority of the socialist system and thus giving the impression that the socialist system could permanently increase the standard of living.) In the pursuit of their aspirations, the people put the authorities under pressure, which in the 1970s led to great market disequilibria and indebtedness. The systemic and institutional set-up which had arisen in the 1950s was not adapted to changing societal and economic needs, and for this reason it was not possible to turn the aspirations of the people into a motivational force (see also Pajestka, 1986, pp. 415–20).

His way of arguing, combined with other indications, conveyed a strong impression that the author blamed the difficulties on forces of the past which projected their shadows on to the present and that political leaders were doing their best to overcome the difficulties.

In his paper on the reform, published three years after the reform had come into effect, J. Pajestka (1985) maintained that the reform, *inter alia*, failed to create an environment which would force enterprises to increase economic efficiency and to expand the time horizon in decision-making. Furthermore, the reform did not create conditions for proper economic calculation, and investment was little subject to the economic mechanism.

C. Józefiak, a Solidarity adviser, and nowadays the director of the prestigious Economic Institute and former Senator, viewed the process of the reform differently from J. Pajestka, let alone Z. Sadowski. Józefiak maintained (1986) that the authorities did not follow the principles of the agreed reform.[12] To him, the greatest deviation was in the abandonment of the promised reorganisation of the central institutions and the failure to redefine their jurisdiction. A far-reaching restriction of government interference in enterprise affairs was expected. To this end the number of branch ministries was to be restricted, an occurrence which did not take place. Józefiak's criticism was also directed against giving the Planning Commission greater rights than had been anticipated. Furthermore, he questioned the tendency to build up a management authority between the ministries and enterprises.

The author was also critical of excessive government regulation at the expense of market forces, and particularly of the great share of official prices and the authorities' instructions on how to calculate non-official prices.

The drafting of the five-year plan for 1986–90 was also attacked by C. Józefiak. To him, the commitment to priorities first (in this case metallurgy, fuels and energy), followed by a discussion of the whole plan, was the wrong way to approach planning. He saw the result of interest group pressures, as well as of the management system itself, in this behaviour of the planners.

C. Józefiak's conclusion was pessimistic, admitting some progress in reforming the system, but insisting that it remained centralistic, though partially directly and partially indirectly centralistic.

J. Mujżel, a former director of the Institute of Planning, took a position which one could qualify as middle of the road. He (1984) evaluated the reform positively on the whole, mainly in comparison to the 1973 reform. Still, he had many critical observations, among others, that the solution of many systemic problems was left to the administration and, therefore, it could be expected that individual-ised instead of universal rules would be the practice. He also objected to the lack of banking reform and of free access to foreign currencies for import purposes, the predominance of price formation according to the old formula (cost + profit), excessive use of taxes, etc.

In summarising the evaluation, J. Mujżel mentioned that the re-form faced great obstacles in spite of the advantage it had in being accepted as a method of overcoming the economic crisis. The main obstacles were the limited democratisation of the system and its technocratic orientation. Furthermore, reforms affect certain group interests and the bearers of these interests necessarily defend them-selves. Finally, it is worthwhile mentioning that J. Mujżel felt that one of the indirect obstacles was the insufficient development of economic science.

Role of Planning

The economic reform, approved in 1981, also included changes in planning. The representatives of Solidarity and its sympathisers on the committee for the reforming of planning advocated a planning

system which could be denoted more or less as indicative. The
majority of the committee opted for a system very similar to the
Hungarian. A. Karpiński (1986),[13] who headed the committee for
some time, called the new concept informative–determinative
(*informacyjno-decyzyjny*). This name was supposed to reflect the
committee's judgment that the plan should provide information
needed for their planning purposes to enterprises but, at the same
time, should contain decisions binding only on the government and
financial institutions. The new planning system was designed as a
two-level planning system (central plan and plans of enterprises, but
not of branch ministries), with a greater role for the market within
the framework of the plan, the democratisation of planning, and a
greater role to strategic planning (ibid., pp. 272–6).

The role of planning so defined was disliked by many economists,
mainly followers of Solidarity. Perhaps the promise of democratisation of planning was the one thing which soothed their discontent.
When it turned out that some of the principles of the economic
reform, including planning, were not implemented as promised, the
criticism of planning strengthened.

Of course, only a few critics of planning approached the subject
from one position. Many critics were convinced, either on the basis of
what they regarded as solid theoretical proofs or by intuition, that
only the market mechanism could cope with Polish problems. Others
still believed in central planning, provided that the EM, and with it
planning, underwent important changes. Needless to say, there were
many economists who felt that some cosmetic changes in planning
were sufficient to make it work.

In the text to come, the views of the first two groups will be
discussed. The first group was perhaps best represented by C.
Józefiak and A. Lipowski, who tried to show why planning was an
impediment to the efficient working of the economy. Both preferred
a market economy, but only A. Lipowski stated this openly, and both
saw the culprit primarily in the conflicting group interests, which
according to them had been produced by planning.

C. Józefiak had already tried, in 1981, to explain in his paper,
'Central plan and interests of the managerial groups', how conflicting
group interests arise in a centrally planned economy. In his 1984
article he elaborated on his views. His criticism was directed primarily at centralised planning, but, from his suggested cures and their
evaluation, one has the strong impression that his criticism refers to
almost all kinds of planning.

The traditional planning system generates conflicting interests between different levels of management concerning the size of output targets and inputs, including labour, and conflicting interests between branches of the economy and within branches and regions. The representatives of interest groups enter into a coalition or into competitive relations. To advance their own interests the interest groups try to push their representatives into important positions in decision-making. Since, in the centralised system, no mechanism exists in the economy to solve the conflicting interests within the framework of rationality, great damage can be inflicted on the economy. One could add that CP bodies themselves are not immune to the consequences of conflicting interests. When investment funds are allocated from the centre, the propensity to invest is very high and the central planners are under strong pressure from interest groups. The decision-makers about the allocation of investments would have to be people of high integrity and authority to be guided only by the interests of the economy. Józefiak maintains that in many cases not 'objective economic criteria [decide] but the power relationship between competing interest groups' (1984, p. 134).

C. Józefiak also argues against planning by alluding to the stochastic nature of economic processes. It is difficult – he claims – to foresee from the centre all the possible factors which may have an effect on the development of the economy, and all attempts to cope with this problem have been unsuccessful.

A. Lipowski (1988, pp. 219–40) shows that decision-making about important economic issues is much influenced by political considerations, and what is called the national interest is often group interest. Since what is presented as national interest depends on the changing relationship between group interests and other factors, elements of uncertainty are introduced in the economy.

In a 1986 article, A. Lipowski argues that, in a non-market economy, the criteria governing distribution of funds for investment purposes are not efficiency considerations, but political power relations between pressure groups. To him this is the normal way, it is how a real socialist system works. In addition, the author argues that no synthetic criterion of rationality on the macro-economic level exists. The needs of the future in the absence of the market and the possible manifestation of consumer preferences cannot be properly predicted. On top of this, strong incentives, which may encourage enterprise managers to behave rationally, are missing in a centralised system. All this, combined with the enormous influence of group interests, must devalue planning. In his book Lipowski backs up his conclusion with the statement that planning in the 1970s in Poland had a purely ceremonial nature which he regards as something natural (1988, p. 233).

K. Porwit, perhaps the best-known planning theoretician, can be regarded as a good representative of the second group. He was, and it seems he still is, a follower of planning. He took, however, the position that planning depends on the nature of the economic system. Since he was in favour of a radical economic reform, he also wanted a radical overhaul of planning. He expressed his views in a great number of articles.

In his 1983 article, he maintains that the market 'should be the coordinating mechanism when . . . current adaptive processes and development undertakings with relative short cycles of realisation' are involved. When important changes in technology must be tackled and when 'development processes with relatively long cycles of realisation' are the issue, planning should be the coordinator.

In his 1984 article, K. Porwit stresses that economic equilibrium and economic efficiency cannot be achieved if a considerable part of the economy is not regulated by market forces. In order to allow the market to work, rational prices are needed. These are also a precondition for working out a realistic plan.

In his conclusion, he makes it clear that to him planning (*planowosc*) is superior to the processes emanating from the market, since it enables future considerations to be applied to current activities.

Role of the Market

The debate on planning was also a reflection of the attitude of debaters to market forces, since, by rejecting one of the coordinating mechanisms, the other must be applied. However, not much specific attention has so far been devoted to the market. This will be rectified below.

Many debates on the merit of the market as a coordinating mechanism took place in Poland during the period under review. It is impossible to review them all, or even a large part of them. The focus here will be primarily on two debates – a non-public and a public one.

The non-public discussion, which revolved around systemic preferences, gives good insight into the thinking of the leading economists of Solidarity at the end of 1986 or the beginning of 1987 (*21*, 1987, no. 3),[14] at any rate before the announcement of the second stage of the reform. It split the participants into two camps. R. Bugaj and T. Kowalik advocated a third road, something between capitalism and the real socialist system. The rest of the participants wanted, in fact, a transition to capitalism, even if they did not say it in so many words because they were still afraid of the consequences.

T. Kowalik argued that capitalism was not a viable or desirable solution for Poland. Even before the Second World War, Poland had not managed to create a strong middle class, particularly a powerful class of entrepreneurs. The two most entrepreneurial groups, Jews and Germans, no longer exist in Poland. The socialist system did not train entrepreneurs and it created a new man who is estranged from capitalism.

Kowalik was in favour of a non-private system. He probably had in mind a system in which self-managed or workers-owned enterprises were predominant and which was combined with a regulated market mechanism. R. Bugaj concurred with T. Kowalik.

To L. Balcerowicz, a liberal system is the ideal system, but, if it cannot be achieved for political reasons, then he would opt for one closest to the liberal. This is a system in which a free choice exists between a co-operative form of ownership and workers' joint-stock companies. Of course, such a system presupposes a market economy, though a limited one.

Following up on Balcerowicz's assumption that political realities do not allow a full market economy, C. Józefiak prefers a system which is furthest removed from the directive and distributive system, and this is a market economy, controlled by society and with various forms of ownership.

The public debate was touched off by M. Mieszczankowski, one of the editors of the weekly *Życie Gospodarcze*,[15] with his article (1988) titled 'The final structure is not known'. He was induced to write this article, which was, in fact, a challenge to a debate about the final shape of the reform, by the announced principles of the second stage of the reform, particularly by the stand of radical reformers, mainly of the younger generation, who demanded the introduction of a market economy and the adjustment of the forms of ownership to it.

In his article, Mieszczankowski tries to show that the transplantation of capitalist relations into a socialist economy cannot work. Among the reasons for this is that under socialism the purpose of production is use value, whereas it is profit under capitalism. Under the latter there is a self-regulating mechanism which divides up the value added into wage and profit, and surplus value into consumption and accumulation, but it is missing under socialism. If all ownership forms were treated equally, capitalist owners should pay the same wage and content themselves with the same profitability as other owners; but he does not believe that capitalists will accept such a deal.

The debate which followed lasted almost a year and the participants represented a wide range of world outlooks. Even though, to my knowledge, few neo-liberals, if any, participated in it, the debate showed a considerable erosion of support for socialism and an almost allergic reaction to any statements implying socialist superiority. True, no participant in the debate argued openly in favour of the restoration of capitalism; some, for example, T. Jezioranski and M. K. Krzak (1988) (two editors of *Życie Gospodarcze*) maintained that capitalism was neither possible nor desirable. Almost all argued for a dramatic expansion of market forces, and some called specifically for market socialism, while others talked about a third way. Even Z. Madej (1988), who at one time was the chairman of the Planning Commission, argued that marketisation of the economy was the only solution to Polish problems. He also favoured allowing a labour market. A consistent application of market relations with self-management could be one of the socialist alternatives, an idea which was shared by other authors. Madej warned, however, that the great expectations linked to the market might be dashed since the culture of good management was wasted.

K. Porwit (1988) argued that in the new situation three regulative mechanisms were needed: (1) the market mechanism; (2) central regulation, which should also be guided by socio-political criteria with respect to solving distribution problems; and (3) a reconciliation mechanism which would help to solve conflicting interests in distribution of income, fiscal policy as well as social security policy. The new logic of running the economy can be called a third road.

The change in thinking was also evident from the stand on the question of the final goal. In the 1985 panel debate, mentioned above, some criticised the reform for not having a clear goal. In this debate, some regarded the idea of a goal as a new attempt to impose on society a system thought out in advance, a system designed behind a desk. They preferred giving spontaneity free play, recalling how the market economy, the product of a natural development, has performed in comparison to socialism, a mental product.

For completeness, it is important to mention that, though all participants in the debate called for the expansion of market forces –

of course, to different degrees – some still saw a certain role for planning. For example, M. Nasilowski (1988)[16] advocated a system in which the market would in fact be the main coordinator of economic activities; however, planning would play a role, not only in investment in the infrastructure, but also in large enterprises and in the distribution of income. He called such a system market-planning (*rynkowo-planowy*).

As in some other debates, in this too, the market was idealised by some and presented, as it were, as a self-regulating mechanism, able to work with minimal government intervention. As J. Lipiński mentioned in one of his papers (1988),[17] many Polish economists – and this could be applied to many Hungarian economists as well – viewed the market as a perfect competitive institution.

Ownership-Relations Reform

Even before the round-table agreement in April 1989 between the government and Solidarity, many economists, particularly neo-liberals, had come to the conclusion that the time was ripe for a discussion about the reform of ownership relations. In the debate which followed, three groups of views can be distinguished. Turning state enterprises over to private ownership was favoured by the first group; to cross- and institutional or group ownership by the second; and to self-managed enterprises by the third (see also Szomburg, 1989). None of the groups took the position that their solution should be the exclusive one. The views of the first and third group had the most adherents.

The adherents of private ownership mostly professed a neo-liberal ideology; their idols were F. A. Hayek and M. Friedman. They were and are convinced that the market mechanism can only work under private ownership. In other words, what they wanted was not simply a market economy, but a private market economy. Only under such a system, they argued, where the owners can be fully identified – state enterprises were viewed by them as units without a genuine owner – can the economy thrive and prosper. Compared to the current situation, a private market economy will put greater stress on production than on distribution.

Their views were motivated not only by economic but also by political considerations. They believed that the destruction of the present political system could only be complete if state ownership was eliminated (see, for example, Kawalec, 1988).

The neo-liberals were not united in their views. Some wanted to see a very quick liquidation of state ownership and therefore suggested distributing it without charge (see Krawczyk, 1988; Lewandowski and Szomburg, 1988). The latter authors argued that the sale of property would be more advantageous, but this would require waiting too long (according to optimists fifteen years, and according to pessimists one hundred years) and it was important to act quickly in order to extricate the public from 'lethargy and mistrust'. To them such a distribution would mean an expropriation of the state and the 'socialisation of ownership through reprivatisation' (Lewandowski and Szomburg, 1988, pp. 72–3). Their concrete proposal was not as radical as one would expect from the introduction.[18]

Other neo-liberals opposed the idea of distributing property without charge. They were afraid that such an arrangement would create unnecessary inequalities and would not act as a stimulus to higher efficiency. They wanted to sell state assets even if selling took a long period due to the population's lack of capital. The best-known representative of this view was S. Kawalec (1988 and 1989).[19]

The second group – unlike Hungary – did not have many adherents. One of its representatives was M. Święcicki, the secretary general of the Economic Council and minister under the Solidarity government, as a representative of the CP (1988, see also Iwanek and Święcicki, 1987). He believed that the stocks of state enterprises converted into joint stock companies should be distributed among institutions of a non-bureaucratic nature (reformed banks, insurance companies, hospitals, holding companies) and also enterprises. Part of the stocks should be sold to private owners. The main purpose of the holding companies, which hold the stocks of groups of enterprises, was supposed to be to allocate capital, and they were to be controlled by the State Treasury. Święcicki believed that this arrangement could be reconciled with the self-management institution, which could be represented on the board of directors or have the right of veto in matters of great importance for the personnel.

M. Dąbrowski (1988), who was the deputy of L. Balcerowicz for some time, favoured group ownership (ownership of enterprises by workers, cooperatives, municipal enterprises, institutional organisations, etc.) as one of the options beside private ownership.

The third group, which wished to see the existing self-managed system strengthened and expanded, had many adherents, maybe the most, if we add to it adherents of group ownership. This solution was supported on the one hand by the left wing of Solidarity and, on the

178   *Debates on Planning and Market, 1980s–1992*

other, by many members of the Party. The adherents of self-management disagreed with the neo-liberals on many points. First, they did not accept the definition of ownership; second, they did not absolutise the market as the neo-liberals did; and third, some had doubts whether great changes in ownership were needed.

R. Bugaj (1988, p. 100) defines ownership much more generally than neo-liberals do and sees it primarily as an economic concept. To him, ownership is the right to make decisions or participate in decisions about the productive use of the means of production. He does not view ownership, as the neo-liberals do, as an exclusive, indivisible right; according to him, the same means of production may have ownership by 'actors of different categories'.

T. Kowalik (1989) is quite sympathetic to the Swedish social democratic concept of ownership, according to which ownership is the sum of many functions which can belong to many owners. In practice, this means that property may be privately owned, but certain ownership functions can be controlled by the government.

R. Bugaj does not share the great optimism of the neo-liberals about a private market economy. He recalls that a private market economy in itself is not a guarantee of success (1988, p. 103).

Neither R. Bugaj nor T. Kowalik suggested methods for curing the known problems of self-managed enterprises. Some other authors tried to do so. For example, W. Caban (1988) views accumulation as a postponed remuneration, and therefore suggests giving workers dividend-bearing bonds under the same terms as they receive remuneration. Apparently this is supposed to be a partial cure for the preference of workers, particularly those close to retirement, for wages over accumulation. In addition, he assumes that competition will generate efficient work through economic coercion. M. Dąbrowski (1987) sees the solution in selling to workers bonds which must be redeemed at a certain time. Becoming creditors of the enterprise in which they work will make workers interested in accumulation, because only if they are, will the enterprise have enough funds in the future to redeem the bonds.

Z. Fedorowicz (1988) suggests in substance an opposite arrangement. The self-management body is renting the assets for a rent which is equal to the market interest rate.

DEBATES ABOUT TRANSITION TO MARKET ECONOMY

In April 1989, government and Solidarity representatives agreed in round-table negotiations to restructure the political as well as the economic system. As to the latter, the representatives agreed amongst other things to introduce market relations and competition, allow free development of ownership structures including privatisation, develop self-management, and limit central planning to the formulation of government policy.

In the sphere of economic policy, it was concluded that the budget deficit should be reduced by slashing subsidies and selling apartments, shops, productive facilities, and so on. In order to protect the consumers against inflation, 80 per cent of wage indexation was promised. The preservation of the principle of full employment was pledged (*ZG*, 1989, no. 16).

The June 1989 parliamentary elections brought about a shattering defeat for the Party, and the Solidarity leaders managed to manoeuvre it out of political power. The new Solidarity government, headed by Mazowiecki, came under the strong influence of the neoliberals and, without paying due regard to the professed principles of Solidarity, adopted Balcerowicz's stabilisation programme for tackling the deep economic crisis marked by a high inflation rate,[20] a huge budget deficit and great shortages. The stabilisation plan was, in substance, a shock therapy which, in its realisation and consequences, is contrary to the principles adopted in the round-table negotiations. It freed prices with some exceptions (14 per cent of prices in value terms were still controlled), liberalised foreign trade, introduced a new exchange rate and made the *zloty* convertible, imposed a high interest rate (in January 1990 it was 40 per cent quarterly and declined to 4 per cent in June 1990), drastically limited the previous system of tax breaks and subsidies in order to balance the budget, restrained wage growth (in the beginning to 30 per cent of inflation and later to 20 per cent) and abolished control of enterprises with regard to most economic activities (Józefiak, 1990; Kołodko, 1990).

The stabilisation programme has been a success in some respects, but the social cost to Poland now and in the future is and will be very high. In my opinion, the stabilisation of the exchange rate for some time can be regarded as the greatest success. The substantial reduction in the rate of inflation – in 1991 the inflation rate was still 70 per cent (*ZG*, 1992, no. 4) – and the renewal of market equilibrium are not such great accomplishments, if one considers that they were achieved by fighting inflation by inflation and by reducing substantially the standard of living. The stabilisation programme also managed to produce a temporary budget surplus. The creation of rational prices and, in this connection, the elimination of the core of subsidies can also be evaluated as a success. Furthermore, the expansion of the private sector can be regarded as a very positive accomplishment. In brief, shock treatment created preconditions for a market economy. All this was accomplished at the cost of a severe recession GNP declined in 1990 by 11.6 and in 1991 by 9.3 per cent, and industrial production by even more, and unemployment increased to 11.4 per cent at the end of 1991 (see *ZG*, 1992, nos 3 and 5). Real wages declined in 1990 by 32 per cent and in 1991 increased by 1.5 per cent (see S. Gomulka, 1991 and Misiak, 1992) and 30 per cent of peoples' savings were lost in 1990 alone. The decline in purchasing power, which was caused by allowing free prices under conditions of monopolised production, by excessive devaluation of the *zloty*, by severely restraining wage increases and by depriving the population of a great portion of its savings, considerably reduced demand, and this was translated into a decline in production, one of the main reasons why a surplus in the balance of trade was achieved. The decline in production combined with strict monetary policy and the application of a discriminatory tax policy *vis à vis* state enterprises later produced a huge budget deficit. Hopes that shock treatment would bring about a restructuring of the economy did not materialise. When faced with excessive interest rates, which were supposed to force economic units to adjust to market demand, enterprises entered into a mutual extension of credit (Józefiak, 1990).

For completeness, it should be mentioned that the recession in the West and the collapse of trade with the USSR, combined with payments for traded commodities in dollars, must have contributed to the recession.

Stabilisation Programme

The debate started with the publication of the stabilisation programme and gradually intensified, as the results showed a great deal of deviation from the promises made by its architects, and in particular when it turned out that there was no improvement in sight. Some believed that the whole approach to stabilisation was faulty. Some critics approved shock therapy on the whole, but had objections to its intensity and the weight given to individual components. The two groups have much in common as to the suggested cure for the deep recession. They advocate relaxing the monetary policy, eliminating state enterprise discrimination, restraining liberalisation of imports and giving the government a greater role in regulating the economy. Many economists, who initially supported the programme or at least wanted to reserve judgment until such time as the results were in, changed their minds once they saw that even after more than a year the recession was not abating. And, of course, there are economists who still support the programme.

The most articulate representatives of the first group which rejected the stabilisation policy applied are R. Bugaj, T. Kowalik and Z. Sadowski; their criticism has been influenced by ideological and economic considerations. The first two signed a declaration called 'Towards the direction of an alternative programme' (*ZG*, no. 18, 1990) which criticised the stabilisation programme for not respecting sufficiently the employees' interests and for allowing the private sector and managers to gain undue influence. The declaration also called for the institution of different forms of employee ownership.

R. Bugaj perhaps presented his views best in a panel discussion with M. Dąbrowski (1990), the then deputy minister of finance and one of the architects of the stabilisation programme. Bugaj argued for a gradual, not shock, cure of the Polish diseases, because he was convinced that the anti-inflationary policy, which in fact meant fighting inflation with inflation, must necessarily produce a deep recession, much deeper than the government predicted. Once the country gets into a recession, it will take a long time to extricate itself, because Poland does not have market institutions.

T. Kowalik (1990A) believes that it was a mistake to design a stabilisation programme which produces a recession. He also criticises the neo-liberals for not wanting to interfere in the economy once it is plagued by a slump because they assume that market forces themselves will bring the recession to an end.

Z. Sadowski (1991) takes a clear-cut position in favour of a gradual systemic transformation. He believes that the systemic change has a chance of success if it is made in a way that does not disrupt the working of the economy and does not reduce the standard of living. To this end, he suggests maintaining a 'considerable scope of state intervention'. Prices should be freed gradually and deflationary policy should be moderate.

In a later article (1991A), titled 'Directions of Revision', Sadowski calls for a relaxation of monetary policy and the removal of tax and

credit discrimination against state enterprises. He sees this discrimination as one of the reasons why no recovery has yet started. The
existing cost inflation, which makes it difficult to curb imports under
conditions of a fixed exchange rate, is another reason for the decline
in output. Z. Sadowski calls for equal treatment of all enterprises,
regardless of their ownership form. J. Kaleta (1991), who is also very
critical of the government's discriminatory policy, believes that the
motivation for it is purely ideological.

In the 1991A article, Sadowski also counsels replacing full liberalisation of imports with a prudent liberalisation, combined with
protection for some production. The government should be involved
in working out a concept of economic restructuring. Budgetary funds
for investment should be mainly used for the infrastructure.

The following four economists (J. Mujżel, G. Kołodko, D. Rosati
and K. Porwit) can be regarded as representative of the second group.
In an interview J. Mujżel (*ZG*, 1990, no. 12), in his capacity as
deputy chairman of the Economic Council, the highest advisory organ
of the government, indirectly criticised Balcerowicz's programme for
deviating from the philosophy of the 1989 round-table agreements and
for adopting right-wing liberal concepts. He did not view the programme as being faulty as a concept, but expressed many doubts
whether it could be successfully implemented.

In one of his 1991 papers, Mujżel expands his criticism, though it is
still very cautious. According to him, some transformation provisions
should be carried out rapidly, even in one stroke, and some gradually, such as devaluation of the currency, elimination of subsidies and
reduction of tariffs. It was a mistake for those provisions which
should be applied gradually to be included in shock treatment. As to
the treatment of recession, his suggested cure is similar to that of Z.
Sadowski.

G. Kołodko (1990, 1990A), the director of the research institute of
the ministry of finance, implicitly accuses Balcerowicz et al. of deliberately bringing about hyperinflation in 1989 in order to have a
good excuse for shock therapy. He criticises the stabilisation programme for being too ambitious; to him the idea of bringing down
inflation to 1 per cent within half a year was illusory, irresponsible
and doomed to failure. He sees the failure in, among others, the loss
of the population's savings, which could have been used for buying up
small assets and shares in enterprises. The severe recession, going far
beyond what was promised, is unacceptable in itself, but, in addition,
it has not brought about the expected restructuring of the economy

and has mostly affected the consumer goods industries. To remedy the situation, Kołodko suggests an active government interventionist policy aimed at reviving supply, mainly by stimulating investment.

In his 1991 article, he condemns government economic policy, which he rightly characterises as neo-liberal–monetarist, and calls for its replacement by an interventionist–fiscal policy. His main objection is that the monetarist policy, whose one objective has been to bring about a balanced budget, has generated the opposite, a huge budget deficit – by its deflationary policy, one could add. The main effort of the government – in his opinion – must be directed at renewing a balanced budget, which cannot be achieved without putting the economy on a growth path. To this end, it is necessary to nurture the state sector; it is an illusion to expect the private sector alone to be able to accelerate output.

D. Rosati (1990) believes that the stabilisation programme was too restrictive and therefore produced a deep recession. Too much stress was put on fighting inflation while the fact that the cause of inflation changed from being the result of excessive demand in 1989 to cost-push in 1990 was ignored, and too little attention was paid to recovery. The programme liquidated not only forced, but also voluntary, savings. Excessive wage restriction had more of an anti-production than an anti-demand effect and hampered a substitution of capital for labour. The restrictive budgetary policy produced a surplus at a time of recession. In order to make the exchange rate stable, the *złoty* was devalued more than was necessary and, as a result, contributed to inflation. Last but not least, the monetary policy was also too restrictive.

In his introduction, K. Porwit (1991) defends the government transformation programme and expresses the view that the recession is an inheritance of the old system. Still, he has some criticism of the government. To him, it is concerned too much with macro-economic and too little with micro-economic policies and distribution of income. Growth in economic efficiency will not come about automatically as a result of privatisation; micro-economic policy is needed. Apparently he has in mind some kind of industrial policy. He also urges a fight against the negative aspects of capitalism, unemployment among other things.

S. Kurowski is a special case. He has been an anti-communist all his life and has vented his feelings openly and suffered for this. One would expect him to be an excited supporter of Balcerowicz's programme. And in the beginning he really was, though he had critical comments about some of its components. His position was reflected in the economic programme worked out for the right-wing faction of Solidarity (*GN*, 1991, no. 10–11) by a collective of economists, headed by him. But he has gradually changed his mind; it is not known whether any reasons, other than academic ones, have played a role. In his 1991 article written together with M. Przigodzki, he launches a scathing attack on Balcerowicz's programme: in his view it is a programme for the liquidation of the economy. The market equilibrium achieved is at a very low level of consumption, and as a result production has to decline. Attempts to extricate the economy from this mess generate inflation. Enterprises do not have the means for the needed modernisation, and the recession hampers a restructuring of the economy. Their suggested cure for the recovery of the economy is, in a nutshell, the following: to increase the money supply and regulate by taxes the prices of enterprises which are producing final goods and are in monopoly positions. This is necessary in order to prevent inflation. Anyhow, a 2–3 per cent monthly inflation, which Kurowski regarded in the past as unacceptable, is now not a catastrophe. Interest rates should be reduced and credit gradually expanded in order to stimulate economic activities. Custom tariffs should be increased in order to protect domestic production.

In his later article (1991) Kurowski attacks, this time indirectly, the IMF, arguing that the stabilisation programme, adopted with IMF blessing and nudging, produces a deep recession, not by accident, but by its being deliberately built into the programme in order to produce external equilibrium, primarily so that Poland is able to repay its external debts. He even hints that there is some kind of conspiracy between the government and the IMF in this regard. According to him, Poland receives in return for this co-operation a reduction in debts, and the services of foreign advisers who are, however, paid partially from the aid given to Poland. This exaggeration, which was criticised by D. Gotz-Kozierkiewicz (1991) who is not a government supporter, reflects the spread of anti-Western feelings, fed by the continuing worsening of the economic situation.

There are many economists, though their number is declining, who support Balcerowicz's programme. W. Wilczyński, a member of the Economic Council, is one of them. He admits that the economy has shortcomings, but he finds their origin in the inadequate reaction of the public rather than in the programme itself. He suggests deregulating the economy with simultaneous strengthening of the role of the central bank – in other words, strengthening or at least not relaxing monetary policy. Fighting inflation must be the primary concern. Indexation of wages, which has lagged far behind price rises, should be gradually eliminated. He warns against Neo-Keynesianism. In brief, he puts the fate of the Polish economy in the invisible hands of the market (1991).

J. Winiecki, who is quite well known in the West for his writings and who was always an opponent of the former regime, also supports Balcerowicz's programme, primarily by belittling its recessional effects. Among other things, he argues that the figures quoted about the decline in production are exaggerated, since they are based on figures reported by the managers of the old regime who had a tendency to inflate output figures. In addition, in the changed conditions enterprise managers no longer hoard inventories as they did before because now they behave rationally. He published these views abroad and at home (1991, 1991A). In my opinion, this does not seem to be a very sophisticated apology. Let me mention only two arguments. Considering that the decline in industrial output has been really dramatic, the small percentage of doctoring in the past, as estimated by the author himself, cannot make a difference in the whole picture. J. Lipiński (1991) shows that enterprise behaviour has not yet changed for various reasons and that it is an exaggeration to talk about rational purchases by enterprises.

It is interesting that the majority of the Economic Council including its chairman, W. Trzeciakowski, a well-known fighter for a market economy and a minister in Mazowiecki's government, criticised government policy very sharply (*ZG*, 1991, no. 47). The Council believes that the successes achieved have been extracted at excessive cost because the government has focused too much on fighting inflation, opened the economy more than necessary, assumed that it is possible to use the legal system to turn a monopolised economy into a market, trusted only shock treatment without considering the cost, relied too much on the invisible hand and eliminated the role of government from the economy. It warns the government that a continuation of the tough monetary policy will not produce the expected efficiency results, and counsels the promotion of restructuring investments and the expansion of small and middle-sized private enterprises with the help of temporary higher tariffs, and preferential and guaranteed credits.

It is no exaggeration to say that the Council gave the government, and indirectly the IMF, a failing grade. The government was subjected to even harsher criticism by a special committee chosen at an extraordinary congress of the Polish Economic Association (*ZG*, 1991, no. 44). Without going into details, let me just mention that the committee maintained that the government, by its policy, created a greater economic crisis than the one which took place in 1979–82.

Privatisation

In August 1990, a privatisation law was passed. A state enterprise (here, middle-sized and large enterprises are meant) can be turned into a joint stock company if this is requested by the director and the employees' council or by the founding body, with the consent of the above-mentioned institutions. The Minister for Ownership Changes, who is in charge of privatisation affairs, must approve it after he has consulted the personnel of the enterprise in question. The shareholder of the enterprises thus turned into joint stock companies is the State Treasury until the shares are sold. 20 per cent of the shares should be offered to employees at 50 per cent of the nominal price. One-third of the members of the newly elected Supervisory Council of the privatised enterprise should represent the workers (Act on Privatisation, 1990). This is supposed to be a substitute for lost self-management rights. The law allows privatisation bonds, free of charge, to be issued in equal amounts to all citizens to be used for buying shares.

The debate on privatisation has preceded and followed the passage of the law. The main problems contested have been: the pace of privatisation, the method used – should shares be only sold or also distributed without charge? – and to what extent should the pluralism of ownership forms, promised in the round-table agreement, be honoured. I will start with the last problem.

The privatisation law is a clear violation of the 1989 round-table agreements which assumed a plurality of ownership forms. In the agreements, the preservation of self-managed enterprises was listed in first place among the principles of the new economic system. Obviously, the neo-liberals are in favour of fully fledged private enterprises and have managed to design the law accordingly.

C. Józefiak argued (1990) that the law was a good compromise between capitalist and workers' ownership, in that 20 per cent of the shares can be bought by employees. Self-managed enterprises would be contrary to what exists abroad and would not create a mature market economy.

On the other hand, J. Mużel (1990) and R. Bugaj and T. Kowalik

(1990) called for a plurality of ownership forms that include self-managed enterprises and enterprises owned by workers. Interestingly enough, the Economic Council, which was appointed by the Mazowiecki government, also called for plurality of ownership relations (see *ZG*, 1990, no. 42).

The government pushed for rapid privatisation; Balcerowicz wanted to have small and medium-sized enterprises privatised by the end of 1991, and large enterprises put into the pre-privatisation stage by encouraging them to turn into joint stock companies. This pre-privatisation stage was regarded by the government as commercialisation (Economic Council discussion, *ZG*, 1990, no. 41). In its submission to the IMF about its intended economic policy for 1991–3, the government again committed itself to accelerating privatisation (see Mujżel, 1991). The government sees privatisation almost as a panacea, as if all its problems can be solved once privatisation is achieved. As in the case of stabilisation, ideology hampers the ability to see ownership through the economic prism.

Many economists, for example, G. Kołodko (Economic Council discussion, *ZG*, 1990, no. 41) and J. Mujżel (panel discussion, *ZG*, 1990, no. 21), counselled against rushing into the denationalisation of large enterprises, arguing that there was a lack of capital and danger of a further decline in production. Surprisingly, S. Kurowski and Przigodzki (1991) also came out against the acceleration of privatisation, arguing that this would destroy the economy. They counselled gradual privatisation, depending on the availability of capital and cadres. On the other hand, M. Dąbrowski (1991) advocated the acceleration of privatisation in order to be able to accelerate the market reform. To this end, he suggested using non-equivalent transfer of assets and simplified methods of estimating assets.

Despite government efforts to accelerate 'large' privatisation, it is progressing very slowly and will take a long time for the major part of the state sector to be privatised. Therefore many economists demand (for example, Z. Sadowski, 1991; Mujżel, 1990A and 1991) the commercialisation of state enterprises. This is supposed to be different from the one suggested in law, in that enterprises are to get full autonomy, which, in practice, means the transfer of a part of property rights to enterprises. In addition, they urge the government to accelerate the privatisation of small and middle-sized enterprises.

Some economists would like to see privatisation spreading, through the rise of new, private businesses. According to Z. Sadowski (1991B), if new enterprises could spread quickly, the problem of the privatisation of state enterprises would perhaps not be so large a problem.

As already indicated, the idea of distributing shares without charge, which was propagated by neo-liberals, has been included in the new privatisation act. It is supposed to speed up the process of privatisation and it is perhaps also a bandage for the wound caused by the shock therapy.

R. Bugaj and T. Kowalik (1990) attacked this approach, arguing that it would lead to the concentration of assets in a few hands and would reduce share prices. They discounted the idea that free access to shares would noticeably increase entrepreneurship in Poland. After enumerating the pros and cons of free, direct or indirect distribution of shares, Z. Sadowski (1991B) rejects it, whereas J. Mujżel (1991) suggests limiting it radically.

CONCLUDING REMARKS

Poland was the only country in the Soviet bloc where the regime was faced with opposition organised by workers (Solidarity). The regime, which claimed to represent primarily the interests of the industrial workers, was challenged by a new trade union, not controlled by the CP. While the industrial blue-collar workers, or certain segments of them, in other countries of the Soviet bloc made up the mainstay of the regime, the Polish workers were increasingly alienated from the regime and regarded it as a force standing against them.

Mainly after the declaration of martial law, many intellectuals joined Solidarity formally or informally. They had similar or perhaps even stronger reasons than their colleagues in the other countries under review for disliking or resenting the regime. Many Poles saw the existing system as a product imposed by a country which had occupied a large part of their homeland before 1918. In addition, the Polish leaders were not very reform-minded. W. Gomulka, and likewise his successor, E. Gierek, resisted radical reforms. The Polish 1982 reform was, to a great extent, the product of an economic crisis and Solidarity's pressure. Moreover, it was not successful. Furthermore, the economic situation in Poland was on the whole much worse than in other countries under review. This is mainly true after the artificial boom in the first half of the 1970s.

All this led to the radicalisation of the majority of the intelligentsia and to a gradual abandonment of hopes that the system could be reformed. In the case of economists, this meant that a growing number increasingly saw a solution to the grim economic situation in a return to capitalism. Interestingly enough, many chose the option which is furthest from real socialism among the possible capitalist options. They came under the spell of neo-liberalism, which mar- ginalises the role of the government and absolutises market forces, seeing in them a panacea for all economic ills. Naturally, central planning can only have a marginal role in such a system. For many this meant a replacement of K. Marx by F. A. Hayek and M. Friedman as idols.

The neo-liberals put their imprint on Solidarity, which in the begin- ning of its existence adopted the programme of the 1956 reformers. These neo-liberals played an important, if not decisive, role in pushing Solidarity to the right in the following years. They managed to occupy most of the important economic portfolios in Mazowiecki's and Bielecki's governments, and they were able to make the govern- ment accept as its own their ideas about the stabilisation of the economy, privatisation, selft-management, etc. In other words, they made Solidarity (as a political movement) abandon many of its principles.[21] It is quite surprising that a government whose roots are in a trade union would agree to a programme which must end with a deep recession and great hardship for its members. Or was it manipu- lated? Or did its leaders sell out? These are questions which wait for an answer. One is not very surprised that the neo-liberals did not retreat once they witnessed the hardship they brought to their own people, with political instability as a result. Intellectuals, sure of their jobs, are often willing to prescribe medicine for others which they themselves would not like to take. In addition, neo-liberals see a recession as a purgative which rids the economy of its obsolete and inefficient units and creates preconditions for innovation (compare Lipiński, 1991).

In masterminding the shock therapy, the neo-liberals were sup- ported in their effort by foreign consultants and by IMF pressure on the government. In the panel discussion with R. Bugaj mentioned above, M. Dąbrowski (1990) admitted that the IMF pressed hard in the matter of stabilisation, particularly with regard to the control of wages.

Now that the programme has produced a deep recession from which Poland will have great difficulty extricating itself in the coming years, and when inflation has not yet been beaten, some neo-liberals, including foreign consultants, defend their policies by maintaining that the recession has gone beyond their expectations. They should have known that the one-stroke stabilisation policy is a dangerous undertaking whose consequences cannot be predicted, all the more in a country which does not have market institutions in place. Of course, the IMF is also to blame for the recession, which would have been even deeper had the government yielded to its demand for a complete wage freeze. It is worthwhile mentioning that the IMF has not given much thought to the possible consequences of the severe austerity policy which it pushed for.

The new Olszewski government, which was instituted in December 1991, promised to fight the recession, but was ousted before it could take any substantive measures. The two previous governments were reluctant to make substantive changes in Balcerowicz's programme, probably from fear of a negative reaction from the IMF.

The Polish debates in the 1980s have enriched our knowledge about planning and have shown how views on the role of market and self-management have changed. The debates have drawn attention to the vulnerability of planing from an aspect which has been aired very little in other Soviet-bloc countries. It is usually argued that the aims and objectives of the plans express and serve the overall interests of the country. Polish economists have argued that the conflicting interests of different levels of management, regions, industries, industrial branches, and so on make it impossible for the national interest to prevail, and that what is called 'national interest' is, in fact, the interest of the group (or groups) which, due to its (their) political power, is able to impose its (their) will. Judging from the attention given to the idea of conflicting interests in Poland, it seems that the Polish ruling élite apparently has had greater difficulty than other countries in bringing about a reasonable harmonisation of interests.

During the 1980s, views on the role of planning and the market changed dramatically. The idea, which still prevailed at the beginning of the 1980s, that the economy would be served best if it were managed by both coordinating mechanisms in a certain combination – first planning in the leading role, later the market – faded. In the last years of the decade, the view that only a fully fledged market economy could ensure an efficient economy became the dominant view. Interestingly enough, the idea of market socialism has found few followers in Poland.

During the last decade, the attitude to self-management has changed dramatically. The number of followers of self-management has sharply declined. Some have abandoned it because they have always seen it as only an instrument against government interference, and now, when they have a say about what the government can or cannot do, or can identify with the government, self-management has become useless for them. Others, adopting an extreme market ideology, find self-management incompatible with a market economy.

Notes

1. The protocol of understanding was really signed with the strike committee headed by L. Wałesa.
2. T. Kowalik (1990) argues economic experts that in 1980 of Solidarity took positions concerning the economic reform which the Economic Council had formulated in 1956 and which were based on the theories worked out by W. Brus, O. Lange and E. Lipiński.
3. A Schaff (1984) argued that in 1981 Solidarity started to follow an anti-socialist policy.
4. In the second half of 1981, several social scientists came up with demands for changes in the political system. Some asked for a clear, legal definition of the CP's role in the economy (see, for example, Bugaj, Jakubowicz, Mujżel and Topiński, 1981) and some for a restriction of CP organisations in enterprises (see, for example, Grosfeld, 1981, and Grzybowski, 1981).
5. The collective included M. Dąbrowski and A. Lipowski among others.
6. J. Beksiak, who is a former member of the Wakar school, discussed his proposal with many well-known economists, among them L. Balcerowicz, R. Bugaj and C. Józefiak.
7. He relied very much in his computations on M. Rakowski's (1981) calculations. M. Rakowski was an employee of the Planning Board and has nothing to do with the former prime minister.
8. R. Bugaj took a similar view on prices in an article written earlier with Sz. Jakubowicz, J. Mujżel and A. Topiński (1981).
9. In the previously mentioned panel discussion about the economic crisis M. Nasilowski took a similar position.
10. The paper of the two authors gives a good survey of the debate about the causes of the economic crisis.
11. Several leading economists opposed this government price policy, predicting correctly that it would not succeed. However, the government, in its helplessness, preferred to listen to the IMF which urged price increases.
12. Józefiak himself was one of the members of the collective which designed the 'Directions'.
13. Karpiński's book gives good insight into the development of planning in the period 1945–85.
14. L. Balcerowicz, J. Beksiak, R. Bugaj, C. Józefiak, T. Kowalik and A. Topiński participated in the debate.
15. His article in *ZG* was only a shortened version of an article in *Studia*

ekonomiczne, no. 19, 1988, a publication of the Polish Academy of Sciences.

16. M. Nasilowski explained his views on this topic in greater detail in his book (1988A).

17. His paper gives a good survey of how views on the market developed in Poland. The paper was first presented at the Economic Congress in 1987.

18. They suggest issuing bonds to all citizens aged 18 or over in the amount of Zł 1,000.000. The bonds can be used for only one purpose: to buy stocks of enterprises earmarked for privatisation. In key industries, only 50 per cent of stocks should be available for sale.

19. After he became a high official of the government, Kawalec joined those who advocated the free distribution of privatisation bonds (see Kowalik 1990).

20. A good insight into how inflation came about in Poland, and the attempts to cope with it, is given in G. Kołodko's study (1990B).

21. It is necessary to distinguish between Solidarity as a trade union and Solidarity as a political movement or political parties.

9 The USSR

INTRODUCTION

In the first half of the 1980s there was no noticeable change in the Soviet regime. In 1983, L. Brezhnev died and his two successors followed more or less in his footsteps. In 1985, M. Gorbachev, a relatively young CP functionary came to power, and soon a new era started in the USSR.

M. Gorbachev inherited an economy in poor shape. His economic policy and economic reforms, combined with the fight between the centre and the republics over the future structure and shape of the Union, and inter-regional bickering about supplies, brought the economy to the brink of a breakdown. Gorbachev's approach to the ills of the economy was marked with naivete at times (for example, his campaign against alcoholism; for more see below). What is worse is that the Soviet leader did not manage to coordinate properly the political and economic reforms. *Glasnost* was a blessing: it was the foundation for a transformation of the political system; but it was a curse too, when Gorbachev and his associates were not able to reconcile themselves to far-reaching economic reform. The traditional economic system relied heavily on the discipline of the command structure for the fulfilment of plan targets and the distribution of income. *Glasnost* loosened discipline and introduced uncertainty, aroused resentment in the ranks of the ruling élites and put fear into the hearts of bureaucrats for their positions; on top of this, the 1987 reform undermined the existing structure without really replacing it with a new one. In an interview given in London, on the occasion of his dealings with representatives of the largest seven industrialised nations, Gorbachev himself mentioned the latter as one of the reasons for the crisis.

The 1987 economic reform represents the first major attempt to improve the working of the economy since the Second World War. In my opinion, it was much more far-reaching and complex than the 1965 reform. In addition, what is of great importance is that it was combined with political changes. The reform was, however, of a hybrid nature: it combined many principles of the Hungarian economic reform in a watered-down form, with some elements of the former East German system of *Kombinate*. The reform did not bring about the changes needed, and soon new reform blueprints appeared (for detail, see below).

In the first half of the 1980s, economic thinking in the USSR which found its expression in publications, particularly on the relationship between planning and the market, did not advance much. The state's rigid control over intellectual life set a general framework for what could be discussed in publications and how it could be discussed. Dissent in public was not tolerated. The only place where people could express dissenting views was at home, or among trusted friends, or in groups with similar-thinking people.[1] In such an environment it was no wonder that economists were primarily occupied with 'safe' ideas about how to make planning more effective, and with 'chewing over' some of the minor changes in the system of management introduced by Brezhnev's and later Andropov's administration. As far as they ventured into the treatment of the relationship of planning and market, or market relations, no very innovative positions were usually taken.

Gorbachev's advent to power and his commitment to *glasnost* and *perestroika* brought about a dramatic change in Soviet intellectual life. This did not happen, however, all at once. It took Gorbachev some time to elaborate on his pledge to carry out a radical reform. Considering the authoritarian regime in the USSR before Gorbachev and the strict ideological limitations imposed, it was not surprising that even economists who favoured far-reaching reforms did not instantly go public with their views. Yet there were many economists who were conservative by their own choice. Therefore changes in thinking and publications came about only gradually. No doubt, the systemic changes in Hungary and Poland and ongoing debates in those two countries had an impact on the views of Soviet economists.

In this chapter I will first discuss briefly the ideas about the topic under review in the first half of the 1980s, and then turn my attention to the changes in thinking about planning and the market brought about by Gorbachev's administration.

DEBATES IN THE FIRST HALF OF THE 1980s

The views which found their way into publications were largely determined by the nature of the attempts to improve the working of the economic mechanism. In 1979, the Brezhnev administration decided on a package of provisions which aimed at improving planning, the incentive system and investment activities, with the expectation that this would intensify the performance of the economy (*SEG*, 1979, no. 32). In 1983 Andropov's leadership initiated a more comprehensive experiment, which first covered five all-union and republic ministries and was expanded in 1985 to twenty-six ministries (*EG*, 1983, no. 31). The 1983 experiment made supply contract fulfilment with regard to structure, quality and timeliness the main plan fulfilment indicator, and thus replaced net ouput which had been introduced in 1979. The latter still remained as a regulator of wage-bill growth and served for calculation of labour productivity. Normatives were given an important role; they were supposed to be long-term and applied to, among other things, the distribution of profit between enterprises and the state, and wage-bill growth. The 1983 package extended the role of enterprises in decision-making and in the financing of investment.

In the period under review, the economists' attention was focused primarily on how to 'intensify' the working of the economy in accordance with the set goals of the 'reforms' of the first half of the 1980s. If we confine ourselves to our topic under review, it can be said that the debates revolved around two areas especially: improvement in planning and, even more, improvement in the system of indicators, which is a component of planning in an administrative system. These were areas which economists could quite safely discuss and even make critical comments about, as long as they did not draw direct or indirect conclusions about the need for a far-reaching restructuring of the economic mechanism, say, along the principles of the Hungarian economic reform.

Of course, professional journals also published studies on the economic mechanism, but the number of those which were critical of the mechanism were relatively few and timid. It is interesting that the criticism of the EM usually went further than the demands for remedy, as if the authors wanted to smooth away the impression they had created by the criticism of the system. Nothing could appear which challenged the foundations of the socialist economic system, but even research pieces which questioned some of the main principles of the existing system of management had no great chance of appearing. Only studies which stayed within the official framework of thought were printed.

The Economic Mechanism

The state of thinking about the economic system and the economic mechanism was perhaps best reflected in a three-volume book on *The Economic System of Socialism*, compiled by a huge collective which included, among others, some of the best known reformers (L. Abalkin, A. Aganbegian, T. Zaslavskaia) and which appeared in Moscow in 1984 (*Ekonomicheskii . . .*, 1984).[2] Because of lack of space, only the ideas in the volumes on planning and commodity–money relations will be mentioned here. As to planning, the volumes express the traditional idea that the law of planning is the objective reflection of collective ownership and enables a proportional and balanced regulation of the whole economy by a national plan. Under capitalism, individual labour becomes social only after it is validated by the market, whereas under socialism, labour has a direct social character (Vol. 1, pp. 460–3). The substance of this statement is that central planners – unlike capitalist managers – are able to determine correctly *ex ante* the allocation of resources, including labour, in accordance with the needs of the economy, a statement which practice refutes.

Volumes 1 and 3 also contain chapters on commodity-money relations; they are primarily focused on the traditional topics which are mostly treated conventionally. The authors reject the view that socialism is a special type of commodity production. 'Socialism as a special system of collective life cannot be defined by the availability of commodity production which is only one of the characteristic features' (Vol. 1, p. 478). Under socialism, the law of value works in combination with other laws characteristic of socialism (basic law and law of planning); it plays an important role as a law of commodity–money relations, but it does not regulate the economy. It is used in a planned way for the development of the economy (Vol. 1, p. 473).

When it comes to a discussion of the utilisation of the commodity–money relations, the authors maintain that these relations are manifested in domestic and foreign trade (Vol. 3, p. 449), a finding which is in the traditional spirit. What is perhaps new is the stress placed on the utilisation of value categories (wages, price, interest) as instruments for the assertion of national, collective and *individual interests* (Vol. 3, p. 457). This innovative approach is then offset by a chapter devoted to the criticism of reformist and revisionist views (Vol. 3, pp. 619–30).

The second example of the state of economic thinking is a collective work of CMEA economists, edited by Soviet and East European economists, dealing with the economic mechanism of socialist countries (*A szocialista . . .*, 1984). One would expect that such a book would devote quite a lot of attention to the role of the market, all the more because Hungarian and Polish economists took part in writing it. In reality, very little attention is devoted to the market. In the first chapter, where the tendencies prevailing in the economic mechanisms of the socialist countries are discussed, no mention is made of the growing importance of the market in Hungary and Poland. The only thing mentioned which has anything to do with market relations is the increasing role of the small-scale private sector (p. 41). It is clear that the Soviet editors did not allow the inclusion of market relations in the volume for political reasons.

T. Zaslavskaia's unpublished 'Novosibirsk manifesto' (1983)[3] gives a good insight into how radical economists viewed systemic problems and how they wanted to solve them. In the light of the existing situation in the USSR, her paper was, no doubt, a courageous act and what is even more important, she correctly pinpointed some of the reasons for the ills of the economy. She showed that, with the increase in the sophistication of production and in the demand for qualified labour, subjective factors grew in significance, and administrative methods became more and more useless. Her attack on a long-held dogma about the existence of the identity of interests between society and social groups, even more her contention that persons in high positions had vested interests in maintaining the existing system of management and therefore were against reforms, was a daring step. However, when it came to suggesting cures, she was not very specific or radical: she counselled a transition to economic methods of output regulation, more rights for enterprises, and legislation enabling small private businesses to be created. She made no mention of the need to apply market forces, let alone give them a decisive role.

The published research concerning systemic problems was even less daring in evaluating the existing economic mechanism than Zaslavskaia's manifesto was. The suggested cures were often more specific, but not revolutionary. The most radical demands were to extend greater autonomy to enterprises, make contracts between suppliers and buyers a significant instrument of the economic mechanism, evaluate enterprises according to their contributions to final national economic results and to introduce rational prices. Some economists gave priority to improving planning.

Perhaps R. Karagedov was one of the most radical economists in the demand for systemic changes (1985). After evaluating critically the 1983 experiment, he suggested introducing a two-level management of the economy: the centre and associations (enterprises). Operative functions should be left to enterprises and the centre should focus on long-term development. The autonomy of enterprises could be limited only by law. Enterprises operating on the basis of the principle of self-financing should have the right to make decisions about investment and should be given greater rights in the determination of prices.

It is clear that, in Karagedov's reform blueprint, market forces were given more weight. On the other hand, he also made it clear that important goals of economic policy should not be made dependent on a 'commodity–money mechanism'. He argued that the centre should interfere by direct methods of planning in major investment and personal incomes, and in some other areas.

P. Bunich (1985), N. Fedorenko (1985) and E. Kapustin (1984), like Karagedov, wanted to restructure the EM by giving greater autonomy to enterprises. P. Bunich argued that consumer goods enterprises in particular should have greater autonomy. N. Fedorenko, director of the reputable Central Mathematical Economics Institute of the USSR, called for greater rights to enterprises, reduction of output targets, and a larger role for contractual relations. To him, the greatest problem of the economy was a lack of coordination between plan targets and economic levers, mainly prices. He advocated, on the one hand, the need for prices to stem from the plan (an old idea of optimal planners) and, on the other, a role for enterprises in the determination of prices. The author explicitly stressed that his reform suggestions did not aim at achieving market socialism.

Among the many articles which L. Abalkin published in the period under review, one specifically dealt with the theoretical problems of the economic mechanism (1983). In it he argued that the existing EM was not suitable for intensive economic growth, an ambition of the authorities, and that it hampered technological progress. He also warned that changes in indicators would not do the trick, and that a profound *perestroika* was needed.

Judging on the basis of his criticism, one would expect far-reaching reform demands. In reality, the reform proposals were modest; perhaps the author wanted to remain in the realm of the possible. L. Abalkin advocated changes in planning; he urged the application of the primacy of the national-economic approach in planning, and thus an abandonment of the practice of compiling the national plan from branch plans. Evaluation of the activities of ministries should be based on their contribution to the final economic results. He also advocated basing the planning of output deliveries on contracts between suppliers and buyers, thus making the institution of overfulfilment redundant.

Evaluation Indicators

This segment will concentrate on the debates about the 1983 experiment only. As mentioned, this was a safe topic for debate, and many economists participated in it. The debate was of importance because it gave a good insight into the working of the economic mechanism in practice. Economists mostly used the debate to criticise some of the established indicators, of course after expressing praise for the experiment as a whole. Only a few participants used the debate to formulate their concept of restructuring the EM, and therefore it cannot be used as a rich source of information about general systemic problems.

Many debates concentrated on the state of contracts between suppliers and buyers, the fulfilment of which was supposed to be one of the main indicators of performance. Some called for making the contracts instruments of plan compilation, while others complained that the contracts did not reflect demand and did not eliminate plan targets. There were also complaints that the 1983 experiment did not bring about a change in planning practice (see for example, the debate in the editorial board of *PKh*, 1985, no. 4).

The debates focused extensively on economic normatives and their shortcomings. Some economists criticised the fact that the normatives were not uniform, while others wanted to have normatives adjusted to the level of technology and the productivity of enterprises. A lot of criticism was expressed about the lack of normative stability; it was maintained that contrary to promises the normatives for wage–bill growth were set for only two years, and for only one year for distribution of profit (Ibid, and panel discussion in the editorial board of *EKO*, 1985, no. 11).[4]

Some economists came up with suggestions about how to improve the system of indicators. It is worth mentioning that P. Bunich timidly forwarded the idea of introducing net increment of profit as the main indicator (1985A). He did not, however, combine this

suggestion with a call for the elimination of output targets, as was
sometimes done.

FIRST PHASE OF THE GORBACHEV ADMINISTRATION

The Gorbachev administration can be divided into two phases: the
first lasted up to 1989 and the second up to Gorbachev's resignation.
The first can be characterised in two catch words, which Gorbachev
himself coined, namely *glasnost* and *perestroika*, of course in their
first stage. The new communist leader committed the Party to bringing about a radical reform, engulfing not only the economy but also
all societal life. A new era of political liberalisation was gradually
introduced: censorship was relaxed and human rights were substantially expanded. In 1987, the promised radical reform was approved;
while not really radical, it still meant progress compared to what had
existed before.

Glasnost and the economic reform created not only an environment for the freer expression of views, but what is no less important,
it generated new impulses to economic contemplation and thinking.
For most economists, as will be shown later, the CP line, which was
determined by M. Gorbachev and his associates and which, in the
economy, meant the principles of the 1987 economic reform and
related provisions, was the framework within which criticism was
exercised. Probably the old custom of not deviating much from the
official positions still prevailed; it is difficult to say whether caution or
conservatism or both were the reason for this phenomenon. One
should not be surprised that social scientists approached new moves
with suspicion and fear: they well knew that published ideas, deviating much from accepted standards, could be used against them,
especially if the regime changed for any reason. In addition, it is not
easy for intellectuals, particularly if they are older, to change radically their world outlook and their way of thinking. Unlike Polish and
Hungarian economists, Soviet economists were in much greater and
longer isolation from Western economic thought. Moreover, many
Polish and Hungarian economists regarded socialism as a foreign
product imposed on them by the Soviets and therefore *a priori*
objectionable. Soviet economists did not have such objections.

There were, of course, economists who professed and published
ideas going beyond the conceptual framework of the reform. They
challenged not only the existing economic mechanism, but also some

aspects of the socialist economic system, previously an unprecedented occurrence. But few economists doubted the reformability of the economic mechanism, not to mention the economic system.

It has already been mentioned that the 1987 Soviet reform was a combination of many principles of the Hungarian 1968 reform in a watered-down form, with some elements of the East German system. The Soviet reform envisaged a substantial expansion of enterprise autonomy. Enterprises were to be allowed to work out five-year and annual plans – however, not entirely according to their own considerations. On the one hand, they had to consider non-binding state control figures which were of an informational nature, and on the other, to comply with mandatory state orders (contracts), normatives and limits. State orders were a new institution, probably taken over from China.[5] They had to absorb through time a smaller and smaller part of the output capacity of enterprises and were to be allotted to enterprises on the basis of a tender; the remainder of enterprise capacity had to be filled by contracts with buyers. The reform also promised to create a favourable environment for competition. The formation of prices was to be determined very much according to the 1968 Hungarian economic reform. Similarly, wage regulation had to become less controlled by the centre. For the first time, a small number of associations was given the right to enter into direct trade relations with foreign partners. The promise of self-management for enterprise workers was perhaps the best sign of changed times. Gorbachev's predecessors resented the very idea of self-management, let alone its implementation, for fear that this might endanger the leading role of the CP. The decision to establish new state production associations, which had to take over the job of the chief departments of branch ministries, a move along the line of *Kombinate*, gave the reform a slight East German flavour (for more, see Adam, 1989, ch. 10).

The reform can be evaluated on the whole as a failure. It did not bring about a turnaround in the economy; on the contrary, it made the economic situation worse. For more, see below.

Economic Reform

The reform debates were intensive, lively and critical. In some cases, the criticism was harsh. For the first time, the political system was also questioned, not so much the leading role of the CP as the way the system was applied. There were calls for a reduction of Party meddling in the affairs of enterprises, and for democratic elections (see, for example, the debate in the Economic Institute, *VE*, 1988, no. 6).[6] What is interesting is that usually no new economic reform blueprints were put forward. For example, G. Popov (1988), the present mayor of Moscow and one of the leaders of the democratic movement who dared to criticise the 1987 reform, did not come up with a reform blueprint. Many economists criticised the old concept of centralism and called for a new relationship between the centre and enterprises; however, most economists accepted on the whole the solutions envisaged in the 1987 reform. Many censured planning and blamed it for the shortcomings in the economy; again, most economists expressed more or less satisfaction with the changes envisaged in planning. On the other hand, many maintained that, without the expansion of commodity–money relations, a new relationship between the centre and enterprises was impossible. It is worth mentioning that some economists started to use the term market instead of commodity–money relations. As will be shown later, some made a distinction between the two terms and others used them interchangeably. Most criticisms were made in the name of socialism and were motivated by a desire to make the socialist system more efficient and more directed to the needs of the population. Economists still believed that socialism was the desirable and only possible system under the existing conditions.

True, there were certainly economists who had great misgivings about the system but were not yet ready to air those misgivings, out of fear or because the professional journals were not ready to publish them. No doubt, even among those critics, there were some who wanted to give the reform a chance.

In the following sections I will discuss first the views of those who more or less steadfastly supported the 1987 reform, and then the views of its critics. L. Abalkin, A. Aganbegian, S. Sitarian and E. Figurnov can be regarded as representatives of the first group. In his article, written before the 1987 June plenum of the Central Committee of the Party, Academician L. Abalkin, the director of the prestigious Institute of Economics and an adviser to M. Gorbachev, maintained that *perestroika* would bring about a restructuring of the foundation of the system in ownership relations and planning. He was not specific as to ownership, but elaborated on planning. The relationship between centralisation and enterprises should change. The objectives of the plan should be achieved by economic methods, and planning should be democratised. Abalkin wrote, 'nowadays we view enterprises and working collectives not only as objects of planning but also as subjects of planning activity'. He repeated his old thesis that the objective of planning should be the whole economy. Of course, he did not forget to stress that the expansion of commodity–money relations was crucial for the success of the reform. As to binding targets, he took the position that light industry enterprises should not be subject to output targets (1987).

In a debate mentioned above, L. Abalkin shared the views of some debaters who maintained that a radical economic reform could not succeed without an adequate restructuring of the political system, that there must be a clear separation between economic and political management and, finally, that the reform should proceed from the bottom up.

In a debate in the club of directors (*EKO*, 1987, no. 3), Academician A. Aganbegian, one of the main architects of the 1987 reform, expressed his views about the direction desirable in the upcoming economic reform. Alluding to the plenary meeting of the CC of the CP in June 1986, he maintained that planning should be limited to important targets, such as contribution to the budget and major investment projects. To him, the greatest problem was how to orient production so as to satisfy consumer demand.

In his article, which aims at explaining the principles of the 1987 reform (1987), A. Aganbegian maintains that the new reform is based on socialist ownership, planned development, distribution according to work and activisation of commodity–money relations. The principle of 'more socialism' is the guideline of the reform. The radicalness of the reform lies in the replacement of administrative methods by economic ones.

In his article, entitled 'Centralised Management and the Market', E. Figurnov (1988) maintained that the new centralism, marked by democratisation and economic methods, could not work without the support of the market. The market had always existed in the USSR. Neglecting it hurt the economy. Figurnov claimed that the 'Market for producer goods, prices, credit, long term normatives for the distribution of enterprise revenues in the new system become the instruments of planned centralised management'.

Discussion of the critics will start with the moderate and then proceed to the more radical. In his article dealing with *khozraschet* and centralised management, P. Bunich (1988) maintained that full *khozraschet* could only function if enterprises were independent and workers participated in management. He viewed the 1987 reform as radical; the introduction of co-operatives was evidence in this regard (see also his 1988A). Control figures, state orders and limits were the necessary and sufficient instruments of centralism. He resented normatives, and with good reason, because they resulted from plans rather than the other way round, and therefore he regarded them as administrative methods.

G. Popov (1988) subjected the 1987 reform to very sharp criticism. To him, self-financing, as well as self-management, would turn out to be a fiction. State orders were only a new instrument for controlling the activities of enterprises. Normatives were derived from the plan, and this would introduce arbitrariness in their setting. The concept of the reform was designed in such a way that the poorest performers would be kept afloat at the expense of thriving enterprises. All economic levers were derived from the administrative plan, instead of the new five-year plan being equipped with a new mechanism.

Whereas P. Bunich and G. Popov focused their criticism on the 1987 economic reform, N. Shmelev's attack in his two articles (1987, 1988) was directed at various aspects of the economic system and economic life. To him, monopolisation and lack of enterprise interest in technological progress were the greatest ills of the economy. Shortages in the economy were caused by disrespect for economic laws. The renewal of market equilibrium for consumer goods depended on healthy commodity–money relations in agriculture. Therefore he suggested adjusting agricultural procurement prices as well as leasing land to peasants in some areas. He advocated the expansion of the individual–cooperative sector in order to ensure competitive conditions. The market should be expanded in order to turn it into a buyers' market. Subsidies should be eliminated in order to achieve rational prices; the expenditures saved should be used for wage increases. As to planning, he suggested limiting it to strategic planning and the distribution of investment funds in order to ensure proportionality. Plans should be based on contracts between buyers and suppliers. He also touched on many taboos: he suggested exploring the effect of allowing a small reserve army and called for reduced military spending. His 1987 article in particular triggered an uproar in conservative ranks.[7]

Ownership Relations

The 1965 Soviet economic reform did not give any opportunity for a debate on ownership; collective ownership was regarded as the basis of socialism which it was not advisable to challenge. The 1987 economic reform and speeches connected with it, mainly M. Gorbachev's, gave a stimulus to such a debate. In his report to the plenum of the CC in June 1987, M. Gorbachev suggested that workers must become active co-proprietors, in that they should be involved in the management of collective property, and that more democracy in the economy was 'indivisibly linked with active use of various forms of co-operative and individual enterprise projects alongside state ownership' (Gorbachev, 1987, p. 41). Of course, the new legal provisions on ownership, which meant an encroachment on the dogmatic concept of socialist ownership, may have stimulated debates even more. In 1986, the individual labour activity law was passed, according to which families could engage in small business. In 1988, a new law on co-operatives (henceforth new co-operatives) was passed. Since the law allows non-members to be employed, it has become a cover-up for private enterprise. Co-operatives, like state enterprises, are allowed to issue shares. Finally, leasing of land as well as industrial assets is allowed (for more, see Hanson, 1990, pp. 83–94).

The ownership debates in the period under review were by no means a challenge to collective ownership. Even N. Shmelev, who in his reform suggestions in 1987 and 1988 went the furthest, did not really challenge collective ownership.[8] The same is true of G. Lisichkin (1988), who attacked Stalin for his brand of socialism. He rejected Stalin's idea that collective ownership was more efficient than private, but only because, in his opinion, what existed as collective ownership was so in name only. Most of the participants in the debate criticised the fact that workers, who were supposed to be co-owners or co-possessors, had no say in the use of the means of production. They alluded to the negative consequences of this phenomenon, and called for turning state ownership into societal ownership.[9] The promised introduction of self-management was regarded as the realisation of this demand. It was believed that self-management could best be realised under conditions of joint-stock ownership or under a leasing system. To many, co-operative ownership and ownership based on individual labour were an integral part of societal ownership. A few economists opposed changes in ownership, arguing that the shortcomings of the economy should be sought in areas other than ownership.

First, mention should be made of the attitude of the all-union conference of October 1988 on problems of socialist ownership, which was sponsored by the Institute of Economics and the Scientific Council of the Academy of Sciences. L. Abalkin, in his address, which was published in the form of an article (1988A), posed the important question: can socialism achieve the advantages of capitalism (high economic efficiency, quick adaptability to technological progress and quick response of supply to demand) without being forced to give up the advantages of socialism (full employment, social security, collectivism)? His answer was in substance affirmative, provided the system was able to mobilise 'man's social and labour activism', a point which he often stressed. And the subjective factor could only be generated by encouraging a genuine proprietary approach to work.

When it came to drawing conclusions from his analysis, he was not very specific. He made it clear that he was against absolutisation of state ownership, that it was desirable to transform it into societal ownership and that ownership should be adjusted to the level of socialisation of activities, but not much further.

The study, worked out by the Institute of Economics and submitted to the all-union conference, stressed the great importance of overcoming the deformation of socialist ownership which lay in the replacement of societal by state ownership. Not only the state, but also collective and individual ownership should be regarded as an integral part of societal ownership. It also called for developing joint-stock ownership and ownership based on leasing. Forms of ownership based on exploitation should be shunned. The study recommended the expansion of the new co-operatives, but at the same time pointed out their conflicting nature in allowing the employment of non-members in the co-operatives.

In the recommendations adopted by the conference, criteria of a socialist nature (*sotsialistichnost*) for ownership forms were listed: these were, among others, the absence of exploitation, democratic relations, highest economic efficiency, equal access to different activities, and social guarantees.

L. Nikiforov (1988), with whose article *Voprosy ekonomiki* opened a long debate about ownership in its columns, argues that 'perfection' of ownership is the key to improvement in the economy. To him, societal appropriation is realised not only when the owner is the state, but also when the owners are collectives or individuals. To make state ownership societal, two conditions must be met: (1) the state must reflect the interests of all society, which is almost impossible; and (2) it must consider the different interests of classes, groups and collectives, which is impossible under conditions of state appropriations. A solution to this problem lies in allowing all workers and collectives to be part of ownership relations, which to him is what the 1987 reform was all about.

V. Shkredov (1988) and A. Butenko (1988) came to a similar conclusion using different arguments. Shkredov complained that the complete nationalisation, carried out in the 1930s, has not undergone any changes since then. As a result, people have lost interest in the working of the economy. In the period from the 1930s to the beginning of the 1950s, the state countered this phenomenon by brutal measures of coercion. When these provisions were acknowledged as socially inadmissible and rescinded, the government lost control. A. Butenko, doctor of philosophy, complained that some people use collective property for selfish interests and that workers had no say in its use. Analysing collective ownership, he came to the conclusion that it was common (shared by everyone) and at the same time ownerless. Both Shkredov and Butenko saw a solution in self-management.

In a joint article N. Vladova and N. Rabkina (1988) took the opposite position, arguing against changes in ownership. They were in favour of commodity–money relations which, according to them, are the basis for full *khozraschet*, but not of the market, which requires real owners. Reduction in state ownership would, they warned, disorganise the economy. The shortcomings of the economy were not caused by ownership, but by the existing narrow wage differentials and the applied investment policy.

SECOND PHASE OF THE GORBACHEV ADMINISTRATION

The second phase was different in principle from the first. In a nutshell, it can be said that its most important feature was the adoption of the market as the chief and decisive coordinating mechanism. The decision to introduce a market economy meant that planning was relegated to the role of an adjunct of the market. Initially, it seemed that the new economic system would be market socialism in the sense that the market economy would be based on a preponderance of state ownership; judging on the basis of many documents and the speech of M. Gorbachev at the meeting of the CC of the Party (*P*, 1991, 26 July), which discussed the CP's new programme, one can assume that the Soviet government still believed in some kind of market socialism. The abortive *coup d'état* which took place in August 1991 meant the end of socialism.

The second phase was also marked by another important difference. The expansion of *glasnost*, the weakening of the CP which culminated in its dissolution after the attempted *putsch*, and the growing feeling of greater certainty that the old, repressive system was a thing of the past, created an environment in which intellectuals were no longer limited in their thinking by the CP line. There was a dramatic change in attitude to all important questions of economic and political life.

The 1987 reform, as could be expected, did not stop the worsening of the economic situation, and even contributed to it. The conceptual contradictions in the reform were an important reason for the failure. One of the principles of the reform was self-financing; however, enterprises did not receive the autonomy needed in order to make this principle an incentive to higher economic efficiency. Output targets *per se* were not assigned to enterprises, but state orders, which were mandatory, took their place to a great extent so that enterprises were limited in their decisions about output mix. The reform promised a competitive environment, but, at the same time, concentration of industry continued, to mention some of the contradictions.

There was also resistance to the reform in the ranks of the central bureaucracy who were afraid of losing power, though the bureaucracy as such remained untouched by the reform. The concept of economic normatives was an unsound idea in itself; the branch ministries made the normatives, as well as the state orders, factors which worked against the objectives of the reform.

The main reasons for the worsening economic situation were the growing budget deficit and the rapid wage increases which were not matched by production. Both, combined with price increases, accelerated the rate of inflation. The growing budget deficit was due to increasing price and enterprise subsidies, social and, of course, high military expenditures. The ill-thought-out fight against the high consumption of vodka, which resulted in annual losses of at least 10 billion *rubles* to the state budget, was also a factor.

The factors mentioned, combined with the growing deficit in the balance of trade which slowed down imports of consumer goods, with food hoarding, prompted primarily by the announced plans for huge impending price increases, and with an inept distribution system, which became even worse with the loosening of workplace discipline, created great shortages in many places. The situation was aggravated by the Moscow and Leningrad mayors, who had forbidden non-residents to shop in their cities, a provision which triggered a retaliation from the rural areas.

It is impossible in this study to discuss the provisions made in order to cope with the worsening economic situation. Huge price increases carried out in March 1991 were perhaps the most important provision.

The decision of the highest authorities to embark on a market economy was reflected in the thinking of economists and, vice versa, the ideas of Soviet economists influenced the economic policy; in the second stage of the Gorbachev administration the influence of academic economists increased considerably.

Economic Reform

The failure of the 1987 economic reform generated a whole series of reform blueprints. It is beyond the scope of this study to record, let alone discuss, all the proposals. Therefore some of them will be mentioned only briefly. In the autumn of 1989, a moderate bill for the transition to a market economy was passed by the Supreme Soviet. This act, which was associated with the names of N. Ryzhkov and L. Abalkin, was short-lived. When M. Gorbachev came under increasing pressure because of the worsening economic situation, and because of the republican and local elections which weakened his position, he resorted, on the one hand, to the establishment of the office of presidency, for which he was the only candidate, and on the other, promised a 'radicalisation of the radical reform'. And so came into being the '400 days' proposal, conceived under the guidance of G. Yavlinskii. Though this proposal was not accepted by N. Ryzhkov, the prime minister of the day, it later became the basis for S. Shatalin's 500 days programme. In the meantime (May 1990) N. Ryzhkov submitted a more radical proposal, which, in contrast to the original, had a shorter transitional period and allowed for huge price increases as a first step in the reform. The price reform proposal was one of the reasons why N. Ryzhkov's proposal was rejected. It is interesting that Yeltsin criticised the proposal because of the price increases it envisaged (see Kondratenko, 1991).

Shatalin's reform blueprint (*Perekhod* . . ., 1990)[10] caught the attention of Soviet intellectuals as well as foreign observers of the USSR for several reasons. This was a blueprint prepared at the request of Gorbachev and Yeltsin, which in itself was a newsworthy event in light of the power struggle between the two. In addition, it envisaged the creation of preconditions for a market economy, including considerable privatisation within 500 days. B. Yeltsin embraced Shatalin's programme (which was approved by the Russian Supreme Soviet) because it was in line with his political objectives, whereas Gorbachev's leadership rejected it and replaced it with its own 'Basic guidelines for the stabilisation of the economy and transition to a market economy' (1990) (hereafter 'Guidelines'[11]), though it took over many ideas from Shatalin's programme (for more, see Kondratenko, 1991). In April 1991, the government submitted an anti-crisis programme to the Supreme Soviet. A subsequent programme, worked out by G. Yavlinskii in co-operation with a group of Harvard University professors headed by H. Allison, was rejected by the Union government.

Both Shatalin's programme and the 'Guidelines' were programmes for the transition to a market economy. They also had in common the sequencing of the proposed reforms: both intended first to stabilise the currency and substantially reduce the budget deficit, then start with destatisation (a term for depriving the state of its absolute power over state enterprises, see also p. 219) and privatisation, and, only when relative stabilisation was achieved, was price reform to be instituted. The incomes of the population were supposed to be protected from inflation by indexation. The system of state orders (contracts) was to be continued for some time in order to prevent output declining dramatically. It is clear that both programmes tried to avoid shock treatment.

The two programmes varied in several respects, the most important being that Shatalin's programme was based on republican sovereignty, whereas the 'Guidelines' were based on the assumption that the Union, though considerably decentralised, still had a very important economic role to play. In Shatalin's programme, the republics were supposed to dispose of their own resources, to determine the level of taxes, forms and methods of privatisation, to regulate prices, and so on. The republics were to allot funds to the Union for programmes in which they were interested. No explicit mention was made of a common monetary policy, one of the main preconditions of a single, all-union market. Yet the need for such a market was suggested, and the fact that the republics should agree on certain economic policies was also mentioned (*Perekhod* . . . 1990, pp. 12–13).

The 'Guidelines' recognised the sovereignty of the republics, but reserved the right of taxation; the level of taxes was to be agreed with the republics. In addition, the republics had to empower the Union to carry out an agreed monetary and credit policy, regulate prices on key products and services, etc. Finally, the Union had to be in charge of the single fuel and energy system, military production and such like (1990).

In addition, Shatalin's programme was supposed to be carried out in 500 days, to be divided up into four stages and start immediately, whereas the 'Guidelines' did not include a detailed timetable for the transition and assumed a gradual solution of the problems.

The two programmes also differed in their approach to privatisation, in the changes suggested for reforming the individual building blocks of the system and, finally, in the rhetoric. In Shatalin's programme, destatisation and privatisation were to be applied rapidly to the major part of the economy, whereas the 'Guidelines' were vague on the issue as far as the so-called large privatisation was concerned. The 'Guidelines' attacked the old system less and, when they did so, the terminology was milder than in Shatalin's proposal. Gorbachev, who introduced the 'Guidelines', underscored that they were compatible with socialism.

Though the 'Guidelines' were approved by the Supreme Soviet, they were soon eclipsed by the anti-crisis programme, introduced by the Union government in April 1991 (*EiZh*, 1991, no. 18). This programme was a mixture of economic policy provisions and systemic changes. V. Pavlov, the prime minister of the day, who presented the programme in the Supreme Soviet, maintained that it was a compromise between the old system and a pure market economy, and that it combined the market with administrative methods, a compromise which was intended to ensure that unemployment would be moderate.

The programme did not envisage the instant liberalisation of prices, apparently for fear that it would produce further price increases, on top of the huge increases initiated by the government in March 1991.[12] Instead, taxes were to be increased in order to mitigate market disequilibrium and ensure additional funds for social programmes. However, in the Union prognosis and programme which replaced annual plans, the government envisaged a considerable reduction in the number of fixed prices, and the introduction of internal convertibility of the ruble (*EiZh*, 1991, no. 27).

V. Pavlov made it clear that there was no intention of privatising everything. He promised, however, to accelerate the so-called small privatisation; two thirds of small-scale businesses and service facilities should be in private hands in 1992. Middle- and large-sized enterprises should be turned into joint-stock companies and 10 per cent of them into worker-owned companies. Workers and enterprises should be encouraged to buy shares; the money used for such purchases would not be taxed. He also stressed the importance of attracting foreign capital.

The Yavlinskii–Allison reform plan (1991) varied from others, including Shatalin's programme, in that it was closer to what is called 'shock therapy' and did not contain wage indexation. It was based on the sovereignty of the republics, but it envisaged a single market with a uniform monetary policy and a Central Bank. The reforms were to be backed up with Western aid. The plan's blueprint was spread out over a longer period (1991–7) and divided into two stages. The first stage (1991–3) was devoted to the creation of the legal and economic institutions of the market. In this stage, the renewal of a balanced budget, price liberalisation with few exceptions, wage regulation by taxes, liberalisation of most foreign trade, and internal convertibility were to be achieved. (It is not clear whether all these provisions were to be carried out by a certain date, as happened in Poland.) In addition, privatisation of small and middle-sized enterprises was to be put into motion. Large enterprises were to be turned into joint stock companies whose shares would be sold. There was to be no distribution of assets without charge. Land reform which gives land to efficient peasants was to be put into effect.

The second stage (1994–7) was to be marked by structural changes in the economy, the stepping-up of large privatisation and other important measures needed for the good working of a market economy. At the end of this stage, the Soviet economy should be integrated into the world economy.

The two different blueprint reforms (Shatalin's on the one hand and the 'Guidelines' and anti-crisis programme on the other) had support in the economic community; after all, the drafting of the reform blueprints was mostly the work of economists. The radical group, which advocated a speedy transition to a market economy and a rapid democratisation of the country, an integral part being sovereignty for the republics, supported Shatalin's programme and later the Yavlinskii–Allison programme. Many members of this group assumed a market economy where the government role would be minimal. Such views can be characterised as neo-liberal. The moderates supported the 'Guidelines' and later the anti-crisis prog-ramme.

In addition to the two camps, there was a third one, the conserva-tive, to which even the Union government proposals seemed too radical. Even before Shatalin's programme and the 'Guidelines' appeared, A. Aganbegian (1990A), at the helm of a committee evaluating alternative suggestions for a reform at the request of the Union government, talked about three groupings, which were some-what similar to those already mentioned.[13]

With the deepening economic crisis, the increasing frustration over the poor working of the economic mechanism and the growing gap in technology between the USSR and the West, a rapid radicalisation of systemic thinking was going on. Increased familiarisation with West-ern economic thought, personal contacts with Western peers and, what was perhaps more important, the changes in Poland and Hun-gary must also have acted in the direction mentioned.

The development of the views of L. Abalkin, who can be regarded as a moderate and still a follower of market socialism in 1990, may serve as a good example of the rapid radicalisation of views. In 1987, he took up positions which shaped the 1987 economic reform, being one of its main architects. Studying his publications which have appeared in the meantime, one can see clearly a rapid shift in his thoughts regarding the desirable reforms. In a sense, the evolution in his ideas mirrored the changes in the attitude of the Soviet govern-ment to the economic reform which he helped to mould in 1989–91 as the deputy prime minister for economic reforms.

I will discuss only those of his many studies which, in my opinion, show an important change in his thought. In his 1989 article titled 'The market in the socialist economic system', he no longer talks about commodity–money relations, which in itself indicates a shift in his thinking. He believes that the market is characteristic, not only of capitalism, but also of other social systems. The market under social-ism has specific features: it is not based on hired labour but on the labour of workers, proprietors of the means of production, on social-ist ownership, social guarantees and developed systems of planning. To him, the market should not be the only mechanism determining the proportions of production. Major scientifico-technical, social and economic programmes, and production and social infrastructure, should be planned. Planning should also have an impact on the microsphere.

In his 1990 article, which discusses the need for a radical reform, he makes important leaps in his outlook on many questions related to the economic system. He stresses the need to modernise property relations which is an old requirement. What is new is the principle adopted that none of the diverse forms of ownership should receive *a priori* support. There are, however, qualifications: forms of ownership which allow exploitation and alienation and prevent workers from participating in management are not admissible.

His concept of the socialist market has also changed; its scope is considerably widened. However, the function of the government is to remain important; it should have an exclusive role in the 'formation and development of the production and social infrastructure' and in the setting of rules for economic behaviour with the help of norms of socialist management. Since it is not clear what the author means exactly by 'norms of socialist management' and in addition, since he talks about the need to work out a new five-year plan, it is difficult to say how close his concept of the government role in the economy is to that of the West. At any rate, it is quite remote from what it had been, even in a reformed system. It is also important to stress that L. Abalkin does not want to achieve the transition to a market economy with the aid of shock treatment.

In his contribution to the discussion of the Party programme at the CC meeting (*P*, 1991, 29 July), L. Abalkin argues that what is needed is a highly efficient economy, adaptable to technological progress and sensitive to the social needs of human beings. Whether such an economy should be called capitalist or socialist is irrelevant.[14]

Needless to say, there were more radical and more conservative views than those of L. Abalkin. First, S. Shatalin's views will be discussed. In my opinion, it would be wrong to call him a neo-liberal, though, in the spectrum of views, his positions were more radical than those of L. Abalkin. Of course, as in the case of other economists, it is possible to notice a radicalisation of his views too. In a conference which was attended by many leading economists, Shatalin took the position that all forms of ownership should be treated equally, and further development would be linked to a gradual shrinking of state ownership (*P*, 1989, 15 September). In a 1990 interview, he took a more radical position, suggesting that state ownership should primarily be preserved in the infrastructure and argued against those who advocated the view that non-state ownership should prove its right to existence and demanded that state ownership should prove its usefulness.

In another interview (1990A) S. Shatalin takes the position that the government (republican) should intervene only when legal norms are violated. Otherwise, it should concern itself with the infrastructure and social issues. It should support business if it is interested in its development. He expresses opposition to shock treatment.

I have not come across a 1991 publication by S. Shatalin, except his open letter to Gorbachev (1991) in which he criticises the president for rejecting the programme associated with his (Shatalin's) name in order to satisfy the conservatives. The letter shows only one thing – he sticks to a transition to a market economy.

Perhaps E. Yasin's views best represent the radicals or even the neo-liberals. Of course, his views developed gradually, but most of the time they were ahead of other views in radicalism. In an article written together with his younger colleagues (Yasin et al., 1989) he called for the replacement of economic normatives by taxes and for a radical price reform, which would introduce flexibility, except for prices for primary resources and indispensable consumer goods.

In a paper entitled 'Socialist market or a fair of illusions?', which was accepted for publication only as a discussion paper (1989), he put price reform in the centre of reforms aimed at a transition to a market economy. He suggested following the Chinese example by introducing dual prices for enterprise products: regulated prices for products produced on government orders, and contractual and free prices for products produced by enterprises over and above government orders. In addition, retail prices, mainly those which were subsidised, should be increased.

In his 1990 paper, E. Yasin maintained that the 1987 reform, based on central planning and self-management, failed, and the only solution was a transition to a market economy. In enumerating the preconditions for a working market, he mentioned among others free prices, demonopolisation, competition, stable fiscal and monetary systems, and destatisation. As to a transition to a market economy, he advocated starting with a renewal of market equilibrium, whose achievement would be linked with free prices with a few exceptions, and later a continuing with the construction of the market mechanism. His opposition to shock treatment was substantiated by political reasons – by his conviction that the public would not accept such a measure.

In a paper published several months later (1991), he advocates harsh provisions which can be called shock treatment, except that convertibility of the *ruble* is at the end of the process. In brief, the programme includes instant elimination of the budget deficit, a restrictive monetary policy to the extent that it creates a shortage of money, freeing of prices with a few exceptions, minimal indexation of wages and incomes, and a suspension of most social programmes. The author argues that the economic situation has worsened to such an extent that only radical measures can rescue it.

At the other end of the spectrum, there were views of many shades, from views advocating market socialism to the extreme which can be called conservative, since they tried to preserve the maximum from the old system. I will mention here only two. A. Sergeev, head of the department of the Academy of Labour and Social Relations, suggested in a debate about privatisation (1991) that modified and differentiated mechanisms of planning (five-year for basic industries and no plans for light and consumer industries; they should work on the basis of contracts) should be applied instead of a leap into a spontaneous market.

I. Bratishchev et al. (1991) who, along with A. Sergeev, opposed general privatisation and instead proposed the transfer of assets to enterprise collectives (for more see pp. 221–2) took the position that in the competitive sector enterprise collectives should be free to plan, sell and divide up their receipts. There was, however, in their blueprint, one important restriction among others: enterprise collectives should not be allowed to change the general production orientation of the enterprise without the approval of the authorities. If the value of the enterprise declined or the enterprise did not fulfil the obligations it had taken on itself, the authorities could take the unit into their direct management for two years. In the non-competitive sector, enterprises should be managed by the authorities. This blueprint resembled the Hungarian system of 1985.

Planning

This will be a short section. Much of what can be said about the debates on planning has been discussed in earlier pages and will be discussed again in the sections on ownership and the concept of socialism. It is clear that, once a decision is taken to transform the economy into a market economy, central planning is at best relegated to the position of an adjunct of the market. It is known that the XIIIth five-year plan was in the process of preparation in 1989–90 and, according to the decree of M. Gorbachev of December 1989 (*CDSP*, 1990, no. 2, pp. 25–6), was supposed to be presented to the Supreme Soviet no later than 1 September 1990. It seems that this decree, like many other decisions, was overtaken by events. In L. Abalkin's report to the Supreme Soviet about practical steps for a transition to a market economy, no mention at all was made about the future role of planning (1990A). And in the Union prognosis and programme for 1992 (*EiZh*, 1991, no. 27), no reference was made to the five-year plan.

No doubt, central planning as a system of administrative assignment of output targets was completely discredited, and the 1987 reform had already meant a certain deviation from it. In the years following, further changes occurred in central planning.[15] With the decision to make the transition to a market economy, central planning increasingly lost its role and influence, partly because planning as such was exposed to guilt by association. This does not mean that central planning in a modified form cannot be useful, mainly in the transitional period to a market economy.

In the debates about the future economic system, planning was paid less and less attention in the course of the three years under review. Some felt that the role of planning was self-explanatory once they expressed themselves in favour of a transition to a market economy. No doubt, many of the radicals, particularly those who wanted to reduce the government to the job of being a night watchman, believed that planning had nothing to offer in a market economy. At the other end of the spectrum of views, there were economists who still wanted to preserve the old system in a slightly modified form.

Here I would like to mention only middle-of-the-road views, starting with Academician O. Bogomolov. In a paper (1989) in which he expressed his views on the future concept of socialism, he suggested replacing mandatory planning by indicative programming in order to ensure the independence of enterprises. This was at a time when the idea of indicative planning was still strange to most economists.

S. Dzarasov, head of the department of political economy of the Academy of Sciences, takes a pragmatic approach to planning (1990). He believes that it should be applied to the extent that it is effective. According to him the transition to a market economy does not preclude the planning of basic, particularly science- and investment-intensive branches.

V. Ivanchenko, one of the economists who devoted regular attention to planning had taken in the past a very conservative position. In his 1988 article, he had already criticised the 1987 reform for not bringing changes to the main functions of planning. In 1991, he discussed the role of planning under conditions of a market economy in the USSR. To him, a regulated economy should combine market and planning; the latter should regulate macroproportions and balance the economy, whereas the former should determine microproportions. Problems such as the restructuring of the economy, the promotion of technological progress, the conversion of military production etc. cannot be achieved without planning.

Ownership Relations

Some progress in ownership changes was achieved in the period from 1989 to September 1991, when this section was written. In 1990, a Union law on ownership was passed (*EiZh*, 1990, no. 12). It did not explicitly allow private ownership but the formulations used seem to indicate an implicit permission. At the same time, the law prohibited forms of ownership which produced alienation or exploitation. In February 1991, the Union government published a draft law on destatisation and privatisation (*EiZh*, 1991, no. 7).

The idea of destatisation, as long as it was understood in the narrow sense, that is, without privatisation (for more, see below), had already caught on during the first phase of the Gorbachev administration. This view was shared by advocates of the transition to a market economy and by those who did not want a changeover to a market economy but wanted to improve the economic mechanism. Of course, there were still economists who did not want any important change in state ownership.

The idea of privatisation was embraced only slowly and with reluctance, and perhaps only by a minority of economists. To many economists, privatisation meant an end to socialism, which they still cherished despite the many disappointments. For example, in his critical paper on the law of ownership, A. Aganbegian, who cannot by any means be labelled as a conservative, did not even mention private ownership when enumerating the possible forms of ownership in the USSR (1990).

Of course, the publication of the draft law on destatisation and privatisation promoted the idea of privatisation and increased the number of supporters of this idea. The discussion of the new Party programme, which sanctioned the transition to a market economy and privatisation, acted in the same direction. To many economists private ownership became not only acceptable but desirable. The exploitation argument had no longer any bearing on their thinking. Some members of this group argued that in modern times capitalism was not exploitative; others found the whole idea to be nonsensical and not deserving of any attention. In the first phase of the Gorbachev administration, economists saw their ideal in what they called societal ownership, which they identified with socialist ownership, and included under this collective name all forms of ownership permissible at that time. The new non-agricultural co-operatives, though many of them were a cover-up for private ownership, were also included in socialist ownership in order to lend them respectability. In the second phase, the labelling of something as socialist gradually ceased to be a recommendation. Private ownership became the slogan of the day; its advantages were stressed and overstressed.

The 1987 economic reform introduced self-management in enterprises, and in the minds of economists this became instantly the vehicle with which societal ownership could be achieved. In the dramatic shift in systemic thought, the idea of self-management was dropped or marginalised. True, the idea did not have much time to sink in as in Poland, but still, the way in which it was dropped attested to the great changes in the USSR.

As already indicated, destatisation can be understood in a broader and a narrower sense. In the narrower sense, it means that conditions are created under which the state cannot interfere operatively in enterprise affairs, in other words, enterprises become subject to a market regime. However the state remains the formal owner. This arrangement is called commercialisation. This is how N. Shcherbakov, the first deputy of the prime minister of the Union, who was responsible for the draft law on destatisation and privatisation, explained it in a meeting about the draft (*EiZh*, 1991, no. 26).[16] Destatisation can be achieved by converting enterprises into joint-stock companies or even, preferably, by turning leased enterprises into joint-stock companies. The broader definition includes not only destatisation but also, or even primarily, privatisation. This is how Shatalin's programme (*Perekhod* . . ., 1990, pp. 68–9), and Nikiforov and Kuznetsova (1991) understood it. The latter two authors viewed destatisation as a depriving of the state of its monopoly power, not only in the economy, but also in political and cultural life as well.

Privatisation is usually understood as the conversion of state enterprises into non-state enterprises. Selling enterprises to enterprise collectives or turning them into joint-stock companies where the state is not the only shareholder is also regarded as privatisation. The true adherents of privatisation wanted changes in ownership which would create genuine proprietors and would not impose any limits on the use of hired labour. To them, turning enterprises into joint-stock companies where the shareholders were state enterprises was not real privatisation. Opponents of privatisation were primarily against the ideas of the true believers.

Economists who favoured privatisation argued that it was a precondition for a transition to a market economy, which must be based on a preponderance of private ownership. Most believed that there was a direct relationship between ownership and motivation to work. In the debate already mentioned about the draft law (*EiZh*, 1991, no. 27), L. Abalkin expressed doubts about the correctness of this thesis. It was also argued by some economists that privatisation was a way to return to the people what had been taken from them. Shatalin's programme used this argument too.

The followers of privatisation were divided on many issues; I will discuss only two: pace and methods (sale at market prices or without charge). Pace was not such a bone of contention as one would expect. There was more or less an agreement that small-scale privatisation should be carried out by auctions and leases (with the right to buy the assets later) and that it could be accomplished relatively quickly. As to large privatisation, there was more or less agreement that it would take some time, for organisational and financial reasons. Even the Yavlinskii–Allison programme (*CDSP*, 1991, no. 25) did not assume a quick solution. True, V. Shcherbakov, the deputy prime minister of the day, suggested that the Union assets which made up one third of all the assets could be sold in four to five years. However, this calculation was based on the unrealistic assumption that the population would use its savings for buying assets. Reading carefully what the radicals and moderates had to say, one could detect a difference in their attitude: the former advocated privatisation as quickly as possible, whereas the moderates counselled caution, stressing peoples' unreadiness for such an action.

As in the small countries under review, the adherents of privatisation in the USSR were also divided in two camps on the question of whether assets earmarked for privatisation should be distributed without charge. Most debaters were against this; those in favour were primarily the radicals and the leaders of the Russian republic. In the debate mentioned (*EiZh*, 1991, no. 27), V. Shcherbakov argued that distribution without charge would increase social tensions because it was impossible to design a just system for such a distribution. In addition, it would not achieve the goal of privatisation, namely, to make people proprietors.[17] He was supported by L. Abalkin, V. Medvedev and R. Evstigneev. V. Medvedev, assistant to M. Gorbachev, argued that gratis distribution of assets made no economic sense. It could be politically or socially important but it represented a trap. In an article written before the debate (1991), he suggested that the issuing of coupons for the purchase of shares would enhance demand at a time of great shortages, and would not encourage people to engage in entrepreneurial activity.

In this same debate, I. Silaev, the prime minister of Russia, argued in favour of giving everyone 'starting means' as he called it. He justified his stand and that of the Russian government by referring to the absence of financial means for buying up the assets and the reluctance of the population to invest. In other words, the distribution of 'starting means' was supposed to accelerate privatisation.

This idea of giving starting means was elaborated by L. Nikiforov and T. Kuznetsova (1991). In order to give all workers, including retirees, an opportunity for an equal start, everyone should receive a share in republican wealth in the form of bonds, which could be used to buy shares in the worker's own enterprise, or in an enterprise of his choice, or to establish a business.

Opponents of privatisation were of two kinds. Both groups agreed that changes in ownership were unavoidable and, therefore, some solution to the problem must be found which would, at the same time, enable the socialist character of the economy to be preserved. In the first group, two alternatives to privatisation were put forward. In both, enterprise collectives were supposed to play a paramount role, but they differed as to management. This was to be in the hands of the collective in one alternative, and, in the other, in the hands of hired management. The second group was more in favour of a compromise which would, on the one hand, preserve state ownership in a modified form, and on the other hand, would allow genuine private ownership to a degree.

The views on the first alternative were well articulated by a group of academics, already mentioned, from different branches of the social sciences (I. Bratishchev et al., 1991). They did not object to destatisation but were against massive privatisation, though not against limited private ownership. To them the property which was in the hands of the state belonged to the people and the state had no right to sell it or distribute it without charge (they called it privatisation with a bribe). They favoured entrusting the management of the property to enterprise collectives (see also p. 216).

A. Sergeev's views expressed in the debate mentioned (*EiZh*, 1991, no. 26) could be regarded as representative of the second alternative. He argued against privatisation by maintaining that under Soviet conditions it would be impossible to achieve it even in 50 years. Financial stabilisation, which is the goal of privatisation, could best be achieved by an attack on the illegal underground economy, but such an action was contrary to the policy of privatisation. His alternative to the private economy was a transfer of property to enterprise collectives which would hire the management. Managers would be paid depending on the average wages of the workers, apparently for the purpose of stimulating them to do good work.

V. Kulikov and A. Akhmeduev are good examples of the second group. The former (1990) believed that socialism should be based on different forms of ownership competing with each other. Private ownership should also be allowed, primarily in agriculture and services, but based as much as possible on individual labour. State ownership should be democratised by enterprises becoming independent.

A. Akhmeduev (1991), who probably wrote his paper a year later than V. Kulikov, was prepared to accept a greater compromise. He, too, believed that private ownership should be limited, but allowed to use hired labour.

The Concept of Socialism

It was already indicated in Chapter 6 that in the debates in the USSR about the future economic mechanism, the concept of socialism received more attention than in other countries under review. This is understandable if one considers that the socialist system lasted longer in the USSR than in other countries and therefore permeated the consciousness of intellectuals more than anywhere else. The greater isolation of Soviet intellectuals from Western thought because of greater restrictions on travel abroad and access to literature also had its effect. Perhaps the most important factor was, as mentioned, that socialism in the Soviet Union was an indigenous phenomenon, whereas in the smaller countries under review it was regarded as an imported product from a country which was in low esteem and hated in Poland and Hungary for historical reasons.

It is understandable that if radical reforms, which were contrary to what real socialism was associated with in the intellectual mind, were on the agenda, the question about the fate of socialism would necessarily arise. Is the idea of socialism going to be dropped entirely, or is a new vision of socialism going to replace the old? These were legitimate questions. Needless to say, the vision of socialism changed on the whole with the radicalisation of the reforms. The average vision of socialism in 1989, when the trend was to a market economy which was still supposed to be socialist, was, of course, quite different than in 1991 after the CC meeting where a social democratic programme was largely adopted, or even more after the August 1991 *putsch*. As already indicated, views on the desirable concept of socialism varied. While many economists stuck to the idea of socialism, though in a modified form, many others turned their backs on it.

The redefinition of socialism was coupled with the abandonment of, or alterations in, many theories and ideas which underpinned real socialism. In the course of time, not only Lenin's but also Marx's many propositions were challenged. Marxism was not only cleared of many dogmas imposed on it by Stalinism, but many of its fundamental theories were questioned too.

Ideas about the concept of socialism were scattered throughout many articles dealing with the economic mechanism. But there were also many studies devoted only to the concept of socialism. Those ones which were the work of collectives of social scientists deserve special attention. For the beginning of the period under review, perhaps the best were the concepts worked out, at the request of *Pravda* ('Contemporary Concept . . .', 1989), by the social science division of the Praesidium of the Academy of Sciences. They were based on a discussion in which many well-known social scientists took part.[18] Another was the work of the editors of the theoretical journal of the Party, *Kommunist* ('New Aspects . . .', 1989) in consultation with the above-mentioned division of the Academy of Sciences.

What most studies on the concept of socialism had in common was that they were mostly a scathing criticism of real socialism which was largely the work of Stalin; they denounced the Stalinist model of socialism as a distorted model, unacceptable to modern society. What they offered instead was a concept of renascent socialism which varied, mainly as the crisis continued to deepen. Some still stuck to the ideas of Marx and Lenin (see, for example, Rakitskaia, 1990), while others tried to blend theoretical socialism with general civilisation components. And still others found the idea of socialism repulsive.

Academician O. Bogomolov (1989) maintained that real socialism of the Stalinist type was discredited and was to blame for the economic crisis. This was reflected in, among others, a lag behind the West in the most important indicators of economic performance.

Radaev and Auzan's (1989) criticism was even sharper: they called the Stalinist model state socialism; by this they meant a system in which the state is hypertrophically involved in social life. They regarded such a system as a primitive kind of socialism, a transitional phenomenon which came about because it was introduced at a time when economic and cultural conditions were not yet mature enough for genuine socialism. The less a country is developed, the more socialism takes on totalitarian features. The authors believed that the existing social and economic crisis was a result of the contradictions in state socialism.

When the authors came to characterise state socialism in more detail in the economic sphere, they mentioned the following, among others: distribution of income according to the position held in the hierarchy; and reproduction characterised by shortages which partly result from accumulation for the sake of accumulation.

The authors of the study in *Pravda* ('Contemporary Concept . . .', 1989) were no less critical; what is worth mentioning from their portrayal of state socialism, and what is not listed above, is: coercive organisation of labour; the system not equipped with a self-correcting mechanism; and the system having a tendency to autarky.

Up to now, I have discussed views criticising distortions in socialism. However, socialism was also challenged in its foundations. G. Shakhnazarov (1991) indirectly questioned Marx's interpretation of history as a motion from a lower to a higher level of social systems, driven by contradictions between productive forces and production relations. According to him, there is no proof that the development was linear from a lower to a higher level. In other words, the long-held thesis in the USSR that socialism was a higher stage in the development of mankind was challenged. To Shakhnazarov, revolutionary changes in productive forces and production relations were not the only factors of development. L. Abalkin (1991) called for a re-evaluation of Marxist–Leninist theories, such as, the class approach to society and the role of the state.

A. Yakovlev, one of the architects of *perestroika* and former member of the Politbureau of the Party, criticised the fact that the concept of socialism was still dominated by the dispute with capitalism: 'this dispute [about which classes exploit others] has long since become meaningless, for what must be brought to the fore is a vision of the economy as being a society's *life-support* system' (1990).

Most contributions to the debate about the future conception of socialism had in common several principles. Perhaps the most important was that the focus of socialism must be people and only socialism which was oriented to people and their interests was worth the name of socialism. In order to achieve this goal, democratisation of economic and political life was needed. Government must result from the people's will and must work for their interests. The government was for the people and not the opposite. Socialism can develop only in co-operation with capitalism. It must be an integral part of the world economy; it cannot develop outside the world economy. There is only one civilisation and socialism must be part of it (for example, 'New Aspects . . .', 1989).

In many studies the idea was put forward that the market was the best spontaneous human invention, no better alternative has yet been discovered, and, to ensure freedom for all, diverse forms of ownership must be instituted.

There was, of course, a difference in the characterisation of renascent socialism between the beginning of the period under review and the end. In the beginning many saw in Lenin's ideas, mainly from the period of NEP, guidelines for a renewal of socialism (for example, 'Contemporary concept . . .', 1989).

Interestingly enough, the article in the journal *Kommunist* ('New aspects . . .', 1989) contained few references to Lenin. But still the characterisation of future socialism was rather in the spirit of the first stage of the Gorbachev administration. Referring to Gorbachev's speech in July 1989 at the all-union conference of the CP, the authors maintained that socialism is 'a society based on principles of humanism, socialist democracy and social justice, different forms of collective ownership, self-regulation of the economic life with the coordinating role of the economic centre' (p. 7). The authors did not reject private ownership, but the emphasis was on self-managed, non-private ownership. The role of the market was stressed, but at the same time the need for regulation including planning was underscored.

With the passage of time, the features of real socialism, even in a modified form, faded away more and more in the suggested concepts of socialism. Let us recall L. Abalkin's speech at the meeting of the CC about the CP programme, in which he more or less blurred the difference between capitalism and socialism (see p. 214).

In his article, G. Shakhnazarov (1991) maintained that the present ideal was a system in which the economy would be market oriented, combined with high efficiency and competing diverse forms of ownership (capitalist principle), and would be equipped with a strong social safety net (socialist principle).

These were the views of the moderates. In 1991, to most radicals socialism was no longer a system which they wanted to be associated with.

CONCLUDING REMARKS

This chapter has shown that, in the period under review, Soviet systemic thinking developed at a different pace in individual phases. In the first half of the 1980s, the systemic thinking was more or less stagnant and was not much different from what had existed in the 1970s. In most publications, the old dogmatism prevailed. Even contributions which were permeated with some dissenting views were very modest in their demands. No doubt, dissenting views had tremendous difficulty finding their way into publications and, if they did, their authors could expect some sanctions. It is important to stress that most economists accepted the regime and believed that it had a legitimate claim to their loyalty. Even in the worsening economic situation, they always found reasons to absolve the regime. If they criticised living conditions – and they often did – they confined themselves to peripheral issues and consciously or unconsciously avoided pinpointing the real reasons for the shortcomings. Needless to say, there were people who did not mince words when the conversation turned to economic life, but this was almost always in small groups of friends, or, more often, in family circles.

In the second half of the 1980s, and especially in 1990–1, systemic thinking went through a dramatic development: it became radicalised in a relatively short period of time. The rapidly worsening economic situation was an important reason for this development. More and more economists started to believe that only radical solutions could save the economy from a catastrophe.

The wavering and hesitancy of M. Gorbachev when he was faced with a choice between different reform proposals also contributed to radicalisation. Had he had a definite, reasonable concept of how the reformed system should look, a strategy to achieve it and the willingness to put his prestige on the line for such a concept and strategy, perhaps the decline of the economy could have been stopped, the fight with Yeltsin reduced and, with it, the unreasonable radicalisation prevented.

The fight for power between M. Gorbachev and B. Yeltsin, complicated by the fight between the conservatives and the radicals and between the Union and the republics, contributed also to radicalisation. It made it almost impossible for them to agree on a reasonable economic reform and, if an agreement was achieved, it was short lived, as, for example, the Shatalin programme. In this fight both M. Gorbachev and B. Yeltsin looked for help in the West. B. Yeltsin, in order to disarm Western suspicion of him and diminish M. Gorbachev's head start, adjusted his views very much according to the wishes of the West. And the West was interested in radicalisation, hoping in this way to achieve its goals in the USSR.

M. Gorbachev's lack of a clear concept and strategy also had another effect. He will, no doubt, enter into history as a great reformer. The dismantling of the Soviet authoritarian regime will be associated with his name. But M. Gorbachev did not achieve what, no doubt, he wanted to achieve: to reform the Soviet system into a democratic socialist system. Many historians will surely try to answer the question why his dream was not turned into reality. In the beginning, he was at the helm of the reform movement, mainly in the political sphere. Because he did not have a clear vision of what he wanted, because it became very difficult to coordinate political and economic reforms and because there was unprecedented political relaxation not matched with economic changes, he undermined the small chance of success the economic reform had, and, after a while, lost the lead and was carried by events instead of controlling them.

It is clear that M. Gorbachev could not have come up with a radical economic reform in 1985; he would have been ousted by his colleagues in the Politbureau. This is not to say that nothing could have been done to make the economy healthier. The campaign initiated by Gorbachev to increase motivation for work, which was a good idea, should not have been waged at the cost of a huge increase in the budget deficit. In two or three years, the public could have been prepared by education and propaganda for the gradual denationalisation of small-scale businesses and service facilities, and especially for the leasing of land, according to the Chinese example. A great portion of small scale businesses could have been sold at auctions in 1987 and 1988 and provisions undertaken to support the rise of private businesses by extending credits and other incentives. After proper preparation, privatisation of a large part of middle- and large-sized enterprises could have been put on the agenda. (For more about the possible model of transformation, see Chapter 11.)

The model suggested in Chapter 11 contrasts with shock treatment or even with Shatalin's programme. The authors of Shatalin's proposal were correct when they attacked the 'Guidelines' (1990), arguing that urgent provisions were needed. However, the transition to a market economy in the USSR could not and cannot be accomplished in 500 days; such an action requires much more time. The Yavlinskii–Allison proposal was more realistic in this respect. Shatalin et al. assumed that most legislation would be prepared in 100 days; this is an impossible venture if the legislation is supposed to be discussed in a democratic way (with the republics and different interest groups) and to be free of any contradictions and loopholes.

The aborted *coup d'état*, which was intended, among other things, to thwart the signing of the Union agreement because the plotters did not agree with the creation of a loose Union, brought about the opposite; it largely contributed to the destruction of the planned new Union structure which had been put together with such great diplomatic skills. It also opened the way for Yeltsin – who on the one hand, organised a successful resistance to the plotters and on the other, helped by his behaviour to bury the Union – to outmanoeuvre Gorbachev. The Commonwealth of Independent States, the brainchild of Yeltsin, meant an end to Gorbachev's presidency.

It was clear that Yeltsin, who was less committed to an ideology than Gorbachev, would be more willing to accommodate Western ideas about economic reform than his rival, all the more because the West was willing to promise help only on condition that the USSR embarked on a radical reform. Therefore it is no great surprise that Yeltsin's Russia and, with it, the former countries of the USSR, have resorted to shock treatment in the form of the freeing of prices as the first step in the transformation effort (see interview with A. Shokin, deputy prime minister of Russia, *CDSP*, 1991, no. 44). This is a very risky provision considering Russia's collapsed distribution system, financial instability, rapid depreciation of the *ruble* and huge monopolisation of the economy. It will probably produce hyperinflation, huge unemployment and may provoke social unrest. In brief, it may have even more negative consequences than the shock treatment had in Poland. The therapy surely has support among domestic neoliberals and the West, which believes that the sooner the old economic structures are destroyed, the better. However, such calculation may easily turn out to be counterproductive. If it brings about a huge decline in production and in the standard of living and, in addition, causes high unemployment, the old political forces or the extreme right forces may gain popular support for an attempt to return to or gain power respectively.

Notes

1. 'During those years I had learned that Russia was a split-level society, with an official public facade and another reality in private' (H. Smith, 1990, p. 11).
2. A qualification to this statement is in order. The views expressed in the volumes were not, of course, shared by all economists; many undoubtedly had more radical views; perhaps even some of the contributors, who, however, went along for various reasons.
3. According to the author (Zaslavskaia, 1990, p. 2), this was the name given in the West to the paper which she presented in a seminar.
4. The discussion took place after Gorbachev's advent to power and was influenced by it, but it was still focused on the 1983 experiment.
5. In China, products resulting from output capacity not under the state control could be sold at market prices. No such arrangement existed in the USSR.
6. It seems that participants in debates express more radical views than in their own publications, one reason being perhaps that in a collective people lose their normal fear.
7. D. Doder and L. Branson (1990) maintain that Ligachev's supporters demanded a prohibition on the types of articles written by N. Shmelev.
8. N. Shmelev suggested, however, leasing land to peasants.
9. I use the term 'societal' for the Russian *obshchestvennyi*, since I feel that the term 'social' may lead to confusion.
10. Shatalin's programme was the work of a collective, to which G. Yavlinski, N. Petrakov and E. Yasin, among others, belonged. Originally, L. Abalkin was also supposed to be a member, but, because of conceptual disagreements, he left the collective.
11. A good overview of the Guidelines . . .(which are also known by the name 'presidential' or 'programme of Aganbegian' who was its architect) is given in a joint study of four institutions, among them the International Monetary Fund and the World Bank (*The Economy* . . ., 1990).
12. For more about price increases, see *P*, 1991, 20 and 21 March.
13. He distinguishes the 'extra-market development' group (conservative), which wanted to preserve the old system with some modifications, the 'market extremism' group, which believed that the government role in the economy should be minimal, and the 'regulated market' group, which favoured government policy and which was also favoured by A. Aganbegian himself.

14. This statement should be taken with a certain reservation since it is based on an abbreviated report in *Pravda*.
15. The debate among functionaries of the Planning Commission gives a good survey of the changes carried out and intended in central planning (*PKh*, 1990, no. 4).
16. The meeting in which M. Gorbachev, S. Pavlov, I. Silaev and L. Abalkin, among others, attended was reported in *EiZh*, 1991, nos 26 and 27.
17. In the name of the Union government, Shcherbakov suggested that only assets depreciated by more than 70 per cent and apartments under certain conditions could be distributed without charge.
18. This was conceived on the basis of a seminar in which L. Abalkin, O. Bogomolov and T. Zaslavskaia, among others, participated.

10 Czechoslovakia

INTRODUCTION

In Czechoslovakia, the normalisation process (a catchword for a return to the pre-reform situation) which started in April 1969, after A. Dubček and his supporters were ousted from the leadership of the CP, imposed strict control over the intellectual life of the country. Not all groups acquiesced in this without active opposition to the deprivation of human rights. A small segment of the intelligentsia, composed of different professions, seized many opportunities to demonstrate to the authorities that it was prepared to fight for its rights with peaceful means, even at the risk of imprisonment. The most notable demonstration of this determination was the establishment of the Charter 1977, an organisation which committed itself to monitoring the extent to which Czechoslovakia honoured the obligations which it took on when it signed the United Nations Accord on human rights.[1]

As in other countries of the former CMEA, the economic situation in Czechoslovakia began to worsen in the second half of the 1970s. It was, however, in the lucky situation of being much less indebted to the West than its neighbours and therefore, for political and ideological reasons, could better resist pressure for major economic reform. It followed the Soviet pattern more or less slavishly. In 1979 the Soviets came up with some minor changes in their system of management. Czechoslovakia followed suit in 1980. In 1984, a much more comprehensive 'reform' was initiated by Andropov's administration. In no time, Czechoslovakia had imitated the USSR. It even imitated Gorbachev's 1987 economic reform, though it resented his *glasnost*.

The 1987 Czechoslovak economic reform, which was not supposed to be implemented fully until 1991, was not a radical reform when measured by the standard of the 1966–9 reform (for more, see Adam, 1989, pp. 190–207), but at least it was a sign that the authorities were reacting to domestic and external pressures. The reform brought about a measure of political relaxation and a more favourable environment for research and the exchange of views. This was at a time when most radical reformers had started to lose or had already lost their belief in the reformability of the economic mechanism. There were probably some who believed in market socialism. The radical reformers were not of the same view as to how to solve the economic problems. All agreed that a market economy was the solution, but they varied in their views on how to achieve it, which became clear once the transition to a market economy was put on the agenda and economists were free to express their ideas. The solidarity which had existed among the radical reformers, in the face of an oppressive power, disappeared once the pressure was gone.

In 1988–9, the Czechoslovak leaders realised increasingly that their rule was coming to an end. Of course, they tried everything imaginable to rescue as much as possible of the system or at least to postpone the end. They sent one delegation after another to Moscow seeking help. They were even willing to transfer power under certain conditions to some communist who was not discredited. According to reliable sources, they invited Z. Mlynář, a secretary of the Central Committee of the Party in 1968 and presently a professor in Austria, to Prague for such negotiations. When the M. Németh government in Hungary decided to allow East German tourists, numbered in thousands, to go to West Germany, instead of to their own country, the Czechoslovak government also came under pressure to do the same. And it did. This was a good sign to the Czechoslovak dissenters that the Communist leadership was demoralised and no longer able or willing to undergo a real fight to sustain its rule. On the other hand, the usually careful Czechs were prepared to put up a fight for their rights. This was confirmed during the anniversary of the International Student Day. When student demonstrations were confronted by the police and some students were beaten, huge masses joined the students, and the communist government was forced to accept the demands of the dissenters which meant an end to communist rule.

Since during most of the 1980s there was not an environment in Czechoslovakia for the free exchange of views, I will discuss this period briefly in so far as it concerns our topic. This will leave more space for a discussion of the evolution of views on the eve of the 'velvet' revolution, and especially for contrasting ideas about the transition to a market economy.

THE 'REFORMS' OF 1980 AND 1984

The focus of the 1980 'reform' ('provisions for the perfection of the system of planned guidance of the economy', as it was officially called) was on an improvement in planning for the purpose of ensuring economic equilibrium, and growth in economic efficiency. This was to be achieved primarily by enhancing the time horizon of plans, integrating prognostication into planning, improving the methods of drafting plans and their disaggregation, increasing the effectiveness of control and improving the evaluation of plans, and also by an application of modern technology, better utilisation of resources and closer integration into an international division of labour. These were not new principles – one could find them in various speeches of CP functionaries; what was new was that they were elaborated and specified. Perhaps the most important changes were the dropping of gross value of output and its replacement by adjusted net output[2] as an indicator, the alteration of some wholesale prices to better reflect price movements in world markets, and the adoption of the principle of continuous price changes (*SHN*, 1980, nos 11, 12).

The 1984 changes underscored the importance of economic efficiency and called for the integration of demanding international standards in the efficiency criteria. In the drafting of plans, a greater utilisation of value categories (prices, exchange rates, credits) was suggested. A greater role was assigned to profit and normatives (*SHN*, 1984, nos 42 and 43). In neither of the documents was the market given an explicit role; it was, however, implicitly assumed that the market would increase in importance.

The direction of the 'reforms' more or less set the framework for research and also for the debates. Some saw the solution to the problem of promoting economic efficiency, the main purpose of the reforms, primarily in improving central planning, others in extending greater autonomy to enterprises. After the 1984 'reform', mainly after Gorbachev committed the USSR to *perestroika*, the idea of greater autonomy for enterprises started to be more and more stressed.

The debates about the improvement of central planning revolved to a great degree around the system of indicators. This was a natural phenomenon since the nature of indicators determines to a great degree the behaviour of enterprises and puts its imprint on the system of management. Therefore authors who wanted changes in the economic mechanism pushed for changes in the system of indicators. Often a suggestion for a change in indicators, mainly if profit was suggested, was a shorthand call for transformation of the management system.

Needless to say, in the period discussed the authors still believed in the reformability of the management system. After all, even in Hungary and Poland, where the reform movement had progressed much further, the reformability of the system was still not challenged.

I will first discuss the debate on indicators and then turn to the more general debate on planning.

Performance Indicators

The debate on indicators was initiated by V. Kyzlink (1983) and continued almost the whole year in the columns of the weekly *Hospodářské noviny* (*HN*). V. Kyzlink suggested using net profit as a gauge of the performance of enterprises. This had to bring an end to the practice of giving each enterprise efficiency tasks which corresponded to its conditions. Perhaps he also assumed that such an arrangement would make the assignment of output targets superfluous. To make net profit the basic indicator, the author called for prices to be made an objective category, by linking them to world market prices or to create separate prices for CMEA countries.

M. Matějka (1983) posed the question whether introduction of profit, as a single indicator, would not deny a role to the plan. His answer was negative. The activities of enterprises should move in the framework of a physical plan. He did not forget to mention that the planning of products from the centre should be limited only to cases where the authorities were able to do the job better than individual enterprises.

J. Vejvoda (1983) admitted that under existing conditions it was impossible to make prices an objective category unless domestic prices were based on world market prices. Such a solution was unacceptable to him since this would mean an introduction of competitive capitalist relations and an elimination of peoples' ownership.

It is interesting that J. Matějka (1983), who was a functionary of the government committee for the affairs of planned management of the economy, criticised Vejvoda and did not try to defend the adopted indicator, adjusted net output, which, as could be expected, did not become a stimulus for higher economic efficiency.

Improvement of Planning

M. Toms (1983) was a good representative of economists who did believe that by improving planning the economic mechanism could be made more efficient. He explicitly rejected the idea that just the expansion of the autonomy of enterprises could solve the problem of low efficiency. The views of Soviet optimal planners resonated in his thinking, and he looked for a solution in the concept and exactingness of the plan itself. To this end, he advocated an elimination of the duality in planning, namely, the use of plan indicators and indicators of efficiency; the indicator of economic efficiency – net profit – should permeate all planning considerations and become the fundamental aspect in drafting plans in all their stages, including the evaluation of the plan's fulfilment. Since rational prices are a precondition for profit to be a reliable indicator, the author suggested replacing the two concepts of prices – cost prices and prices of optimal plan – by a single price concept which would include social labour cost and other costs as well as the degree to which social needs were satisfied. The meaning of the latter was, however, not explained.

The book edited by and mostly written by J. Dvořák (1985) was quite critical of the 1980 reform as well as of the system of management. The authors criticised the system for, among others, the instability of the economy, caused to a great degree by its low adaptability to the technological changes taking place. However, they did not suggest any radical solutions, but rather improvements in planning. So they agreed with the introduction of net profit as the main indicator, thus giving to indirect methods (prices, taxes, credit) an opportunity, but warned that these must be combined with direct methods, mainly with the regulation of wages (1985, pp. 180–9).

One of the many deficiencies of the administrative system was that the formulation of the central plan depended on enterprises for information primarily about their productive capacities and the labour intensity of products produced by them. When plan fulfilment was the main indicator, this encouraged enterprises to conceal reserves. The authors suggested that the problem could be solved if the centre could also get information about norms of utilisation of resources and comparative studies of performance in the best enterprises at home and abroad (pp. 172–3). This suggestion seems to be theoretically possible, but must surely be practically impossible.

I. Okáli and his colleagues (1983)[3] can be regarded as representative of the believers in a greater role for enterprises, primarily in the determination of output mix. Suppliers and buyers were to agree about the structure of goods to be shipped and inform the planners about their contracts before the plans started to be drafted; thus the contracts would become part of the plan-compilation process. If it turned out that the contracts were in conflict with the plan, they could be adjusted. The authors hoped that such a procedure would bring to an end a situation in which the suppliers seemed to represent collective interests, and that it would put both partners (suppliers and buyers) in an equal position.

In this concept, market relations are given a certain role. However, the authors made it clear that they did not intend to relegate planning to an indicative function. The centre was still supposed to set directly qualitative tasks (probably profit), limits and, of course, macro-economic regulation (1983, p. 339).

A. Červinka (1985) goes much further than the Slovak authors. To improve the working of the economic mechanism, it is important to find an optimal division of decision-making between the centre and enterprises. According to him, the centre works well if it concentrates on setting long-term development goals, ensuring macro-economic proportions and creating a favourable environment for the working of enterprises. Enterprises themselves should determine what to produce on the basis of effective demand at home and abroad.

An inconsistency is noticeable at the end of the article where Červinka calls for a reduction in output targets. It is not out of the question that the author's last statement was only a tribute to the existing ideology in order to avoid a conflict with the authorities. Such tactics were not infrequently used by intellectuals.

V. Kadlec, education minister and rector of the School of Economics in 1968, expressed his views about the economic mechanism and economic situation in *Listy* (1983), appearing in Munich. According to him, the recessional phenomena in Czechoslovakia were the direct result of unprofessional central plans. These produced, to mention the most important ills of the economy, market disequilibria as a result of inflationary incomes that were not matched by goods and services; disequilibrium between the ambitious planned targets in investment and the real resources available for their implementation; and a demand which outstripped the potential supply of labour. He also blamed planning for the rise of a new class of people who made fortunes from shortages. His criticism was not directed at planning as such. He wanted, however, at the same time to allow the working of the market, at least to the extent demanded in the Action programme of the 1968 economic reform.

ON THE EVE OF THE VELVET REVOLUTION (1987–1989)

The period 1987–9 was in several respects different from the previous one. The external conditions, relevant to Czechoslovakia, changed considerably. The Congress of the Soviet CP which took place in 1986 committed the country to a radical reform and in the June 1987 meeting of the CC of the Party, M. Gorbachev's blueprint for the economic reform was approved. Czechoslovak leaders could ignore what was happening in Hungary and Poland, but not the systemic changes in the USSR; after all, the official propaganda had coined and used for many decades the slogan, 'the USSR is our example'. The Czechoslovak leaders reluctantly came up with an economic reform.

In 1987 the Czechoslovak CC of the CP and the government approved the principles of a new reform (*SHN*, 1987, no. 5; and *SHN*, 1988, no. 8). The reform blueprint meant progress compared with what had existed before, but it lagged far behind the Hungarian or for that matter the Polish reform. It was similar to the Soviet in that it was still marked by many features characteristic of a centralised system. The reform still envisaged output targets, though in a much-reduced number of cases, and limits in the case of deficit inputs and in foreign trade. Normatives were to play an important role. Limited self-management in enterprises was also promised.

The reform was also supposed to bring some changes in planning, the most important being the reduction of the role of physical planning. Financial flows should play an active role in the drafting of plans and not simply adjust to the set physical targets and proportions. Equilibrium of the economy must result from the equilibration of financial flows and material balancing.

Even if the Czechoslovak Communist leaders did not accept Gorbachev's *glasnost*, they could not avoid some political relaxation. The new atmosphere brought back into a full, active, intellectual life many former top economic reformers of 1968, such as K. Kouba, O. Turek and Č. Kožušník, to mention just a few. These people had been forced to spend the last twenty years in manual, or some low administrative, positions, a long enough time to ponder the past, including their world outlook. No wonder that most of them changed their attitude to the system which they had helped to build, but which had mismanaged the economy and destroyed their lives, aspirations and dreams. Most of them also turned their backs on the idea of socialism itself.

This was also a period of dramatic events, mainly in 1988–9. In 1988 the Hungarian Communist leaders committed themselves to a transition to a market economy and, in 1989, to a multi-party system. In Poland in 1989, the CP and Solidarity agreed on a multi-party system and market economy (for more see Chapters 7 and 8). Of course, all these events were possible because dramatic changes were taking place in the USSR. All these changes raised expectations in Czechoslovakia that the antiquated system at home would eventually come to an end. The question was only what would come in its place and when and how it would come. The position one took on all these questions had necessarily an impact on one's thinking and the nature of one's publications.

Before 1987, in Hungary and Poland, the idea of irreformability of the system had already begun to spread rapidly. More and more economists came to believe that only a transition to a market economy could solve the problems which confronted the countries. The change in thinking in the neighbouring countries surely contributed to the rapid growth of followers of this idea in Czechoslovakia, an idea which was openly defended by many, even before the 'velvet' revolution. This does not mean that socialism was rejected by all economists. Many remained faithful to the system and called only for changes in the economic mechanism, while others believed in market socialism, and still others used market socialism as a shield against accusations of heresy.

The dramatic changes in thinking did not find their way into publications until 1988 and 1989. In 1987, the Party still did not allow open dissenting views to be published. Therefore, the 1987 economic reform was evaluated positively even by economists who surely did not agree with it. In making judgments about publications one must bear this fact in mind.

In this section I will first discuss how some economists reacted to the 1987 reform, then views about the desirable reforms.

The 1987 Reform

In the eyes of many economists, the reform was regarded as too little too late. M. Matějka, professor of the School of Economics (1988), may have fired the first salvo in the head-on attack. He was soon followed by Z. Vergner, former director of the planning commission research institute (1989), and others.

M. Matějka first subjected to criticism the idea of planning in the form it was conceived in the textbooks on the political economy of socialism. He argued that the capacities ascribed to planning were wishful thinking rather than anything else. It was impossible to secure proportional development of production from the centre. Material balancing was only applied to a limited number of products. In addition, he maintained that efforts to secure proportionality with the help of planning must necessarily impede the development of the economic structure. Also in the author's view, to want to guide the economy by five-year plans necessarily meant dooming the economy to retardation in technology (no explanation why is given).

Both M. Matějka and Z. Vergner criticised mainly the administrative elements of the reform. So they felt that the assumed continuing rationing of producer goods, though to a reduced extent, would introduce irrationalities into the economy. M. Matějka argued that, in light of the intended reduction of compulsory output targets, the authorities would not have a guide for allocating producer goods. Z. Vergner believed that limits on allocated producer goods would necessarily lead, as in the past, to hoarding and an inefficient use of producer goods.

Both also criticised the planned continuation of wage control and even more the supposed wholesale price reform, based on old methods. Z. Vergner also objected to the failure of the reform to eliminate the separation of price circuits. He finished his contribution with a reminder that 'socialism was a continuation of commodity production under changed ownership relations'.

M. Matějka's attack did not remain long without response. The latter came from the secretary of the government committee for the affairs of planned management of the economy, J. Matějka (1988). His main argument was that M. Matějka misinterpreted the gist of the reform and that limits were only a temporary solution. It was a sign of changed times that nobody of stature among the conservative economists who had consulted or assisted J. Matějka came to his help.

Of the economists who did not take part directly in the debate but who criticised the 1987 reform, mention will be made of M. Hrnčíř's and K. Dyba and K. Kouba's contributions. Hrnčíř (1988), a senior researcher of the Economic Institute, showed that the 1987 reform blueprint continued in the old tracks and did not represent a genuine restructuring of the economic mechanism as was promised. In the reform blueprint, central planning was defined as a type of vertical coordination and regulation. In analysing what this meant in the traditional system, the author pinpointed the weak elements of the system and their consequences, one being monopolisation of the economy. He correctly found the normative method, on which the reform was to be based, to be defective, and he came to the conclusion that the reform would have little positive impact on the economy.

K. Dyba and K. Kouba[4] (1989) first discussed the 1958 and 1968 reforms. They stressed that the 1968 reform continued even after the Soviet-led invasion, and that proposals were prepared and some of them approved for the expansion of market forces, including a capital market, which were thwarted by the political changes. Their main criticism of the 1987 reform lay in their contention that the reform was of a hybrid nature, combining ideas of 'perfecting (as in the late 1950s) with some features of the market-oriented reform from the late 1960s'. In more concrete terms, they faulted the authorities for their intention to preserve administrative prices, for strengthening monopolisation instead of breaking it up, for not going far enough in reforming foreign relations, and for not revising the old strategy of economic growth.

Desirable Reforms

Disregarding the conservative views which wanted to preserve in substance the existing system, it is possible to divide the ideas of 1988–9 on how to restructure the economic system into three groups. At one end of the spectrum were views which in some respects were near to the principles of the Hungarian reform, rather of the 1960s, and at the other end were the followers of a free market economy.

The latter, even if they did not say so in so many words, viewed the socialist system as a bankrupt system which did not lend itself to a reform since it was based on faulty foundations. True, they did not call for privatisation of the economy, but only because they felt that it was untimely. It would be wrong to assume that this was a uniform group. Many members saw in the market economy the best possible solution, but not a panacea to all the ills of the economy. And therefore they counted on an important role for the government. Others believed that the transfer of the economy to the 'invisible hand' would solve all the problems. In their view government intervention should be minimal. They took more or less the position of their mastermind, M. Friedman.

The middle of the spectrum was dominated by views which could be characterised with some qualification as market socialism. It is not clear whether those who professed market socialism regarded it as preferable under existing conditions or favoured it as a permanent solution – as a third way.

J. Dvořák and Z. Hába can be regarded as representative of the first group. In his early 1988 article, J. Dvořák evaluated the 1987 reform positively, though he also had some critical comments. Considering this contribution, but mainly the one in 1989, one can get an idea, though not a complete one, about the author's view on the desirable direction of the reform. In his 1988 article, J. Dvořák, among others, called for profit to be made a genuine gauge of performance and for an end to basing prices on costs. He also stressed the more innovative suggestions in the 1987 reform, such as an active role for value relations in compiling state plans, a shift to strategic planning and a substantial reduction in targets.

In his 1989 article, the author suggested a new approach to full employment. Enterprises should be concerned only with the efficient use of the work force; full employment, as well as the placement of dismissed workers, should be the concern of the state. It is clear that all changes mentioned assumed a certain role for market forces.

Unlike J. Dvořák, Z. Hába (1987, 1987A) did not specifically mention the Hungarian reform, and his papers were probably written before the publication of the 1987 reform, but after the 1986 CC decision to institute a reform. Both his papers dealt with market relations. The one published in *Nová mysl* concentrated exclusively on this topic, and therefore this will be discussed. To him commodity–money relations should be an integral part of the socialist economic mechanism. Their relegation to a formality in the past had damaged the economy. Market forces cannot, however, play the same role under socialism as under capitalism because of collective ownership. It is important to create conditions for market forces which would enable them to support the aims and goals of a socialist society. The plan cannot effectively encompass all activities; many of them can be performed efficiently only by decentralisation, and thus the market comes into play. The market should, however, be a planned market.

V. Komárek's and L. Rusmich's views can be classified as market socialism with some qualifications, mainly with regard to the latter. V. Komárek's[5] prolific research and publication activity was primarily directed at the structural changes needed in the economy in order for Czechoslovakia to join the group of countries with the most efficient economies. Of course, he also devoted attention to systemic questions. His views are best articulated in his 1989 paper in *Politická ekonomie*. According to him, one of the greatest mistakes of socialism was to negate the law of value and repress the market mechanism. An efficient development of the economy can only be achieved by a transfer to a market economy. Such a step does not mean abandoning socialism.

The market can ensure short-term proportionality much better than planning can. The role of planning is to regulate the market, but the market should regulate the activities of enterprises. In his paper in *Hospodářské noviny* (1989A) he contends that this regulation of the market will enable 'the negative economic impact of the market, primarily mass unemployment and inflation', to be averted.

Komárek also called for the renewal of different forms of socialist ownership and for allowing people to participate in the management of the economy and society.

L. Rusmich, nowadays a senior research fellow of the Institute for National Economic Research, belongs to the group of researchers who always fought for the application of market forces in the economy even at times when it was not popular to do so.[6] In a paper written by M. Hrnčířová and him (1989), the authors treat the market as a neutral coordinating mechanism which works in different systems. Socialism is to them a higher type of commodity production. However, market relations should be limited; planning should regulate the market with the goal of preventing monopolisation, capital and labour markets. Though socialism has not yet proven its superiority over capitalism, they hope that socialism, as a more humane society, will replace capitalism, but 'it will absorb its civilisation contributions and develop them'.[7]

Prior to the 'velvet' revolution Z. Šulc (1990), a prolific economist who was silenced for twenty years, took a position which was somewhere between the second and third group of views. He believes that the correct division of systems is into two – 'a central distributive mechanism' and 'a regulated money market mechanism' – and that the two systems cannot be mixed. In a centrally distributive system, economic units behave in the same way regardless of ownership relations, whether they are based on capitalist or socialist ownership. He backs up his statement by alluding to the behaviour of enterprises under the Nazi planned economy. Central planning in the market economy, which he prefers, should be binding only on the government, which should regulate the economy primarily by fiscal policy.

He discusses the preconditions needed in order to make enterprises fully entrepreneurial units without substantial privatisation.

The third group gained in influence as the crisis in the political system deepened. Many who belonged to the third group play important roles at present in shaping the economy.

O. Turek, a senior research fellow of the Forecasting Institute, for the most part explained his views in three papers. In the 1988 article which is a criticism of the 1987 reform on a general level, the author revealed his views by comparing the two possibilities of coordinating economic activities and by making it clear that he favoured coordination by market prices. Coordination of economic activities under socialism – according to him – becomes more and more difficult with the changes taking place in advanced economies.

In his 1989 article O. Turek discussed economic performance and social comfort (by which he means in substance a social safety net). He believes that the extent of social programmes should be determined by the performance of the economic system. There is also an indirect relationship between economic performance and social programmes. It seems to him that the less consideration a country gives to social programmes, the more efficient its economy can be. He believes that Sweden is losing its place in world economic rankings because of its stress on social policy, whereas Japan's economy is robust because its economic policy favours the strong actors in the economy. One of the important motivations for a transition to the administrative system (socialism) was the desire for social guarantees, which hampered economic reforms. A return to a market economy, which is a precondition for an efficient economy, must be – according to the author – combined with a weakening of some social guarantees.

In his earlier article (1989), written with T. Ježek,[8] the authors discuss the role of the state. According to them, the state's primary responsibility is to formulate the rules and conditions under which business can work. The role of the state should be limited in business; if engaged in business it must comply with the general rules and conditions valid for enterprises.

K. Kouba expressed his views about the desired reforms in mainly foreign publications. One, written with K. Dyba, which criticised the 1987 reform and thus indirectly indicated the authors' views on the nature of desirable reforms, was discussed above. Here it remains to discuss the paper which was published in the Hungarian theoretical journal *Közgazdasági Szemle* (1990).[9]

In this article, he maintained that the economic reforms were not successful since none managed to bring about a rational price system. Most price reforms were based on the assumption that prices should serve economic policy or be an instrument for plan fulfilment. K. Kouba, who aspired to transform the existing economic system into a market economy, understandably regarded the replacement of central planning by free prices as the essence of the transformation.

After subjecting the existing price system to criticism, the author expressed the view that the price liberalisation should be gradual and simultaneous with the creation of competitive markets. At the same time, it was necessary to produce an equilibrated exchange rate.

K. Dyba approached the problem of restructuring the economic system from the viewpoint of international economic relations, which is his specialisation. He (1989) tried to prove that the performance of the Czechoslovak economy was closely linked to the fluctuations in the world economy. The worsening of the economic performance after the second half of the 1970s was the result of the inadequate adaptability of the Czechoslovak economy to the development of the world economy, the main reason being that the planners did not distribute investment funds 'according to the changing comparative advantages of export opportunities'. To cure the situation it was necessary, argued the author, to open the Czechoslovak economy fully, and this was possible only in a marketised economy where administrative planning was in substance abolished.

V. Klaus, the main architect of the current concept of transition to a market economy, was – as could be expected – a zealous adherent of marketisation. In an article written with D. Tříska (1988), both authors professed to be macro-economists; by using this name, they wanted to dissociate themselves from 'traditional reformists', who, in their view, claimed to favour a pro-market orientation, but in reality did not want a fully fledged market, based on consumer sovereignty and a capital and labour market.

In his 1989 article V. Klaus discussed the institutional changes needed for a transition to a market economy. To him, the planning centre must be separated from the economic centre and should not have either financial funds or direct contact with enterprises. It should be responsible for, among others, the strategic development of the economy, for probes into the working of the economy and for evaluation of government interventions. The monetary centre must also be separated from the economic centre, and – as explained in the 1988 paper – must ensure macroeconomic equilibrium, the latter being linked to an optimum stock of money. He counselled against a policy of gradual changes, arguing that 'short pain is better than long lasting pain'.

'Structuralists' and 'Systemists'

In the period under review, the comparisons of performance and of the potential of the Czechoslovak economy with those of its neighbours and with advanced capitalist countries became popular research topics. The motives for such research were not only strictly scientific; they had certain other purposes, one being to prove the need to restructure the economy or the economic system, or both. This interest in comparative studies increased once the Forecasting Institute had published the first partial results of its research into the state of the Czechoslovak economy compared to other economies, especially those of the industrially advanced countries, and the trends in its development until 2010 (called by the authors, 'complex prognosis').

This was a government-approved research task which was completed in 1988. Its purpose was to map out a strategy for restructuring the economy and society. The results of the research were forwarded to the political and economic leaders. The theoretical journal *Politická ekonomie* (1989, no. 5) published 16 papers on the complex prognosis, in which the authors expressed their own views on different aspects of the Czechoslovak economic system and economy.[10]

All the authors of the complex prognosis, headed by V. Komárek, as well as other authors, agreed that the Czechoslovak economy needed restructuring. According to V. Komárek (1989), the Czechoslovak economic performance ranked among highly developed countries in 1985. Its per capita GDP, calculated in terms of purchasing-power parity, was only 15–25 per cent lower than that of Great Britain, Austria and Belgium, and 15–40 per cent higher than that of Greece, Portugal and Ireland.[11] However, the quality and structure of the produced goods did not match those of advanced countries, and therefore restructuring of the economy was needed. The author suggested adopting the strategy of small, developed European countries, which in practice would mean restricting traditional heavy industry and some branches of light industry.

Some economists were principally against the suggestion that Czechoslovakia should imitate capitalist countries (see Vintrová, 1989), and others saw restructuring as a cure for the economic ills. The latter were called 'structuralists' by many economists (see Klaus and Tříska, 1988); many of them resorted to such positions because they did not believe that the establishment would consent to a far-reaching reform of the economic mechanism. This is not to say that 'structuralists' were against reforms; however, when compared to the 'systemists' who saw the solution for the sick economy in a transition to a market economy, they put greater stress on restructuring the economy. Some of the 'systemists' believed that once market forces were allowed free play, structural problems would be automatically solved. O. Turek and T. Ježek (1989) took such a position. They warned that, in the absence of market structures and rational prices, any structural policy would mean a jump into the unknown, since the planners were in no position to formulate rational goals. Structural changes should be left to enterprises.

On the other hand, judging from the role he assigned to planning, it can be assumed that V. Komárek (1989) counted on the active participation of the government in bringing about the desired structure of the economy. It seems that M. Hrnčíř (1989) took a middle position between the two views mentioned.

TRANSITION TO A MARKET ECONOMY

After the 'velvet' revolution, which took place in November of 1989 and meant an end to the one-party state, the new government committed itself to a transition to a market economy based on private ownership. After parliamentary elections on 8/9 June 1990, which brought to power the Civic Forum in Czech lands and its partner in Slovakia, the Public Against Violence,[12] as well as their coalition partners, the new government headed by M. Čalfa announced in its programme that it was committed to a radical economic reform. This envisaged the liberalisation of prices and foreign trade combined with internal convertibility, the creation of competition and the privatisation of a substantial part of the state sector (*HN*, 1990, 4 July).

In the scenario of the economic reform submitted by the government to the parliament on 1 September 1990, the government programme took on concrete forms. It became clear that the neo-liberals, who occupied the important economic portfolios, had managed to a great extent to impose their philosophy on the economic reform. True, the government called for a stabilisation programme which would not produce high inflation nor an increase in foreign indebtedness. Avoidance of inflation was declared to be the most important macro-economic policy task to which all other policies, including employment, must be subordinated (*HN*, 1990, 4 September). As will be shown, the way in which the reform was implemented was contrary to this declared government policy.

On 1 January 1991 Czechoslovakia introduced a package of far-reaching transformation provisions, which, compared to the Polish ones of 1990, could be characterised as a slightly moderate form of shock treatment. The package comprised all the elements of the Polish therapy, but some of the components were less radical. Some publications characterise the Czechoslovak package as cautious; in doing so they probably have in mind the Polish experience. However, compared to the Hungarian programme and considering the economic situation in Czechoslovakia, it can hardly be evaluated as cautious. More about this later.

In 1990 the government increased consumer prices considerably in order to reduce subsidies, bring relative prices closer to their social costs and eliminate the separation of price circuits. In January 1991, prices were set free and subsidies eliminated, with some exceptions. For some foodstuffs, such as flour and its products, meat and milk, as well as energy, transportation, and so on, maximum prices were set (*HN*, 1991, 3 January), with the intention of freeing them in the course of time.

At the same time, internal convertibility of the Czechoslovak crown was introduced. This provision, which was the most controversial, linked the exchange rate of the crown to a basket of hard currencies. The initial exchange rate was set at 28 crown for one dollar. As in Poland, exporters must surrender all the foreign currencies received for their products, and importers of goods are guaranteed the foreign currencies they need. Unlike Polish private persons who can freely convert their *zlotys* into hard foreign currencies, people in Czechoslovakia can claim only foreign currencies up to the amount set by the authorities.

Simultaneously, foreign trade was liberalised with some exceptions. In order to curb imports, a 20 per cent surcharge, which was later reduced to 15 per cent, calculated in terms of duty value, was imposed on consumer goods. Exports of some goods were linked to licenses (*HN*, 1991, 2 January).

In order to avert a price–wage–price inflationary spiral and renew market equilibrium, a restrictive monetary and fiscal policy, accompanied by strict wage control, was imposed, with the consent, more or less, of the trade unions. Until it becomes possible to apply more

effective monetary tools (probably the information given to enterprises by the ministry of finance meant regulation by money supply)
the main instruments of control are supposed to be credit limits for
individual banks and the interest rate (maximum 24 per cent) (*HN*,
1991, 2 January). If wages exceeded the set guideline (for the first
quarter it was set at 5 per cent) enterprises are obliged to pay very
high penalties (*Práce a mzda*, 1991, no. 4–5, pp. 68–9).[13]

As to privatisation, the scenario of the economic reform envisages
a quick small privatisation (covering small and middle-sized businesses and service facilities) with the help of cash auctions. Large
privatisation, which is going to affect large enterprises, should proceed in two stages: commercialisation and sale. The first stage
amounts to the converting of enterprises into a legal form (mostly
joint-stock companies) so that they can be sold. To accelerate the
process of privatisation, investment vouchers, with which they will be
able to buy shares of enterprises to be privatised, will be distributed
to the population for a nominal charge.

The provisions made on 1 January 1991 laid down preconditions
for a market economy. A more rational price system has come into
being and subsidies have been eliminated to a great degree. The
exchange rate is stable. Shortages, which existed previously, have
been eliminated. Consumers have greater choice of products. The
private sector is expanding. However, the successes have been
achieved at a very high social cost. Inflation surged and production
declined. The figures listed further on are estimates from the Statistical Office. According to them, the index of consumer prices increased by 54.1 per cent in 1991. This increase was due largely to the
new, undervalued exchange rate of the crown, huge reduction in
subsidies and to the huge monopolisation of the economy. For completeness, it is necessary to add that the government managed to slow
down inflation on the average to a half per cent monthly in the second
half of 1991. An inflation rate of 10–20 per cent for the next year is
estimated. Real wages declined by 25.3 per cent; if the decline in real
wages in 1990 is added (5.5 per cent), the total decrease amounts to
32.2 per cent. Industrial output declined in 1991 by 22.8 per cent as a
result of a huge decline in demand. Unemployment increased to 6.6
per cent in 1991; in Slovakia it was much higher (Šujan 1992).

Strategy of Transformation

Before parliament passed the government proposal for reform, it
requested five economic institutions to appraise the proposals. So

there were group reactions to the transformation policy. In addition, the policy touched off a long debate among individual economists which still continues.

First, I will briefly discuss two group proposals – one of the Forecasting Institute (*HN*, 1990, 11 September) and one of the Czechoslovak Forum (*Principle Features* . . ., 1990). Neither of them had great effect on the transformation policy. The writers of these documents had no political power to back up their views, and in addition, many of them, being former communists, were vulnerable, a circumstance which V. Klaus, the finance minister, used to discredit them.

The two proposals did not differ much; both counselled against instant currency convertibility and an exchange rate based on market equilibrium level (meaning black market level); instead, they suggested a short-term coexistence of two exchange rates – one official, based on the cost of reproducing hard currency (17 crowns for one US$) and the other free, resulting from auctions of hard currency in the free market. The document of the Forecasting Institute argued that convertibility of Czechoslovak goods and services should first be achieved. Exporters were to surrender a large portion of their receipts to the State Bank. This would allow certain raw materials and consumer goods to be imported without quantitative limitations. Enterprises which acquired foreign currency in the free market would be allowed to import freely.

These proposals promised to stimulate exports without contributing to inflation. It was assumed that in the course of stabilisation the two exchange rates would merge into one rate.

The views of individuals can be classified into three groups: the first does not agree in principle with the approach to the transformation of the economy, the second agrees with the applied concept but has serious objections to individual solutions, and the third group supports government policy.

The adherents of the first group have in common the idea of combining the transition with structural changes without bringing about a decline in output and the standard of living. Therefore this group is against restrictive monetary and fiscal policy. In addition, it believes that government should be involved in structural changes. Finally, it favours gradual transformation.

M. Matějka can be regarded as one of the representatives of the first group; he explained his views in a series of articles in *Právo lidu*, a daily of the Social Democratic Party, and in *HN*. To begin with, his economic philosophy differs substantially fom V. Klaus', who is the mastermind of government policy. Unlike V. Klaus, he does not believe in the omnipotence of the market; he argues that the government must play an active role in the development, technological advancement and restructuring of the economy and maintains that this is what the government does in advanced capitalist countries, particularly in Japan (1990).

Taking this philosophy as his base, M. Matějka believes that the transformation concept should have been linked to a development programme which would have included what he calls a micro-economic policy, meaning an industrial, trade and regional policy. He counselled in favour of a gradual transformation of the economy. 'This is an evolutionary path of great diligence', writes the author (*Právo lidu*, 1991, 2 March).

Matějka agrees with the Japanese study done for the Czechoslovak State Bank that claims the economy should be opened gradually as the competitiveness of commodities increases. The author takes the same view with regard to price liberalisation (*Právo lidu*, 1991, 1 and 13 March).

V. Kadlec is also very critical of the transformation blueprint. In his 1990 article, he expresses concern about the insufficient preparation of the blueprint; this he sees in the lack of quantification and of information on the possible impact of the planned provisions on output, standard of living and social tolerance. There is no information about internal debt (by this he means neglect of the infrastructure and environment and the technical lag behind Western countries), which must be repaid at least partially in order to achieve 'equilibrated, dynamic and efficient growth of national income'. He is also critical of the authorities for trying to discourage discussion about crucial provisions. All this creates the impression that the authorities are trying to conceal possible negative consequences. V. Kadlec warns of the possible risks of the planned price liberalisation and convertibility of the crown.

In an interview given to *Rudé právo* (1991), V. Kadlec returns to the criticism expressed in his 1990 article about the transformation concept. He makes it clear that he prefers a gradual transformation, even if it means continuing limits, allocations and subsidies for some time. He writes, 'I have not yet heard an acceptable explanation as to why it is necessary to take all the reform steps almost simultaneously. I think it would be advantageous to stretch them out over a longer period of time'. A gradual reform would prevent chaos and the cheating of consumers by monopolies and speculators. 'I am not afraid of certain temporary centralisation. I am afraid of incompetency', says the author, probably having the government in mind. He also criticises the devaluation and insufficient consideration for social problems in the transformation process.

From what has been said about V. Komárek's views, one could expect that he would not agree with the government concept of a transition to a market economy. And indeed, he soon made it clear that he was against instant price liberalisation and convertibility of the crown. Instant price liberalisation – according to him – would destabilise the consumer goods and services market which was functioning quite well. It was necessary to focus on a renewal of the market for producer goods, which was marked by shortages. Once it was renewed, the domestic market could be linked to the world market along with the introduction of the convertibility of the crown. The marketisation of the producer goods sector should be achieved through restructuring and by restricting industrial branches, disadvantageous for the economy in the long run. V. Komárek rejected the idea that the market must necessarily determine restructuring, arguing that analyses made of the Czechoslovak economy were thorough enough to avoid mistakes. For the purpose of restructuring, it would be necessary to combine the general rules and tools of the market with selective tools of government regulation. He expressed the belief that such a policy would be combined with economic growth and an increase in the standard of living (1990A).[14]

In the Forecasting Institute's new study, which in substance was an evaluation of government transformation policy, V. Komárek subjected government policy to sharp criticism (1991). He maintained that the economic reform was excessively politicised and ideologised, and instead of being based on strictly professional research, was hastily compiled from 'eclectic sets of textbooks of current standard macroeconomics combined with stereotyped proposals of anti-inflationary and pro-export monetary programmes earmarked for developing countries . . . These in substance simple reform schemes were exported to Central and East European countries and propagated by such theoreticians as for example Prof. J. Sachs' (1991, p. 138).

According to Komárek, it was a great mistake to want to introduce market relations instantly, with the help of free prices and floating exchange rates, in an economy which has a long history of internal and external disequilibrium. Such an attempt must lead to a reproduction of deficits on a lower level with the inescapable consequence of recession and indebtedness (p. 137).

He devotes a lot of space to the negative consequences of freeing prices and introducing internal convertibility. One of the aims of government policy has been to make enterprises more efficient. To this end, subsidies have been cut and a restrictive monetary policy has been applied. However, the freeing of prices has brought a bonanza to enterprises and has worked against economic efficiency. (This bonanza was short-lived. Soon an opposite development came into being; due to high taxes and a decline in demand most enterprises got into a difficult financial situation.) Due to improved profitability, enterprises can afford greater declines in productivity than in employment, despite declining sales and output.

The second group is represented by many known economists. The main objection of this group is to internal convertibility. Most adherents of the group are against the high rate of devaluation; some object to the implementation of convertibility in one stroke.

I will begin with Z. Šulc's two articles in which he explains his concept. He is against both shock therapy and gradual transformation (which would last 4–10 years) and apparently prefers a middle-of-the-road approach. Shock therapy threatens to produce a high rate of inflation and a gradual transformation, under conditions of piecemeal price liberalisation, would create unequal conditions for enterprises and require wage regulation, which is unacceptable to him. According to him, what is needed first is to construct an infrastructure for the market in the form of a renewal of the linkage between price circuits, set the rules for conducting business, and prepare an overhaul of the tax system. The renewal of the linkage between price circuits does not mean that all prices will be liberalised. For the sake of achieving market equilibrium and to mitigate the social consequences, some prices should remain fixed, some limits should be preserved and some subsidies to enterprises retained, all only temporarily. The transformation programme should be financed by a tax on state enterprise assets (1990A).

As to convertibility, Z. Šulc's position is the same as that of the Economic Forum, not surprisingly, since he was probably the most important author of the Forum's report (see p. 249). He warns that a high rate of devaluation[15] will make many enterprises unprofitable and less adaptable to new conditions; it will bring about a decline in output, an increase in unemployment and probably more indebtedness. It will most likely increase exports only insignificantly, since the problem there is a lack of convertible commodities (1990B).

O. Turek's objections were primarily to the intended high devaluation of the crown. He rejected the argument that the new exchange rate should be near to the black market rate; instead, he suggested basing the new exchange rate close to the purchasing-power parity of the crown. Unless such a policy was adopted, he warned, the purchasing power of the crown would move as a result of inflation to the exchange rate (1990).

In his contribution to the Forecasting Institute's study mentioned above, O. Turek (1991A) again warned of the possible danger of the dramatic devaluation of the crown. In his opinion, the reformers did not take into consideration the fact that the devaluation might produce a stronger encouragement of import expansion as a result of its (devaluation) inflationary impact than export and that, as a result, the authorities might possibly tackle the problem either by engaging in import control or by resorting to another devaluation, thus opening the way to a spiral, devaluation–price increases–devaluation. Should a new devaluation threaten, he would prefer import controls and the imposition of temporary, higher tariffs (1991A, pp. 41–2).

O. Turek also counsels relaxation of the restrictive monetary and wage policy. This is important in order to stimulate an increase in demand, which is unnecessarily low, and thus arrest declining economic activity. In this connection, it is worth mentioning that the author believes that the population's willingness to make necessary sacrifices is in a certain sense misused by the economic policy which undermines the population's assent to the economic reform (p. 45).

J. Klacek (1990), presently the director of the prestigious Economic Institute of the Academy of Sciences, expressed objections to a one-stroke liberalisation of prices and especially to a one-stroke convertibility of the crown. Liberalisation of prices should be made dependent on the extent of competition in individual branches.

L. Rusmich (1991) called for a rapid price reform but one not implemented at a single stroke. To him convertibility should complete the transition process. The exchange rate should be set somewhere in the middle between two extremes, one being a rate based on purchasing power parity – this would make 80 per cent of export unprofitable – and the second being calculated on the basis of market equilibrium – this would ruin a large portion of Czechoslovak industry and increase indebtedness.

The last two views are not typical of the second group; they can be judged as views belonging somewhere between the first and second groups.

In discussing the views of the third group, I will start with the economic philosophy of V. Klaus, the architect of the transformation policy, which has perhaps best been explained in his polemic with the authors of the Forecasting Institute's study mentioned above. First, however, I will discuss his speech to the annual conference of the World Bank (1990). In it, he made clear that Czechoslovakia would like to put an end to the cautious 'muddling through' and gradual attempts to improve the system. A partial reform is, in his opinion, worse than no reform at all. The main tool of economic reform must be macroeconomic policy, meaning restrictive monetary and fiscal policy.

In his polemical article (1991), V. Klaus made it clear that he is against gradual transformation of the economy, and against any industrial policy or the state's role in the restructuring of the economy. He apparently believes that once the state has made the correct provisions (such as restrictive macropolicies and liberalisation of prices and foreign trade), the rest should be left to market forces. He does not admit that his transformation policy has brought about a dramatic decline in economic activity. According to him, this is due to external factors and 'an inevitable tax for the 40 years of squandering . . . overemployment . . . plundering of the economy, living at the expense of the past and future, etc.'. The preceding statement is, to say the least, strange, in light of the known consequences of shock treatment. The author dismisses M. Pick's contention (1991) about the premature opening of the economy and its consequences, and V. Komárek's view that currency convertibility should be introduced only after convertible commodities are available. The production of convertible commodities is inconceivable 'without the opening of the economy to the world and this without the introduction of the convertibility of the crown'. However, at a conference in Vienna, where the issue of currency convertibility was discussed (see note 8 of Chapter 11), V. Klaus took a different position. 'After a year in which the Czechoslovak economy has been largely reformed – indeed transformed – I no longer mention the sequencing issue at all. I am deeply convinced that the idea of sequencing is just a technocratic or rationalistic notion based on unrealistic beliefs in social engineering' (*IMF Survey*, 1991, 2 December, p. 362).

K. Kouba (1990A)[16] agrees in substance with the reform concept. He stresses that Czechoslovakia, compared to other countries, has favourable conditions (one being limited indebtedness) for a transition to a market economy. This transition must be quick, since the central management of enterprises has been abolished and a rational price system, which would guide the economy, does not exist. In addition, it is necessary to take advantage of the existing popular consensus for reforms.

He suggests that the liberalisation of the vast majority of prices requires, on the one hand, regulation of aggregate demand, and on the other hand, demonopolisation of the economy and the creation of a competitive environment.[17]

Privatisation

There is agreement among economists that, in order to have a market economy, a powerful private sector is needed. There is, however, disagreement about the pace, degree and methods, including the distribution of investment vouchers with which shares can be bought. The main reason for the disagreement is the divergency of views on the role which ownership plays in the determination of economic efficiency. More concretely, some believe more or less that private property in itself, regardless of its size, economic and social environment and the skills of the owners, is a necessary and sufficient precondition for economic efficiency. They believe that once private ownership is installed, all other preconditions for its efficient working will fall into place.[18]

Those who profess such ideas – and their number is not small – are, of course, in favour of rapid and mass privatisation[19] and are willing to accelerate it by the distribution of investment vouchers (for examples of such attitudes, see Tříska, 1990; Ježek, 1990). It can be said that such thinking shaped the government policy explained above.

Needless to say, these views are by no means shared by all economists. First, let me mention the view of the Forecasting Institute in its appraisal of the government proposal (see p. 251). It indirectly counselled gradual privatisation. In order to achieve reasonable prices for the assets, the number of enterprises to be sold should not exceed domestic and foreign demand. It was resolutely against the free distribution of investment vouchers. Privatisation should proceed in three stages: (1) commercialisation, the conversion of state enterprises into independent enterprises; (2) supplementation of enterprises with capital, domestic and foreign, and preparation for sale; and (3) the sale itself. As to foreign capital, the authors of the document preferred in the initial period its involvement in establishing new enterprises or expanding the assets of existing ones.

The views of individuals can be divided into three groups, if the official views are disregarded. The first two groups have in common the advocating of a gradual restructuring of ownership and an active role for a Fund of national property. They differ as to the restructuring and also the nature of the Fund's role. The third group is in favour of rapid privatisation under existing conditions, but in some respects its concept of privatisation differs from the government's.

One group professes leftist views. It would apparently like to maintain a relatively strong public sector and therefore regards the present government approach to privatisation as a squandering of state assets for the sake of ideological objectives. Z. Hába (1990) perhaps articulates the group's views best. He favours a plurality of ownership forms competing with one another and refutes the idea that only a private owner can be a fully valuable market actor. He suggests transforming the assets of most 'destatised' enterprises (meaning enterprises separated from state control and budget) into a Fund of national property (a huge, quasi-holding company) which would lease assets for use to domestic as well as foreign entrepreneurs for a certain recompense. The author would like to see self-management in many enterprises.

The second group is marked by views which vary in some respects. Because of lack of space, I will only discuss the ideas of Z. Šulc and L. Rusmich, who devoted much attention to this topic. Z. Šulc believes that, for practical economic reasons, 'large' privatisation cannot be rapid and should be gradual. Therefore it is important that 'destatised' enterprises be commercialised and behave as much as possible like market units (1990C). In a later article, he elaborated on this idea and indirectly advocated the transfer of 'destatised' enterprise assets into the Fund of national property, an institution which is separated from the state. The main task of the Fund is to monitor the performance of enterprises (without directly managing them), see to it that unprofitable enterprises become profitable or face liquidation, and prepare most enterprises for sale when the right occasion arises (1990D).

Šulc's concept of 'large' privatisation apparently has to create an environment for an orderly privatisation at market prices and for some market behaviour in 'destatised' enterprises, which, due to the intended, rapid privatisation, are in a state of uncertainty and disorganisation.

Let me first mention briefly L. Rusmich's ideas about the relationship of market and ownership. He is not of the view that market relations cannot arise unless they are based on private ownership.

Genuine societal ownership (which is not an instrument of power, as it was in the old system) is not an obstacle to market relations since it does not deprive market actors of their independence, and the division of labour is not eliminated (1991, pp. 16–17). He believes that there is a close relationship between freedom of choice in the market place and democracy, and the latter should be applied to enterprises too (pp. 28–9).

'Destatised' enterprises should be managed by the Fund of national property in the sense that it would allocate investment funds to enterprises. The funds needed should come from enterprises in the form of rent payments and dividends (pp. 40–1). If 'destatised' enterprises cannot be made profitable, they should be sold or leased to domestic private entrepreneurs. Foreign capital should also be used, mainly in the case of reconstructed enterprises which want to be active in exports (pp. 42–3).

Č. Kožušník (1991A) is perhaps the best representative of the third group. He does not view privatisation in such rosy terms as government circles do, though he is a staunch adherent of a market economy based on private ownership. He is aware that privatisation in itself cannot solve all the problems. No doubt, a private owner has a more responsible approach to property and tries to achieve maximum income. It is not enough to want, one must also know how to use his property in order to achieve high returns, writes the author.

Kožušník criticises the government for not having a strategy of privatisation. According to him, institutional ownership should play an important role; the fact that it has a dominant role in highly developed countries is not accidental, but the result of a long-lasting spontaneous process which is worth imitating. Institutional ownership 'reflects, among others, the reality that in "large" undertakings skills and professionalism are more important than direct ownership relations' (1991A, p. 106).

The author's advice is to take advantage of the co-operative form in the privatisation process, mainly in converting state farms. He also favours the participation of workers in ownership; he believes that it would be advantageous for them to buy shares with their investment vouchers in the enterprise in which they work. He expects that this will increase workers' interest in a better performance in their enterprise.

The project of distribution of investment vouchers for a nominal price[20] touched off a great debate.[21] It seems that most economists, even some of those who support the government package for transformation, are against such a policy (see for example K. Kouba, interview, 1990, *HN*, no. 30). Those who favour such a step argue that this will help to accelerate privatisation and the establishment of a capital market, and instil an entrepreneurial spirit in the population. T. Ježek (1990) even argues that investment vouchers are also needed in order to find out what the relative prices of shares are. This is not a convincing argument in light of the general opinion that free distribution will bring about a massive sale of shares and a decline in their prices. It is doubtful whether prices after such a decline will correctly reflect the relative values of assets in an economically justified manner.

Some opponents of the free distribution of investment vouchers argue that the idea is based on the assumption that ownership is the decisive motivation for efficient performance, which is only fully true in the case of small enterprises where the owner and manager are the same person. They regard it as illusion to expect that such an action will promote entrepreneurship. Some believe that it will lead to inflation and greater polarisation of society.

J. Klacek et al. (1991) believe that privatisation by investment vouchers was scaled down compared to the original intentions. They claim that foreign investors dislike this method so much that they will not invest in enterprises where it is applied. In addition, this method does not mean an influx of new technology and know-how. They also warn of the danger of feeding inflation if the vouchers are used to any great extent.

O. Turek (1991) would like to solve the problem of lack of capital, which is one of the reasons why the idea of distribution of vouchers came into being, with mortgage credits, extended by banks, which should get funds for this purpose from the Fund of national property. This is an idea which has more followers, but which has not yet been elaborated into an operative form.

V. Klusoň (1990, 1990A), a senior research fellow of the Economic Institute, who has researched the problem of privatisation more than many others, argues that there are neither valid ethical (some argue that enterprises belong to society and therefore everyone is entitled to share in the assets) nor economic reasons for free investment vouchers. He sees the solution to the lack of domestic capital in an open door to foreign capital.

CONCLUDING REMARKS

It has already been indicated that the Czechoslovak intellectuals were not in such a lucky position as their colleagues in Poland and Hungary with regard to research and freedom of expression. The normalisation process in Czechoslovakia put an end to the freedom of expression which social scientists had enjoyed during the Prague Spring and which they had used for discussing, *inter alia*, the shape of the economic reform. This also meant an interruption in the process of crystallisation of ideas about a possible combination of planning and market in such a way that genuine market relations could arise. The gradual dismantlement of the economic reform and a return to the traditional system, imposed on economists new topics of research and publications. Economists were pushed into the role of apologists for the economic system and the reforms of the management system. Some accepted this role because they believed in the system, others because it served their career, and some found ways to express their dissenting views without endangering their positions. After all, pro-fessional publications had more tolerance for dissent than the daily papers had. There were, of course, economists who were silent or muzzled. Therefore it is understandable, if we confine ourselves to our topic, that the debates until 1987 revolved around the problems of improving planning and the system of indicators. Market relations, if discussed, were treated as an adjunct to central planning. The discussions about planning were not useless. Some of the contribu-tions shed new light on the working of the traditional system, a matter of historical value.

In 1987, political relaxation started and was soon reflected in critical publications, one of the reasons being that the new political atmosphere made possible the return to research of many economists silenced for twenty years. Understandably, the topics were different from the previous period. Criticisms of central planning, and reason-ings about why a market economy was needed and how it could be introduced, were now the focus of the debates. The new atmosphere enabled Czechoslovak economists to catch up with their Hungarian and Polish peers in topics discussed and attitudes, with one important exception, ownership.

After the 'velvet' revolution, the problems of the transition to a market economy are in the forefront of debates. Even economists who favoured or favour the old system, as it was or with many modifications, must adjust to the new reality if they want to join the debates; other systemic topics are not topical and are therefore irrelevant. To my knowledge, few publications about the possible role of planning in a market economy exist. Planning has become taboo and it is not advisable to say something positive about it. Everything which is closely connected with and characterises the old system, even if in a modified form, is rejected out of hand, regardless of its merit. In the 1950s, there was a tendency to reject everything which characterised capitalism as an economic system. Nowadays, the same tendency is evident, but, of course, it works in the opposite direction.

The government, including V. Klaus, assured the population several times that Czechoslovakia would not imitate Poland and that shock treatment would not be applied because there was no need for it. Despite such assurances, it was applied, though in a more moderate form than in Poland. It has brought about certain positive aspects (see p. 248), but at an unacceptable social cost. What is worse is that the social cost is, of course, highly unevenly distributed. The brunt of the recession, into which the country was plunged by shock treatment, is borne by the majority, while a small group profiteers. The distribution of vouchers will probably contribute to this immense redistribution of wealth and income. (For more, see Chapter 11.)

There was no economic, let alone political, justification for applying shock treatment for the sake of transforming former socialist economies into market economies, especially in Czechoslovakia. Poland suffered from hyperinflation and therefore some, not very strong, arguments could be made for such a therapy. Czechoslovakia was in a quite different situation. Č. Kožušník, a staunch advocate of the market economy (see his 1990) and a top reformist of the 1960s, characterised the economic situation before the 'velvet' revolution in the following way: 'Despite some recurring gaps, the shelves of our stores were not empty, inflation was moderate, foreign debt was bearable, employment was full and the standard of living rather stagnated, and as far as it declined, this was not alarming' (1991). What a different situation there is nowadays as a result of shock treatment!

Shock treatment should have also been shunned for the sake of maintaining a united country. The deep recession, which affected Slovakia much more severely than the Czech lands, contributed to the alienation of the Slovaks from the Czechs.

Of course, the IMF, the World Bank and their sponsors, the Western powers, are to be blamed to a certain degree. They pushed shock treatment because they were afraid that in the case of a gradual solution, the political leaders of the post-socialist countries would not have sufficient resolve to persevere once they encountered political difficulties in the process of implementing the transformation package. They are also to be blamed for encouraging the authorities to abandon some of the principles of their own reform scenario, such as an active structural policy in the transitional period and the freeing of prices to the extent that demonopolisation of the economy is achieved. J. Klacek et al. (1991), who discuss these problems in their evaluation of the reform, maintain that the Czechoslovak federal government changed its position and accepted the international financial institutions' philosophy that structural changes are a matter for the market mechanism.

The main blame, however, falls on the shoulders of the government and its exponents. Had the government not acquiesced with the influence of the neo-liberals, and had they resisted the shock treatment, the IMF would have been forced to retreat. After all, Hungary has not opted for shock therapy and yet has not lost the financial support of the IMF. In Czechoslovakia, V. Klaus has often used the IMF as an instrument for pushing the government in the direction he desires.

In the paper mentioned, Č. Kožušník (1991), who is very unhappy with the results of the shock therapy and characterises them as features of a 'fateful tragedy', expresses the view that the IMF's concept, which, according to him, is designed for countries with a market mechanism and is not appropriate for former centrally planned economies, has found fertile soil in Czechoslovakia because revolutions tend to resort to radical solutions. The radicalism, which hampers people's ability to think rationally and pragmatically, is the result of the wrongs, humiliation and persecution which people had to endure in the old system. Radicalism also leads to impatience and to a tendency to adjust reality to ideology regardless of the cost.

Č. Kožušník also blames the shock treatment on the fact that no other alternative was elaborated into an operative form. He apparently has in mind the circumstance that V. Komárek, who was the deputy prime minister for economic affairs in the first post-'velvet' revolution government for some time, failed to come up with a viable operative plan for the transition to a market economy. And with this he created the opportunity for the followers of shock treatment. It is worthwhile to add that Klaus and his associates could prevail because he is a clever politician who has managed to create for himself a powerful political constituency and a party, and has had the support of the West.

Notes

1. All periodicals, non-periodicals and publishing houses were under the strict control of the authorities, who did not tolerate any dissenting views, so that critical or seemingly critical views had no chance of seeing the light. Because of this, intellectuals, inspired by the Soviet example, resorted to *samizdat* (Mencl et al., 1990, p. 333). Up to the second half of the 1980s, the Czechoslovak *samizdat* was quite limited in size (it included very little economic literature) and influence. A few economists found an outlet for their views in foreign journals and magazines, mainly in the bi-monthly periodical of Czechoslovak *émigrés, Listy*. In the beginning, they wrote under assumed names, later under their own.

2. Adjusted net output was not a pure net indicator since it included depreciation.

3. The articles were the result of a research task of the Slovak Academy of Sciences.

4. K. Dyba is the former director of the prestigious Institute of Economics and the present minister of the Czech lands for economic policy. K. Kouba is a senior research fellow of the Forecasting Institute and one of the best known Czechoslovak economists.

5. V. Komárek has been the director of the Forecasting Institute from its establishment in the middle of the 1980s. The institute was really a signal from the political leadership about its determination to ease control over intellectuals. Several top economists from the Prague Spring again found jobs in their field in the Institute.

6. See Rusmich's book (1988).

7. It would be wrong to assume that this paper was to the liking of the authorities because it talked about socialism. In fact, they saw it as an attack on the system – which it really was.

8. T. Ježek is the minister of the Czech government in charge of privatisation.

9. The article was prepared for the Czechoslovak and Soviet conference in Prague which took place in September 1989. In an earlier conference in Moscow, Kouba presented an abbreviated version of this paper. In his paper prepared in the middle of 1989 for a conference in Hungary, K. Kouba (1990B) stresses that the 1987 reform lacks a strategy of transition. To him such a strategy must include a policy of monetary and fiscal discipline.

10. In 1990, V. Komárek et al. published *Prognóza a program* (*Prognosis and Programme*). It is not clear whether the book is a verbatim copy of what was submitted to the government.

11. V. Komárek's figures did not agree with figures forwarded by other authors. For example, F. Nevařil, an official of the office of the prime

minister, estimated that the per capita GNP for 1984 was $3345. According to him, the Austrian GNP per capita was 247 per cent higher, and this was without taking into consideration the much lower participation rate completed working hours there. J. Kolář and K. Zeman (1989) came up with estimates which are close to V. Komárek's.

12. Both parties have disintegrated in the meantime.
13. Increases to 3 per cent are free of penalty; for increases between 3 and 5 per cent, the penalty is 200 per cent, and above 5 per cent, 750 per cent of the amount paid out in wages beyond the allowable sum.
14. In an earlier interview (1990), V. Komárek urged the introduction of a competitive environment through privatisation and a fight against monopolisation.
15. In his considerations, Šulc assumed a rate of 24 crowns for one dollar, but in reality, the exchange rate adopted was 28 crowns for a dollar.
16. K. Kouba was the chairman of a group of experts who worked out a reform proposal for the government of the Czech lands.
17. In a personal conversation, I was told by K. Kouba that he favoured the postponement of price liberalisation by several months in order to do something first about demonopolisation.
18. My views on positions expressed are explained in Chapter 11.
19. T. Ježek (1990) wants to carry out privatisation in three years. In his opinion, the more enterprises can be sold at once the better for the working of the capital market.
20. An investment voucher is sold for *Kčs* 1000, which was approximately 28 per cent of the average monthly wage in 1991. In an interview with *Rudé právo* (1992, 3 January), T. Ježek maintained that 50 to 60 per cent of state enterprises would be distributed to holders of investment vouchers. In order to reduce the risk to voucher holders, they need not buy shares of enterprises directly; instead, they can purchase investment units from an investment privatisation fund (a kind of mutual fund).
21. Even Czech economists who live abroad participated in the debate (for example, O. Šik).

Part III
Concluding Remarks

11 Observations

This chapter is going to be a mixed bag. On the one hand, I would like to express my views in a systematic way on some issues which were discussed in the preceding chapters and, on the other, discuss problems which have not been raised hitherto, but which are somehow connected with our topic. I will try to explain why the views on planning and market changed during the period under review, answer the question whether reform of the system was possible, touch on some problems connected with the transition to a market economy, and, finally, I will discuss the possible role of planning in a market economy.

REASONS FOR CHANGES IN THINKING

The preceding chapters have shown that in the debaters' concept of reforms the market increasingly grew in importance. In the 1960s, in the minds of most reformers, planning was viewed as the main coordinating mechanism, or at least as one of the two complementary coordinating mechanisms. Only a few economists called for a fully fledged market economy. In the second half of the 1980s, the situation changed dramatically in Poland and Hungary, the two countries which spearheaded the reform movement. In both countries, but mainly in Hungary, calls for a transition to a market economy were initially disguised as calls for market socialism. And now, all the countries under review are in the process of transition to a market economy based on private ownership.

One could argue that the calls for the institution of a market economy came only after the reforms had not produced favourable changes in the working of the economy, and when it had become clear that the socialist system was irreformable. However, such argumentation is not very convincing in light of the known fact that the latest reforms in the countries had no chance of passing the test of viability, since they lasted only a short time. And such historical experiments need to be in operation far long in order for an objective judgment to be made. In addition, the reforms proceeded under very difficult economic conditions which were caused not only by systemic factors, but also by economic policy decisions and external factors.

The huge indebtedness in both Poland and Hungary, which burdened the economies immensely, was not of a systemic nature. Czechoslovakia, which for most of the 1980s opposed far-reaching reforms, was much less indebted than the two countries mentioned. If systemic factors played a role in a country becoming indebted, their influence, it can be said, was rather negative.

There was a time when the socialist regime had the support of a large segment of the population. It is difficult to pin down exactly the time when the socialist system started to gain acceptance. In the USSR, this may have happened in the second half of the 1930s when the first positive results of industrialisation, which imposed tremendous sacrifices on the population, became evident, and the material situation of the population improved at a time when capitalist economies were coming out from the Great Depression. Also in the 1950s, the system was largely accepted, because the people accepted the propagandist thesis about its permanence. The fact that the Soviet Union became one of the two superpowers also worked in this direction. In the first half of the 1950s in East European countries, the population did not favour the new system. Even in Czechoslovakia, where the Communist Party had a larger percentage of followers than in the neighbouring countries, the ambitious medium-term plans, which were carried out at the expense of the standard of living of the population, combined with other measures, such as liquidation of small businesses and forced collectivisation, turned great segments of the population against the regime. In the second half of the 1950s, when, in all the countries under review, the communist leaders put greater stress on the standard of living, and the material situation of the population began to improve, people slowly started to accept the system, all the more because Hungarian events convinced them that the socialist system was there to stay. In the first half of the 1970s, most socialist countries experienced a golden age, the peak of their development. Afterwards, the economic situation worsened, and with it the dissatisfaction of the population and their opposition to the socialist system grew.

No doubt, the economic situation (understood very broadly, that is, including the material situation of the people of the countries as a whole and their socio-economic groups in particular) had a great impact on the thinking of economists. Economic life itself gives birth to new ideas, mainly if the economy experiences some trouble. People look for some new solutions in order to cope with the difficulties. But this could not have been the only influence. In the first half of the 1960s, socialist economies were in poor shape; nevertheless there were no calls for a transition to a market economy. It took time for such ideas to become the demand of the day.

There were many other factors besides economic ones which bred new ideas: political, ideological, external, ethnic, generational, and so on. Before elaborating on this, it is worth mentioning that in every society creative people exist who are driven by some internal instinct to analyse economic life and suggest improvements, regardless of whether these are needed or not.

Under Stalin's rule, dissent could not develop. Cruel repression was only one of several methods used to make intellectuals adhere to the CP line in their thinking. Ideology was a powerful tool too; combined with propaganda which was governed by the principle that the end justifies the means, it managed to make many people agree voluntarily with, or even defend, the objectives of the Stalinist policy. A great many people, including intellectuals, were receptive to Marxist ideas about socialism, a planned economy, state ownership, full employment, etc., whether in their true or distorted form.

Needless to say, the XXth Congress of the Party in 1956, at which N. Khrushchev denounced Stalin as a criminal, was a watershed in the development of systemic thinking in the socialist countries. Interestingly enough, the occurrences at the congress had greater impact on the smaller countries than on the Soviet Union. Khrushchev's propaganda of coexistence between the socialist and capitalist systems brought about some additional political relaxation, and the Iron Curtain was raised a little in the USSR as well. Debates there about the economic mechanism itself started in the 1960s, but it was understood that they could not go much beyond the CP line, let alone challenge socialism's foundations. It is not clear whether there would have been a majority of economists willing to do so even if they had been allowed to. After all, they were under the spell of their education and ideology. Only the most receptive scholars resonated to the reforms in Hungary and Czechoslovakia.

The situation in the smaller countries was different. The Communist regime was not able to impose its will on, and control the thinking of, intellectuals, including economists, and insulate them from the outside world to the extent it did in the USSR. This was true primarily of Poland and Hungary (where after the 1956 uprising repression followed for several years and then was replaced by a more relaxed regime).

The economic reforms of the 1960s also made some cracks in

Eastern Europe's insulation from the West; they opened the way for a limited exchange of views between East European and Western scholars. Tourism may have had an even greater effect. This new phenomenon, which swept the world and developed into a powerful industry, could not be disregarded in the smaller countries. On the one hand, the countries wanted to share in the earnings from tourism (even the USSR was interested as long as it was one-sided) and on the other, the governments came under pressure to allow tourism. First, foreign travel was allowed to socialist countries only; later, it was expanded to Western countries for a select few. Tourism gave an opportunity for comparisons of domestic living conditions with those in the West, where tourists headed if they could go to non-socialist countries at all. Although tourists are usually not reliable judges when it comes to comparisons, this is of no relevance here, because what is of importance for the thinking is the perception. If one considers that private tourists from the smaller countries usually had to survive on canned food brought from home, content themselves with substandard accommodation and not even consider buying some of the 'miraculous' goods offered by the West, it is easily understandable that they did not return home with a great love for the regime. Radio Free Europe, with its sophisticated propaganda aimed at stressing the weaknesses of the regime, contributed to the travelling population's heightened frustration, which was not diminished by the fact that smaller countries lacked hard currencies.

These circumstances were not sufficient to bring about a fundamental reversal in the attitudes of East European economists to the socialist system. In the 1960s and 1970s, few academic economists had a chance to go to the West or meet foreign scholars. Many still hoped that the system could be made more efficient by, among other things, taking over some elements of the capitalist system, and, mainly, by allowing market forces to play a greater role. (The stress on the market was understandable since the West's prosperity was attributed to market forces.) Nevertheless, every meeting with the West chipped away a layer from their belief in the socialist system.

The 1980s, mainly the second half, saw a rapid loss of faith in socialism. The factors already mentioned had an increasing impact, mainly the rapid growth of tourism and the spread of contacts with the West. Constant comparisons of the economic performance of the socialist economies with that of countries which, before WWII, were on approximately the same economic level, comparisons which mostly turned out negatively for the socialist countries, had a devastating influence on the morale of East European intellectuals, in particular economists.[1] In the 1980s, such comparisons were made not only in Poland and Hungary, but even in Czechoslovakia. The rapid spread of the second economy in all countries under review had an eroding effect on the real-socialism ideology. I. Szelényi (1990), a well-known Hungarian sociologist, maintains that not Gorbachev, but the rising middle class brought down the socialist system in Hungary. The information revolution, which cannot be easily kept out, even with an Iron Curtain, also played an important role. Of course, the most important factor was the economic situation which was deteriorating, mainly in Poland. Both Poland and Hungary struggled with great difficulties in order to be able to honour their obligations resulting from their huge debts. In addition, in Poland, the situation was complicated by the incessant fight between the government and the outlawed Solidarity. The economic mess was increasingly interpreted as proof of the inability of the socialist system to cope with the crisis. Such an interpretation offered itself all the more because on the one hand, the reforms did not produce a turnaround and on the other, the economic literature delivered more and more arguments – some well founded and some ill founded – that the socialist system even in its reformed structure could not work efficiently. The slow reaction of the political leaders to the economic crisis and their unwillingness to engage in a meaningful political reform were interpreted as evidence that the system was irreformable.

The change in thinking had also to do with a generational factor. The new generation in the smaller countries, which had grown up under the socialist system, was in many respects different from the older generation, which still remembered the Great Depression and the rise of Hitler to power, the latter's expansionist policy and his aggressive war, which engulfed almost the whole world and brought to an end the independence of Poland and Czechoslovakia. The older generation, especially in Czechoslovakia, saw the USSR as the liberator and was, for this reason, more receptive to socialist ideas and more tolerant of the shortcomings of socialism. The new generation, which was on the whole better educated, approached the socialist system critically and pragmatically without any great feelings of sympathy for it. It viewed the system as an obstacle to 'stretching its wings', which was true especially for young professionals, including economists.

Anti-Soviet nationalistic feelings, which smouldered under the surface to different extents in different times, resurfaced once the economy started to falter. Poland and Hungary had good historic reasons for not liking the Russians, who had thwarted or helped thwart their national aspirations in the past. Resentment of the USSR, as the successor to Russia, was reinforced by the fact that it had used the liberation of East European countries to impose its political and economic system on them. Socialism was therefore viewed as a foreign product, imposed from the outside. Regular interference by the Soviet Union exacerbated the situation.

The shabby treatment of the intelligentsia (here those of its members who were in positions of responsibility in the Party and government are disregarded) was one of the most important factors which led to the dramatic change in its thinking. Even in Poland and Hungary, where the intellectuals were relatively better treated than in other socialist countries (for example, Czechoslovakia), they could not be satisfied with their position. They were for long denied the principal freedoms essential for their self-realisation. More than other segments of the population, the intelligentsia was troubled by the lack of democratic institutions and human rights and also, in the smaller countries, by Soviet encroachment on their national sovereignty. In addition, it had serious grievances: it regarded the narrow wage differentials for skill as signs of disrespect for its professions and interests. All this was sufficient to make the majority of the intelligentsia resentful of the socialist regime. On top of this, there was the institution of nomenclature which excluded, for political reasons, many highly educated people from positions of responsibility. In Czechoslovakia, members of the intelligentsia who were actively involved in the fight for the 1968 economic reform were prevented from working in their professions; many were forced to take manual jobs.

Finally, the Soviet factor in all its variety should not be forgotten. If not for *glasnost*, many of the changes in Poland and Hungary could not have taken place. The Polish government was willing to engage in a political dialogue with Solidarity and the Hungarian one with the rapidly growing opposition (which was also the result of changes in the USSR), once the governments had concluded that the Gorbachev administration was not committed to Brezhnev's doctrine.

The changes in thinking in the USSR were quite rapid in the second half of the 1980s. With the deteriorating economic situation, the views about what to do with the economy radicalised. The economic and political changes in Poland and Hungary surely had an echo in Soviet thinking. The awakening nationalism, made possible and fostered by *glasnost*, worked in the same direction. Understandably, some republican politicians used the new sentiments to strengthen their positions. On the one hand, they engaged in a national fight with the Union and on the other, they initiated radical economic reforms, promising rapid healing of the economy, in order to gain the support of their nations and prestige abroad. The suggested solutions were more and more in the direction of a market economy. When the Soviet leadership decided to introduce a market economy in the Soviet Union, this trend to radicalisation strengthened and accelerated. In 1989–90, most economists still thought in terms of a market economy with the adjective socialist, while in 1990–1 the adjective was progressively dropped. After the aborted *putsch*, socialism was abandoned altogether.

Some factors which led to a change in systemic thinking in the smaller countries had only a small direct impact on Soviet thinking. The impact of tourism was not felt very much in the USSR for the simple reason that it was of limited size. However, Western social scientists can take credit for changes in Soviet thinking.

An important source of ideas is the surrounding world. In modern times, ideas spread quickly across borders. Social scientists are usually more receptive to ideas coming from a country with whose system they sympathise or which they regard as leading in their field. In the smaller socialist countries, at the time when socialism was regarded as the ideal system and different in all aspects from capitalism, the USSR served this purpose. With the spread of reformist ideas, the Soviet Union was gradually replaced in this role by the West. Yet it did not entirely lose its importance for new ideas. It served as a licence place for some ideas. An idea which passed Soviet censorship was regarded as correct and could be disseminated at home without fear of charges of heresy.

From the foregoing it is clear that social scientists looked more and more for inspirations in the West. It is also known that it was an old Western, especially American, dream to bring down the socialist system in the USSR and Eastern Europe. Security reasons were undoubtedly the main motive, but systemic fears were not far behind. In Western plans – which probably existed – for achieving this goal, an important role was certainly attributed to the conversion of the intelligentsia to the idea of a market economy and democracy. The West used primarily three instruments to win over the inelligentsia: control of the purse strings, especially in the hands of the IMF; scholarships; and invitations to universities and conferences.

The activities of the IMF in Hungary and later in Poland were not, of course, motivated by a desire to strengthen the existing socialist system. Had they been, they would have been contrary to the desires of its main sponsors, particularly the USA. The question is: had the IMF acted in a way designed to undermine the socialist system? It is difficult to give a positive answer which can be backed up with watertight evidence. The fact that the IMF promoted methods used in market economies, and socialist governments accepted them, had necessarily an effect on systemic thinking. In addition, the IMF, in pursuit of its policy, dealt not only with the appropriate authorities, but also came into contact with a broader collective of social scientists. The purpose of this strategy was, among others, to find support for its proposals, whose by-product was the dissemination of the gospel of private enterprise.

Scholarships as well as university invitations for visits and conferences helped convert East European and Soviet scholars to adherents of the market economy. It is interesting that most converts adopted right-wing ideologies and became ardent followers of M. Friedman and F. Hayek, a fact which later played an important role in the formulation of policies in the transitional period to a market economy. Many dogmatic communists turned into dogmatic marketeers, some out of conviction, some because they distinguish themselves with a dogmatic way of thinking, and some in order to conceal their past. Most social democrats in the smaller countries, who were forced to join the CP in the 1940s, remained faithful to their original ideas.

Of course, the West would have been in no position to influence Soviet and East European thinking to the extent it did, if it had not been for developments in the countries themselves in the 1980s. In the clash of two ideologies, the capitalist ideology triumphed because the economic and political reality in the capitalist countries was less in contradiction with the promises made by governments than was the case in the socialist countries.[2] The existing democratic freedoms, including freedom of choice in capitalist countries, a phenomenon of great importance, mainly to the intelligentsia and the segment of the population gifted with an entrepreneurial spirit or eager to be involved in business, helped to tilt the scales in favour of the capitalist ideology. The advantages of real socialism (such as full employment, comprehensive social safety net) lost their attractiveness in face of the rapidly declining standard of living. The increasing propaganda, coming from inside the countries as well as from foreign sources, that adoption of the market economy would bring prosperity almost approaching the Western level had an effect too.[3]

WAS THE SYSTEM REFORMABLE?

L. Balcerowicz allegedly characterised the socialist system as a system which leads from capitalism to capitalism. If the characterisation was not meant as a joke, it meant to say that socialism was doomed to failure. In my opinion, socialism in the *traditional* form, as represented by a one-party state, almost absolute socialist ownership, an administrative economic mechanism and economic policies with stress placed on the preferential development of heavy industry, was really what was doomed to failure. This does not mean that a reformed system was also necessarily destined for the same fate. The question to be asked is: what kind of reforms were needed in order to make the system viable, and were such reforms possible? It is clear that this is purely an academic question. The collapse of the socialist system cannot be undone; it has been discredited to such a degree that any attempt to introduce a system which is remotely reminiscent of the old one will be resisted for a long time.

Before answering these important questions, let me make clear that in my view the collapse of the socialist system in Hungary and Poland was inevitable under the conditions which came about as a result of developments in the two countries, but mainly in the USSR, in the second half of the 1980s. The reforms of the 1960s *did not and could not go far enough when there was relatively strong support for socialism*. The Czechoslovak reform was destroyed by the pressure of the Soviet-led invasion. The Hungarian reform was halted and reversed to some extent in 1972 through domestic and mainly foreign pressure. When Hungary and Poland in the 1980s again engaged in reforms, the situation was different from the second half of the 1960s. Both countries groaned under the burden of their huge international debt and their standard of living was declining.

Gorbachev's advent to power and his commitment to a radical economic reform strengthened the hands of the radical reformers in both countries; they used the new opportunity for new reform demands, to which the authorities reluctantly acquiesced.

The governments expanded the role of the market and created conditions for its application to capital and labour. Furthermore, they

allowed the expansion of the private sector and committed themselves to treating all forms of ownership equally. Despite the
changes, the economic situation continued to worsen and with it the
political situation. The political leaders slowly realised that the
regime was in a deep crisis and that Gorbachev was no longer committed to Brezhnev's doctrine. They looked for a compromise with the
opposition: in the economic sphere, by promising to institute market
socialism. Sensing that the regime was no longer protected by the
Soviets, the opposition, which in Hungary was headed by the intelligentsia, and in Poland by labour and the intelligentsia, was no
longer interested in reforms; what it wanted was to bring down the
regime. Its job was made easier because the crisis affected the CPs
themselves, in that they started to disintegrate rapidly. In addition,
the opposition had the support of the West.

One can assume that had the situation, particularly in the Soviet
Union, developed in a different way, the socialist system in Hungary
and Poland would probably have survived at least for some time, and
the reforms would have had a better chance. Had socialism survived
for longer, market socialism could have been tested for its viability,
say in Hungary, in a country with an ethnically homogeneous population. In Yugoslavia the working of the market mechanism was detrimentally affected by bickering among the republics and by its own
extreme form of self-management.

Let me now return to the questions posed above by first discussing
briefly the fundamental changes needed in the political system. It
would have been necessary to turn the one-party state into a democratic state based on a multi-party system. The representatives of the
socialist system, who contended that their system was for the good of
the people, would have to prove that the majority of the citizens
really wished such a system. Of course, such a fundamental change
cannot be carried out all at once; there must be some transitional
period in which gradual steps are taken towards the final goal, a
democratic society. Gradualness is also needed in order to make an
economic reform successful. A radical economic reform is not a
matter of one-shot provisions. In addition, the political and economic
reforms must be well synchronised, otherwise there is a great danger
that the economy will be thrown into chaos, as recent Soviet experience shows, and will make the power-holders reluctant to go through
with political reforms or encourage them to reverse already-made
reforms.

Is there a chance that a system which was rammed down people's throats could be approved in democratic elections? The development in post-socialist countries showed that there was such a chance. In Bulgaria, Romania and Albania, the former CP received parliamentary majorities in the first democratic elections which took place in an international anti-communist atmosphere. It is also important to remember that elections took place under unfavourable economic conditions, for which the CP could be blamed. If the change in the political system could have occurred in favourable economic conditions, the chances for the socialist system might have been much better. This is, of course, true only of the first elections. More about this later.

The question can be asked: is it realistic to assume that political leaders would voluntarily risk their power and privileges? Judging this question on the basis of conventional wisdom, the answer must be negative. However, enlightened leaders of Gorbachev's and Kádár's type may voluntarily agree with or can be won over for such reforms, especially if they feel that without reforms they are exposed to great risks.

The economic reform would have had to bring about a system which would have prevented the diseases of the traditional socialism – such as low economic efficiency, shortages, low quality of products, reluctance for innovations, to mention the most important shortcomings – without giving up most of its advantages. The best way to eliminate the shortcomings is replacing the institutions which caused them with new ones which will encourage economic actors to practise different behaviour. And this means in the first place to replace detailed central planning with a system of market socialism. The market is an impersonal coordinating mechanism; this is its strength, but also its weakness. Its working determines what, how, and for whom goods are produced without the need for government intervention. The market is also a stimulus to minimise costs, because only in this way can profit be maximised. This last statement is fully valid under conditions of perfect competition, a state which in reality does not exist. The weakness of the market is that, if left to itself, it produces fluctuations in economic growth, unemployment and large inequities in distribution of income, and is indifferent to social justice and societal priorities. It is the role of government to cope with these weaknesses of the market. Nowadays in all capitalist countries, but in some more than in others, government economic policies rely on interventions in the economy, beyond what *laissez faire* economists of Friedman's type would like to see. Recent development, even in the

USA, shows that many people want a government which actively influences the economy and which does not rely only on market forces.[4]

It is obvious that if the reformed system is supposed to be market socialism, it must have many features in common with a capitalist economy. The market must be applied not only to consumer and producer goods, but also to capital and labour. A stock market, the typical symbol of capitalism in the eyes of many socialists, must be an integral part of the reformed system. Without it, the market cannot properly fulfil its function. However, this does not mean that it must be turned into a quasi-casino, a centre of speculation, as it is in the USA to a great extent. There are methods to make the stock market purely a centre for raising capital for investment.

The reformed system must be based on the idea that the gap in the level of economic efficiency and technological progress which divides the former socialist countries from the West can gradually be narrowed by opening up the economy. This cannot, however, be carried out in a one-shot operation. To do so would mean exposing the domestic economy to devastating foreign competition. The opening of the economy must be a gradual process; the more convertible commodities (commodities which can compete in demanding foreign markets) a country is able to produce, the closer it will arrive at the goal of integrating the economy with the world economy. The expansion of convertible commodities will also pave the way to currency convertibility.

It is clear that, in a reformed socialist system, the government role must be even greater than in capitalist countries. It cannot rely only on fiscal and monetary policies, though they must be the main tools; it must also use non-market methods, among them, planning. In the last section of this chapter, I offer several ideas about planning in a market economy. In a reformed socialist system, its role must be much more extensive: planning should be involved in formulation of an industrial as well as regional and infrastructural development strategy and in solving environmental and social problems. Ownership problems will be discussed in the next section below.

The question is: what should the role of socialism be in the reformed system, beyond what has already been mentioned? A socialist system, to be worth its name, must differ from a capitalist system, primarily in its approach to social policy, the distribution of wealth and income, employment and the environment. In social policy (understood in the narrow sense, meaning without a price policy serving social purposes, as it was in the traditional socialist system) no fundamental change is needed in its comprehensiveness compared to the previous one. But democratic methods must be used to determine the structure and organisation of individual social programmes. The public must have an important say in shaping them. Perhaps a more difficult question is how to ensure sufficient funding for certain programmes, mainly health care. During recent years, some social programmes have been considerably underfunded.

Nowadays, all capitalist countries have social programmes. But still there should be a difference in approach to social problems between a capitalist and a renascent socialist system. In the latter the interest of society or its weaker segments should get priority over private interests in solving social problems.[5]

In the traditional socialist system, wage differentials for skill were very narrow, and this hampered innovation and initiative. In a reformed system, wage differentials for skill would have to be wider, but not to the extent they are in some capitalist countries. To this end, a reformed system must influence wage differentials by taxes, or if necessary by setting ceilings, even for chief managers in the private sector.

Distribution of income in capitalist countries is carried out only partially by market forces. If a chief executive of an American corporation makes the board of directors approve a salary for himself or herself which is 50 to 150 times higher than the average wage of a worker in the same company (see 'Corporate élite', 1991), that has little to do with market forces. In most cases, he would not receive such a high salary in another company where he does not have well-disposed directors who are often corrupted by him.

A reformed system must aspire to achieve an economic situation in which every one who wants to work can find a job. Obviously, unemployment cannot be avoided in the transitional period. But the government, which should become responsible for employment, must do its best to hold down unemployment to the lowest possible rate. To this end, it must not use stabilisation methods which necessarily generate huge unemployment. More about this in the next section.

In the traditional socialist system, the full employment policy was carried out at the expense of economic efficiency. A reformed system cannot afford such a policy. It must look for ways to promote the idea of full employment without hurting economic efficiency. Much can be done without international co-operation, as Swedish experience shows. This refers primarily to a comprehensive programme for retraining workers. But there are methods for promoting employment which one country alone cannot do, if it does not want to be in a disadvantageous position in the world market. I have in mind primarily a gradual and considerable shortening of the work time. An internationally concerted slowing down of the technological drive, which displaces workers at a rate greater than new job opportunities can be created, can also help.

In my opinion, a reformed system can be a much more efficient system than the old one. I have, however, doubts whether it can be a stable system. Such a system will be what we call a third road system, something between the old traditional socialist system and capitalism. It will have to exist in a capitalist sea which cannot be expected to be well disposed to countries with a third road system. Multinational companies may regard such a system as a threat to their interests and may discriminate against countries which apply it, especially if the third road system is limited to smaller countries. The discrimination may make it difficult for the regimes of such countries to preserve the loyalty of their citizens.

PROBLEMS OF TRANSITION TO A MARKET ECONOMY

In this section I will express my views primarily about two important questions of the transition to a market economy, namely, the strategy of transformation except for privatisation, and privatisation.

Strategy of Transformation

In Chapter 6 as well as in the country studies chapters, I explained what kind of objectives and problems are involved. The question is, how can they be solved without generating an upheaval in the economy? No doubt, such far-reaching provisions cannot be made without causing some hardship to the population in the form of unemployment and a decline in the standard of living. It is important to minimise the social cost and distribute the burden of transition as equitably as possible. When decisions were being made in Poland and Czechoslovakia about the strategy of transformation and stabilisation, neither social costs nor equitable distribution of the burden were high on the list of criteria. The neo-liberals, who managed to gain the prevailing influence in economic matters in most governments, were convinced, in the spirit of their ideology, that there was only one path to a market economy and that was through shock treatment. They viewed material hardship as a surgeon views pain, a necessary by-product of the operation; they did not have great compassion for the population they exposed to hardship.[6] If the first criterion did not bother them much, the second, equitable distribution of the burden, was actually contrary to what they wanted to achieve, the creation of a strong property-owning middle class. The transition was also supposed to be a process of 'primary accumulation'.

The neo-liberals had the support of the IMF and the World Bank because their transformation strategy was in fact the transformation programme of the two financial institutions. Not only this; the international financial institutions encouraged and enticed former socialist countries to accept such programmes by promising financial and technical help (compare S. Gomulka, 1991A). It is probably this fact which helped the neo-liberals to gain such an influence.

In Chapter 8 I have already discussed the positive and negative aspects of shock treatment in Poland and backed up this analysis with some figures. One must ask the question: would Poland not have been better off with a gradual transformation to a market economy, which would have stretched out the introduction of the market, but would not have imposed such immense hardships on the population? More than two years have elapsed since the stabilisation programme was introduced, and there has not been a turnaround in economic growth, and inflation is still very high. There is a danger that Poland will be in a state of stagnation for many years. In addition, shock treatment has generated political instability which in turn has had a negative effect on the economy. Czechoslovakia is much better off than Poland, but its population, considering the economic situation before November 1989, has also been exposed to unnecessary hardship (see Chapter 10).

The hardship figures in both countries are much worse than the architects of the programmes estimated. True, the recession in the West, once it came into being in the second half of 1990, contributed to the hardship because it made exports to the Western markets more difficult. The collapse of the trade with the former USSR and GDR was an even more important factor. However, these facts accounted to only a small degree for the hardship figures which were much higher than expected.

The architects of the transformation programme should have known that, if such far-reaching provisions are undertaken simultaneously,

their outcome cannot be predicted with great accuracy, simply because it is difficult to predict the reactions of enterprises and individuals to such austerity programmes. In Czechoslovakia above all,
where the transformation started later, they also had to take account
of the recession and the Polish experience with shock treatment.
Caution would have been in order. Yet international financial institutions also pushed for one-time solutions; they wanted to bring the
former socialist countries to the point from which return to some kind
of a socialist system would be very difficult.

In the literature, many alternative transformation programmes
have been suggested. I agree with those economists who argue that
the transition to a market economy, including economic stabilisation,
should be governed by the principle of gradualness. Experience
hitherto, mainly in Poland, confirms this. There is no reason to
engage in risky, one-shot programmes which expose the population
to great hardship in order to make sure, among other things, that
there will be no return to the old system. As already indicated above,
there is no such danger. On the contrary, exposing the population to
great hardship may generate strong nostalgia for the old system, a
phenomenon which is quite evident in Poland.

It is certainly of interest to know that the Interaction Council,
which groups former statesmen, with Helmut Schmidt, the former
chancellor of Germany, at the helm, and which has at its disposal a
group of renowned experts, took more or less a similar view in a
statement at their meeting in Prague, chaired by Pierre Trudeau, the
former prime minister of Canada.[7] 'The transformation of one system
predominantly based on central planning and state ownership into
another, predominantly based on market principles, private ownership and encouragement of initiative and enterprise, may well take
over a decade. *Countries cannot expect to reap immediate benefits.
Transformation does not happen overnight'*, reads the statement (*Final Statement*, 1991, p. 1).

In the ensuing text a model of gradual transformation is suggested.
Of course, only the principles applied should be the same in all the
countries; their implementation, sequence of the provisions and their
timing should depend on the concrete situation in each individual
country. The transition process should start with measures which
would withdraw the money overhang where such exists and at the
same time boost market forces. It is necessary to begin, as soon as
possible, with the sale of retail stores, small-scale production units

and service facilities. In order not to be hampered in this action by the need to compensate the original owners of the nationalised assets, the rule should be adopted that compensation is to be given only in the form of cash or long-term bonds. Furthermore, the sale of state apartments should be started. To encourage apartment dwellers to buy apartments, their prices should be set below the 'market price' and it should be made clear that it is the government's intention to increase rents gradually to an economically justifiable level.

The evolution of the market should also be supported by the creation of incentives for the opening of new businesses. Great opportunities are available, mainly in the service sector, which was very much neglected under the old regime, but also in the small-scale production of goods. One such incentive should be the extension of credit under favourable conditions.

The liquidation of the money overhang can be helped by government-sponsored investment in the insufficiently developed infrastructure. People will certainly buy bonds issued for the financing of such investment, if the return on the invested funds is guaranteed and the interest rate is set at a higher level than for bank deposits. Investment in bonds can in some cases be sweetened by promising preferential access to the services which will arise from such an investment (for example, a telephone connection). Investment in the infrastructure, as well as in services, in addition to satisfying an effective demand and thus contributing to a restructuring of the economy in a desired direction, has the advantage of creating new job opportunities, at a time when employment in other sectors is shrinking.

It is obvious that, without a rational price system, the market cannot work properly. This does not mean that prices should be freed all at once. If high inflation, combined with a huge decline in output, is to be avoided, the freeing of prices must be carried out in stages, according to a well thought-out plan. This is all the more necessary since the freeing of prices must be combined with a gradual elimination of most subsidies.

The inflationary effect of freeing prices depends to a great degree on the extent of the competitive environment. All the countries under review have entered the transition period with a highly monopolised economy. No doubt, a genuine, far-reaching, selective deconcentration is needed. It should be selective because in some branches economic and technological considerations justify concentration. The need for the creation of a competitive environment is a further reason why the transformation policy should not start with a comprehensive liberalisation of prices.

The receipts from the sale of state assets and the elimination of subsidies will help to reduce the budget deficit. A gradual increase in the interest rate for housing loans to the market level can also be a contribution to the renewal of budget equilibrium. Fiscal discipline, combined with a reasonable monetary policy, must be enforced.

Wages should not be freed. Their growth should be a matter of an agreement among the government, employers and trade unions. If an agreement to hold down the growth of wages to the approximate increase in the cost of living cannot be reached, the government should interfere. What should be done about wages in the private sector? As long as the private sector contributes only a tiny percentage to the total output, there can be no objection to letting it handle wages according to its own considerations. It must, however, comply with rules referring to minimum wages. Once the private sector becomes a bigger player in the economy, it must be subject to the same rules as the state sector.

Foreign trade must also be liberalised gradually as the number of convertible commodities increases. In the meantime, it is necessary to protect the domestic market in non-competitive branches of industry from being flooded by foreign goods. In their naive excitement about the market, Polish neo-liberals have excessively liberalised imports, and recently L. Wałęsa complained that foreigners were destroying Polish industry. In my opinion, he should blame first government policy and, second, Poles who use their foreign currency holdings to import cheap foreign goods instead of investing them in Poland.

Only when this process of competitiveness-promotion has manifestly taken hold can convertibility of the currency follow. To resort to convertibility much earlier would require setting the exchange rate at an inflationary level and exposing the economy to the probable need for a frequent currency devaluation, thus turning it into a constant source of inflation.[8]

The introduction of a realistic exchange rate should also be gradual. It should be recalled that after WWII several Western countries had two or three exchange rates for some time.

Large privatisation is a long process and cannot affect all enterprises. It is in the interest of the economy to avoid an atmosphere of expectancy and passivity, even in enterprises which are scheduled to be privatised. One of the first provisions in the transitional period should be to make enterprise operations as efficient as possible. It seems that the best way to do this is to give them full autonomy (with property rights remaining in the hands of the state), with the understanding that they must be self-financed and that they cannot expect a government bail-out whenever they are in trouble. This does not mean that the government should leave enterprises to themselves. The post-socialist economies need substantial restructuring; it would be foolish to expect that the market alone can do this. The government must play an active role in restructuring the economy. (For more, see below, p. 291.)

Last but not least, market institutions (such as a two-tier banking system, capital and labour market, stock market), including a legal system conducive to market relations, must be built up. Without such a market infrastructure, economic policies, including monetary and fiscal policies, cannot be expected to have the desired impact. The shock treatment in Poland has also had such devastating effects because it was applied at a time when the market infrastructure was missing.

Privatisation

As is known, almost all productive assets were nationalised or collectivised in most former socialist countries. This was a great blunder and, no doubt, one of the factors which doomed the traditional system to failure. Sweeping socialisation of the means of production was motivated primarily by ideological considerations, and not by economic ones. Lenin's statement that small-scale production constantly breeds capitalism certainly played an important role in the eagerness to socialise everything possible. In some countries, the circumstance that the private sector paid higher wages than the state sector could afford was not without effect on the approach to small-scale industries. In brief, private ownership was suspect, and state ownership was given preference, regardless of its economic merit.

Nowadays, we are witnesses to an opposite approach to ownership in the former socialist countries. The authorities' behaviour is based on the assumption that a market economy can only work if private ownership predominates and is treated preferentially. Many neo-liberals would privatise everything. Even many of those economists who in the past took the position that all forms of ownership must be treated equally and given the chance to compete under equal conditions, now demand preferential treatment for private ownership. This is not surprising, considering that such thinking is widespread in the West.

True, many take such a position because they believe that private ownership is superior to state ownership. In my opinion, it is wrong to make such generalisations. No doubt, private ownership is superior when the manager is at the same time the owner; it can be assumed that an owner who risks his capital will work to the best of his ability to make his operations as efficient as possible. (Whether he will succeed depends on, among other things, his skills, knowledge, initiative, perseverance and so on.) This is the case of small- and middle-scale enterprises where a direct link between ownership and management exists. The situation is not so clear when there is a separation between ownership and management, which is the case in corporations. Some questions are in order: Do private shareholders have a decisive control over corporations? Can they impose their will on managers and make the latter respect their interests? Can they remove managers who are inept or who work against the shareholders' interests? No doubt, there are laws on the books which allow shareholders to do all this. The question is: what is the practice? In the East European countries and the former USSR, where many economists believe that market economies work as textbooks suggest they should work, the question is answered positively. In the West, the answers to this question are controversial. In their *From Marx to the Market*, W. Brus and K. Laski take an affirmative position: they write, 'The latter – the controlling or almost controlling owners – are the main carriers or potential carriers of the entrepreneurial function through direct strategic decisions taken by the boards of directors, through supervision of the management actions, and through personnel policy. Here one can hardly claim a divorce between ownership and entrepreneurship' (1989, p. 141). In addition, they distinguish between managerial and entrepreneurial functions, the difference being that the latter also include risky decisions which only owners can make. They draw the conclusion that 'state enterprises can hardly be expected to become the same kind of players in the market as private, individual or collective enterprises' (1989, p. 142). In his *The New Industrial State* (1967, pp. 90–1), J. K. Galbraith takes a different position; he maintains that managers in American corporations are able to manipulate shareholders, mainly because of the great dispersion of stock ownership. Who is correct? To my knowledge, there are no statistical figures on this matter, and, if there were, they could not be very reliable, considering the complexity of the nature of the question. What exists is of an anecdotal character.

Some comments on Brus and Laski's statement are in order. They implicitly assume, judging from the text, that the controlling owners all pull in the same direction, and therefore managers have a hard time manipulating them. In reality, controlling owners may have a variety of interests, one reason being their involvement in more than one corporation and therefore they may not all take the same attitude to the management of a certain corporation. In addition, not all the members of the board of directors, which is usually equipped with great authority, are representatives of the owners. In Burrough and Hellyar (1990), which discusses the fate of the American huge corporation RJR Nabisco, one can find a classic example of how the chief executive of the corporation was able to manipulate the board of directors by giving them various privileges.

One could make a further point about Brus and Laski's statement. They do not regard all institutional investors as the carriers of the entrepreneurial function; they put some of them in the same group as dispersed shareholders. It is known that institutional investors are nowadays the main shareholders; B. Horvat (Możejko, 1990) estimates their share at 75 per cent. Even if we limit ourselves to comments made here and consider J. K. Galbraith's findings, it seems plausible to argue that the influence of private shareholders is not nearly as powerful as some believe it to be. And where it is, is there proof that individuals outside the corporation can make the best decisions when hundreds of millions or billions of dollars are involved? Wealth in itself does not provide the expertise needed in order to make rational decisions about sophisticated production and investment problems.[9]

For all the reasons mentioned, it seems to me that in the case of large enterprises managed by hired personnel, there need not necessarily be a difference between privately owned and state-owned firms as to entrepreneurship. Z. Šulc's view (see p. 242) about the relationship between the economic system and the impact of ownership on economic efficiency supports this statement. There is, however, one important qualification. The state-owned firms must have far-reaching autonomy. They must be treated like other forms of ownership in terms of taxes, subsidies, economic regulation and so on. If they have to perform certain economic functions for the state, these should not be performed at the cost of efficiency.

In my opinion, an economy fares best if different forms of ownership (private, employee-owned, state, including self-managed) will compete with each other. None of the ownership forms should get priority for ideological reasons. There is no reason why state-owned firms could not exist in insurance and banking, not to say in production. American insurance firms have not given any proof that they are superior to potential state insurance.[10] Health insurance firms are to a great degree responsible for the rapidly growing health costs in the US. Many American banks, including some large ones, have collapsed, and many are threatened with bankruptcy because of large investment in risky real estate.[11] In East European countries privatisation is very much governed by ideological instead of purely economic considerations. It is portrayed by the ruling élites as if it were the goal of the transformation of the economy. The statement of the Interaction Council, mentioned above, hit the mark by writing 'Although public debate over the last two years has focused heavily on privatisation, *the ends must not be confused with the means*. While introduction of the market economy remains a priority objective, *privatization is but one of the means for its attainment*' (*Final Statement*, 1991, p. 2).

The above approach to privatisation is manifested in the tendency to carry out large privatisation as fast as possible, even at the expense of great losses to the economy. Obviously, the idea of distributing a portion of state assets to the population without charge, or at a nominal charge, has its origin in the desire to accelerate the process of privatisation. Despite all the expectations of the adherents of fast privatisation and the urging of Western financial institutions, large privatisation is proceeding slowly. One important reason for this in Czechoslovakia is the result of the adopted compensation laws, which make it necessary in most cases to ascertain first who the original owners of the assets were. In none of the countries under review is there great interest in purchasing shares of companies to be privatised, either domestically, since there are more attractive investments (real estate, currency speculation), or abroad, because of the fear of instability.

I agree with the critical views on the idea of investment vouchers as they were expressed in the country studies chapters. I would like only to add that the real beneficiaries of privatisation vouchers will probably not be ordinary people, but rich individuals (most of whom gained their wealth in illegal ways during the old system or in the new). Ordinary people who have little knowledge of the stock market will be an easy prey to speculators. Distribution of privatisation vouchers will be an important link in the ongoing process of immense redistribution of income and wealth and the creation of a prosperous middle and upper class.

Many neo-liberals see the slow process of privatisation as a significant factor in the existing difficulties in the economy. Had the architects of transitional programmes had more sense of the possible, had they not been carried away by wishful thinking and had they accordingly adjusted the working of enterprises, the countries' economies could now be in better shape. The uncertainty which has been created in enterprises has contributed, no doubt, to the economic difficulties. The tax and credit discrimination which has been applied against state enterprises, mainly in Poland, has also worked in this direction. Furthermore, privatisation could have been helped, had the governments pursued aggressively a policy of creation of new private enterprises. (For more, see pp. 282–3.)

POSSIBLE ROLE OF PLANNING

With the collapse of the socialist system, the idea of socialism itself has been discredited and with it the idea of planning *per se*. There was a period in the Soviet Union and East European countries when almost divine qualities were attributed to planning, and the market was demonised. Now the situation is reversed.

Does this mean that planning has no usefulness in the transitional period or later in a fully fledged market economy? No doubt, the great majority of the ruling élites in the former socialist countries answer this question positively. The approach to planning is determined by the role which one attributes to government in the management of the economy. If one believes that government involvement should be confined to the creation of an environment conducive to the working of the market and, in economic policies, to the primary use of monetary policy, which is the view of neo-liberals, then, of course, planning has no place in such a scheme.[12]

However, in all the countries under review, despite frequent *laissez faire* rhetoric, the government intervenes beyond what M. Friedman, the high priest of pure marketisation, suggests, and beyond what is usual in Western market economies. Some planning activity is also going on in East European countries, though under different names, such as programmes and prognoses, but these, of course, are binding only on the governments. The nature of the transitional period dictates a greater involvement of the government than there is in some other countries.

It is obvious that detailed planning, combined with compulsory targets assigned to enterprises, is irreconcilable with a market economy. On the other hand, forecasting and *ad hoc* interventions in the economy for the sake of mitigating fluctuations in the economy cannot be regarded as planning. I agree with economists who understand by planning the pursuit of some future aims, the coordination of these aims in order to achieve them, and the existence of a plan (see Tinbergen, 1964, p. 8; Oules, 1966, pp. 28–9). J. Hayward (1978, p. 11) advances a definition of planning (shared also by Chaloupek and Teufelsbauer, 1987, p. 316) which is acceptable, though broad, and, as the author himself states, which is intended to cover all kinds of planning systems. Planning 'is attempted through the strategic use of instruments of economic and social policy by the government, in concert with other economic and social organisations, to attain explicit quantitative and/or qualitative objectives in the short, medium and long term'. Even if the definition does not mention the word 'plan', it is clear from further on in the text that a plan is assumed.

In a discussion of the role of planning, it is necessary to distinguish between its function in the transitional period to a market economy and that in an established market economy. In the transitional period, planning is not only helpful, but it is almost imperative in order to ease marketisation of the economy (compare Dallago, 1991). As already mentioned, it is now clear that privatisation in the countries under review will proceed over a long period and that the governments, even as formal owners, will be involved in the economy. They directly or indirectly control a great amount of investment, credit and the interest rate (compare Brada, 1990), and therefore they can have an important role in the urgently needed transformation of the economic structure. Such activity may have a greater effect on the economy if it is properly planned on the basis of research into the development of world and domestic markets, and the economic actors are informed about government intentions ahead of time. Planning can also act in a positive way in opening up the economy to world markets. It can even be used to pull the former Soviet and East European economies out of the recession in which they find themselves at present. Finally, it can be used for actions which create conditions for its own far-reaching elimination, for example, privatisation of the state sector.

Planning's role in a market economy must necessarily be much smaller. I will proceed from a less controversial through to a more controversial suggestion.

Firstly, in my opinion, the most important planning activity in a market economy should be what can be called 'strategic planning'. It means letting planning focus on structural changes – more precisely, using planning for the optimisation of the economic structure (compare Karpiński, 1989). This does not mean subjecting structural changes to some plan objectives. It means only that some important production and certain technologies, which are of importance for the restructuring of the economy from the viewpoint of domestic and foreign demand and for an increase in the competitiveness of domestic products in foreign markets, are picked out for special care.

The role of the plan, be it long- or medium- term, which is binding only on the government, is to identify the important production and technologies and outline ways of handling them. Up to this point, there may be agreement among economists; even opponents of planning do not mind if the government supports very significant productions and/or technologies. The question is: should the government become the investor or should it decide who the investor is on the basis of tender, and contribute to the financing of investment by subsidy and/or guaranteed loans?

Most adherents of full marketisation of the economy are against direct government involvement in investment. On the one hand, they are afraid that such involvement may impede the working of the market and, on the other, they distrust government's ability to do things right. As is known the greatest shortcomings of the administrative system were, namely, its inability to ensure smooth changes in the structure of the economy in accordance with changes in demand at home, and to maintain an acceptable pace in technological development.

In my opinion, government involvement in a limited number of investments may produce better results than a pure system of subsidies which, in the final analysis, does not commit the receiving parties to achieving any concrete results.

It is vital for the countries under review to lessen substantially the technological gap which divides them from the West. To rely on market forces alone to do the job is a gamble. In some countries, such as Japan[13] and South Korea, the government has been instrumental in promoting technological progress, and there is no reason why this could not be done in the former socialist countries.

Secondly, I would suggest that planning may play an important role in the reconciliation of conflicting interests, primarily between employers and employees. Many market economies leave the harmonising of conflicting interests to the market and combat its negative effects with monetary policy, mainly increases in interest rates which produce unemployment. If the countries are determined not to allow high rates of unemployment, it is not advisable to rely on the market alone; they must have an incomes policy in place. To make such an incomes policy rational, it must be based on realistic forecasts and plans for the development of the economy.

Incomes policy need not mean the imposition of specific solutions or the introduction of a mandatory price and wage policy (see Adam, 1990). If the employers and employees can agree without upsetting the economy, there is no reason for the government to intervene. In many cases, awareness that the government can intervene may be a sufficient encouragement for the two bargaining parties to come to a viable compromise. However, if the two parties cannot agree, or if the agreement is such that in the long run it will produce inflation, the government should step in.

The following suggestion is the most controversial. It deals with the possible coordinating role of the planning authority (its elected body in preference to the executive body) in formulating medium- and long- term economic and social policy. Short-term economic policy, particularly when it refers to *ad hoc* intervention in the economy, should be left in the hands of functional ministries, mainly the ministry of finance. Of course, the formulation of medium- and long-term economic and social policy cannot be the realm of the planning authority only; all other ministries must have an important input since they know best the problems on their own ground and can best defend their interests.

On the other hand, it should be remembered that the planning authority has two advantages which make it fit for the coordinating function. Due to their planning activities, the planning authorities have, more than other institutions, a comprehensive body of information based on research about the state of the economy and its various components, and forecasts about possible development.

Second, compared to other central economic institutions (for example, the ministry of industry or agriculture), the planning authority is the most neutral to group interests. In its coordinating role, it should reconcile conflicting interests without allowing any serious injury to national interests. This is not an easy task, because some

members of the elected planning authority are representatives of
certain group interests. However, the planning authority can count
on some help. On the one hand, market forces may keep group
interests partly in check. On the other, the public airing of significant
economic and social policy problems, and scrutiny of the activities of
the planning authority, in accordance with the principle of democratisation of planning, may work in the same direction.[14]

*   *   *

In the first ten chapters I have discussed the development of views on
planning and market in the last thirty odd years in the four countries
under review. I have tried to show the changes in thinking on the
topic of this book and the reasons for these changes, as well as the
differences in thinking in individual countries and the origin of these
differences. In the space which was available to me, I could, of
course, focus only on the most relevant aspects of the topic discussed.
Needless to say, the first ten chapters were influenced by my own
views on the topic which are explicitly presented in the last chapter. I
do not expect that my interpretations of the debates in the countries
under review and my views expressed in the last chapter will be
generally accepted; I look forward to a constructive debate in the
hope that this will shed further light on the topic.

In my own opinion, socialism, all aspects of its development,
including the evolution of thought about the system, and its failure
will be a topic of research for some time to come. This interest is
generated not only by theoretical inquisitiveness, but also by some
popular curiosity about an alternative system to capitalism, socialism,
which failed. If my book, which I present now to the readers, is of
some help to a better understanding of real socialism, I will feel that
my work was not in vain.

Notes

1. Gy. Horn, the present leader of the Hungarian Socialist Party, mentioned in an interview (*Nsz*, 22 October 1991) that his first doubts about
socialism occurred at the end of the 1960s when he had a chance to read a
comparison of the performance of the Czechoslovak and Austrian economies, prepared by the foreign ministry where he worked. At that time,
only the foreign ministry was allowed to make such comparisons.

2. This should not be understood to mean in any way that the capitalist system is an ideal system.

3. It is understandable that sellers have a tendency to praise their goods and attribute qualities to them which they do not have, or have only to a small extent. Therefore it is not surprising that the market was portrayed by the new adherents of a market economy as a panacea for all the ills of the economy. This may, however, be detrimental if the new converts, holding positions of high responsibility in the new governments, as has happened mainly in Poland and Czechoslovakia, become victims of their own propaganda.

4. Henry Kaufman, the former chief economist of the well-known big American brokerage house, Solomon Brothers, a very influential economist in his own right, was asked in a television programme, 'This week with David Brinkley' (21 December 1991), to explain the reasons for the American recession. To him, the current recession is the result of old sins, such as introducing too liberal a regime for financial institutions. He apparently had in mind the fact that institutions are not regulated enough by the government and are free to invest in real estate according to their own consideration.

5. Two examples will make clear what I have in mind. In Canada at the end of the 1960s there were several occasions when whole families died as a result of fire. In one case a family of eleven died in Quebec. Almost all the victims were poor, living in dilapidated dwellings. But the Canadian government did little to remedy the situation; it relied on the market. And indeed, the market came up with smoke detectors, which were quite expensive in the beginning and therefore unaffordable for the poor. A socialist government worth its name would have initiated research to create a fire warning gadget and made it available to the poor at a subsidised price or without charge. In addition, it would make the installation of smoke detectors in all housing units compulsory; therefore their price could be relatively low.

   It is clear that in the USA the Bush administration did not want a national health care system for ideological reasons, though it is proven that private health care insurance companies are inefficient and an obstacle to general access to health care. Needless to say, such an attitude is unacceptable to a socialist government.

6. The neo-liberals usually stress only the positive aspects of shock treatment. The IMF and Western advisers behave in the same way. In his many interviews, J. Sachs, who was an adviser to the Polish minister of finance and now is an adviser to the Russian government, always stresses the achievement of market equilibrium, but avoids talking about the social costs. In addition, as a proof of success in Poland he uses an argument which is faulty and not dignified for a Harvard University professor, namely, that the value of average incomes in terms of dollars increased substantially compared to the period preceding shock treatment. He forgets that before shock treatment, Poles could get at least twice or three times as many goods for one dollar.

7. In addition to those mentioned, the Interaction Council includes, among others, Gerald Ford, the former president of the USA, Valery Giscard

d' Estaing, former president of France, and Lord Callaghan, former prime minister of Great Britain.

8. The *IMF Survey* published, in its issue of 2 December 1991, a report about a volume of papers, *Currency Convertibility in Eastern Europe*, edited by J. Williamson, and highlighted the quotation from the text on which the contributors agreed, namely 'currency convertibility makes sense when the essential features of a market economy are already in place'. It is interesting that the writer of the report did not directly argue with this view.

9. R. Campeau, for example, a Canadian tycoon, learned it the hard way. Having a lot of money from successful real estate investments, he decided to purchase a big chunk of retail business in the USA with the help of bank loans and junk bonds in the amount of $ 6 billion. The investment turned out to be a disaster, one reason being, as experts agree, that he had only money and no understanding of the retail business.

10. In three Canadian provinces, state car insurance exists; it was introduced by a social democratic administration. In British Columbia, it has been preserved even under a very conservative government.

11. In the USA, credit card holders must pay approximately 18 per cent interest on the unpaid balance on their account. Now that the market interest rate has dramatically fallen, consumer associations demanded a reduction in the interest rate paid by card holders. George Bush also came up with the same demand. Then the banks made it clear that a substantial reduction would endanger their stability, since 25 per cent of their profits come from interest on credit cards. In other words, the low income segments of the population – higher income groups pay their debts on time – must finance the stability of the banks.

12. Of the four countries under review, Poland is the only one where the Planning Office has not been abolished. In Hungary, it was abolished by the new government resulting from free elections, in Czechoslovakia it was eliminated in 1991, and in the Soviet Union Gossplan was turned into the ministry of economy and prognosis.

13. In the television programme '60 minutes', broadcast on 21 April 1991, reporter M. Wallace complained about the American lag in technology in some areas. According to his inquiries, American high-tech weapons used in the Gulf War could not have worked without their Japanese technological components. He mentioned, what is generally well known, that the Japanese government is directly involved in promoting technological progress.

14. In my discussion in 1991 with high officials of the smaller countries under review, involved in what may be called planning, it turned out that their ministry was the centre which prepares a lot of economic policy proposals.

Bibliography

For space reasons only full reference to books, regardless of the language in which they are published, are listed. References to periodicals and newspaper articles are listed without titles unless they are published in English. If, from an edited volume of studies, several studies are used, besides the author, the editor(s) of the volume as well as the first word of the title are indicated. The full reference to the volume is listed under the name of the editor(s).

ABALKIN, L. (1983) *K*, no. 14.
ABALKIN, L. (1986) *The Strategy of Economic Development in the USSR* (Moscow: Progress Publishers). Translation from Russian.
ABALKIN, L. (1987) *PKh*, no. 5.
ABALKIN, L. (1988) *VE*, no. 6.
ABALKIN, L. (1988A) *EG*, no. 45.
ABALKIN, L. (1989) *VE*, no. 7.
ABALKIN, L. (1990) *VE*, no. 1.
ABALKIN, L. (1990A) *EiZh*, no. 49.
ABALKIN, L. (1991) *P*, no. 7.
Act on Privatisation (1990) *ZG*, no. 16.
'Action Programme of the Communist Party of Czechoslovakia' (1969), in *Rok šedesátý osmý* (Prague: Svoboda).
ADAM, J. (1979) *Wage Control and Inflation in the Soviet Bloc Countries* (London: Macmillan; New York (1980): Praeger Publishers).
ADAM, J. (1989) *Economic Reforms in the Soviet Union and Eastern Europe since the 1960s* (London: Macmillan; New York: St. Martin's Press).
ADAM, J. (1990) 'Inflation and Unemployment', in Hungarian *Gazdaság*, no. 1; in Czech *PE*, no. 8; in Russian (1991) *VE*, no. 1; and in Polish *E*, no. 4–6.
ADAM, J. (1991) 'The possible new role of market and planning in Poland and Hungary', in Aslund, A. (ed.) *Market Socialism or the Restoration of Capitalism* (Cambridge University Press).
AGANBEGIAN, A. (1987) *EKO*, no. 11.
AGANBEGIAN, A. (1990) *VE*, no. 2.
AGANBEGIAN, A. (1990A) *P*, 27 August.
AKHMEDUEV, A. (1991) *VE*, no. 4.
ALBINOWSKI, S. (1981) *Trybuna Ludu*, no. 223.
ALTMANN, F. L. (1987) *Wirtschaftsentwicklung und Strukturpolitik in der Tschechoslowakei nach 1968* (Munich: Olzog Verlag).
ANTAL, L. (1982) 'Thoughts on the Further Development of the Hungarian Mechanism', *Acta Oeconomica*, Vol. 29, no. 3–4.
ANTAL, L. (1983) *Medvetánc*, nos 2–3.
ANTAL, L. (1983A) 'Carrying on with the Economic Reform', *The New Hungarian Quarterly*, no. 91, Autumn.
ANTAL, L. (1984) in *Vita* . . . (Budapest).

ANTAL, L. (1985) 'About the Property Incentive', *Acta Oeconomica*, Vol. 34, no. 3–4.
ANTAL, L. (1985A) *Gazdaságirányítási és pénzügyi rendszerünk a reform útján* (Budapest: KJK).
ANTAL, L. (1988) *Tervgazdasági Fórum*, no. 4.
ANTAL, L., L. BOKROS, I. CSILLAG, L. LENGYEL and Gy. MATOLCSY (1987) 'Fordulat és reform' ('Turning Point and Reform') *KSz*, no. 6.
ÁRVA, L. (1989) *KSz*, no. 9.
ASTAKHOV, B., L. VOZNESENSKY, F. VOLKOV and A. JUDKIN (1988) 'Questions of Commodity Production and the Law of Value under Socialism', *PoE*, October.
A szocialista országok gazdasági mechanizmusa (1984), collective work of Soviet, Czechoslovak, Hungarian, GDR, Polish, Bulgarian and Mongolian economists (Budapest: KJK). Translation from Russian.
ASZTALOS, L. Gy., L. BOKROS and Gy. SURÁNYI (1984) *KSz*, no. 4.

BÁGER, G. (1989) *Tervgazdasági Fórum*, no. 4.
BAKA, W. (1981) interview, *Zycie Warszawy*, 10 July.
BALASSA, Á. (1984) in *Vita . . .* (Budapest).
BALASSA, Á. (1987) *Tervgazdasági Fórum*, no. 3.
BALÁZSY, S. (1954) *Többtermelés*, no. 11.
BALÁZSY, S. (1984) *KSz*, no. 5.
BALCEROWICZ, E. (1991) *GN*, no. 7–8.
BALCEROWICZ, L. et al. (1980) *ZG*, nos 51–2.
BALCEROWICZ, L. et al. (1981) *Przeglad Techniczny*, nos 47 and 48.
BÁRSONY, J. (1986) *KSz*, no. 4.
BÁRSONY, J. (1989) *KSz*, no. 5.
BAUER, T. (1982) *Mozgó Világ*, no. 11.
BAUER, T. (1983) *KSz*, no. 11.
BAUER, T. (1984) in *Vita . . .* (Budapest).
BAUER, T. (1989) *F*, no. 50.
BEKSIAK, J. (1968) *Nowe Drogi*, no. 3.
BEKSIAK, J. (1981) *Biuletyn AS*, no. 4, February.
BEREND, T. I. (1983), in I. Síklaky (ed.), *Koncepció és kritika* (Budapest: Magvető).
BEREND, T. I. (1988) *A magyar gazdasági reform útja* (Budapest: KJK).
BEREND, T. I. (1990) *The Hungarian Economic Reforms 1953–1988* (Cambridge University Press).
BERGSON, A. (1960) Comment to Zauberman Alfred's paper 'The Soviet Debate on the Law of Value and Price Formation', in G. Grossman (ed.), *Value and Plan. Economic Calculation and Organization in Eastern Europe* (Berkley: University of California Press).
BIELASIAK, J. (1983) 'The Party: Permanent Crisis', in A. Brumberg (ed.), *Poland: Genesis of a Revolution* (New York: Vintage Books).
BIRMAN, A. (1964) 'For a Profound Elaboration of Problems of Management', *PoE*, no. 5. Russian original in *PKh* (1963) no. 3.
Blue Ribbon Commission (1990) *Hungary in Transformation to Freedom and Prosperity*, (Budapest).

BOBROWSKI, Cz. (1957) in *Dyskusja o polskim modelu gospodarczym* (Warsaw: Książka i wiedza).
BOGOMOLOV, O. (1989) *K*, no. 11.
BOKOR, J., O. GADÓ, P. KÜRTHY, T. MEITNER, S. SÁROSINÉ and J. WILCSEK (1957) *KSz*, no. 4.
BOKROS, L. (1989) *F*, no. 38.
BORNSTEIN, M. (1964) 'The Soviet Price Reform Discussion', *Quarterly Journal of Economics*, vol. LXXVIII, pp. 15–48.
BOSIAKOWSKI, Z. (1963) *E*, no. 6.
BRADA, J. C. (1990) 'Indicative Planning in Socialist Economies: Does It Have a Role?', *Journal of Comparative Economics*, vol. 14.
BRÁNIK, J. (1967) in Bránik, J. (ed.), *Řízení národního hospodářství* (Prague: Svoboda)
BRATISHCHEV, I. et al. (1991) *EiZh*, no. 21.
'Bridge' (1990) 'Híd-csoport', *Kg*, no. 7.
BRUS, W. (1956) *GP*, no. 7.
BRUS, W. (1972) *The Market in a Socialist Economy* (London: Routledge & Kegan Paul). Translation from Polish (1961).
BRUS, W. and K. LASKI (1989) *From Marx to the Market: Socialism in Search of an Economic System* (Oxford: Clarendon Press).
BUGAJ, R. (1988) in *Propozycje Przeksztalcen Polskiej Gospodarki* (Warsaw: Zeszyty Naukowe).
BUGAJ, R. et al. (1981), proposal to the I. Congress of Solidarity, in Programme, *Tygodnik Solidarnosc*, no. 29. See also the report in no. 26.
BUGAJ, R., Sz. JAKUBOWICZ, J. MUJZEL and A. TOPIŃSKI (1981) *ZG*, no. 15.
BUGAJ, R. and T. KOWALIK (1986) *Wiez*, no. 10.
BUGAJ, R. and T. KOWALIK (1990) *ZG*, no. 39.
BUNICH, P. (1985) *VE*, no. 9.
BUNICH, P. (1985A) *EKO*, no. 2.
BUNICH, P. (1988) *VE*, no. 8.
BUNICH, P. (1988A) *Sotsialisticheskii trud*, no. 8.
BURROUGH, B. and J. HELYAR (1990) *Barbarians at the Gate. The Fall of RJR Nabisco* (New York: Harper & Row).
BUTENKO, A. (1988) *EKO*, no. 2.

CABAN, W. (1988) *ZG*, no. 39.
CAMPBELL, R. (1968) 'The Economic Reform in the USSR', *American Economic Review*, May.
ČERVINKA, A. (1985) *HN*, no. 44.
CHALOUPEK, G. and W. TEUFELSBAUER (1987) *Gesamtwirtschaftliche Planung in Westeuropa* (Frankfurt: Campus Verlag).
CHANDLER, A. D. (1990) *Scale and Scope, The Dynamics of Industrial Capitalism* (Harvard University Press).
CHERNYSHEVA, V. (1964) 'Summary of Discussion on Problems of Price Formation', *PoE*, no. 4. Russian original in *VE* (1963) no. 7.
CIEPIELEWSKI, J. (1987) in J. Ciepielewski (ed.) *Dzieje Panstw Socjalistycznych* (Warsaw: PWN).
'Contemporary Concept of Socialism' (1989) *P*, 14, 16 and 17 July.

'Corporate élite' (1991) *Business Week*, 25 November.
CSABA, L. (1991) interview in *F*, no. 7.
CSAPÓ, L. (1967) *KSz*, no. 9.
CSIKÓS-NAGY, B. (1964) *KSz*, no. 9.
CSIKÓS-NAGY, B. (1966) *Ekonomický časopis*, no. 9. Translation from Hungarian.
CSIKÓS-NAGY, B. (1968) *PSz*, no. 10.
CSIKÓS-NAGY, B. (1982) 'Development Problems of the Hungarian Economy', *The New Hungarian Quarterly*, no. 88, Winter.
CSIKÓS-NAGY, B. (1988) *Tervgazdasági Fórum*, no. 3.
CSILLAG, I. and K. A. SOÓS (1990) *F*, no. 4.

DĄBROWSKI, M. (1987) *ZG*, no. 29.
DĄBROWSKI, M. (1988) in *Propozycje Przeksztalcen Polskiej Gospodarki* (Warsaw: Zeszyty Naukowe).
DĄBROWSKI, M. (1991) *GN*, no. 7–8.
DĄBROWSKI, M. and R. BUGAJ (1990) *Tygodnik Solidarnosc*, no. 3.
DALLAGO, B. (1991) *Kg*, no. 5.
DIACHENKO, V. (1966) 'A Lever of Economic Stimulation', in Sharpe II. Russian original in (1965) *EG*, no. 45.
Directions of the Economic Reform (1981) (*Kierunki reformy gospodarczej*), (Warsaw: Książka i Wiedza).
'Diskuse . . .' (1957), ('Discussion about the law of value and the formation of prices') *PE*, no. 7.
DOBB, M. (1966) *Soviet Economic Development since 1917* (London: Routledge & Kegan Paul).
Documents adopted by the Congress of the Polish Economic Association (1981) *ZG*, no. 12.
DODER, D. and L. BRANSON (1990) *Gorbachev, Heretic in the Kremlin* (New York: Viking).
DVOŘÁK, J. (1988) *HN*, no. 4.
DVOŘÁK, J. (1989) *HN*, no. 3.
DVOŘÁK, J. et al. (1985) *Soustava plánovitého řízení, efektívnost a intenzifikace československé ekonomiky* (Prague: Svoboda).
DYBA, K. (1989) *PE*, no. 5.
DYBA, K. and K. KOUBA (1989) 'Czechoslovak Attempts at Systemic Changes: 1958, 1968, 1988', *Communist Economies*, vol. 1, no. 3.
'Dyskusja na II zjezdie ekonomistow polskich' (1956), ('Discussion on the II Congress of Polish Economists') *E*, no. 5.
Dyskusja o polskim modelu gospodarczym (1957), a collective work (Warsaw: Książka i wiedza).
DZARASOV, S. (1990) *VE*, no. 2.

Economic crisis, panel discussion (1981) *Tygodnik Solidarność*, no. 16.
The Economy of the USSR, Summary and Recommendations (1990) (Washington: The World Bank).
Ekonomicheskii stroi sotsializma (1984), collective work, E. I. Kapustin (chief editor), three volumes (Moscow: Ekonomika).
ELLMAN, M. (1971) *Soviet Planning Today* (Cambridge University Press).

ELLMAN, M. (1973) *Planning Problems in the USSR. The contribution of mathematical economics to their solution 1960–71* (Cambridge University Press).
ERNST, P. (1968) *Nová mysl*, no. 11.

FALLENBUCHL, Z. (1986) 'The Economic Crisis in Poland', in *East European Economies: Slow Growth in the 1980s* (Washington: US Congress).
FALUSNÉ SZIKRA, K. (1988) *KSz*, no. 4.
FEDORENKO, N. (1985) 'Planning and Management: What should they be like?', *PoE*, no. 8. Russian original (1984) *EKO*, no. 12.
FEDORENKO, N., P. BUNICH and S. SHATALIN (eds) (1970) *Sotsialisticheskie printsipy khoziaistvovaniia i effektivnost obshchestvennogo proizvodstva* (Moscow).
FEDOROVICH, M. (1962) *EG*, 3 and 10 Nov.
FEDOROWICZ, Z. (1988) *Trybuna Ludu*, 15 Sept.
FEJTÖ, F. (1974) *A History of the People's Democracies, Eastern Europe since Stalin* (Harmondsworth: Penguin).
FELKER, J. L. (1966) *Soviet Economic Controversies* (Cambridge Mass: MIT Press).
FERBER, K. and G. REJTÖ (1988) *Reform (év)fordulón* (Budapest: KJK).
FIGURNOV, E. (1988) *K*, no. 7.
Final Statement of the Interaction Council (1991) (New York).
'Fordulat és reform' ('Turning point and reform') Antal, L., L. Bokros, I. Csillag, L. Lengyel and Gy. Matolcsy (eds) (1987) *KSz*, no. 6. Also published in a slightly modified form in *Medvetánc*, no. 2, 1987.
FRISS, I. (1967) *KSz*, no. 6.

GALBRAITH, J. K. (1967) *The New Industrial State* (Toronto: Signet Books).
GATOWSKI, L. (1966) 'The Role of Profit in a Socialist Economy', in Sharpe I. Russian original (1962) *K*, no. 18.
Gazdaságpolitika és gazdasági fejlődés Magyarországon (1988), a study of the Planning Office, Budapest.
GLÓWCZYK, J. (1968) *ZG*, nos 14 and 15.
GOLAN, G. (1973) *Reform Rule in Czechoslovakia, The Dubček Era 1968–1969* (Cambridge University Press).
GOMULKA, S. (1991) *ZG*, no. 18.
GOMULKA, S. (1991A) 'The Causes of Recession Following Stabilization', *Comparative Economic Studies*, no. 2, Summer.
GORBACHEV, M. (1987) *On the Tasks of the Party in the Radical Restructuring of Economic Management* (Moscow: Novosti).
GORDON, J. (1962) *GP*, no. 2.
GOTZ-KOZIERKIEWICZ, D. (1991) *ZG*, no. 49.
GRABOWSKI, C. (1961) *Handel Wewnetrzny*, no. 5.
GROSFELD, J. (1981) *Tygodnik Powszechny*, no. 46.
GROSSMAN, G. (1966) 'Economic Reforms: A Balance Sheet', *Problems of Communism*, no. 6.
GRZYBOWSKI, S. (1981) *Przegląd Techniczny*, no. 6.

Guidelines . . . ('Ósnovnye napravleniia po stabilizatsii narodnogo khoziaistva i perekhodu k rynochnoi ekonomike') (1990) *P*, 18 October.
HÁBA, Z. (1987) *Nová mysl*, no. 9.
HÁBA, Z. (1987A) *PE*, no. 8.
HÁBA, Z. (1990) *HN*, no. 34.
HAGELMAYER, I. (1968) *Pénzügyi Szemle*, no. 4.
HANSON, Ph. (1990) 'Ownership Issues in *Perestroika*', in J. E. Tedstrom (ed.) *Socialism, Perestroika and the Dilemmas of Soviet Economic Reform* Boulder (Westview Press).
HAYWARD, J. (1978) 'Introduction; Inertia and Improvisation: The Planning Predicament', in Hayward, J. and O. A. Narkiewicz (eds) *Planning in Europe* (London: Croom Helm).
HERER, W. and W. SADOWSKI (1988) *Zderzenia z barierami rozwoju* (Warsaw: PWE).
HETÉNYI, I. (1989) *Tervgazdasági Közlemények*, no. 2.
HETÉNYI, I. (1989A) *Tervgazdasági Fórum*, no. 2.
HOCH, R. (1989) *TSz*, no. 11.
HOLUBNYCHY, V. (1982) *Selected Works of*, ed. I. S. Koropeckyj (Edmonton: Canadian Institute of Ukrainian Studies).
HORÁLEK, M., M. SOKOL, Č. KOŽUŠNÍK and O. TUREK (1968) *SHN*, no. 14.
HORVÁTH, D. T. (1991) *Kg*, no. 8.
HRNČÍŘ, M. (1988) *PE*, no. 12.
HRNČÍŘ, M. (1989) *PH*, no. 3.
HRNČÍŘOVÁ, M. and L. RUSMICH (1989) *HN*, no. 18.
Hungary in Transformation to Freedom and Prosperity (1990), Proposal of the Blue Ribbon Commission (Indianapolis: Hudson Institute).
Hungary (1991), OECD Economic Surveys (Geneva).

'IMF study examines the legacy of economic reform in Hungary' (1991) (report about *Economic Reform in Hungary since (1968)*, by A. Boote and J. Somogy) *IMF Survey*, 12 August.
Information on the Privatisation of State Owned Enterprises (1990) (Budapest: State Property Agency).
IVANCHENKO, V. (1988) *PKh*, no. 6.
IVANCHENKO, V. (1991) *PKh*, no. 2.
IWANEK, M. and M. SWIĘCICKI (1987) *ZG*, no. 26.

JAKUBOWICZ, S. (1981) *Przeglad Techniczny*, no. 15.
JÁNOSSY, F. (1969) *KSz*, nos 7–8.
JĘDRYCHOWSKI, S. (1982) *Zadluzenie Polski w krajach kapitalistycznych* (Warsaw: Książka i Wiedza).
JEŽEK, T. (1990) interview in *HN*, no. 45.
JEZIORANSKI, T. and M. K. KRZAK (1988) *ZG*, no. 8.
JÓZEFIAK, C. (1981) *Odra*, no. 3.
JÓZEFIAK, C. (1984), in J. Mujzel and S. Jakubowicz (eds) *Funkcjonowanie gospodarki polskiej* (Warsaw: PWE).
JÓZEFIAK, C. (1986) *21*, no. 1, May.

JOZEFIAK, C. (1990) *ZG*, nos 36 and 37.
JUDY, R. W. (1973) 'The Economists', in G. Skilling and F. Griffiths (eds) *Interest Groups in Soviet Politics* (Princeton University Press).

KADLEC, V. (1983) *Listy*, no. 5.
KADLEC, V. (1990) *HN*, no. 50.
KADLEC, V. (1991) interview in *Rudé právo*, 11 January.
KALECKI, M. (1963) *Zarys teorii wzrostu gospodarki socjalistycznej* (Warsaw: PWN).
KALECKI, M. (1982) *Socjalizm, funkcjonowanie i wieloletnie planowanie.* Collected Works, vol. 3 (Warsaw: PWE).
KALETA, J. (1991) *ZG*, no. 26.
KANTOROVICH, L. (1960) 'Mathematical Methods of Organising Planning and Production', *Management Science*, no. 4. Translation from Russian of a 1939 paper.
KANTOROVICH, L. (1965) *The Best Use of Economic Resources* (Oxford: Pergamon).
KANTOROVICH, L. (1966) 'Principle of Optimality', in Sharpe II. Russian original (1965) *EG*, no. 45.
KAPUSTIN, E. (1984) *VE*, no. 12.
KARAGEDOV, R. (1985) *EKO*, no. 5.
KARPIŃSKI, A. (1986) *40 lat planowania w Polsce. Problemy, ludzie, refleksje* (Warsaw: PWE).
KARPIŃSKI, A. (1987) in J. Ciepielenski (ed.) *Dzieje panstw socjalistycznych* (Warsaw: PWE).
KARPIŃSKI, A. (1989) *Nowe Drogi*, no. 8.
KATSENELINBOIGEN, A. (1979) *Soviet Economic Thought and Political Power in the USSR* (New York: Pergamon Press).
KAWALEC, S. (1988) in *Propozycje Przeksztalcen Polskiej Gospodarki* (Warsaw: Zeszyty Naukowe).
KAWALEC, S. (1989) *Zmiany*, no. 5.
KLACEK, J. (1990) in *Poznámky k ekonomické reforme* (Prague: Economic Institute of the Czechoslovak Academy of Sciences).
KLACEK, J. et al. (1991) *PE*, no. 9–10.
KLAUS, V. (1989) *PE*, no. 5.
KLAUS, V. (1990) *Finance a úvěr*, no. 8.
KLAUS, V. (1990A) in *Transformace centrálně plánovaných ekonomik v ekonomiky tržní* (Prague: Publication of the Economic Institute of Charles University, no. 3.
KLAUS, V. (1991) *THN*, no. 37.
KLAUS, V. and D. TŘÍSKA (1988) *PE*, no. 8.
KLUSOŇ, V. (1990) *HN*, no. 45.
KLUSOŇ, V. (1990A) *HN*, no. 46.
KOCANDA, R. and P. PELIKÁN (1967) *PE*, no. 2.
KODET, Z. (1965) *PE*, no. 4.
KOLÁŘ, J. and K. ZEMAN (1989) *HN*, no. 46.
KOŁODKO, G. (1990) *Polish Hyperinflation and Stabilization 1989–1990* (Warsaw: Working papers of the Institute of Finance, no. 10).
KOŁODKO, G. (1990A) *ZG*, no. 12.

Bibliography 303

KOŁODKO, G. (1990B) *Inflacja, Reforma, Stabilizacja* (Warsaw: Studentska Oficyna Wydawnicza ZSP).
KOŁODKO, G. (1991) *ZG*, nos. 46–47.
KOMÁREK, V. (1989) *PE*, no. 5.
KOMÁREK, V. (1989A) *HN*, no. 19.
KOMÁREK, V. (1990), interview in *HN*, no. 5.
KOMÁREK, V. (1990A) *HN*, no. 25.
KOMÁREK, V. (1991) in *Prognostické* . . . (Prague).
KOMÁREK, V. et al. (1990) *Prognóza a program* (Prague: Academia).
KOMENDA, B. (1966) *PE*, no. 9.
KOMENDA, B. (1969) *Nová mysl*, no. 7.
KOMENDA, B. and Č. KOŽUŠNÍK (1964) *PE*, no. 3.
KONDRATENKO, R. (1991) *PE*, no. 3.
KOPÁTSY, S. (1969) *PSz*, no. 11.
KOPÁTSY, S. (1988) 'Alakítsuk át részvénytársaságokká a versenyszféra nagyvállalatait', unpublished paper, 23 March.
KOPÁTSY, S. (1989) *Húsz év után* (Budapest: Pénzügykutató Részvénytársaság).
KOPÁTSY, S. (1990) *Nsz*, 19 September.
KORNAI, J. (1980) *Economics of Shortage* (Amsterdam North Holland).
KORNAI, J. (1982) *Gazdaság*, no. 3.
KORNAI, J. (1986) 'The Hungarian reform process: visions, hopes and reality', *Journal of Economic Literature*, December.
KORNAI, J. (1989) *Indulatos Röpirat a gazdasági átmenet ügyében* (Budapest: Heti Világgazdaság Kiadói Részvénytársaság).
KORNAI, J. (1990) *The Road to Free Economy. Shifting from a Socialist System. The Example of Hungary* (New York, London: W.W. Norton).
KORNAI, J. (1990A) *A gazdasági vezetés túlzott központosítása*, Second edition (Budapest: KJK). First edition was published in 1957.
KORNAI, J. (1990), interview in *Mozgó Világ*, no. 4.
KORNAI, J. and MATITS, A. (1987) *A vállalatok nyereségének bürokratikus újraelosztása* (Budapest: KJK).
KOSTA, J. (1973) 'The main features of the Czechoslovak Economic Reform', in V. Kusin (ed.) *The Czechoslovak Reform Movement 1968* (Oxford University Press).
KOSTA, J. (1974) *Sozialistische Planwirtschaft, Theorie und Praxis* (Opladen: Westdeutscher Verlag).
KOSTA, J. and B. LEVČÍK (1967) *Österreichische Osthefte*, no. 6.
KOTZ, L. (1987) in K. SZABÓ (ed.) *Vagyonérdekeltség – reform* (Budapest: KJK).
KOUBA, K. (1965) *PE*, no. 4.
KOUBA, K. (1967) *PE*, no. 9.
KOUBA, K. (1968) in K. KOUBA et al. (eds) *Úvahy o socialistické ekonomice* (Prague: Svoboda).
KOUBA, K. (1969) *Nová mysl*, no. 3.
KOUBA, K. (1990) *KSz*, no. 3.
KOUBA, K. (1990A) in *Transformace centrálně plánovaných ekonomik v ekonomiky tržní* (Prague: Publications of the Economic Institute of Charles University, no. 3.

KOUBA, K. (1990B) *PE*, no. 5.
KÖVES, A. (1991) *Kg*, no. 11.
KÖVES, A. (1992) *Nsz*, 8 January.
KOWALIK, T. (1986) 'On crucial reform of real socialism', *Forschungsberichte*, no. 122 (Vienna: The Vienna Institute for Comparative Economic Studies).
KOWALIK, T. (1987) 'Three Attitudes and Three Dramas', in G. Fink, G. Poll and M. Riese (eds) *Economic Theory, Political Power and Social Justice, Festschrift Kazimierz Laski*, Vienna: Springer-Verlag.
KOWALIK, T. (1987A) *ZG*, no. 17.
KOWALIK, T. (1989) *E*, no. 3.
KOWALIK, T. (1989A) *Zmiany*, no. 1.
KOWALIK, T. (1990) *ZG*, no. 35.
KOWALIK, T. (1990A) *ZG*, no. 28.
KOŽUŠNÍK, Č. (1968) *Ekonomická revue*, no. 4.
KOŽUŠNÍK, Č. (1968A) *Nová mysl*, no. 5.
KOŽUŠNÍK, Č. (1990) *HN*, no. 1.
KOŽUŠNÍK, Č. (1991) *NH*, no. 6.
KOŽUŠNÍK, Č. (1991A) in *Prognostické* . . . Prague.
KOŽUŠNÍK, Č. and Z. KODET (1967) *Nová mysl*, no. 6.
KRAWCZYK, R. (1988) *Przeglad Katolicki*, no. 13.
KRONROD, Ya. (1957) *PE*, no. 9. Russian original (1957) *VE*, no. 2.
KRONROD, Ya. (1958) *VE*, no. 10.
KUÇZYŃSKI, W. (1984) *Europäische Rundschau*, no. 1.
KULIKOV, V. (1990) *PKh*, no. 5.
Kupa Programme (1991), official document of the Hungarian ministry of finance, March.
KUROWSKI, S. (1957) in *Dyskusja o polskim modelu gospodarczym* (Warsaw: Książka i wiedza).
KUROWSKI, S. (1981) *Tygodnik Powszechny*, no. 37.
KUROWSKI, S. (1991) *ZG*, no. 47.
KUROWSKI, S. et al. (1981), proposal to the Congress of Solidarity, in *Programme, Tygodnik Solidarność*, no. 29.
KUROWSKI, S. and PRZIGODZKI, M. (1991) *ZG*, no. 27.
KÝN, O. (1964) *PH*, no. 12.
KÝN, O. (1968) *Ekonomická revue*, no. 4.
KYZLINK, V. (1983) *HN*, no. 11.

LANG, M. (1970) *SHN*, no. 27.
LANGE, O. (1960) in O. Lange (ed.) *Zagadnienia ekonomii politycznej* (Warsaw: Książka i Wiedza).
LANGE, O. (1973) *Socjalism*, Collective Works, vol. 2 (Warsaw: PWE).
LANGE, O. and F. TAYLOR (1938) *On the Economic Theory of Socialism* (Minneapolis: University of Minnesota Press).
LASKI, K. (1961) *Nowe Drogi*, no. 1.
LASKI, K. (1967) *Nástin teorie socialistické reprodukce* (Prague: Svoboda) Polish original (1965).
LENGYEL, L. (1987) *Medvetánc*, no. 2.
LENGYEL, L. (1988) in L. LENGYEL (ed.) *Tulajdonreform* (Budapest: Pénzügykutató Részvénytársaság).

LENGYEL, L. (1989) *Végkifejlet* (Budapest: KJK).
LENGYEL, L. (1991) interview in *TSz*, no. 12.
LEONTIEV, L. (1966) 'The Plan and Methods of Economic Management', in Sharpe I. Russian original (1964) *P*, 7 September.
LERNER, A. (1947) *Economics of Control* (New York: Macmillan).
LEWANDOWSKI, J. and J. SZOMBURG (1988) in *Propozycje Przeksztatcen Polskiej Gospodarki* (Warsaw: Zeszyty Naukowe).
LEWIN, M. (1975) *The Political Undercurrents in Soviet Economic Debates* (London: Pluto Press).
LIBERMAN, E. G. (1966) 'Plan, Profits, Bonuses', in Sharpe I. Russian original (1962) *P*, 9 September.
LIBERMAN, E. G. (1966A) 'Planning Production and Standard of Long-Term Operation', in Sharpe I. Russian original (1962) *VE*, no. 8.
LIBERMAN, E. G. (1966B) 'Once Again on the Plan, Profits and Bonuses' in Sharpe I. Russian original (1964) *P*, 20 September.
LIPIŃSKI, J. (1988) *E*, no. 3–4.
LIPIŃSKI, J. (1991) *GN*, no. 1–2.
LIPOWSKI, A. (1986) *ZG*, no. 18.
LIPOWSKI, A. (1988) *Mechanizm rynkowy w gospodarcze polskiej* (Warsaw: PWE).
LISICHKIN, G. (1988) *Novyi mir*, no. 11.
LISIČKIN, G. (1967) *Plán a trh* (Prague: Svoboda). Russian original (1966).
LISKA, T. (1963) *KSz*, no. 9.
LISKA, T. (1988) *Ökonosztát* (Budapest: KJK).
LÓRÁNT, K. (1988) *Tervgazdasági Fórum*, vol. IV, no. 2.
LUKASIEWICZ, A. (1987) 'Oskar Lange on Socialist Development Planning', *Oeconomica Polona*, no. 3.

MADEJ, Z. (1981) interview in *ZG*, no. 28.
MADEJ, Z. (1988) *ZG*, no. 14.
MAIZENBERG, L. (1966) 'On a Solid Basis' in Sharpe II. Russian original (1965) *ZG*, no. 45.
MALYSHEV, I. (1960) 'Some Problems of Price Formation in a Socialist Economy' in *International Economic Papers*, no. 10. Russian original (1957) *VE*, no. 3.
MARX, K. (1962) *Capital*, Vol. III (Moscow: Foreign Language Publishing House).
MATĚJKA, J. (1983) *HN*, no. 16.
MATĚJKA, J. (1988) *HN*, no. 48.
MATĚJKA, M. (1983) *HN*, no. 17.
MATĚJKA, M. (1988) *HN*, no. 43.
MATĚJKA, M. (1990) *HN*, no. 23.
MATOLCSY, GY. (1989) *F*, no. 21.
MEDVEDEV, V. (1991) 'How To Carry Our Privatisation' in *CDSP*, no. 22. Russian original (1991) *Izvestiia*, 4 June.
MENCL, V., M. HÁJEK, M. OTAHAL and E. KADLECOVÁ (1990) *Křižovatky 20. století* (Prague: Naše Vojsko).
MIESZCZANKOWSKI, M. (1981) *Polityka*, no. 43.
MIESZCZANKOWSKI, M. (1984) *ZG*, no. 30.
MIESZCZANKOWSKI, M. (1988) *ZG*, no. 1.

MINC, B. (1961) *E*, no. 1.
MINC, B. (1969) in *Dyskusja o funkcjonowaniu gospodarki socjalistycznej* (Warsaw: PWE). First published (1968) *Polityka*, no. 5.
MISIAK, M. (1992) *ZG*, no. 23.
MÓRA, M. (1991) *KSz*, no. 6.
MOŻEJKO, E. (1990) *ZG*, no. 47.
MUJŻEL, J. (1968) *ZG*, no. 30.
MUJŻEL, J. (1969), in *Plan a rynek*, (Warsaw: Ksiazka i Wiedza.)
MUJŻEL, J. (1984), in J. MUJŻEL, and S. JAKUBOWICZ (eds) *Funkcjonowanie gospodarki polskiej* (Warsaw: PWE).
MUJŻEL, J. (1990) *ZG*, no. 7.
MUJŻEL, J. (1990A) *GN*, no. 7–8.
MUJŻEL, J. (1991) *GN*, no. 6.

'Náčrt ďalšieho postupu ekonomické reformy' (1969) in *Ekonomický časopis*, no. 3.
Náčrt základní koncepce rozvíjení ekonomické reformy (1969) (Prague: Economic Institute of the Czechoslovak Academy of Sciences).
NAGY, T. (1964) *KSz*, nos 7–8.
NAGY, T. (1967) *KSz*, no. 2
NAGY, T. and Sz. ESZE (1963) in SZAMUELY (ed.) (1986)
NASILOWSKI, M. (1988) *ZG*, no. 29.
NASILOWSKI, M. (1988A) *Socjalistyczny system gospodarowania w Polsce* (Warsaw: PWE).
NEMCHINOV, V. S. (1966) 'The Plan Target and Material Incentive' in Sharpe I. Russian original (1962) *P*, 21 September.
NEMCHINOV, V. S. (1966A) 'Making Enterprises Interested in More Intensive Plans' in Sharpe I. Russian original (1962) *VE*, no. 11.
NEMCHINOV, V. S. (1966B) 'Socialist Economic Management and Production Planning' in Sharpe I. Russian original (1964) *K*, no. 5.
NEMCHINOV, V. S. (1972) *Společenská hodnota a plánovaná cena* (Prague: Svoboda). Translation from Russian.
NÉMETH, M. (1988) *Tervgazdasági Fórum*, no. 3.
NET (Siec) (1981) *Biuletyn AS*, no. 34, 28–30 August.
NEVAŘIL, F. (1988) *PE*, no. 8.
'New Aspects of Socialism' (1989) in *K*, no. 13.
'The New Program of the Communist Party of the Soviet Union' (1965) in A. P. Mendel (ed.) *Essential Works of Marxism* (New York: Bantam Books).
NIKIFOROV, L. (1988) *VE*, no. 3.
NIKIFOROV, L. and T. KUZNETSOVA (1991) *VE*, no. 2.
NIKITIN, P. (1960) *Politická ekonomie*, popular textbook (Prague). Russian original (1959).
NOVE, A. (1968) *The Soviet Economy* (London: Allen & Unwin).
NOVE, A (1982) *An Economic History of the USSR* (Harmondsworth: Penguin Books).
NOVE, A. (1983) *The Economies of Feasible Socialism* (London: Allen & Unwin).
NOVOZHILOV, V. V. (1964) 'Cost-Benefit Comparisons in a Socialist

Economy' in V. Nemchinov (ed.) *The Use of Mathematical Methods in Economics* (Edinburgh: Oliver & Boyd). Russian original (1959).
NOVOZHILOV, V. V. (1970) *Problems of Cost-Benefit Analysis in Optimal Planning* (White Plains: International Arts and Sciences Press). Russian original (1969).
NYERS, R. (1965) *TSz*, no. 7.
NYERS, R. (1968) *Gazdaságpolitikánk és a gazdasági mechanizmus reformja* Selected papers and interviews (Budapest: Kossuth Könyvkiadó).
NYERS, R. (1984), *Vita* . . . (Budapest).
NYERS, R. (1986) *Tervgazdasági Fórum*, no. 2, and interview in *Valóság*, no. 5.
NYERS, R. (1988) Introduction to T. Liska, *Ökonosztát* (Budapest: KJK).

OKÁLI, I. et al. (1983) *Ekonomický časopis*, no. 4 and 5.
OSIATYŃSKI, J. (1988) *Michal Kalecki on Socialist Economy* (London: Macmillan). Translation from Polish (1983) (Warsaw: PWN).
OULES, F. (1966) *Economic Planning and Democracy* (Harmondsworth: Penguin Books).
Outline of the economic reform, concept for the reform committees (1988) *F*, no. 49.
Outline of the further development of the economic reform (1969) *Ekonomický časopis*, no. 3.

PAJESTKA, J. (1967) panel discussion, *Nowe Drogi*, no. 1.
PAJESTKA, J. (1969) in *Plan a rynek* (Warsaw: Książka i wiedza).
PAJESTKA, J. (1984) in H. Król (ed.) *Reforma po starcie* (Warsaw: PWE).
PAJESTKA, J. (1985) *ZG*, no. 37.
PAJESTKA, J. (1986) in J. Pajestka (ed.) *Gospodarka w procesie reformowania* (Warsaw: PWE).
Party Resolutions and Decisions (1978) *(A Magyar Szocialista Munkáspárt határozatai és dokumentumai 1963–1966)* (Budapest: Kossuth Könyvkiadó).
PASZYŃSKI, A. (1981) *Przegląd Techniczny*, no. 4.
PAVLOV, V. (1991) 'Anti-crisis programme', *EiZh*, no. 18.
PELIKÁN, P. (1967) *PH*, no. 1.
Perekhod k rynku. Kontseptsiia i programma (1990) (Moscow: Ministry of Information). Also known as Shatalin's programme.
PÉTER, Gy. (1954) *KSz*, no. 3.
PETŐ, I. and S. SZAKÁCS (1985) *A hazai gazdaság négy évtizedének története, 1945–1985*, vol. 1 (Budapest: KJK).
PETSCHNIG, M. Z. (1991) *Valóság*, no. 11.
PETSCHNIG, M. Z. and E. VOSZKA (1991) *KSz*, no. 10.
PICK, M. (1991) in *Prognostické* . . . (Prague:
PLACHTINSKÝ, D. (1966) *Ekonomický časopis*, no. 9.
'Polish Economic Association's Reform Blueprint' (1980) ('PTE o reformie'). Supplement to *ZG*, no. 46.
POPOV, G. (1988) 'Conservatives and Avantgardists', *CDSP*, no. 52. Russian original (1988) *Sovetskaia kultura*, 5 January.
PORWIT, K. (1968) *ZG*, no. 44.

PORWIT, K. (1983) 'Problems of the Planning System in Poland', *Oeconomica Polona*, nos 3–4.
PORWIT, K. (1984), in J. MUJZEL and S. JAKUBOWICZ (eds) *Funkcjonowanie gospodarki polskiej* (Warsaw: PWE).
PORWIT, K. (1988) *ZG*, no. 18.
PORWIT, K. (1991) *GN*, no. 6.
Principle Features of a Transition to Market Economy (1990). Document prepared by the Economic Forum, Prague.
Prognostické reflexe problémů přechodu k demokracii a k tržní ekonomice (1991). Study of the Forecasting Institute of the Czechoslovak Academy of Sciences, Prague, May.
'Programme' (1981) ('Program NSZZ "Solidarność"'), *Tygodnik Solidarność*, no. 29.
Programme of the Polish government (1987) *Trybuna Ludu*, 27 October.
Project (1981) (*Podstawowe zalozenia reformy gospodarczej, projekt*) (Warsaw: Ksiazka i Wiedza).
Protocol of Understanding (1980) (*Protokoly porozumien Gdansk, Szczecin, Jastrzebie*) (Warsaw: Krajowa Agencja Wydawnicza).
PRŮCHA, V. et al. (1974) *Hospodářské dějiny Československa v 19. a 20. století* (Prague: Svoboda).

RADAEV, V. and A. AUZAN (1989) *VE*, no. 9.
RAKITSKAIA, G. (1990) *VE*, no. 2.
RAKOWSKI, M. (1991) *ZG*, no. 25.
RAKOWSKI, M. F. (1991) *Jak to sie stalo* (Warsaw: Polska Oficyna Wydawniczna 'BGW').
Report of the Consultative Economic Council for 1986 (1987) *ZG*, nos 7 and 8.
RÉVÉSZ, G. (1990) *Perestroika in Eastern Europe, Hungary's Economic Transformation, 1945–1988* (Boulder: Westview Special Studies).
Rok šedesátý osmý (1969) (Prague: Svoboda).
ROSATI, D. (1990) *ZG*, no. 37.
RUSMICH, L. (1988) *Zbožně-peněžní vztahy v rozvinutém socialismu* (Prague: Academia).
RUSMICH, L. (1991) in *Formování finančního a měnového mechanismu v podminkách tržní ekonomiky*, publication 34 of the Central Institute of National Economic Research, Prague.

SADOWSKI, Z. (1985) *Nowe Drogi*, no. 5.
SADOWSKI, Z. (1987) 'The Principle of Rationality in Oskar Lange's Political Economy in the Light of Later Discussions', *Oeconomica Polona*, no. 3.
SADOWSKI, Z. (1991) *Poland in the Perspective of Global Change* (Warsaw: Polish Association for the Club of Rome).
SADOWSKI, Z. (1991A) *GN*, no. 6.
SADOWSKI, Z. (1991B) *Prywatyzacja gospodarki – warianty i perspektywy* (Warsaw: PEA).
SÁRKÖZY, T. (1982) 'Problems of Social Ownership and the Proprietary Organization', *Acta Oeconomica*, no. 3–4.
SÁRKÖZY, T. (1989) *A tulajdonreformról a társasági törvény után* (Budapest: Kossuth Könyvkiadó).

SÁRKÖZY, T. (1989A) *F*, no. 34.
SCHAFF, A. (1984) *Europäische Rundschau*, no. 1.
SERGEEV, A. (1991) *EiZh*, no. 26.
SHAKHNAZAROV, G. (1991) *K*, nos 4 and 5.
SHARPE, M. (ed.) (1966) *Planning, Profit and Incentives*: vol. I, *The Liberman Discussion*; vol. II, *Reform of Soviet Economic Management* (White Plains: International Arts and Sciences Press).
SHATALIN, S. (1990), interview in *EKO*, no. 7.
SHATALIN, S. (1990A), interview in *CDSP*, no. 17. Russian original (1990) *Izvestiia*, 21 April.
SHATALIN, S. (1991), open letter to Gorbachev, *CSDP*, no. 5. Russian original (1991) *Komsomolskaia Pravda*, 22 January.
SHKREDOV, V. (1988) *K*, no. 12.
SHMELEV, N. (1987) *Novyi mir*, no. 6.
SHMELEV, N. (1988) *Novyi mir*, no. 4.
SÍK, Gy. (1966) *KSz*, no. 4.
ŠIK, O. (1962) *Ekonomika, zájmy, politika* (Prague: Nakladatelstvi politické literatury).
ŠIK, O. (1964) *Nová mysl*, no. 10.
ŠIK, O. (1965) *K problematice socialistických zbožních vztahů* (Prague: Svoboda).
ŠIK, O. (1965A) *PE*, no. 4.
ŠIK, O. (1966) *Economic Planning and Management in Czechoslovakia* (Prague: Orbis).
ŠIK, O. (1967) *Plan and Market under Socialism* (White Plains: International Arts and Sciences Press, jointly with Academia).
SÍKLAKY, I. (1989) *F*, no. 28.
SIPOS, A. and M. TARDOS (1982) *Gazdaság*, no. 3.
SITARIAN, S. (1987) *PKh*, no. 11.
SMITH, H. (1990) *The New Russians* (New York: Random House).
SMOLINSKI, L. and P. WILES (1963) 'The Soviet Planning Pendulum', *Problems of Communism*, Nov.–Dec.
SOBOL, V. (1966) 'A Precise Calculation', in Sharpe II. Russian original (1965) *EG*, no. 45.
SOKOL, M. (1965) *Nová mysl*, no. 2.
SOKOL, M. (1968) *PH*, no. 2.
STALIN, J. (1952) *Economic Problems of Socialism in the USSR* (New York: International Publishers).
'Standpoint . . .' (1987) ('Az MSzMP KB mellett működő Közgazdasági Munkaközösség állásfoglalása') *KSz*, no. 6.
'Standpoint of the Conference of the Party' (1988) ('A Magyar Szocialista Munkáspárt országos értekezletének állásfoglalása a párt feladatairól, a politikai intézmény-rendszer fejlesztéséről') *Nsz*, 23 May.
STARK, D. (1991) *KSz*, no. 3.
STRUMILIN, S. (1960) 'On the Determination of Value and its Application under Socialism', *PoE*, no. 9, January. Russian original in *VE* (1958) no. 8.
SUCHAREVSKII, B. (1966) 'On Improving the Forms and Methods of Material Incentives', in Sharpe I. Russian original *VE* (1962) no. 11.
ŠUJAN, I. (1992) *Ekonom*, no. 4.

ŠULC, Z. (1966) *Rudé Právo*, 26 July.
ŠULC, Z. (1990) *SHN*, no. 2.
ŠULC, Z. (1990A) *HN*, no. 12.
ŠULC, Z. (1990B) *HN*, no. 29.
ŠULC, Z. (1990C) *HN*, no. 18.
ŠULC, Z. (1990D) *Listy*, no. 5.
SULYOK, B. (1968) *PSz*, no. 3.
SUTELA, P. (1991) *Economic Thought and Economic Reform in the Soviet Union* (Cambridge University Press).
SWEEZY, P. (1968) *The Theory of Capitalist Development* (New York: Modern Reader).
SWIĘCICKI, M. (1988) in *Propozycje Przekształcen Polskiej Gospodarki* (Warsaw: Zeszyty Naukowe).
SZABÓ, K. (1985) *KSz*, no. 12.
SZABÓ, K. and M. MANDEL (1966) *KSz*, no. 5.
SZAMUELY, L. (1984) 'The Second Wave of the Economic Mechanism Debate and the 1968 Reform in Hungary', *Acta Oeconomica*, nos 1–2.
SZAMUELY, L. (1986) (ed.) *A magyar közgazdasági gondolat fejlődése, 1954–1978*. Selected articles of the period with an introduction by the editor (Budapest: KJK).
SZEGŐ, A. (1983) *Medvetánc*, nos 2–3.
SZEGŐ, A. and Gy. WIENER (1988) *Tervgazdasági Fórum*, no. 4.
SZEGVÁRI, I. (1990) *F*, no. 6.
SZELÉNYI, I. (1990) *Valóság*, no. 1.
SZOMBURG, J. (1989) *Zmiany*, no. 6.
SZTYBER, W. (1963) *E*, no. 4.

TARDOS, M. (1972) *KSz*, nos 7–8.
TARDOS, M. (1982) 'Development Program for Economic Control and Organization in Hungary', *Acta Oeconomica*, nos 3–4.
TARDOS, M. (1983), in I. SÍKLAKY (ed.) *Koncepció és kritika* (Budapest: Magvető).
TARDOS, M. (1984), in *Vita . . .* (Budapest).
TARDOS, M. (1987), in K. SZABÓ (ed.) *Vagyonérdekeltség – reform* (Budapest: KJK).
TARDOS, M. (1988) *Gazdaság*, no. 3.
TARDOS, M. (1988A) *KSz*, December.
TARDOS, M. (1990) *F*, no. 4.
TARDOS, M. (1991) *Kg*, no. 12.
TINBERGEN, J. (1964) *Central Planning* (Yale University Press).
TOMS, M. (1983) *PE*, no. 12.
TOMS, M. (1985) *HN*, no. 32.
TRAPEZNIKOV, V. (1966) 'For Flexible Economic Management of Enterprises', in Sharpe I. Russian original (1964) *P*, 17 August.
TŘÍSKA, D. (1990) *Finance a úvěr*, no. 9.
TUREK, O. (1988) *PE*, no. 6.
TUREK, O. (1989) *PE*, no. 8.
TUREK, O. (1990) *HN*, no. 10.

TUREK, O. (1991) *NH*, no. 1.
TUREK, O. (1991A) in *Prognostické* . . . Prague.
TUREK, O. and T. JEŽEK (1989) *PE*, no. 5.
TURETSKII, S. (1961) 'Problems of Distribution and Price Formation', *PoE*, no. 5. Russian original (1961) *VE*, no. 4.

URBAN, B. (1969) *Ekonomická revue*, no. 3.

VAAG, L. (1966) 'According to a Single Rate of Profit' in Sharpe II. Russian original (1965) *EG*, no. 45.
VAAG, L. and S. ZAKHAROV (1964) 'Payment for Production Assets and Enterprise Profits', *PoE*, May. Russian original (1963) *VE*, no. 4.
VARGA, I. (1957) *KSz*, nos 10 and 12.
VEJVODA, J. (1966) *PH*, no. 10.
VEJVODA, V. (1983) *HN*, no. 16.
VERGNER, Z. (1989) *HN*, no. 1.
VINCZE, I. (1969) *TSz*, no. 6.
VINTROVÁ, R. (1989) *PE*, no. 5.
Vita a népgazdasági tervezés feladatairól az 1980-as évek Magyarországán (1984) (Budapest: Publication of the Economic Institute of the Hungarian Academy of Sciences).
VLADOVA, N. and N. RABKINA (1988) *VE*, no. 10.
VOSZKA, E. (1991) *Kg*, no. 9.
VOSZKA, E. (1991A) *TSz*, no. 12.

WAKAR, A. and J. G. ZIELIŃSKI (1961) *E*, no. 1.
WAKAR, A. (1965) (ed.) *Zarys teorii gospodarki socjalistycznej* (Warsaw: PWN).
WARD, B. (1958) 'The Firm in Illyria: Market Syndicalism', *The American Economic Review*, no. 4.
WILCSEK, J. (1965) *TSz*, no. 3.
WILCSEK, J. (1967) *KSz*, no. 7–8.
WILCZYŃSKI, W. (1963) *E*, no. 3.
WILCZYŃSKI, W. (1991) *GN*, no. 6.
WINIECKI, J. (1991) 'The Inevitability of a Fall in Output in the Early Stages of Transition to the Market: Theoretical Underpinnings', *Soviet Studies*, no. 4.
WINIECKI, J. (1991A) *GN*, no. 3.

YAKOVLEV, A. (1990) 'Socialism: from Dream to Reality' (Moscow: Novosti).
YASIN, E. (1989) *K*, no. 15.
YASIN, E. (1990) *VE*, no. 7.
YASIN, E. (1991) 'What awaits us if?', *CDSP*, no. 10. Russian original (1991) *Ogonek*, no. 6.
YASIN, E., V. MASHCHINTS and S. ALEKSASHENKO (1989) *VE*, no. 3.
YAVLIŃSKI–ALLISON reform (1991) *CDSP*, no. 25. Russian original (1991) *Izvestiia*, 24 June.

ZALESKI, E. (1967) *Planning Reforms in the Soviet Union, 1962–1966* (Chapel Hill: The University of North Carolina Press).

ZASLAVSKAIA, T. (1983) 'Nobosibirsk Manifesto', unpublished paper.

ZASLAVSKAIA, T. (1990) *The Second Socialist Revolution* (Bloomington: Indiana University Press).

ZAUBERMAN, A. (1960) 'The Soviet Debate on the Law of Value and Price Formation', in G. Grossman (ed.) *Value and Plan, Economic Calculation and Organization in Eastern Europe* (Westport: Greenwood Press).

ZVEREV, A. (1966) 'Against Oversimplification in Solving Complex Problems', in Sharpe I. Russian original *VE* (1962) no. 11.

Index

Note that some common items are not indexed at all (e.g. USSR, Poland, Czechoslovakia and Hungary), and some selectively. 'Cz' stands for Czechoslovakia, 'd' for definition, 'H' for Hungary, 'P' for Poland, 'SU' for the Soviet Union, 'v' for views on planning and market.

318   *Index*

320   *Index*